4th Workshop on Asian Translation (WAT 2017)

Taipei, Taiwan
27 November – 1 December 2017

ISBN: 978-1-5108-5297-6

Printed from e-media with permission by:

Curran Associates, Inc.
57 Morehouse Lane
Red Hook, NY 12571

Some format issues inherent in the e-media version may also appear in this print version.

Copyright© (2017) by the Association for Computational Linguistics
All rights reserved.

Printed by Curran Associates, Inc. (2017)

For permission requests, please contact the Association for Computational Linguistics
at the address below.

Association for Computational Linguistics
209 N. Eighth Street
Stroudsburg, Pennsylvania 18360

Phone: 1-570-476-8006
Fax: 1-570-476-0860

acl@aclweb.org

Additional copies of this publication are available from:

Curran Associates, Inc.
57 Morehouse Lane
Red Hook, NY 12571 USA
Phone: 845-758-0400
Fax: 845-758-2633
Email: curran@proceedings.com
Web: www.proceedings.com

IJCNLP 2017

The 4th Workshop on Asian Translation

Proceedings of the Workshop

November 27 December 1, 2017
Taipei, Taiwan

©2017 Asian Federation of Natural Language Processing

Preface

Many Asian countries are rapidly growing these days and the importance of communicating and exchanging the information with these countries has intensified. To satisfy the demand for communication among these countries, machine translation technology is essential.

Machine translation technology has rapidly evolved recently and it is seeing practical use especially between European languages. However, the translation quality of Asian languages is not that high compared to that of European languages, and machine translation technology for these languages has not reached a stage of proliferation yet. This is not only due to the lack of the language resources for Asian languages but also due to the lack of techniques to correctly transfer the meaning of sentences from/to Asian languages. Consequently, a place for gathering and sharing the resources and knowledge about Asian language translation is necessary to enhance machine translation research for Asian languages.

The Workshop on Machine Translation (WMT), the world's largest machine translation workshop, mainly targets on European languages and does not include Asian languages. The International Workshop on Spoken Language Translation (IWSLT) has spoken language translation tasks for some Asian languages using TED talk data, but these is no task for written language.

The Workshop on Asian Translation (WAT) is an open machine translation evaluation campaign focusing on Asian languages. WAT gathers and shares the resources and knowledge of Asian language translation to understand the problems to be solved for the practical use of machine translation technologies among all Asian countries. WAT is unique in that it is an "open innovation platform": the test data is fixed and open, so participants can repeat evaluations on the same data and confirm changes in translation accuracy over time. WAT has no deadline for the automatic translation quality evaluation (continuous evaluation), so participants can submit translation results at any time.

Following the success of the previous WAT workshops (WAT2014, WAT2015, and WAT2016), WAT2017 brings together machine translation researchers and users to try, evaluate, share and discuss brand-new ideas about machine translation. For the 4th WAT, we proudly include new domains: Newswire and Recipe in addition to scientific paper, patent, and mixed domain for the machine translation evaluation shared tasks. We had 12 teams who submitted their translation results, and about 300 submissions in total.

In addition to the shared tasks, WAT2017 also feature scientific papers on topics related to the machine translation, especially for Asian languages. The program committee accepted 4 papers, which focus on on neural machine translation, and construction and evaluation of language resources.

We are grateful to "SunFlare Co., Ltd." for partially sponsoring the workshop. We would like to thank all the authors who submitted papers. We express our deepest gratitude to the committee members for their timely reviews. We also thank the IJCNLP 2017 organizers for their help with administrative matters.

WAT2017 Organizers

Organizers:

Toshiaki Nakazawa, Japan Science and Technology Agency (JST), Japan

Hideya Mino, National Institute of Information and Communications Technology (NICT), Japan

Chenchen Ding, National Institute of Information and Communications Technology (NICT), Japan

Shohei Higashiyama, National Institute of Information and Communications Technology (NICT), Japan

Isao Goto, Japan Broadcasting Corporation (NHK), Japan

Graham Neubig, Nara Institute of Science and Technology (NAIST), Japan

Hideto Kazawa, Google, Japan

Yusuke Oda, Nara Institute of Science and Technology (NAIST), Japan

Jun Harashima, Cookpad Inc., Japan

Sadao Kurohashi, Kyoto University, Japan

Ir. Hammam Riza, Agency for the Assessment and Application of Technology (BPPT), Indonesia

Pushpak Bhattacharyya, Indian Institute of Technology Bombay (IIT), India

Program Committee:

Chenhui Chu, JST, Japan

Fabien Cromières, JST, Japan

Hideto Kazawa, Google, Japan

Anoop Kunchookuttan, IIT Bombay, India

Qun Liu, Dublin City University, Ireland

Yvette Graham, Dublin City University, Ireland

Yang Liu, Tsinghua University, China

Liling Tan, Universität des Saarlandes, Germany

Masao Utiyama, NICT, Japan

Jiajun Zhang, Chinese Academy of Sciences, China

Technical Collaborators:

Luis Fernando D'Haro, Institute for Infocomm Research, Singapore

Rafael E. Banchs, Institute for Infocomm Research, Singapore

Haizhou Li, Institute for Infocomm Research, Singapore

Invited talk: Turning NMT Research into Commercial Products

Adrià de Gispert

SDL

Abstract

Recently, neural machine translation has revolutionised the field of machine translation, and now results in many research tasks keep improving every year. The new neural models have greatly improved translation quality, but have very different sorts of errors than the traditional statistical machine translation technology. An important challenge is to incorporate this technology improvement into commercial products and ensure that machine translation users get the best value while still keeping the product features they rely on for their work. SDL provides machine translation technology in a variety of products and markets. Our customers have expectations related to decoding speed, support for dictionaries and tags, and other functionality, so they can successfully integrate MT in their workflows. When it comes to commercialising MT, ensuring that these expectations are met is as important as improvements in BLEU score. In this talk I will focus on these important practical aspects in the context of the current NMT developments.

Biography

Dr. Adrià de Gispert is a senior research scientist at SDL Research, as well as a senior research associate at the Engineering Department in the University of Cambridge, UK. He received his PhD on Statistical Machine Translation from Universitat Politècnica de Catalunya (UPC, Barcelona) in 2007. Then he moved to Cambridge, where he has continued working in this field since, both in academia and in industry. He has published more than 30 major research papers on MT, and has contributed to the development of multiple state-of-the-art research and commercial machine translation engines, including phrase-based, syntax-based and neural. He is a Fellow of Clare College, Cambridge.

Table of Contents

Workshop Program

November 27, 2017

9:00–9:20   **Welcome & Overview**

Overview of the 4th Workshop on Asian Translation
Toshiaki Nakazawa, Shohei Higashiyama, Chenchen Ding, Hideya Mino, Isao Goto, Hideto Kazawa, Yusuke Oda, Graham Neubig and Sadao Kurohashi

9:20–10:40   **Research Paper**

Controlling Target Features in Neural Machine Translation via Prefix Constraints
Shunsuke Takeno, Masaaki Nagata and Kazuhide Yamamoto

Improving Japanese-to-English Neural Machine Translation by Paraphrasing the Target Language
Yuuki Sekizawa, Tomoyuki Kajiwara and Mamoru Komachi

Improving Low-Resource Neural Machine Translation with Filtered Pseudo-Parallel Corpus
Aizhan Imankulova, Takayuki Sato and Mamoru Komachi

Japanese to English/Chinese/Korean Datasets for Translation Quality Estimation and Automatic Post-Editing
Atsushi Fujita and Eiichiro Sumita

10:40–11:00   **Coffee break**

11:00–12:00   **System description**

NTT Neural Machine Translation Systems at WAT 2017
Makoto Morishita, Jun Suzuki and Masaaki Nagata

XMU Neural Machine Translation Systems for WAT 2017
Boli Wang, Zhixing Tan, Jinming Hu, Yidong Chen and xiaodong shi

A Bag of Useful Tricks for Practical Neural Machine Translation: Embedding Layer Initialization and Large Batch Size
Masato Neishi, Jin Sakuma, Satoshi Tohda, Shonosuke Ishiwatari, Naoki Yoshinaga and Masashi Toyoda

14:00–14:45 **Invited talk**

Turning NMT Research into Commercial Products
Adrià de Gispert

14:45–15:05 **Poster booster (9 systems)**

15:05–15:10 **Commemorative photo**

15:10–15:30 **Coffee break**

15:30–16:15 **Poster presentation I (System description)**

NTT Neural Machine Translation Systems at WAT 2017
Makoto Morishita, Jun Suzuki and Masaaki Nagata

Patent NMT integrated with Large Vocabulary Phrase Translation by SMT at WAT 2017
Zi Long, Ryuichiro Kimura, Takehito Utsuro, Tomoharu Mitsuhashi and Mikio Yamamoto

SMT reranked NMT
Terumasa Ehara

Ensemble and Reranking: Using Multiple Models in the NICT-2 Neural Machine Translation System at WAT2017
Kenji Imamura and Eiichiro Sumita

A Simple and Strong Baseline: NAIST-NICT Neural Machine Translation System for WAT2017 English-Japanese Translation Task
Yusuke Oda, Katsuhito Sudoh, Satoshi Nakamura, Masao Utiyama and Eiichiro Sumita

Comparison of SMT and NMT trained with large Patent Corpora: Japio at WAT2017
Satoshi Kinoshita, Tadaaki Oshio and Tomoharu Mitsuhashi

16:15–17:00   **Poster presentation II (System description)**

A Bag of Useful Tricks for Practical Neural Machine Translation: Embedding Layer Initialization and Large Batch Size
Masato Neishi, Jin Sakuma, Satoshi Tohda, Shonosuke Ishiwatari, Naoki Yoshinaga and Masashi Toyoda

Kyoto University Participation to WAT 2017
Fabien Cromieres, Raj Dabre, Toshiaki Nakazawa and Sadao Kurohashi

CUNI NMT System for WAT 2017 Translation Tasks
Tom Kocmi, Dušan Variš and Ondřej Bojar

XMU Neural Machine Translation Systems for WAT 2017
Boli Wang, Zhixing Tan, Jinming Hu, Yidong Chen and xiaodong shi

Tokyo Metropolitan University Neural Machine Translation System for WAT 2017
Yukio Matsumura and Mamoru Komachi

Comparing Recurrent and Convolutional Architectures for English-Hindi Neural Machine Translation
Sandhya Singh, Ritesh Panjwani, Anoop Kunchukuttan and Pushpak Bhattacharyya

17:00–   **Closing**

Overview of the 4th Workshop on Asian Translation

Toshiaki Nakazawa
Japan Science and
Technology Agency
nakazawa@nlp.ist.i.kyoto-u.ac.jp

Shohei Higashiyama and **Chenchen Ding**
National Institute of
Information and
Communications Technology
{shohei.higashiyama, chenchen.ding}@nict.go.jp

Hideya Mino and **Isao Goto**
NHK
{mino.h-gq, goto.i-es}@nhk.or.jp

Hideto Kazawa
Google
kazawa@google.com

Yusuke Oda
Nara Institute of
Science and Technology
oda.yusuke.on9@is.naist.jp

Graham Neubig
Carnegie Mellon University
gneubig@cs.cmu.edu

Sadao Kurohashi
Kyoto University
kuro@i.kyoto-u.ac.jp

Abstract

This paper presents the results of the shared tasks from the 4th workshop on Asian translation (WAT2017) including J↔E, J↔C scientific paper translation subtasks, C↔J, K↔J, E↔J patent translation subtasks, H↔E mixed domain subtasks, J↔E newswire subtasks and J↔E recipe subtasks. For the WAT2017, 12 institutions participated in the shared tasks. About 300 translation results have been submitted to the automatic evaluation server, and selected submissions were manually evaluated.

1 Introduction

The Workshop on Asian Translation (WAT) is a new open evaluation campaign focusing on Asian languages. Following the success of the previous workshops WAT2014 (Nakazawa et al., 2014), WAT2015 (Nakazawa et al., 2015) and WAT2016 (Nakazawa et al., 2016), WAT2017 brings together machine translation researchers and users to try, evaluate, share and discuss brand-new ideas of machine translation. We have been working toward practical use of machine translation among all Asian countries.

For the 4th WAT, we adopted new translation subtasks with English-Japanese news corpus and English-Japanese recipe corpus in addition to the subtasks at WAT2016 [1]. Fur-

thermore, we invited research papers on topics related to machine translation, especially for Asian languages. The submitted research papers were peer reviewed by three program committee members and the committee accepted 4 papers, which focus on on neural machine translation, and construction and evaluation of language resources. We also launched the small NMT task, which aims to build a small NMT system that keeps a reasonable translation quality. There are, however, no submissions to the task this year.

WAT is the uniq workshop on Asian language transration with the following characteristics:

- Open innovation platform
  Due to the fixed and open test data, we can repeatedly evaluate translation systems on the same dataset over years. There is no deadline of translation result submission with respect to automatic evaluation of translation quality and WAT receives submissions at any time.

- Domain and language pairs
  WAT is the world's first workshop that targets scientific paper domain, and Chinese↔Japanese and Korean↔Japanese language pairs. In the future, we will add more Asian languages such as Vietnamese, Thai, Burmese and so on.

- Evaluation method
  Evaluation is done both automatically

---

[1] This year we did not conduct Indonesian-English newswire subtask, which is conducted in WAT2016, due to corpus license reasons.

Proceedings of the 4th Workshop on Asian Translation, pages 1–54,
Taipei, Taiwan, November 27, 2017. ©2017 AFNLP

Lang	Train	Dev	DevTest	Test
JE	3,008,500	1,790	1,784	1,812
JC	672,315	2,090	2,148	2,107

Table 1: Statistics for ASPEC.

and manually. For automatic evaluation, we use three metrics: BLEU, RIBES and AMFM. As human evaluation, we evaluate translation results by pairwise evaluation and JPO adequacy evaluation. JPO adequacy evaluation is conducted for the selected submissions according to the pairwise evaluation results.

2 Dataset

WAT2017 uses the Asian Scientific Paper Excerpt Corpus (ASPEC) [2], JPO Patent Corpus (JPC) [3], JIJI Corpus [4], IIT Bombay English-Hindi Corpus (IITB Corpus) [5] and Recipe Corpus [6] as the dataset.

2.1 ASPEC

ASPEC was constructed by the Japan Science and Technology Agency (JST) in collaboration with the National Institute of Information and Communications Technology (NICT). The corpus consists of a Japanese-English scientific paper abstract corpus (ASPEC-JE), which is used for J↔E subtasks, and a Japanese-Chinese scientific paper excerpt corpus (ASPEC-JC), which is used for J↔C subtasks. The statistics for each corpus are shown in Table 1.

2.1.1 ASPEC-JE

The training data for ASPEC-JE was constructed by NICT from approximately two million Japanese-English scientific paper abstracts owned by JST. The data is a comparable corpus and sentence correspondences are found automatically using the method from (Utiyama and Isahara, 2007). Each sentence

pair is accompanied by a similarity score that are calculated by the method and a field ID that indicates a scientific field. The correspondence between field IDs and field names, along with the frequency and occurrence ratios for the training data, are descripted in the README file of ASPEC-JE.

The development, development-test and test data were extracted from parallel sentences from the Japanese-English paper abstracts that exclude the sentences in the training data. Each dataset consists of 400 documents and contains sentences in each field at the same rate. The document alignment was conducted automatically and only documents with a 1-to-1 alignment are included. It is therefore possible to restore the original documents. The format is the same as the training data except that there is no similarity score.

2.1.2 ASPEC-JC

ASPEC-JC is a parallel corpus consisting of Japanese scientific papers, which come from the literature database and electronic journal site J-STAGE by JST, and their translation to Chinese with permission from the necessary academic associations. Abstracts and paragraph units are selected from the body text so as to contain the highest overall vocabulary coverage.

The development, development-test and test data are extracted at random from documents containing single paragraphs across the entire corpus. Each set contains 400 paragraphs (documents). There are no documents sharing the same data across the training, development, development-test and test sets.

2.2 JPC

JPC was constructed by the Japan Patent Office (JPO). The corpus consists of Chinese-Japanese patent description corpus (JPC-CJ), Korean-Japanese patent description corpus (JPC-KJ) and English-Japanese patent description corpus (JPC-EJ) with the sections of Chemistry, Electricity, Mechanical engineering, and Physics on the basis of International Patent Classification (IPC). Each corpus is partitioned into training, development, development-test and test data. This corpus is used for patent subtasks C↔J, K↔J and E↔J. The statistics for each corpus are shown

[2]http://lotus.kuee.kyoto-u.ac.jp/ASPEC/index.html

[3]http://lotus.kuee.kyoto-u.ac.jp/WAT/patent/index.html

[4]http://lotus.kuee.kyoto-u.ac.jp/WAT/jiji-corpus/index.html

[5]http://www.cfilt.iitb.ac.in/iitb_parallel/index.html

[6]http://lotus.kuee.kyoto-u.ac.jp/WAT/recipe-corpus/index.html

Lang	Train	Dev	DevTest	Test
CJ	1,000,000	2,000	2,000	2,000
KJ	1,000,000	2,000	2,000	2,000
EJ	1,000,000	2,000	2,000	2,000

Table 2: Statistics for JPC.

Lang	Train	Dev	DevTest	Test
EJ	200,000	2,000	2,000	2,000

Table 3: Statistics for JIJI Corpus.

Lang	Train	Dev	Test	Mono
H	–	–	–	45,075,279
EH	1,492,827	520	2,507	–
JH	152,692	1,566	2.000	–

Table 4: Statistics for IITB Corpus. "Mono" indicates monolingual Hindi corpus.

in Table 2.

The Sentence pairs in each data were randomly extracted from a description part of comparable patent documents under the condition that a similarity score between two sentences is greater than or equal to the threshold value 0.05. The similarity score was calculated by the method from (Utiyama and Isahara, 2007) as with ASPEC. Document pairs which were used to extract sentence pairs for each data were not used for the other data. Furthermore, the sentence pairs were extracted so as to be the same number among the four sections. The maximize number of sentence pairs which are extracted from one document pair was limited to 60 for training data and 20 for the development, development-test and test data.

The training data for JPC-CJ was made with sentence pairs of Chinese-Japanese patent documents published in 2012. For JPC-KJ and JPC-EJ, the training data was extracted from sentence pairs of Korean-Japanese and English-Japanese patent documents published in 2011 and 2012. The development, development-test and test data for JPC-CJ, JPC-KJ and JPC-EJ were respectively made with 100 patent documents published in 2013.

2.3 JIJI Corpus

JIJI Corpus was constructed by Jiji Press, Ltd. in collaboration with NICT. The corpus consists of news text that comes from Jiji Press news of various categories including politics, economy, nation, business, markets, sports and so on. The corpus is partitioned into training, development, development-test and test data, which consists of Japanese-English sentence pairs. The statistics for each corpus are shown in Table 3.

The sentence pairs in each data are identified in the same manner as that for ASPEC using the method from (Utiyama and Isahara, 2007).

2.4 IITB Corpus

IIT Bombay English-Hindi corpus contains English-Hindi parallel corpus (IITB-EH) as well as monolingual Hindi corpus collected from a variety of sources and corpora developed at the Center for Indian Language Technology, IIT Bombay over the years. This corpus is used for mixed domain subtasks H↔E. Furthermore, mixed domain subtasks H↔J were added as a pivot language task with a parallel corpus created using publicly available corpora (IITB-JH) [7]. Most sentence pairs in IITB-JH come from the Bible corpus. The statistics for each corpus are shown in Table 4.

2.5 Recipe Corpus

Recipe Corpus was constructed by Cookpad Inc. Each recipe consists of a title, ingredients, steps, a description and a history. Every text in titles, ingredients and steps consists of a parallel sentence while one in descriptions and histories is not always a parallel sentence. Although all of the texts in the training set can be used for training, only titles, ingredients and steps in the test set is used for evaluation. The statistics for each corpus are described in Table 5.

3 Baseline Systems

Human evaluations were conducted as pairwise comparisons between the translation results for a specific baseline system and translation results for each participant's system.

---

[7] http://lotus.kuee.kyoto-u.ac.jp/WAT/Hindi-corpus/WAT2017-Ja-Hi.zip

Lang	TextType	Train	Dev	DevTest	Test
	Title	14,779	500	500	500
EJ	Ingredient	127,244	4,274	4,188	3,935
	Step	108,993	3,303	3,086	2,804

Table 5: Statistics for Recipe Corpus.

That is, the specific baseline system was the standard for human evaluation. A phrase-based statistical machine translation (SMT) system was adopted as the specific baseline system at WAT 2017, which is the same system as that at WAT 2014 to WAT 2016.

In addition to the results for the baseline phrase-based SMT system, we produced results for the baseline systems that consisted of a hierarchical phrase-based SMT system, a string-to-tree syntax-based SMT system, a tree-to-string syntax-based SMT system, seven commercial rule-based machine translation (RBMT) systems, and two online translation systems. We also experimentally produced results for the baseline systems that consisted of an neural machine translation system using the implementation of (Vaswani et al., 2017). The SMT baseline systems consisted of publicly available software, and the procedures for building the systems and for translating using the systems were published on the WAT web page[8]. We used Moses (Koehn et al., 2007; Hoang et al., 2009) as the implementation of the baseline SMT systems. The Berkeley parser (Petrov et al., 2006) was used to obtain syntactic annotations. The baseline systems are shown in Table 6.

The commercial RBMT systems and the online translation systems were operated by the organizers. We note that these RBMT companies and online translation companies did not submit themselves. Because our objective is not to compare commercial RBMT systems or online translation systems from companies that did not themselves participate, the system IDs of these systems are anonymous in this paper.

---

[8]http://lotus.kuee.kyoto-u.ac.jp/WAT/

System ID	System	Type	ASPEC				JPC						IITB		JIJI		RECIPE	
			JE	EJ	JC	CJ	JE	EJ	JC	CJ	JK	KJ	HE	EH	JE	EJ	JE	EJ
SMT Phrase	Moses' Phrase-based SMT	SMT	✓	✓	✓	✓	✓	✓	✓	✓	✓	✓	✓	✓	✓	✓	✓	✓
SMT Hiero	Moses' Hierarchical Phrase-based SMT	SMT	✓	✓	✓	✓	✓	✓	✓	✓	✓	✓	✓	✓	✓	✓		
SMT S2T	Moses' String-to-Tree Syntax-based SMT and Berkeley parser	SMT	✓		✓		✓		✓				✓		✓			
SMT T2S	Moses' Tree-to-String Syntax-based SMT and Berkeley parser	SMT		✓		✓		✓		✓				✓		✓		
RBMT X	The Honyaku V15 (Commercial system)	RBMT	✓	✓			✓	✓							✓	✓	✓	✓
RBMT X	ATLAS V14 (Commercial system)	RBMT	✓	✓			✓	✓										
RBMT X	PAT-Transer 2009 (Commercial system)	RBMT	✓	✓			✓	✓										
RBMT X	PC-Transer V13 (Commercial system)	RBMT													✓	✓	✓	✓
RBMT X	J-Beijing 7 (Commercial system)	RBMT			✓	✓			✓	✓								
RBMT X	Hohrai 2011 (Commercial system)	RBMT			✓	✓				✓								
RBMT X	J Soul 9 (Commercial system)	RBMT									✓	✓						
RBMT X	Korai 2011 (Commercial system)	RBMT									✓	✓						
Online X	Google translate	Other	✓	✓	✓	✓	✓	✓	✓	✓	✓	✓	✓	✓	✓	✓	✓	✓
Online X	Bing translator	Other	✓	✓	✓	✓	✓	✓	✓	✓	✓	✓	✓	✓	✓	✓	✓	✓
AIAYN	Google's implementation of "Attention Is All You Need"	NMT	✓	✓														

Table 6: Baseline Systems

3.1 Training Data

We used the following data for training the SMT baseline systems.

- Training data for the language model: All of the target language sentences in the parallel corpus.
- Training data for the translation model: Sentences that were 40 words or less in length. (For ASPEC Japanese–English training data, we only used train-1.txt, which consists of one million parallel sentence pairs with high similarity scores.)
- Development data for tuning: All of the development data.

3.2 Common Settings for Baseline SMT

We used the following tools for tokenization.

- Juman version 7.0[9] for Japanese segmentation.
- Stanford Word Segmenter version 2014-01-04[10] (Chinese Penn Treebank (CTB) model) for Chinese segmentation.
- The Moses toolkit for English and Indonesian tokenization.
- Mecab-ko[11] for Korean segmentation.
- Indic NLP Library[12] for Hindi segmentation.

To obtain word alignments, GIZA++ and grow-diag-final-and heuristics were used. We used 5-gram language models with modified Kneser-Ney smoothing, which were built using a tool in the Moses toolkit (Heafield et al., 2013).

3.3 Phrase-based SMT

We used the following Moses configuration for the phrase-based SMT system.

- distortion-limit
  - 20 for JE, EJ, JC, and CJ
  - 0 for JK, KJ, HE, and EH
  - 6 for IE and EI
- msd-bidirectional-fe lexicalized reordering

- Phrase score option: GoodTuring

The default values were used for the other system parameters.

3.4 Hierarchical Phrase-based SMT

We used the following Moses configuration for the hierarchical phrase-based SMT system.

- max-chart-span = 1000
- Phrase score option: GoodTuring

The default values were used for the other system parameters.

3.5 String-to-Tree Syntax-based SMT

We used the Berkeley parser to obtain target language syntax. We used the following Moses configuration for the string-to-tree syntax-based SMT system.

- max-chart-span = 1000
- Phrase score option: GoodTuring
- Phrase extraction options: MaxSpan = 1000, MinHoleSource = 1, and NonTermConsecSource.

The default values were used for the other system parameters.

3.6 Tree-to-String Syntax-based SMT

We used the Berkeley parser to obtain source language syntax. We used the following Moses configuration for the baseline tree-to-string syntax-based SMT system.

- max-chart-span = 1000
- Phrase score option: GoodTuring
- Phrase extraction options: MaxSpan = 1000, MinHoleSource = 1, MinWords = 0, NonTermConsecSource, and AllowOnlyUnalignedWords.

The default values were used for the other system parameters.

4 Automatic Evaluation

4.1 Procedure for Calculating Automatic Evaluation Score

We evaluated translation results by three metrics: BLEU (Papineni et al., 2002), RIBES (Isozaki et al., 2010) and AMFM (Banchs et al., 2015). BLEU scores were calculated using `multi-bleu.perl` which was distributed

---

[9]http://nlp.ist.i.kyoto-u.ac.jp/EN/index.php?JUMAN
[10]http://nlp.stanford.edu/software/segmenter.shtml
[11]https://bitbucket.org/eunjeon/mecab-ko/
[12]https://bitbucket.org/anoopk/indic_nlp_library

with the Moses toolkit (Koehn et al., 2007). RIBES scores were calculated using `RIBES.py` version 1.02.4 [13]. AMFM scores were calculated using scripts created by the technical collaborators of WAT2017. All scores for each task were calculated using the corresponding reference.

Before the calculation of the automatic evaluation scores, the translation results were tokenized with word segmentation tools for each language. For Japanese segmentation, we used three different tools: Juman version 7.0 (Kurohashi et al., 1994), KyTea 0.4.6 (Neubig et al., 2011) with Full SVM model [14] and MeCab 0.996 (Kudo, 2005) with IPA dictionary 2.7.0 [15]. For Chinese segmentation, we used two different tools: KyTea 0.4.6 with Full SVM Model in MSR model and Stanford Word Segmenter (Tseng, 2005) version 2014-06-16 with Chinese Penn Treebank (CTB) and Peking University (PKU) model [16]. For Korean segmentation we used mecab-ko [17]. For English segmentation, we used `tokenizer.perl` [18] in the Moses toolkit. For Hindi segmentation, we used Indic NLP Library [19]. The detailed procedures for the automatic evaluation are shown on the WAT2017 evaluation web page [20].

4.2 Automatic Evaluation System

The participants submit translation results via an automatic evaluation system deployed on the WAT2017 web page, which automatically gives evaluation scores for the uploaded results. Figure 1 shows the submission interface for participants. The system requires participants to provide the following information when they upload translation results:

- Subtask:
  Scientific papers subtask (J↔E, J↔C),
  Patents subtask (C↔J, K↔J, E↔J),
  Newswire subtask (J↔E),
  Mixed domain subtask (H↔E, H↔J) or
  Recipe subtask (J↔E);

- Method:
  SMT, RBMT, SMT and RBMT, EBMT, NMT or Other;

- Use of other resources in addition to the provided data ASPEC / JPC / IITB Corpus / JIJI Corpus / Recipe Corpus;

- Permission to publish automatic evaluation scores on the WAT2017 web page.

Although participants can confirm only the information that they filled or uploaded, the server for the system stores all submitted information including translation results and scores. Information about translation results that participants permit to be published is disclosed via the WAT2017 evaluation web page. Participants can also submit the results for human evaluation using the same web interface. This automatic evaluation system will remain available even after WAT2017. Anybody can register an account for the system by following the procesures in the registration web page [21].

---

[13] http://www.kecl.ntt.co.jp/icl/lirg/ribes/index.html

[14] http://www.phontron.com/kytea/model.html

[15] http://code.google.com/p/mecab/downloads/detail?name=mecab-ipadic-2.7.0-20070801.tar.gz

[16] http://nlp.stanford.edu/software/segmenter.shtml

[17] https://bitbucket.org/eunjeon/mecab-ko/

[18] https://github.com/moses-smt/mosesdecoder/tree/RELEASE-2.1.1/scripts/tokenizer/tokenizer.perl

[19] https://bitbucket.org/anoopk/indic_nlp_library

[20] http://lotus.kuee.kyoto-u.ac.jp/WAT/evaluation/index.html

[21] http://lotus.kuee.kyoto-u.ac.jp/WAT/WAT2017/registration/index.html

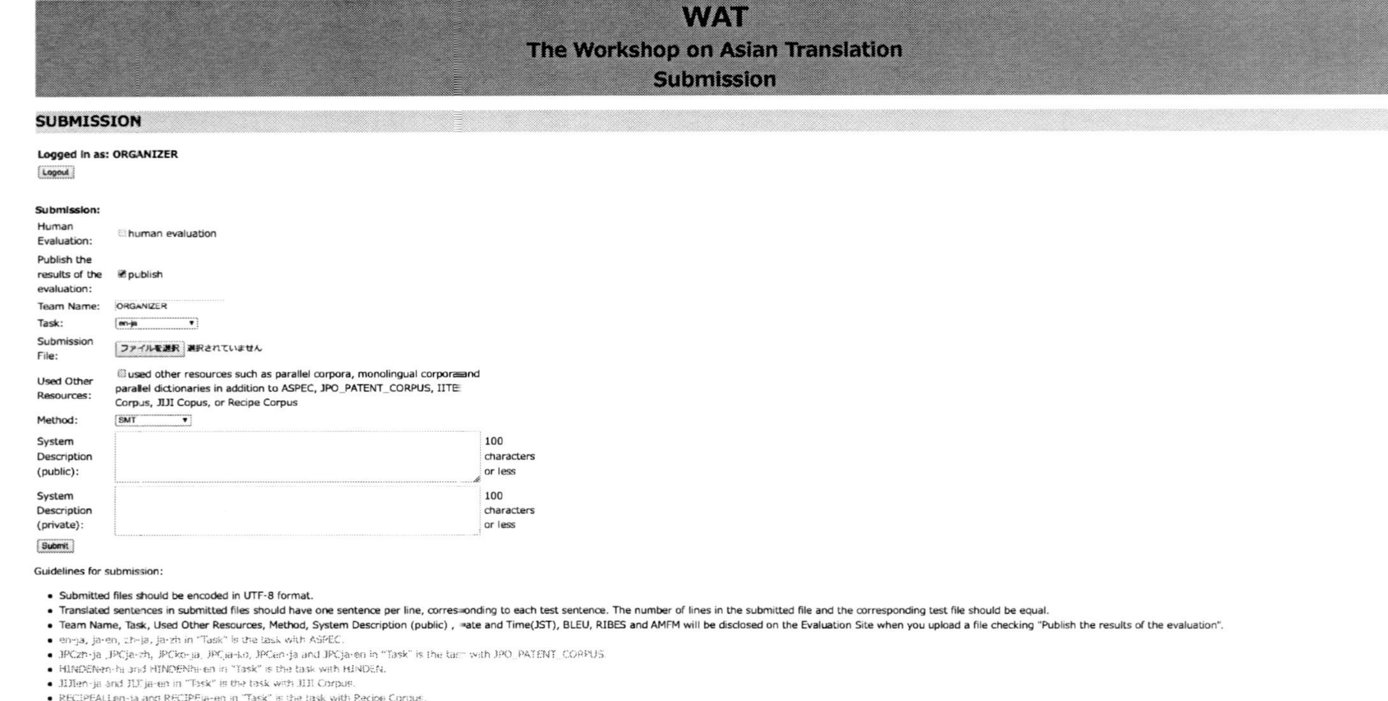

Figure 1: The submission web page for participants

5 Human Evaluation

In WAT2017, we conducted 2 kinds of human evaluations: *pairwise evaluation* and *JPO adequacy evaluation*.

5.1 Pairwise Evaluation

The pairwise evaluation is the same as the last year, but not using the crowdsourcing this year. We asked professional translation company to do pairwise evaluation. The cost of pairwise evaluation per sentence is almost the same to that of last year.

We randomly chose 400 sentences from the Test set for the pairwise evaluation. We used the same sentences as the last year for the continuous subtasks. Each submission is compared with the baseline translation (Phrase-based SMT, described in Section 3) and given a *Pairwise* score.

5.1.1 Pairwise Evaluation of Sentences

We conducted pairwise evaluation of each of the 400 test sentences. The input sentence and two translations (the baseline and a submission) are shown to the annotators, and the annotators are asked to judge which of the translation is better, or if they are of the same quality. The order of the two translations are at random.

5.1.2 Voting

To guarantee the quality of the evaluations, each sentence is evaluated by 5 different annotators and the final decision is made depending on the 5 judgements. We define each judgement $j_i (i = 1, \cdots, 5)$ as:

$$
j_i = \begin{cases} 1 & \text{if better than the baseline} \\ -1 & \text{if worse than the baseline} \\ 0 & \text{if the quality is the same} \end{cases}
$$

The final decision D is defined as follows using $S = \sum j_i$:

$$
D = \begin{cases} win & (S \geq 2) \\ loss & (S \leq -2) \\ tie & (otherwise) \end{cases}
$$

5.1.3 Pairwise Score Calculation

Suppose that W is the number of *wins* compared to the baseline, L is the number of *losses* and T is the number of *ties*. The Pairwise score can be calculated by the following formula:

$$
Pairwise = 100 \times \frac{W - L}{W + L + T}
$$

From the definition, the Pairwise score ranges between -100 and 100.

5.1.4 Confidence Interval Estimation

There are several ways to estimate a confidence interval. We chose to use bootstrap resampling (Koehn, 2004) to estimate the 95% confidence interval. The procedure is as follows:

1. randomly select 300 sentences from the 400 human evaluation sentences, and calculate the Pairwise score of the selected sentences

2. iterate the previous step 1000 times and get 1000 Pairwise scores

3. sort the 1000 scores and estimate the 95% confidence interval by discarding the top 25 scores and the bottom 25 scores

5.2 JPO Adequacy Evaluation

The participants' systems, which achieved the top 3 highest scores among the pairwise evaluation results of each subtask[22], were also evaluated with the JPO adequacy evaluation. The JPO adequacy evaluation was carried out by translation experts with a quality evaluation criterion for translated patent documents which the Japanese Patent Office (JPO) decided. For each system, two annotators evaluate the test sentences to guarantee the quality.

5.2.1 Evaluation of Sentences

The number of test sentences for the JPO adequacy evaluation is 200. The 200 test sentences were randomly selected from the 400 test sentences of the pairwise evaluation. The test sentence include the input sentence, the submitted system's translation and the reference translation.

---

[22]The number of systems varies depending on the subtasks.

5	All important information is transmitted correctly. (100%)
4	Almost all important information is transmitted correctly. (80%–)
3	More than half of important information is transmitted correctly. (50%–)
2	Some of important information is transmitted correctly. (20%–)
1	Almost all important information is NOT transmitted correctly. (–20%)

Table 7: The JPO adequacy criterion

5.2.2 Evaluation Criterion

Table 7 shows the JPO adequacy criterion from 5 to 1. The evaluation is performed subjectively. "Important information" represents the technical factors and their relationships. The degree of importance of each element is also considered to evaluate. The percentages in each grade are rough indications for the transmission degree of the source sentence meanings. The detailed criterion can be found on the JPO document (in Japanese) [23].

6 Participants List

Table 8 shows the list of participants for WAT2017. This includes not only Japanese organizations, but also some organizations from outside Japan. 12 teams submitted one or more translation results to the automatic evaluation server or human evaluation.

---

[23] http://www.jpo.go.jp/shiryou/toushin/chousa/tokkyohonyaku_hyouka.htm

Team ID	Organization	ASPEC JE	ASPEC EJ	ASPEC JC	ASPEC CJ	JPC JE	JPC EJ	JPC JC	JPC CJ	JPC KJ	IITBC HE	IITBC EH	JIJI JE	JIJI EJ	RECIPE TTL JE	RECIPE TTL EJ	RECIPE ING JE	RECIPE ING EJ	RECIPE STE JE	RECIPE STE EJ
Kyoto-U (Cromieres et al., 2017)	Kyoto University	✓	✓	✓	✓															
TMU (Matsumura and Komachi, 2017)	Tokyo Metropolitan University	✓	✓	✓																
EHR (Ehara, 2017)	Ehara NLP Research Laboratory						✓		✓	✓										
NTT (Morishita et al., 2017)	NTT Communication Science Laboratories	✓	✓										✓	✓						
JAPIO (Kinoshita et al., 2017)	Japan Patent Information Organization					✓	✓		✓	✓										
NICT-2 (Imamura and Sumita, 2017)	National Institute of Information and Communications Technology	✓	✓	✓	✓								✓							
XMUNLP (Wang et al., 2017)	Xiamen University										✓	✓	✓	✓	✓	✓	✓	✓	✓	✓
UT-IIS (Neishi et al., 2017)	The University of Tokyo		✓																	
CUNI (Kocmi et al., 2017)	Charles University, Institute of Formal and Applied Linguistics	✓				✓							✓							
IITB-MTG (Singh et al., 2017)	Indian Institute of Technology Bombay										✓	✓								
u-tkb (Long et al., 2017)	University of Tsukuba					✓	✓	✓	✓											
NAIST-NICT (Oda et al., 2017)	NAIST/NICT		✓																	

Table 8: List of participants who submitted translation results to WAT2017 and their participation in each subtasks.

7 Evaluation Results

In this section, the evaluation results for WAT2017 are reported from several perspectives. Some of the results for both automatic and human evaluations are also accessible at the WAT2017 website[24].

7.1 Official Evaluation Results

Figures 2, 3, 4 and 5 show the official evaluation results of ASPEC subtasks, Figures 6, 7, 8, 9 and 10 show those of JPC subtasks, Figures 11 and 12 show those of IITBC subtasks, Figures 13 and 14 show those of JIJI subtasks and Figures 15, 16, 17, 18, 19 and 20 show those of RECIPE subtasks. Each figure contains automatic evaluation results (BLEU, RIBES, AM-FM), the pairwise evaluation results with confidence intervals, correlation between automatic evaluations and the pairwise evaluation, the JPO adequacy evaluation result and evaluation summary of top systems.

The detailed automatic evaluation results for all the submissions are shown in Appendix A. The detailed JPO adequacy evaluation results for the selected submissions are shown in Table 9. The weights for the weighted κ (Cohen, 1968) is defined as $|Evaluation1 - Evaluation2|/4$.

From the evaluation results, the following can be observed:

- The translation quality of this year is better than that of last year for all the subtasks.

- There is no big difference between the neural network based translation models according to the JPO adequacy evaluation results for ASPEC subtasks.

7.2 Statistical Significance Testing of Pairwise Evaluation between Submissions

Tables 10, 11 and 12 show the results of statistical significance testing of ASPEC subtasks, Tables 13, 14 and 15 show those of JPC subtasks, Table 16 shows those of IITBC subtasks, Table 17 shows those of JIJI subtasks and Tables 18, 19 and 20 show those of RECIPE subtasks. $\ggg$, $\gg$ and $>$ mean that the system in

the row is *better* than the system in the column at a significance level of $p < 0.01$, 0.05 and 0.1 respectively. Testing is also done by the bootstrap resampling as follows:

1. randomly select 300 sentences from the 400 pairwise evaluation sentences, and calculate the Pairwise scores on the selected sentences for both systems

2. iterate the previous step 1000 times and count the number of wins (W), losses (L) and ties (T)

3. calculate $p = \frac{L}{W+L}$

Inter-annotator Agreement

To assess the reliability of agreement between the workers, we calculated the Fleiss' κ (Fleiss et al., 1971) values. The results are shown in Table 21. We can see that the κ values are larger for X $\rightarrow$ J translations than for J $\rightarrow$ X translations. This may be because the majority of the workers are Japanese, and the evaluation of one's mother tongue is much easier than for other languages in general.

8 Submitted Data

The number of published automatic evaluation results for the 14 teams exceeded 300 before the start of WAT2017, and 67 translation results for pairwise evaluation were submitted by 12 teams. Furthermore, we selected several translation results from each subtask according to the pairwise evaluation scores and evaluated them for JPO adequacy evaluation. We will organize the all of the submitted data for human evaluation and make this public.

9 Conclusion and Future Perspective

This paper summarizes the shared tasks of WAT2017. We had 12 participants worldwide, and collected a large number of useful submissions for improving the current machine translation systems by analyzing the submissions and identifying the issues.

For the next WAT workshop, we plan to change the baseline system from the PBSMT to NMT because the pairwise scores are saturated for some of the subtasks. Also, we

---

[24]http://lotus.kuee.kyoto-u.ac.jp/WAT/evaluation/

are planning to do extrinsic evaluation of the translations.

Unfortunately, there was no participants for the small NMT task this year. We will brush-up the task definition and invite participants for the next WAT.

Appendix A Submissions

Tables 22 to 41 summarize all the submissions listed in the automatic evaluation server at the time of the WAT2017 workshop (27th, November, 2017). The OTHER column shows the use of resources such as parallel corpora, monolingual corpora and parallel dictionaries in addition to ASPEC, JPC, IITB Corpus, JIJI Corpus, RECIPE Corpus.

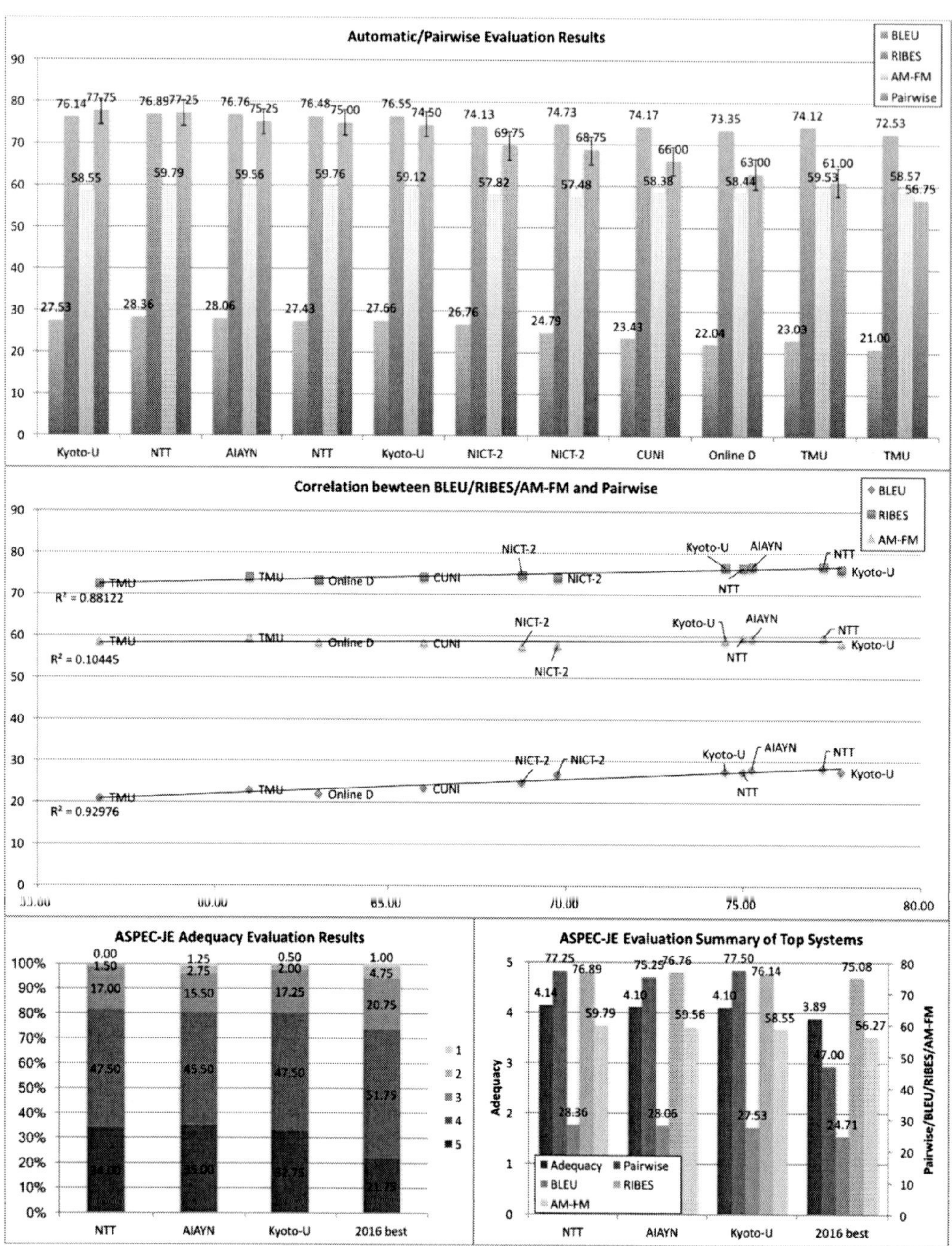

Figure 2: Official evaluation results of ASPEC-JE.

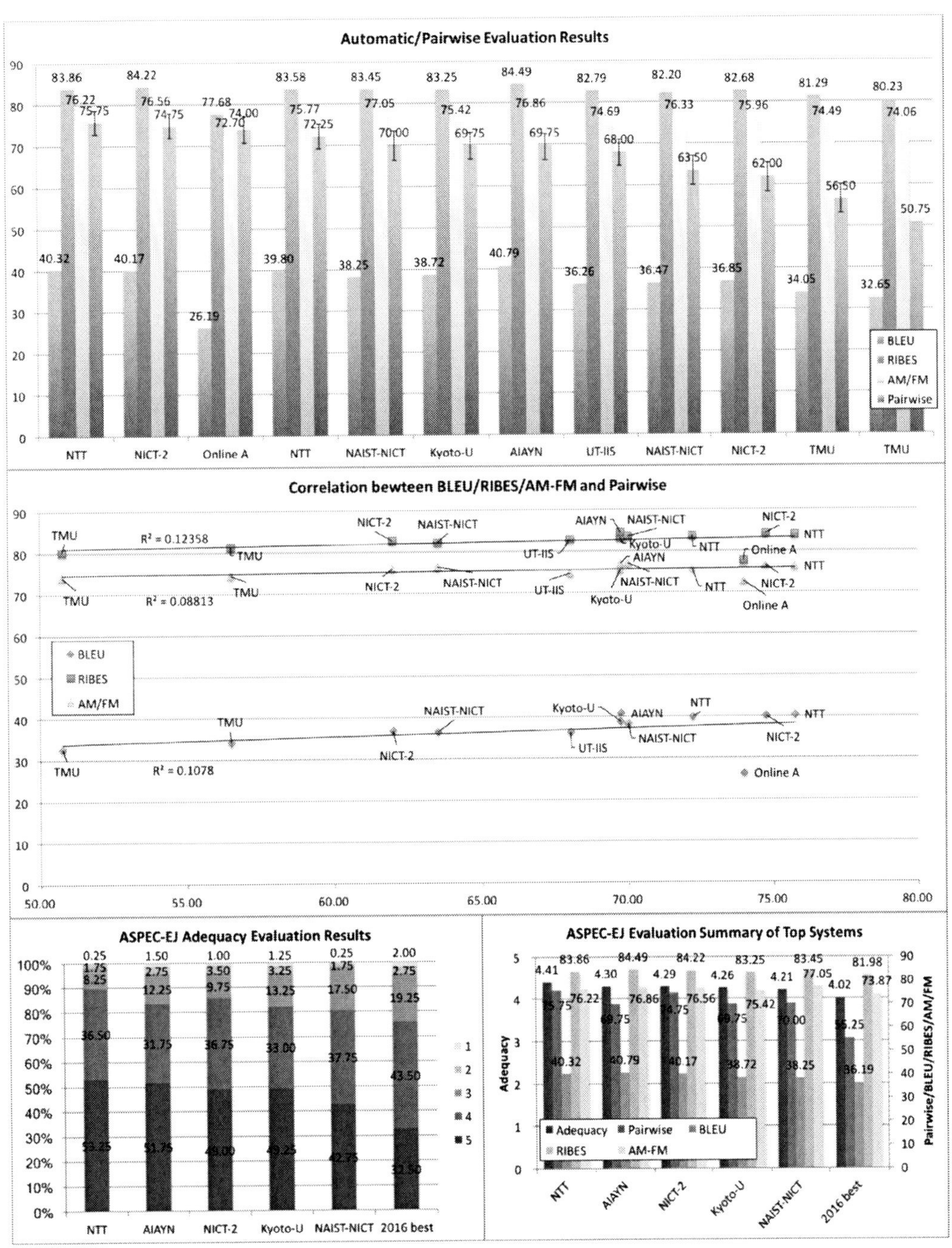

Figure 3: Official evaluation results of ASPEC-EJ.

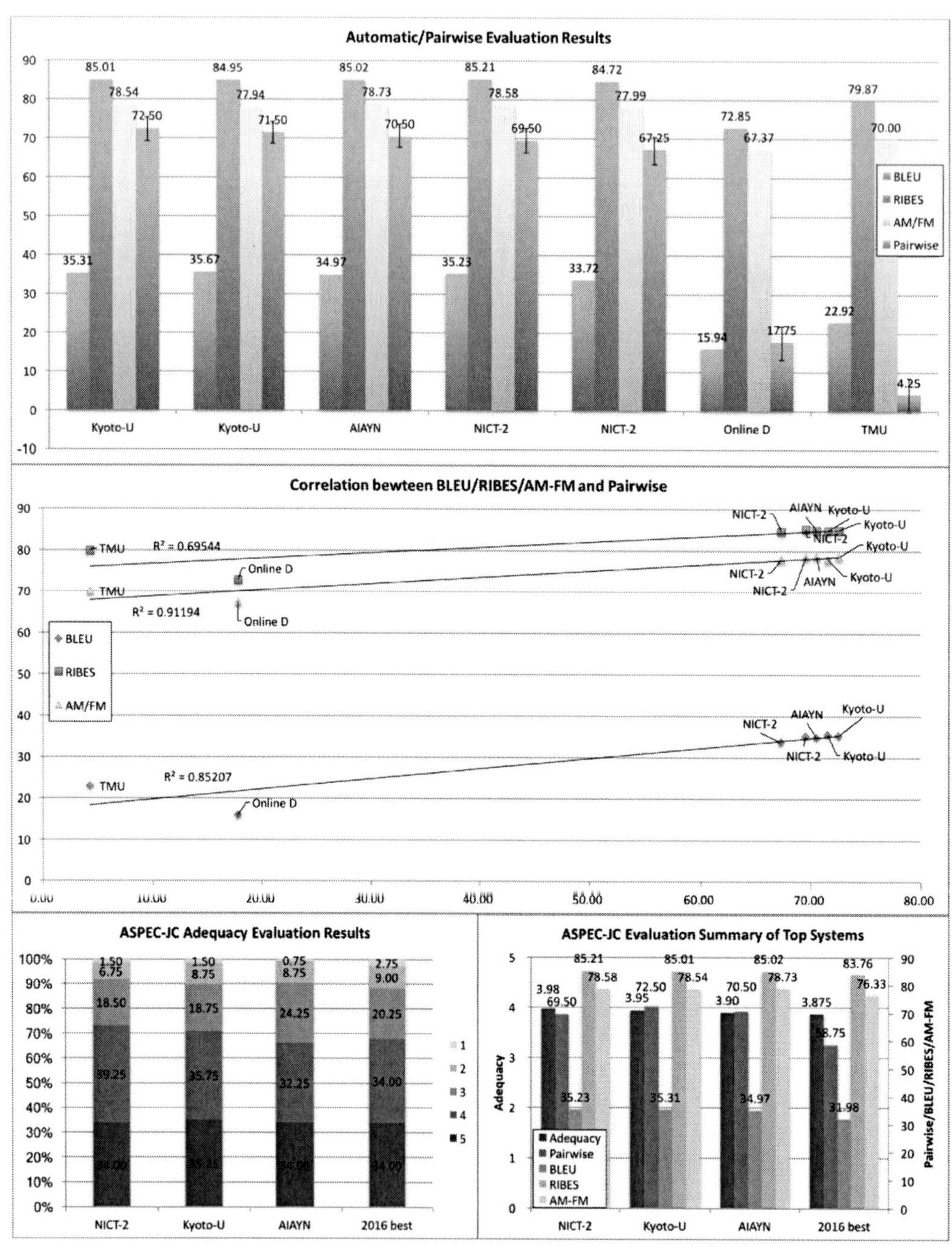

Figure 4: Official evaluation results of ASPEC-JC.

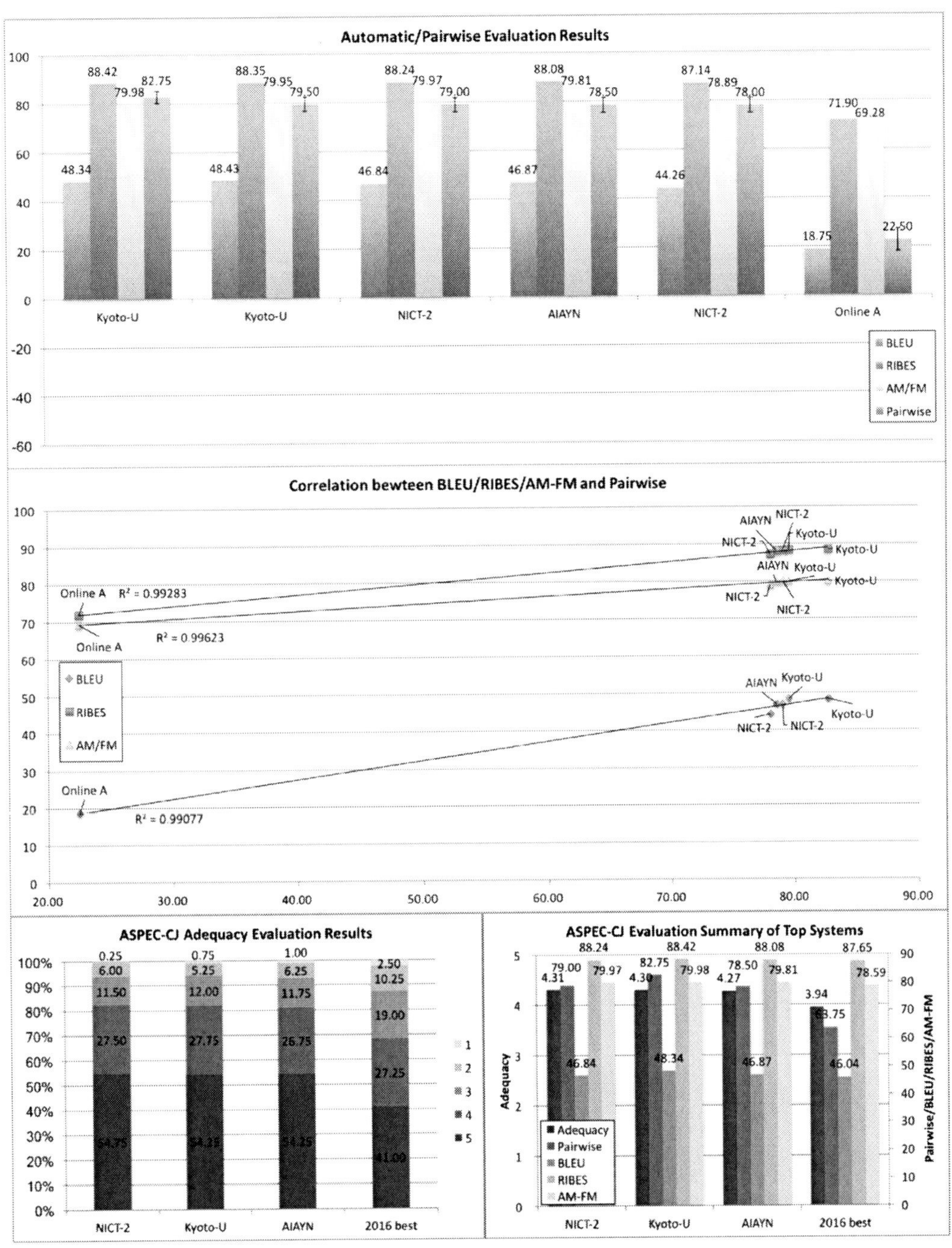

Figure 5: Official evaluation results of ASPEC-CJ.

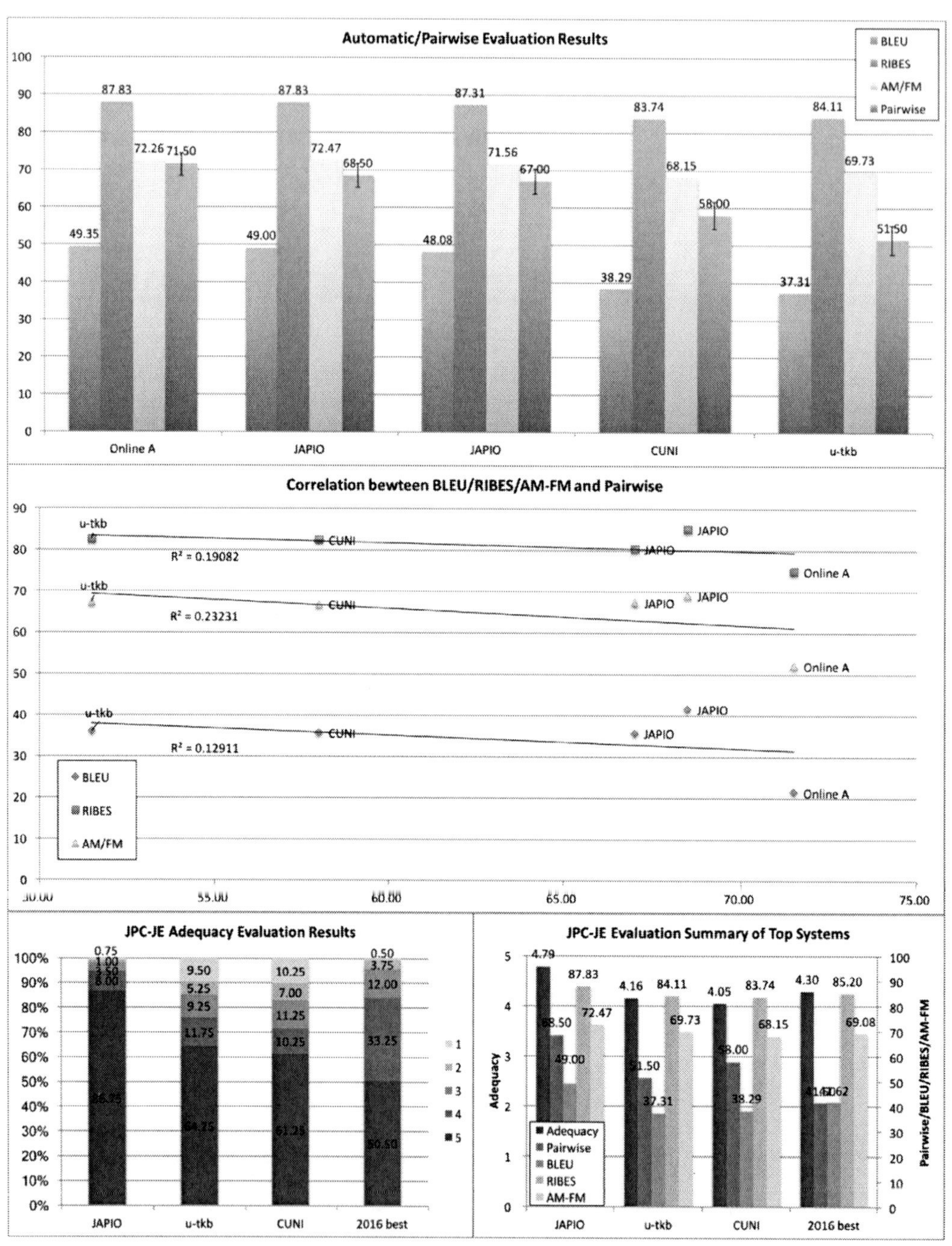

Figure 6: Official evaluation results of JPC-JE.

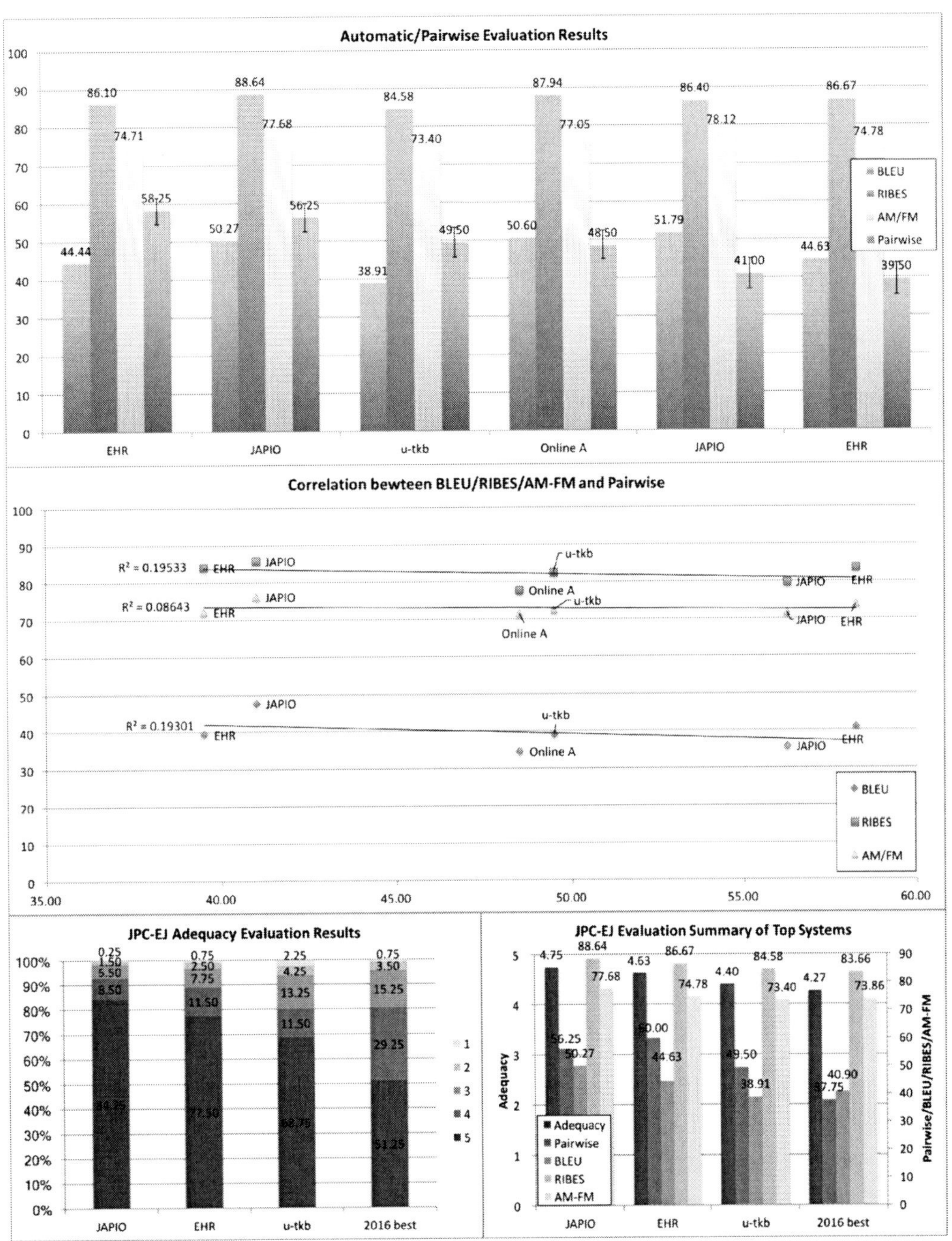

Figure 7: Official evaluation results of JPC-EJ.

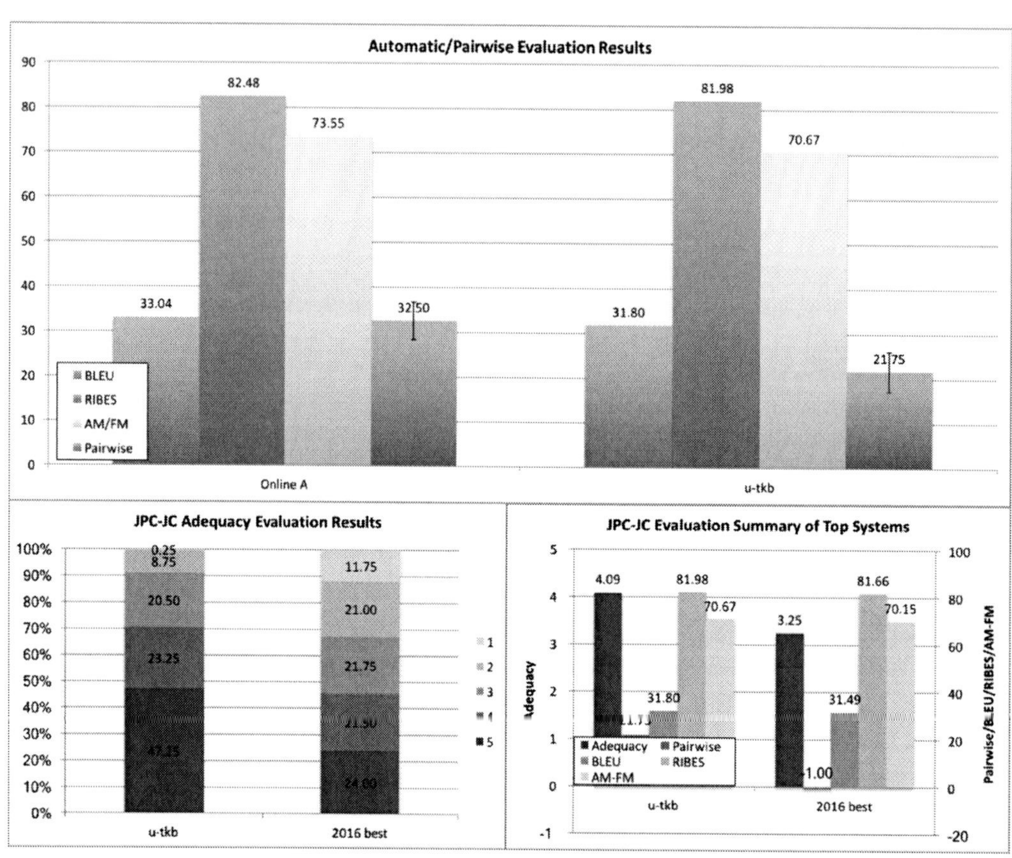

Figure 8: Official evaluation results of JPC-JC.

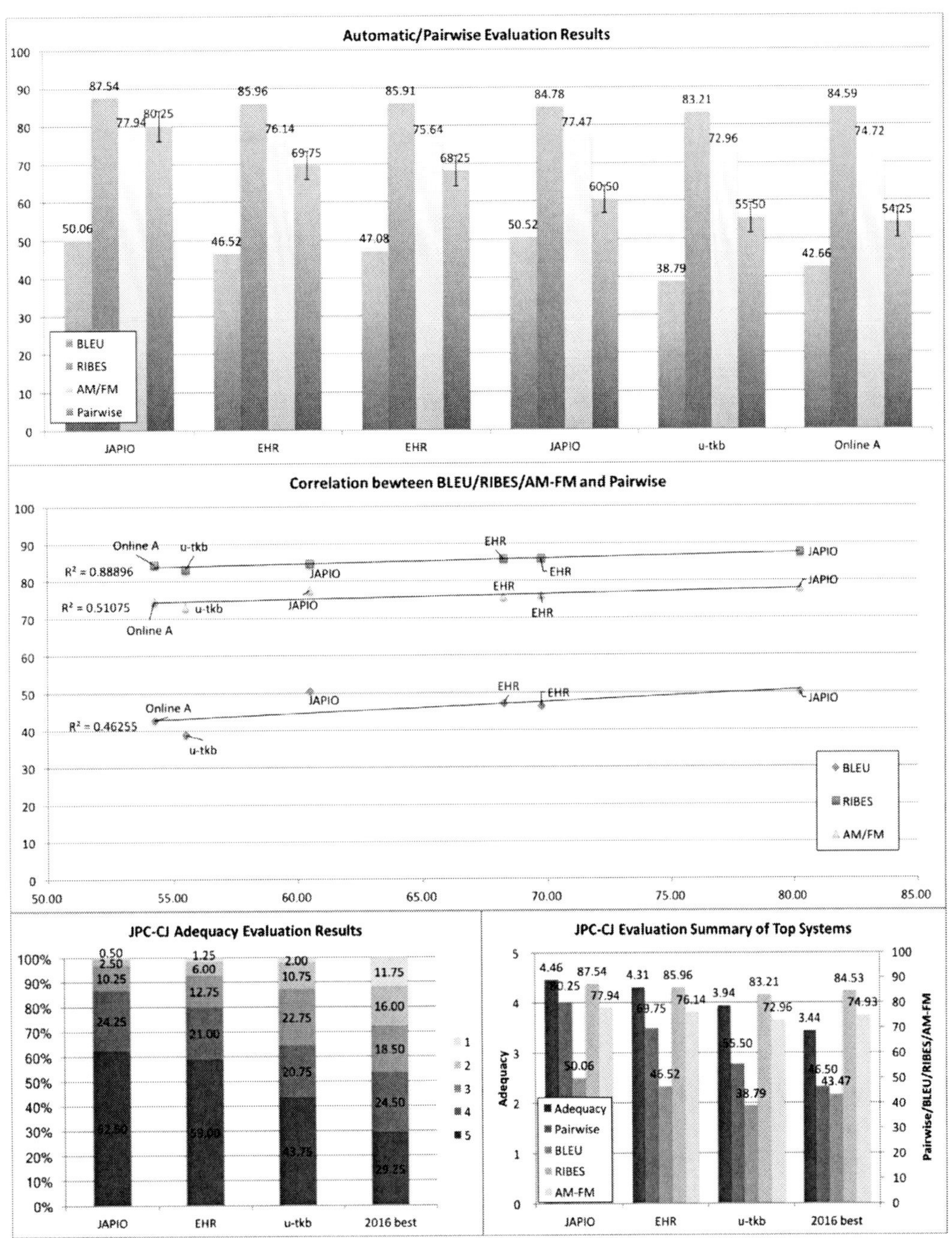

Figure 9: Official evaluation results of JPC-CJ.

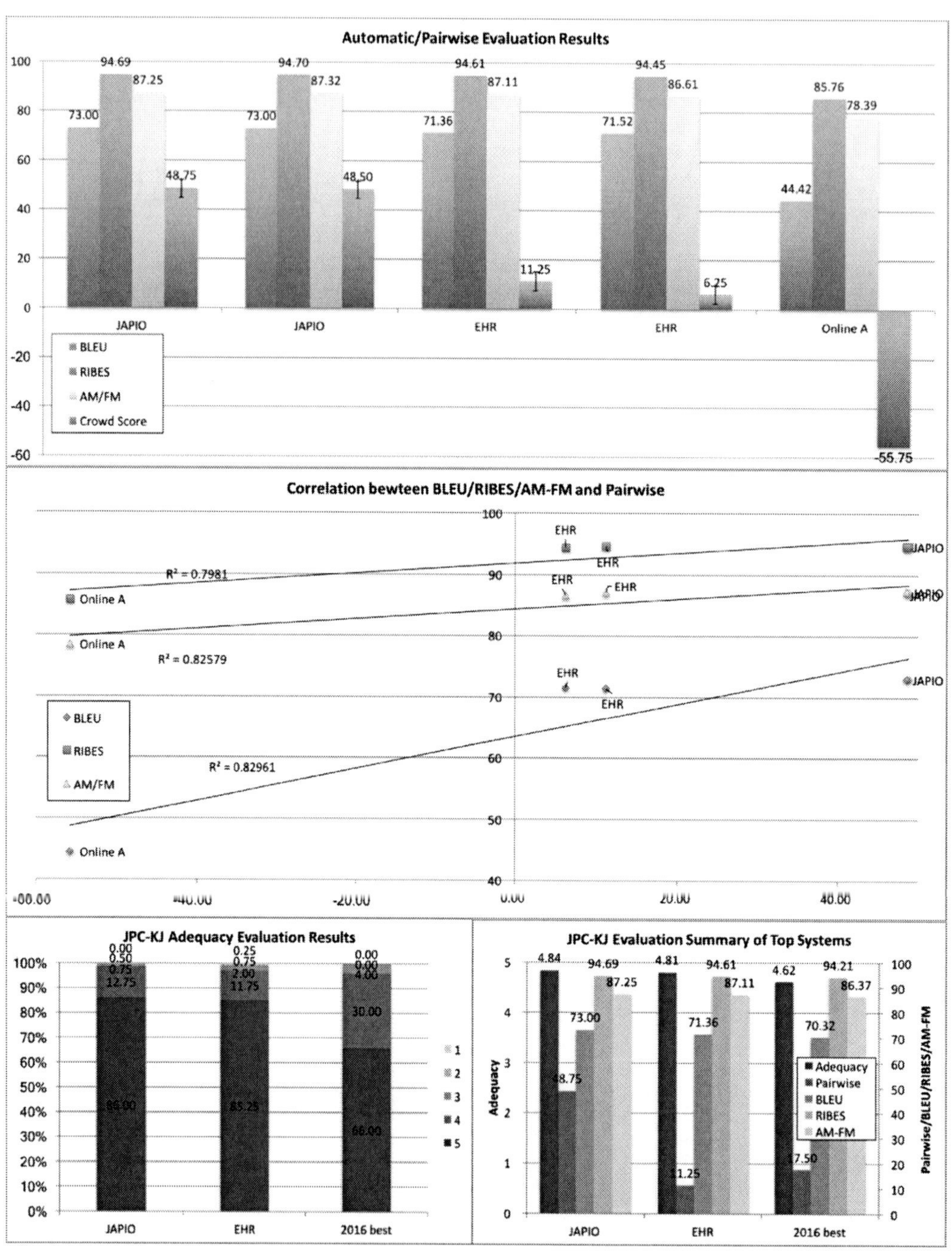

Figure 10: Official evaluation results of JPC-KJ.

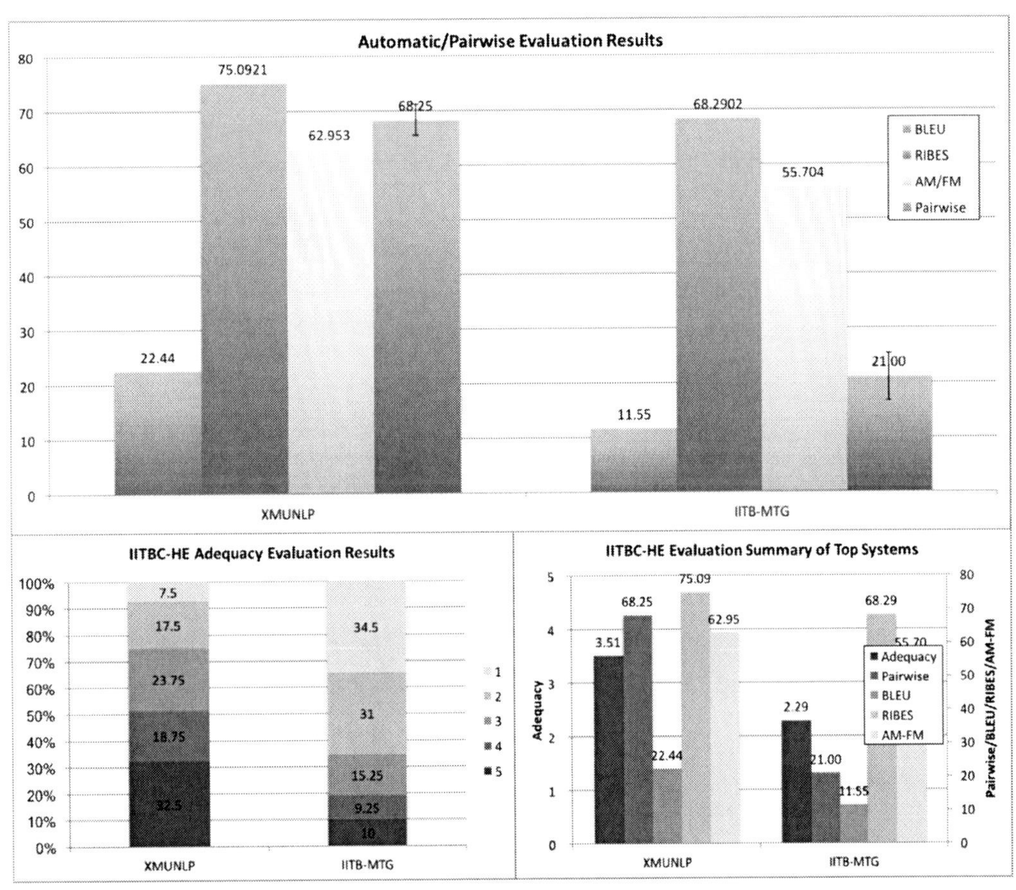

Figure 11: Official evaluation results of IITBC-HE.

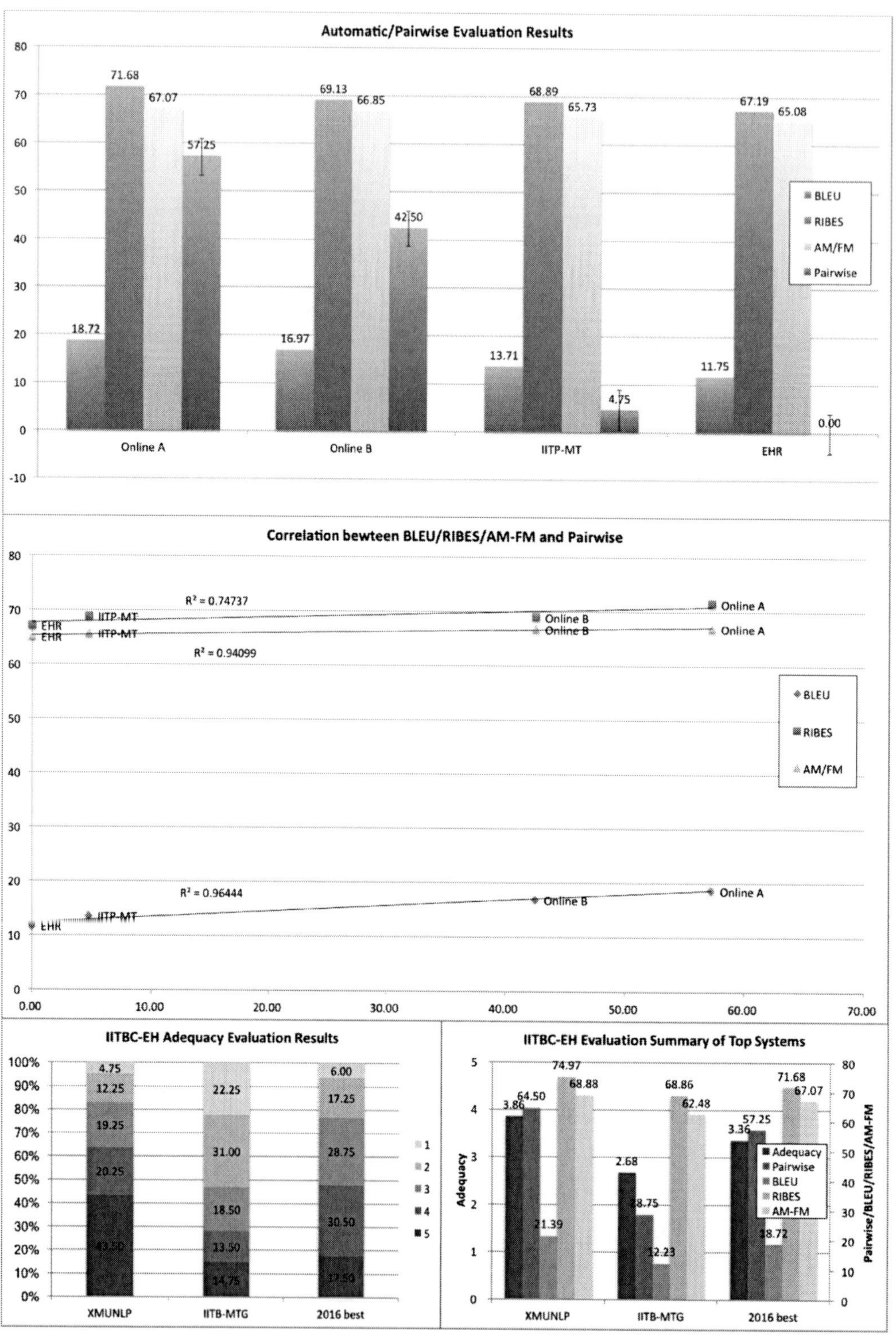

Figure 12: Official evaluation results of IITBC-EH.

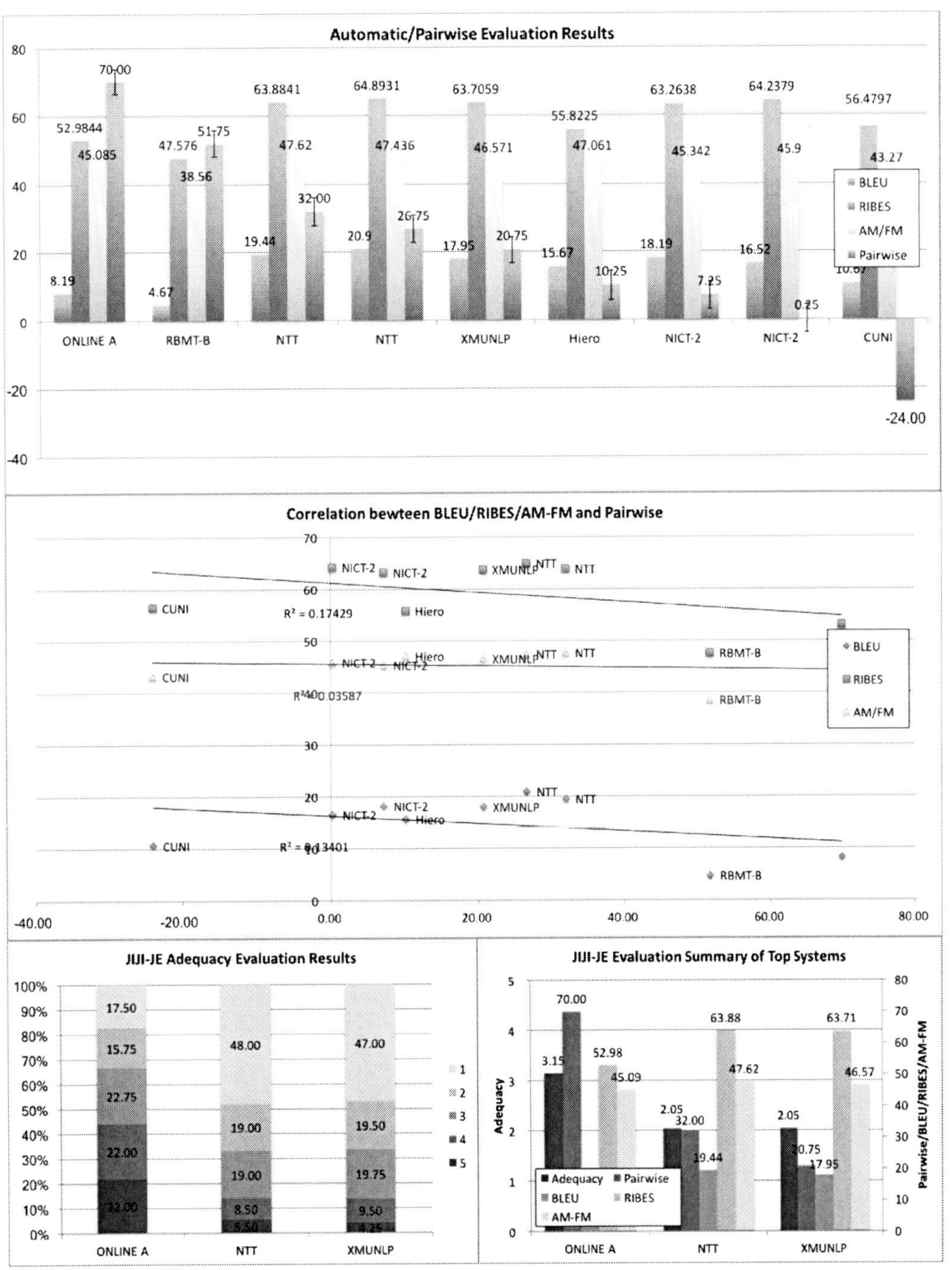

Figure 13: Official evaluation results of JIJI-JE.

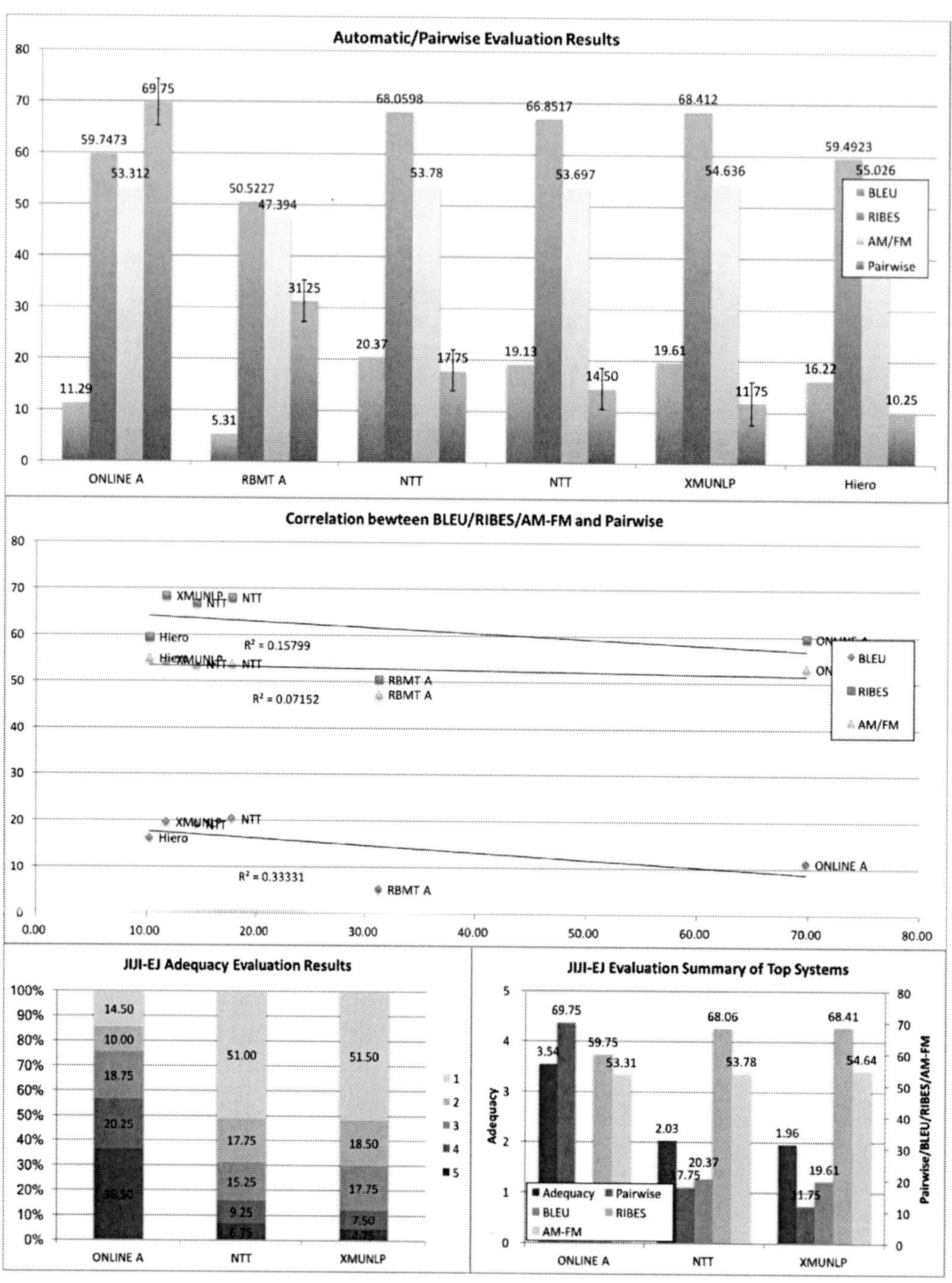

Figure 14: Official evaluation results of JIJI-EJ.

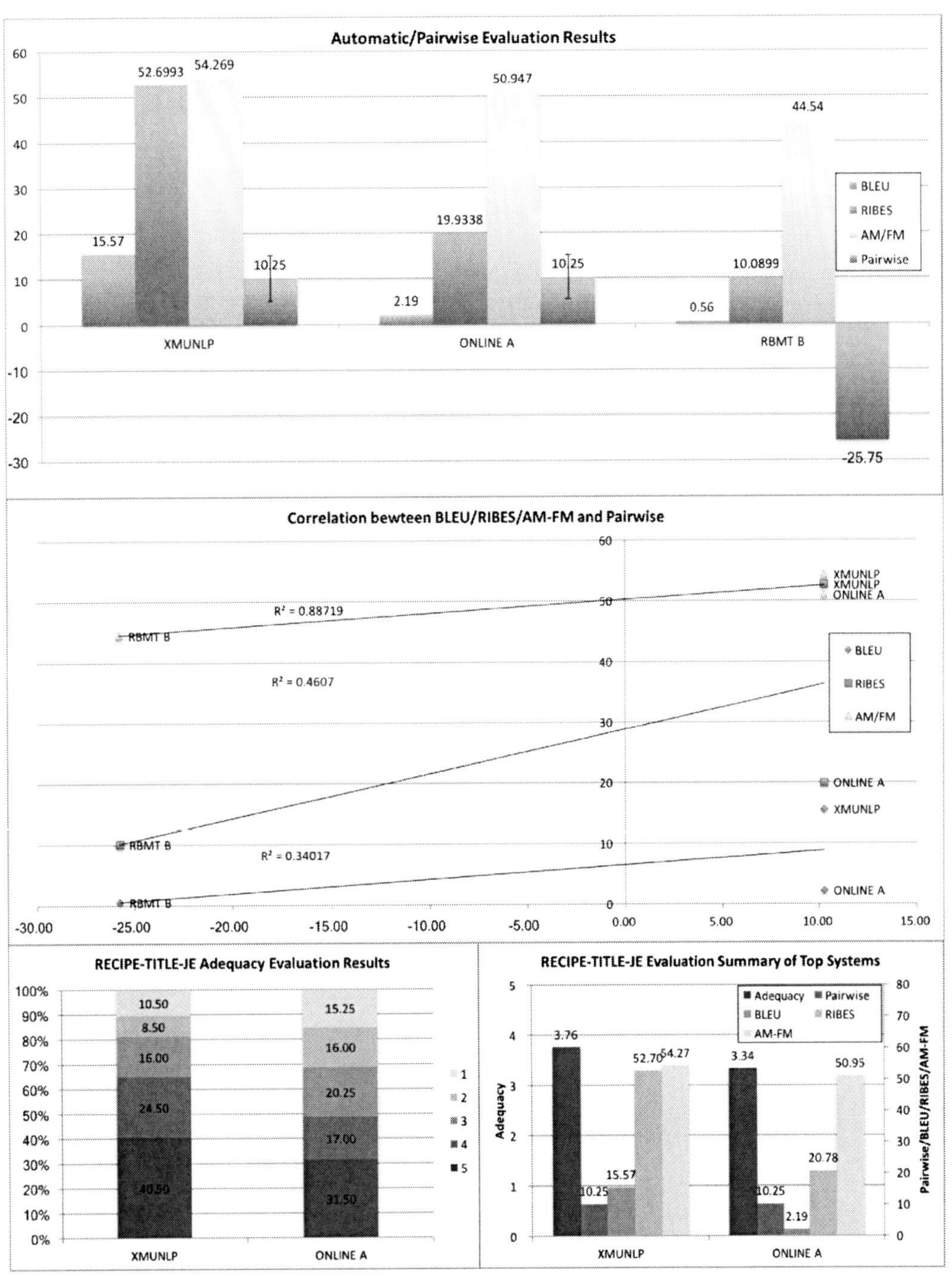

Figure 15: Official evaluation results of RECIPE-TTL-JE.

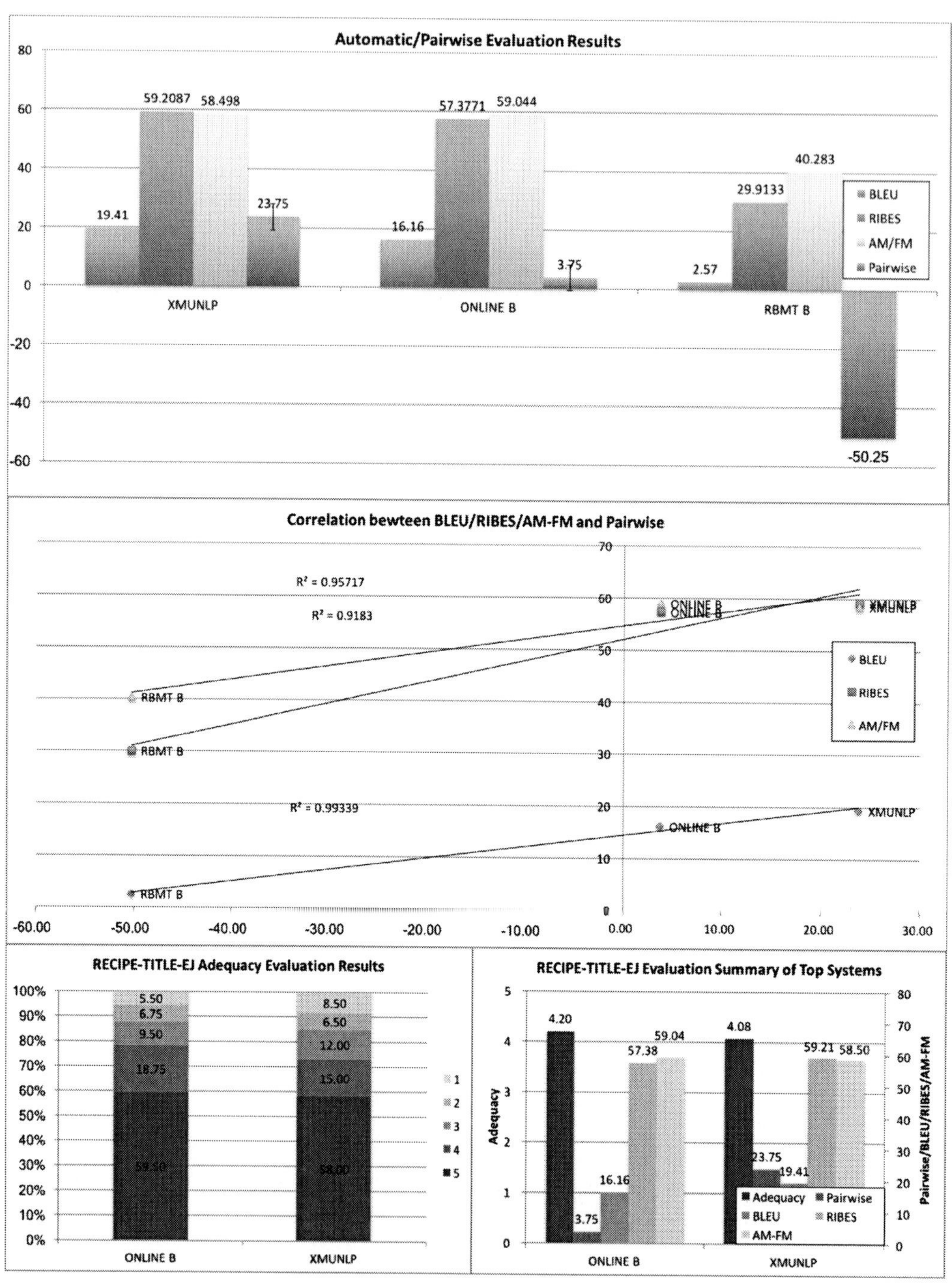

Figure 16: Official evaluation results of RECIPE-TTL-EJ.

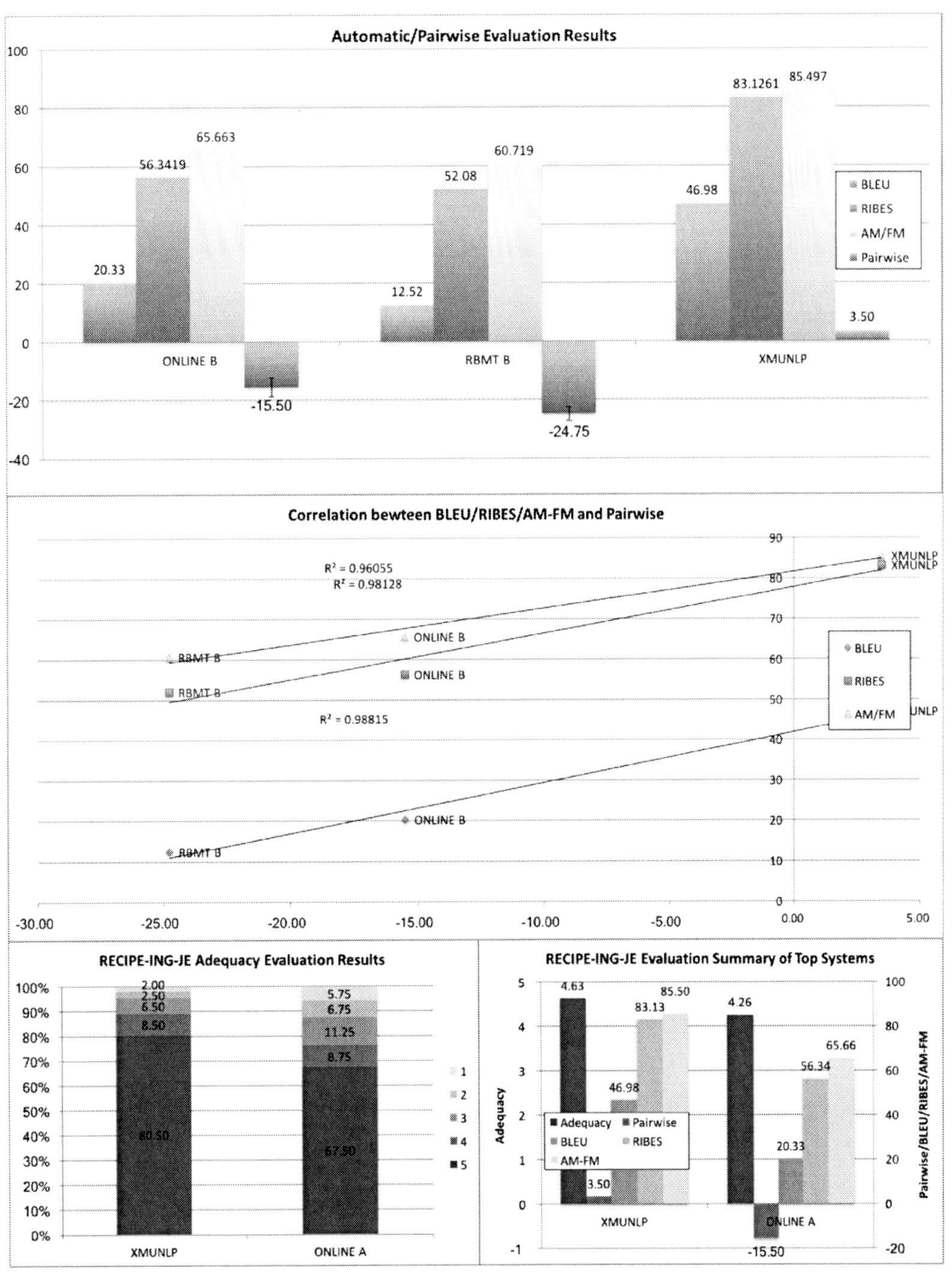

Figure 17: Official evaluation results of RECIPE-ING-JE.

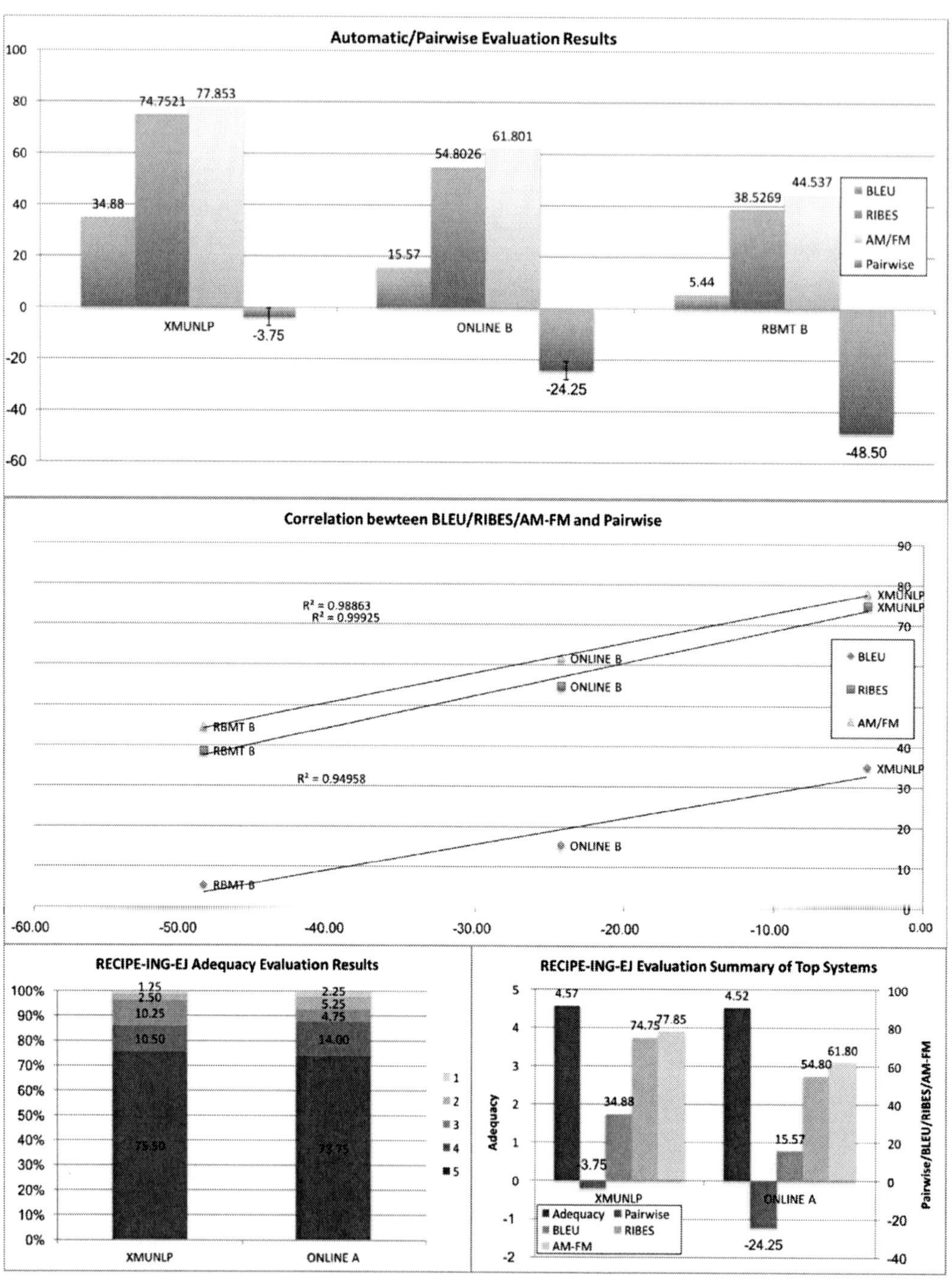

Figure 18: Official evaluation results of RECIPE-ING-EJ.

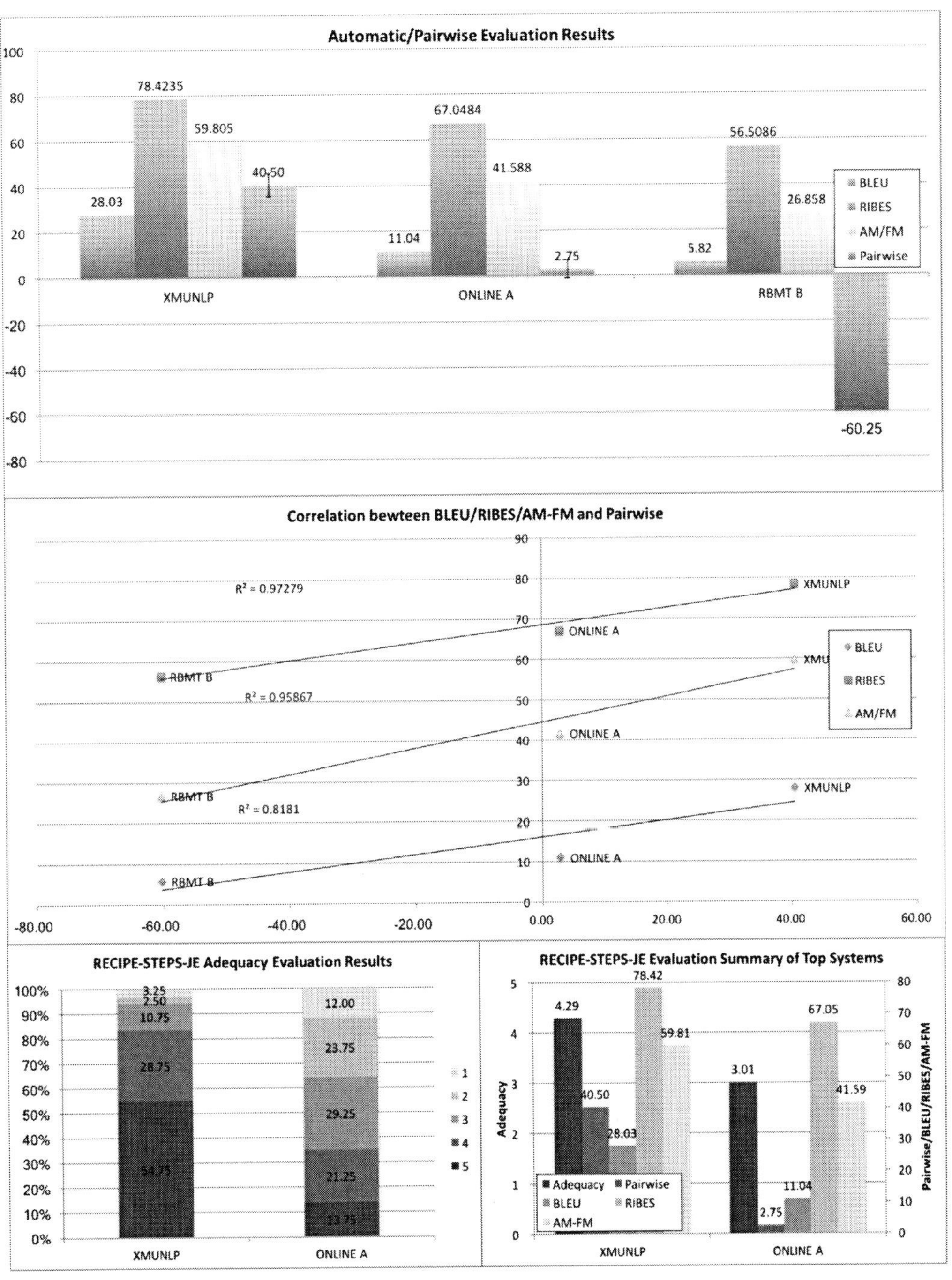

Figure 19: Official evaluation results of RECIPE-STE-JE.

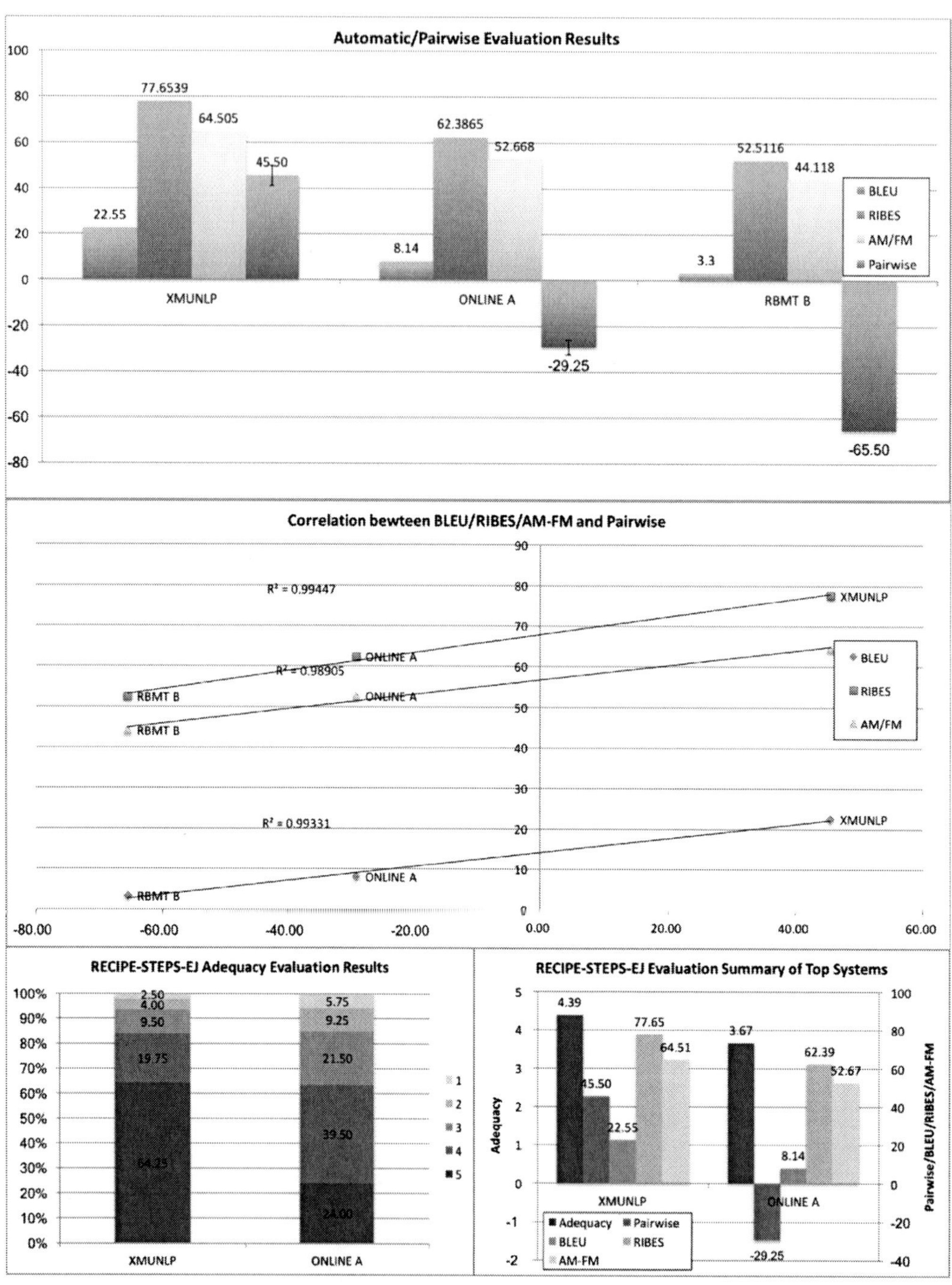

Figure 20: Official evaluation results of RECIPE-STE-EJ.

Subtask	SYSTEM ID	DATA ID	Annotator A		Annotator B		all average	weighted	
			average	variance	average	variance		κ	κ
ASPEC-JE	NTT	1681	4.15	0.58	4.13	0.52	4.14	0.29	0.41
	AIAYN	1736	4.16	0.67	4.05	0.75	4.10	0.26	0.42
	Kyoto-U	1717	4.11	0.69	4.09	0.54	4.10	0.26	0.40
	2016 best	1246	3.76	0.68	4.01	0.67	3.89	0.21	0.31
ASPEC-EJ	NTT	1729	4.54	0.56	4.28	0.49	4.41	0.33	0.43
	AIAYN	1737	4.38	0.83	4.21	0.76	4.30	0.36	0.52
	NICT-2	1479	4.43	0.73	4.16	0.69	4.29	0.35	0.48
	Kyoto-U	1731	4.37	0.84	4.15	0.74	4.26	0.39	0.54
	NAIST-NICT	1507	4.36	0.69	4.06	0.57	4.21	0.26	0.36
	2016 best	1172	3.97	0.76	4.07	0.85	4.02	0.35	0.49
ASPEC-JC	NICT-2	1483	4.25	0.73	3.71	0.98	3.98	0.10	0.18
	Kyoto-U	1722	4.25	0.79	3.64	1.07	3.95	0.12	0.23
	AIAYN	1738	4.26	0.69	3.54	1.03	3.90	0.17	0.27
	2016 best	1071	4.00	1.09	3.76	1.14	3.88	0.20	0.36
ASPEC-CJ	NICT-2	1481	4.63	0.47	3.99	0.98	4.31	0.17	0.23
	Kyoto-U	1720	4.62	0.56	3.97	0.94	4.30	0.16	0.22
	AIAYN	1740	4.59	0.61	3.96	1.04	4.27	0.14	0.23
	2016 best	1256	4.25	1.04	3.64	1.23	3.94	0.23	0.34
JPC-JE	JAPIO	1574	4.80	0.26	4.78	0.51	4.79	0.34	0.42
	u-tkb	1472	4.24	1.26	4.08	2.27	4.16	0.43	0.64
	CUNI	1666	4.12	1.49	3.99	2.35	4.05	0.40	0.63
	2016 best	1149	4.09	0.80	4.51	0.58	4.30	0.25	0.39
JPC-EJ	JAPIO	1454	4.74	0.45	4.76	0.38	4.75	0.32	0.48
	EHR	1407	4.64	0.61	4.61	0.65	4.63	0.42	0.60
	u-tkb	1470	4.39	1.07	4.42	0.99	4.40	0.43	0.61
	2016 best	1098	4.03	0.91	4.51	0.57	4.27	0.23	0.41
JPC-JC	u-tkb	1465	3.99	1.12	4.19	0.94	4.09	0.22	0.32
	2016 best	1150	3.49	1.72	3.02	1.75	3.25	0.27	0.51
JPC-CJ	JAPIO	1484	4.41	0.68	4.51	0.64	4.46	0.26	0.34
	EHR	1414	4.27	0.92	4.35	1.03	4.31	0.33	0.48
	u-tkb	1468	3.84	1.16	4.04	1.36	3.94	0.23	0.43
	2016 best	1200	3.61	1.89	3.27	1.76	3.44	0.26	0.52
JPC-KJ	JAPIO	1448	4.82	0.24	4.87	0.11	4.84	0.55	0.55
	EHR	1417	4.76	0.30	4.86	0.23	4.81	0.35	0.47
	2016 best	1209	4.58	0.32	4.66	0.30	4.62	0.33	0.36
IITBC-HE	XMUNLP	1511	3.43	1.64	3.60	1.74	3.51	0.22	0.45
	IITB-MTG	1726	2.14	1.45	2.45	1.87	2.29	0.30	0.51
IITBC-EH	XMUNLP	1576	3.95	1.18	3.76	1.85	3.86	0.17	0.36
	IITB-MTG	1725	2.78	1.74	2.58	1.87	2.68	0.15	0.38
	2016 best	1032	3.20	1.33	3.53	1.19	3.36	0.10	0.16
JIJI-JE	Online A	1523	3.03	1.60	3.28	2.24	3.15	0.15	0.37
	NTT	1599	1.87	1.25	2.23	1.69	2.05	0.26	0.46
	XMUNLP	1442	1.91	1.26	2.19	1.56	2.05	0.24	0.44
JIJI-EJ	Online A	1518	3.31	1.92	3.78	2.06	3.54	0.23	0.50
	NTT	1679	1.78	1.18	2.28	1.97	2.03	0.29	0.52
	XMUNLP	1443	1.72	1.02	2.20	1.70	1.96	0.33	0.51
RECIPE-TTL-JE	XMUNLP	1637	3.90	1.98	3.62	1.57	3.76	0.30	0.56
	Online A	1534	3.52	2.04	3.16	2.07	3.34	0.36	0.60
RECIPE-TTL-EJ	Online B	1533	4.56	0.55	3.84	2.02	4.20	0.25	0.35
	XMUNLP	1636	4.54	0.62	3.62	2.40	4.08	0.26	0.34
RECIPE-ING-JE	XMULNP	1635	4.68	0.65	4.58	0.85	4.63	0.47	0.67
	Online A	1544	4.29	1.44	4.23	1.57	4.26	0.55	0.76
RECIPE-ING-EJ	XMUNLP	1634	4.71	0.43	4.43	1.03	4.57	0.40	0.53
	Online A	1542	4.50	0.95	4.54	0.91	4.52	0.50	0.65
RECIPE-STE-JE	XMUNLP	1632	4.61	0.76	3.98	0.96	4.29	0.13	0.28
	Online A	1551	3.34	1.54	2.69	1.21	3.01	0.14	0.36
RECIPE-STE-EJ	XMUNLP	1633	4.75	0.36	4.04	1.33	4.39	0.12	0.21
	Online A	1549	4.18	0.42	3.16	1.52	3.67	0.11	0.17

Table 9: JPO adequacy evaluation results in detail.

	NTT (1681)	ORGANIZER (1736)	NTT (1616)	Kyoto-U (1733)	NICT-2 (1480)	NICT-2 (1476)	CUNI (1665)	ORGANIZER (1333)	TMU (1703)	TMU (1695)
Kyoto-U (1717)	-	≫	≫	⋙	⋙	⋙	⋙	⋙	⋙	⋙
NTT (1681)		>	≫	≫	⋙	⋙	⋙	⋙	⋙	⋙
ORGANIZER (1736)			-	-	⋙	⋙	⋙	⋙	⋙	⋙
NTT (1616)				-	⋙	⋙	⋙	⋙	⋙	⋙
Kyoto-U (1733)					⋙	⋙	⋙	⋙	⋙	⋙
NICT-2 (1480)						-	⋙	⋙	⋙	⋙
NICT-2 (1476)							≫	⋙	⋙	⋙
CUNI (1665)								>	⋙	⋙
ORGANIZER (1333)									-	⋙
TMU (1703)										⋙

Table 10: Statistical significance testing of the ASPEC-JE Pairwise scores.

	NICT-2 (1479)	ORGANIZER (1334)	NTT (1684)	NAIST-NICT (1507)	ORGANIZER (1737)	Kyoto-U (1731)	UT-IIS (1710)	NAIST-NICT (1506)	NICT-2 (1475)	TMU (1709)	TMU (1704)
NTT (1729)	-	-	⋙	⋙	⋙	⋙	⋙	⋙	⋙	⋙	⋙
NICT-2 (1479)		-	≫	⋙	⋙	⋙	⋙	⋙	⋙	⋙	⋙
ORGANIZER (1334)			-	⋙	⋙	⋙	⋙	⋙	⋙	⋙	⋙
NTT (1684)				≫	≫	≫	⋙	⋙	⋙	⋙	⋙
NAIST-NICT (1507)					-	-	>	⋙	⋙	⋙	⋙
ORGANIZER (1737)						-	>	⋙	⋙	⋙	⋙
Kyoto-U (1731)							>	⋙	⋙	⋙	⋙
UT-IIS (1710)								⋙	⋙	⋙	⋙
NAIST-NICT (1506)									-	⋙	⋙
NICT-2 (1475)										⋙	⋙
TMU (1709)											⋙

Table 11: Statistical significance testing of the ASPEC-EJ Pairwise scores.

	Kyoto-U (1642)	ORGANIZER (1738)	NICT-2 (1483)	NICT-2 (1478)	ORGANIZER (1336)	TMU (1743)
Kyoto-U (1722)	-	>	≫	⋙	⋙	⋙
Kyoto-U (1642)		-	>	⋙	⋙	⋙
ORGANIZER (1738)			-	≫	⋙	⋙
NICT-2 (1483)				>	⋙	⋙
NICT-2 (1478)					⋙	⋙
ORGANIZER (1336)						⋙

	Kyoto-U (1577)	NICT-2 (1481)	ORGANIZER (1740)	NICT-2 (1477)	ORGANIZER (1342)
Kyoto-U (1720)	⋙	⋙	⋙	⋙	⋙
Kyoto-U (1577)		-	-	-	≫
NICT-2 (1481)			-	-	≫
ORGANIZER (1740)				-	≫
NICT-2 (1477)					≫

Table 12: Statistical significance testing of the ASPEC-JC (left) and ASPEC-CJ (right) Pairwise scores.

	JAPIO (1574)	JAPIO (1578)	CUNI (1666)	u-tkb (1472)
ORGANIZER (1338)	≫	≫	≫	≫
JAPIO (1574)		-	≫	≫
JAPIO (1578)			≫	≫
CUNI (1666)				≫

	EHR (1406)	JAPIO (1454)	u-tkb (1470)	ORGANIZER (1339)	JAPIO (1462)
EHR (1407)	-	≫	≫	≫	≫
EHR (1406)		-	≫	≫	≫
JAPIO (1454)			≫	≫	≫
u-tkb (1470)				-	≫
ORGANIZER (1339)					≫

Table 13: Statistical significance testing of the JPC-JE (left) and JPC-EJ (right) Pairwise scores.

	u-tkb (1465)
ORGANIZER (1340)	≫

	EHR (1414)	EHR (1408)	JAPIO (1447)	u-tkb (1468)	ORGANIZER (1341)
JAPIO (1484)	≫	≫	≫	≫	≫
EHR (1414)		-	≫	≫	≫
EHR (1408)			≫	≫	≫
JAPIO (1447)				≫	≫
u-tkb (1468)					-

Table 14: Statistical significance testing of the JPC-JC (left) and JPC-CJ (right) Pairwise scores.

	JAPIO (1450)	EHR (1417)	EHR (1416)	ORGANIZER (1344)
JAPIO (1448)	-	≫	≫	≫
JAPIO (1450)		≫	≫	≫
EHR (1417)			≫	≫
EHR (1416)				≫

Table 15: Statistical significance testing of the JPC-KJ Pairwise scores.

	IITB-MTG (1726)
XMUNLP (1511)	≫

	IITB-MTG (1725)
XMUNLP (1576)	≫

Table 16: Statistical significance testing of the IITBC-HE (left) and IITBC-EH (right) Pairwise scores.

	ORGANIZER (1526)	NTT (1599)	NTT (1677)	XMUNLP (1442)	ORGANIZER (1396)	NICT-2 (1474)	NICT-2 (1473)	CUNI (1668)
ORGANIZER (1523)	≫	≫	≫	≫	≫	≫	≫	≫
ORGANIZER (1526)		≫	≫	≫	≫	≫	≫	≫
NTT (1599)			≫	≫	≫	≫	≫	≫
NTT (1677)				≫	≫	≫	≫	≫
XMUNLP (1442)					≫	≫	≫	≫
ORGANIZER (1396)						>	≫	≫
NICT-2 (1474)							≫	≫
NICT-2 (1473)								≫

	ORGANIZER (1514)	NTT (1679)	NTT (1603)	XMUNLP (1443)	ORGANIZER (1395)
ORGANIZER (1518)	≫	≫	≫	≫	≫
ORGANIZER (1514)		≫	≫	≫	≫
NTT (1679)			≫	≫	≫
NTT (1603)				-	≫
XMUNLP (1443)					-

Table 17: Statistical significance testing of the JIJI-JE (left) and JIJI-EJ (right) Pairwise scores.

	XMUNLP (1637)	ORGANIZER (1531)
ORGANIZER (1534)	-	≫
XMUNLP (1637)		≫

	ORGANIZER (1533)	ORGANIZER (1528)
XMUNLP (1636)	≫	≫
ORGANIZER (1533)		≫

Table 18: Statistical significance testing of the RECIPE-TTL-JE (left) and RECIPE-TTL-EJ (right) Pairwise scores.

	ORGANIZER (1544)	ORGANIZER (1539)
XMUNLP (1635)	≫	≫
ORGANIZER (1544)		≫

	ORGANIZER (1542)	ORGANIZER (1537)
XMUNLP (1634)	≫	≫
ORGANIZER (1542)		≫

Table 19: Statistical significance testing of the RECIPE-ING-JE (left) and RECIPE-ING-EJ (right) Pairwise scores.

	ORGANIZER (1551)	ORGANIZER (1548)
XMUNLP (1632)	≫	≫
ORGANIZER (1551)		≫

	ORGANIZER (1549)	ORGANIZER (1546)
XMUNLP (1633)	≫	≫
ORGANIZER (1549)		≫

Table 20: Statistical significance testing of the RECIPE-STE-JE (left) and RECIPE-STE-EJ (right) Pairwise scores.

ASPEC-JE		
SYSTEM	DATA	κ
Online D	1333	0.230
AIAYN	1736	0.204
Kyoto-U	1717	0.217
Kyoto-U	1733	0.204
TMU	1695	0.188
TMU	1703	0.191
NTT	1616	0.201
NTT	1681	0.173
NICT-2	1476	0.274
NICT-2	1480	0.257
CUNI	1665	0.241
ave.		0.216

ASPEC-EJ		
SYSTEM	DATA	κ
Online A	1334	0.290
AIAYN	1737	0.338
Kyoto-U	1731	0.321
TMU	1704	0.269
TMU	1709	0.260
NTT	1684	0.353
NTT	1729	0.341
NICT-2	1475	0.315
NICT-2	1479	0.395
UT-IIS	1710	0.305
NAIST-NICT	1506	0.301
NAIST-NICT	1507	0.339
ave.		0.319

ASPEC-JC		
SYSTEM	DATA	κ
Online D	1336	0.189
AIAYN	1738	0.183
Kyoto-U	1642	0.159
Kyoto-U	1722	0.128
TMU	1743	0.171
NICT-2	1478	0.222
NICT-2	1483	0.194
ave.		0.178

ASPEC-CJ		
SYSTEM	DATA	κ
Online A	1342	0.215
AIAYN	1740	0.310
Kyoto-U	1577	0.284
Kyoto-U	1720	0.254
NICT-2	1477	0.191
NICT-2	1481	0.279
ave.		0.255

JPC-JE		
SYSTEM	DATA	κ
Online A	1338	0.424
JAPIO	1574	0.280
JAPIO	1578	0.296
CUNI	1666	0.249
u-tkb	1472	0.380
ave.		0.326

JPC-EJ		
SYSTEM	DATA	κ
Online A	1339	0.410
EHR	1406	0.364
EHR	1407	0.385
JAPIO	1454	0.409
JAPIO	1462	0.280
u-tkb	1470	0.349
ave.		0.366

JPC-JC		
SYSTEM	DATA	κ
Online A	1340	0.185
u-tkb	1465	0.176
ave.		0.180

JPC-CJ		
SYSTEM	DATA	κ
Online A	1341	0.194
EHR	1408	0.201
EHR	1414	0.170
JAPIO	1447	0.257
JAPIO	1484	0.247
u-tkb	1468	0.172
ave.		0.207

JPC-KJ		
SYSTEM	DATA	κ
Online A	1344	0.257
EHR	1416	0.413
EHR	1417	0.459
JAPIO	1448	0.224
JAPIO	1450	0.235
ave.		0.317

IITBC-HE		
SYSTEM	DATA	κ
XMUNLP	1511	0.376
IITB-MTG	1726	0.626
ave.		0.501

IITBC-EH		
SYSTEM	DATA	κ
XMUNLP	1576	0.269
IITB-MTG	1725	0.371
ave.		0.320

JIJI-JE		
SYSTEM	DATA	κ
Hiero	1396	0.117
Online A	1523	0.035
RBMT B	1526	0.004
NTT	1599	0.095
NTT	1677	0.077
NICT-2	1473	0.078
NICT 2	1474	0.064
XMUNLP	1442	0.070
CUNI	1668	0.060
ave.		0.067

JIJI-EJ		
SYSTEM	DATA	κ
Hiero	1395	0.104
RBMT A	1514	0.167
Online A	1518	0.179
NTT	1603	0.189
NTT	1679	0.155
XMUNLP	1443	0.151
ave.		0.157

RECIPE-TTL-JE		
SYSTEM	DATA	κ
RBMT B	1531	0.305
Online A	1534	0.333
XMUNLP	1637	0.366
ave.		0.334

RECIPE-TTL-EJ		
SYSTEM	DATA	κ
RBMT B	1528	0.340
Online B	1533	0.356
XMUNLP	1636	0.341
ave.		0.345

RECIPE-STE-JE		
SYSTEM	DATA	κ
RBMT B	1548	0.290
Online A	1551	0.289
XMUNLP	1632	0.261
ave.		0.280

RECIPE-STE-EJ		
SYSTEM	DATA	κ
RBMT B	1546	0.108
Online A	1549	0.138
XMUNLP	1633	0.162
ave.		0.136

RECIPE-ING-JE		
SYSTEM	DATA	κ
RBMT B	1539	0.537
Online B	1544	0.551
XMUNLP	1635	0.614
ave.		0.567

RECIPE-ING-EJ		
SYSTEM	DATA	κ
RBMT B	1537	0.665
Online B	1542	0.515
XMUNLP	1634	0.618
ave.		0.599

Table 21: The Fleiss' kappa values for the pairwise evaluation results.

SYSTEM ID	ID	METHOD	OTHER	BLEU	RIBES	AMFM	Pair
SMT Hiero	2	SMT	NO	18.72	0.651066	0.588880	+7.75
SMT Phrase	6	SMT	NO	18.45	0.645137	0.590950	—
SMT S2T	9	SMT	NO	20.36	0.678253	0.593410	+25.50
Online D (2014)	35	Other	YES	15.08	0.643588	0.564170	+13.75
RBMT E	76	Other	YES	14.82	0.663851	0.561620	—
RBMT F	79	Other	YES	13.86	0.661387	0.556840	—
Online C (2014)	87	Other	YES	10.64	0.624827	0.466480	—
RBMT D (2014)	96	Other	YES	15.29	0.683378	0.551690	+23.00
Online D (2015)	775	Other	YES	16.85	0.676609	0.562270	+0.25
SMT S2T	877	SMT	NO	20.36	0.678253	0.593410	+7.00
RBMT D (2015)	887	Other	YES	15.29	0.683378	0.551690	+16.75
Online C (2015)	892	Other	YES	10.29	0.622564	0.453370	—
Online D (2016)	1042	Other	YES	16.91	0.677412	0.564270	+28.00
Online D (2016/11)	1333	NMT	YES	22.04	0.733483	0.584390	+63.00
AIAYN	1736	NMT	NO	28.06	0.767577	0.595580	+75.25
Kyoto-U 1	1717	NMT	NO	27.53	0.761403	0.585540	+77.75
Kyoto-U 2	1733	NMT	NO	27.66	0.765464	0.591160	+74.50
TMU 1	1695	NMT	NO	21.00	0.725284	0.585710	+56.75
TMU 2	1703	NMT	NO	23.03	0.741175	0.595260	+61.00
NTT 1	1616	NMT	NO	27.43	0.764831	0.597620	+75.00
NTT 2	1681	NMT	NO	28.36	0.768880	0.597860	+77.25
NICT-2 1	1476	NMT	NO	24.79	0.747335	0.574810	+68.75
NICT-2 2	1480	NMT	NO	26.76	0.741329	0.578150	+69.75
CUNI 1	1665	NMT	NO	23.43	0.741699	0.583780	+66.00

Table 22: ASPEC-JE submissions

SYSTEM ID	ID	METHOD	OTHER	BLEU			RIBES			AMFM			Pair
				juman	kytea	mecab	juman	kytea	mecab	juman	kytea	mecab	
SMT Phrase	5	SMT	NO	27.48	29.80	28.27	0.683735	0.691926	0.695390	0.736380	0.736380	0.736380	——
SMT T2S	12	SMT	NO	31.05	33.44	32.10	0.748883	0.758031	0.760516	0.744370	0.744370	0.744370	+34.25
Online A (2014)	34	Other	YES	19.66	21.63	20.17	0.718019	0.723486	0.725848	0.695420	0.695420	0.695420	+42.50
RBMT B (2014)	66	Other	YES	13.18	14.85	13.48	0.671958	0.680748	0.682683	0.622930	0.622930	0.622930	+0.75
RBMT A	68	Other	YES	12.86	14.43	13.16	0.670167	0.676464	0.678934	0.626940	0.626940	0.626940	——
Online B (2014)	91	Other	YES	17.04	18.67	17.36	0.687797	0.693390	0.698126	0.643070	0.643070	0.643070	——
RBMT C	95	Other	YES	12.19	13.32	12.14	0.668372	0.672645	0.676018	0.594380	0.594380	0.594380	——
SMT Hiero	367	SMT	NO	30.19	32.56	30.94	0.734705	0.746978	0.747722	0.743900	0.743900	0.743900	+31.50
Online A (2015)	774	Other	YES	18.22	19.77	18.46	0.705882	0.713960	0.718150	0.677200	0.677200	0.677200	+34.25
SMT T2S	875	SMT	NO	31.05	33.44	32.10	0.748883	0.758031	0.760516	0.744370	0.744370	0.744370	+30.00
RBMT B (2015)	883	Other	YES	13.18	14.85	13.48	0.671958	0.680748	0.682683	0.622930	0.622930	0.622930	+9.75
Online B (2015)	889	Other	YES	17.80	19.52	18.11	0.693359	0.701966	0.703859	0.646160	0.646160	0.646160	——
Online A (2016)	1041	Other	YES	18.28	19.81	18.51	0.706639	0.715222	0.718559	0.677020	0.677020	0.677020	+49.75
Online A (2016/11)	1334	NMT	YES	26.19	28.22	26.68	0.776787	0.780217	0.782674	0.727040	0.727040	0.727040	+74.00
AIAYN	1737	NMT	NO	40.79	42.55	41.50	0.844896	0.847559	0.851471	0.768630	0.768630	0.768630	+69.75

Table 23: ASPEC-EJ submissions (Organizer)

SYSTEM ID	ID	METHOD	OTHER	BLEU			RIBES			AMFM			Pair
				juman	kytea	mecab	juman	kytea	mecab	juman	kytea	mecab	
Kyoto-U 1	1731	NMT	NO	38.72	40.65	39.37	0.832472	0.835870	0.839646	0.754220	0.754220	0.754220	+69.75
TMU 1	1704	NMT	NO	32.35	35.05	33.72	0.802262	0.809649	0.811057	0.740620	0.740620	0.740620	+50.75
TMU 2	1709	NMT	NO	34.05	36.69	35.32	0.812926	0.818443	0.821563	0.744890	0.744890	0.744890	+56.50
NTT 1	1684	NMT	NO	39.30	42.27	40.47	0.835806	0.839981	0.844326	0.757740	0.757740	0.757740	+72.25
NTT 2	1729	NMT	NO	40.32	42.80	40.95	0.838594	0.841769	0.846486	0.762170	0.762170	0.762170	+75.75
NICT-2 1	1475	NMT	NO	36.35	38.94	37.87	0.826791	0.834448	0.835255	0.759570	0.759570	0.759570	+62.00
NICT-2 2	1479	NMT	NO	40.17	42.25	41.17	0.842206	0.848170	0.849929	0.765580	0.765580	0.765580	+74.75
UT-IIS 1	1710	NMT	NO	36.26	38.93	37.06	0.827891	0.832054	0.836394	0.746910	0.746910	0.746910	+68.00
NAIST-NICT 1	1506	NMT	NO	36.47	38.54	37.30	0.821989	0.827225	0.830116	0.763310	0.763310	0.763310	+63.50
NAIST-NICT 2	1507	NMT	NO	38.25	40.29	39.05	0.834492	0.839321	0.842337	0.770480	0.770480	0.770480	+70.00

Table 24: ASPEC-EJ submissions (Participants)

SYSTEM ID	ID	METHOD	OTHER	BLEU			RIBES			AMFM			Pair
				kytea	stanford (ctb)	stanford (pku)	kytea	stanford (ctb)	stanford (pku)	kytea	stanford (ctb)	stanford (pku)	
SMT Hiero	3	SMT	NO	27.71	27.70	27.35	0.809128	0.809561	0.811394	0.745100	0.745100	0.745100	+3.75
SMT Phrase	7	SMT	NO	27.96	28.01	27.68	0.788961	0.790263	0.790937	0.749450	0.749450	0.749450	—
SMT S2T	10	SMT	NO	28.65	28.65	28.35	0.807606	0.809457	0.808417	0.755230	0.755230	0.755230	+14.00
Online D (2014)	37	Other	YES	9.37	8.93	8.84	0.606905	0.606328	0.604149	0.625430	0.625430	0.625430	-14.50
Online C (2014)	216	Other	YES	7.26	7.01	6.72	0.612808	0.613075	0.611563	0.587820	0.587820	0.587820	—
RBMT B (2014)	243	RBMT	NO	17.86	17.75	17.49	0.744818	0.745885	0.743794	0.667960	0.667960	0.667960	-20.00
RBMT C	244	RBMT	NO	9.62	9.96	9.59	0.642278	0.648758	0.645385	0.594900	0.594900	0.594900	—
Online D (2015)	777	Other	YES	10.73	10.33	10.08	0.660484	0.660847	0.660482	0.634090	0.634090	0.634090	-14.75
SMT S2T	881	SMT	NO	28.65	28.65	28.35	0.807606	0.809457	0.808417	0.755230	0.755230	0.755230	+7.75
RBMT B (2015)	886	Other	YES	17.86	17.75	17.49	0.744818	0.745885	0.743794	0.667960	0.667960	0.667960	-11.00
Online C (2015)	891	Other	YES	7.44	7.05	6.75	0.611964	0.615048	0.612158	0.566060	0.566060	0.566060	—
Online D (2016)	1045	Other	YES	11.16	10.72	10.54	0.665185	0.667382	0.666953	0.639440	0.639440	0.639440	-26.00
Online D (2016/11)	1336	NMT	YES	15.94	15.68	15.38	0.728453	0.728270	0.728284	0.673730	0.673730	0.673730	+17.75
AIAYN	1738	NMT	NO	34.97	34.96	34.72	0.850199	0.850052	0.848394	0.787250	0.787250	0.787250	+70.50
Kyoto-U 1	1642	NMT	NO	35.67	35.30	35.40	0.849464	0.848107	0.848318	0.779400	0.779400	0.779400	+71.50
Kyoto-U 2	1722	NMT	NO	35.31	35.37	35.06	0.850103	0.849168	0.847879	0.785420	0.785420	0.785420	+72.50
TMU 1	1743	NMT	NO	22.92	22.86	22.74	0.798681	0.798736	0.797969	0.700030	0.700030	0.700030	+4.25
NICT-2 1	1478	NMT	NO	33.72	33.64	33.60	0.847223	0.846578	0.846158	0.779870	0.779870	0.779870	+67.25
NICT-2 2	1483	NMT	NO	35.23	35.23	35.14	0.852084	0.851893	0.851548	0.785820	0.785820	0.785820	+69.50

Table 25: ASPEC-JC submissions

SYSTEM ID	ID	METHOD	OTHER	BLEU			RIBES			AMFM			Pair
				juman	kytea	mecab	juman	kytea	mecab	juman	kytea	mecab	
SMT Hiero	4	SMT	NO	35.43	35.91	35.64	0.810406	0.798726	0.807665	0.750950	0.750950	0.750950	+4.75
SMT Phrase	8	SMT	NO	34.65	35.16	34.77	0.772498	0.766384	0.771005	0.753010	0.753010	0.753010	——
SMT T2S	13	SMT	NO	36.52	37.07	36.64	0.825292	0.820490	0.825025	0.754870	0.754870	0.754870	+16.00
Online A (2014)	36	Other	YES	11.63	13.21	11.87	0.595925	0.598172	0.598573	0.658060	0.658060	0.658060	-21.75
Online B (2014)	215	Other	YES	10.48	11.26	10.47	0.600733	0.596006	0.600706	0.636930	0.636930	0.636930	——
RBMT A (2014)	239	RBMT	NO	9.37	9.87	9.35	0.666277	0.652402	0.661730	0.626070	0.626070	0.626070	-37.75
RBMT D	242	RBMT	NO	8.39	8.70	8.30	0.641189	0.626400	0.633319	0.586790	0.586790	0.586790	——
Online A (2015)	776	Other	YES	11.53	12.82	11.68	0.588285	0.590393	0.592887	0.649860	0.649860	0.649860	-19.00
SMT T2S	879	SMT	NO	35.52	37.07	36.64	0.825292	0.820490	0.825025	0.754870	0.754870	0.754870	+17.25
RBMT A (2015)	885	Other	YES	9.37	9.87	9.35	0.666277	0.652402	0.661730	0.626070	0.626070	0.626070	-28.00
Online B (2015)	890	Other	YES	10.41	11.03	10.36	0.597355	0.592841	0.597298	0.628290	0.628290	0.628290	——
Online A (2016)	1043	Other	YES	11.56	12.87	11.69	0.589802	0.589397	0.593361	0.659540	0.659540	0.659540	-51.25
Online A (2016/11)	1342	NMT	YES	13.75	20.64	19.04	0.719022	0.717173	0.720095	0.692820	0.692820	0.692820	+22.50
AIAYN	1740	NMT	NO	45.87	47.30	47.00	0.880815	0.875511	0.880368	0.798110	0.798110	0.798110	+78.50
Kyoto-U 1	1577	NMT	NO	43.43	48.84	48.51	0.883457	0.878964	0.884137	0.799520	0.799520	0.799520	+79.50
Kyoto-U 2	1720	NMT	NO	43.34	48.76	48.40	0.884210	0.880069	0.884745	0.799840	0.799840	0.799840	+82.75
NICT-2 1	1477	NMT	NO	44.26	44.90	44.50	0.871438	0.868359	0.871736	0.788940	0.788940	0.788940	+78.00
NICT-2 2	1481	NMT	NO	46.84	47.51	47.27	0.882356	0.878580	0.882195	0.799680	0.799680	0.799680	+79.00

Table 26: ASPEC-CJ submissions

SYSTEM ID	ID	METHOD	OTHER	BLEU	RIBES	AMFM	Pair
SMT Phrase	977	SMT	NO	30.80	0.730056	0.664830	—
SMT Hiero	979	SMT	NO	32.23	0.763030	0.672500	+8.75
SMT S2T	980	SMT	NO	34.40	0.793483	0.672760	+23.00
Online A (2016)	1035	Other	YES	35.77	0.803661	0.673950	+32.25
Online B (2016)	1051	Other	YES	16.00	0.688004	0.486450	—
RBMT C (2016)	1088	Other	YES	21.00	0.755017	0.519210	—
RBMT A (2016)	1090	Other	YES	21.57	0.750381	0.521230	+23.75
RBMT B (2016)	1095	Other	YES	18.38	0.710992	0.518110	—
Online A (2016/11)	1338	NMT	YES	49.35	0.878342	0.722590	+71.50
JAPIO 1	1574	NMT	YES	49.00	0.878298	0.724710	+68.50
JAPIO 2	1578	NMT	YES	48.08	0.873093	0.715560	+67.00
CUNI 1	1666	SMT	NO	38.29	0.837425	0.681520	+58.00
u-tkb 1	1472	NMT	NO	37.31	0.841136	0.697290	+51.50

Table 27: JPC-JE submissions

SYSTEM ID	ID	METHOD	OTHER	BLEU			RIBES			AMFM			Pair
				juman	kytea	mecab	juman	kytea	mecab	juman	kytea	mecab	
SMT Phrase	973	SMT	NO	32.36	34.26	32.52	0.728539	0.728281	0.729077	0.711900	0.711900	0.711900	—
SMT Hiero	974	SMT	NO	34.57	36.61	34.79	0.777759	0.778657	0.779049	0.715300	0.715300	0.715300	+21.00
SMT T2S	975	SMT	NO	35.60	37.65	35.82	0.797353	0.796783	0.798025	0.717030	0.717030	0.717030	+30.75
Online A (2016)	1036	Other	YES	35.88	37.89	36.83	0.798168	0.792471	0.796308	0.719110	0.719110	0.719110	+20.00
Online B (2016)	1073	Other	YES	21.57	22.62	21.65	0.743083	0.735203	0.740962	0.659950	0.659950	0.659950	—
RBMT D (2016)	1085	Other	YES	23.02	24.90	23.45	0.761224	0.757341	0.760325	0.647730	0.647730	0.647730	—
RBMT F (2016)	1086	Other	YES	25.64	28.48	26.84	0.773673	0.769244	0.773344	0.675470	0.675470	0.675470	+12.75
RBMT E (2016)	1087	Other	YES	21.35	23.17	21.53	0.743484	0.741985	0.742300	0.646930	0.646930	0.646930	—
Online A (2016/11)	1339	NMT	YES	50.60	51.65	50.83	0.879382	0.877336	0.878316	0.770480	0.770480	0.770480	+48.50
EHR 1	1406	NMT	NO	44.44	45.59	44.15	0.860998	0.858466	0.860659	0.747050	0.747050	0.747050	+58.25
EHR 2	1407	NMT	NO	44.63	45.94	44.53	0.866722	0.864256	0.866205	0.747770	0.747770	0.747770	+60.00
JAPIO 1	1454	NMT	YES	50.27	51.23	50.17	0.886403	0.883481	0.885747	0.776790	0.776790	0.776790	+56.25
JAPIO 2	1462	SMT	YES	51.79	52.23	51.75	0.864038	0.861596	0.862200	0.781150	0.781150	0.781150	+41.00
u-tkb 1	1470	NMT	NO	33.91	41.12	39.11	0.845815	0.846888	0.845551	0.734010	0.734010	0.734010	+49.50

Table 28: JPC-EJ submissions

SYSTEM ID	ID	METHOD	OTHER	BLEU			RIBES			AMFM			Pair
				kytea	stanford (ctb)	stanford (pku)	kytea	stanford (ctb)	stanford (pku)	kytea	stanford (ctb)	stanford (pku)	
SMT Phrase	966	SMT	NO	30.60	32.03	31.25	0.787321	0.797888	0.794388	0.710940	0.710940	0.710940	—
SMT Hiero	967	SMT	NO	30.26	31.57	30.91	0.788415	0.799118	0.796685	0.718360	0.718360	0.718360	+4.75
SMT S2T	968	SMT	NO	31.05	32.35	31.70	0.793846	0.802805	0.800848	0.720030	0.720030	0.720030	+4.25
Online A (2016)	1038	Other	YES	23.02	23.57	23.29	0.754241	0.760672	0.760148	0.702350	0.702350	0.702350	-23.00
Online B (2016)	1069	Other	YES	9.42	9.59	8.79	0.642026	0.651070	0.643520	0.527180	0.527180	0.527180	—
RBMT C (2016)	1118	Other	YES	12.35	13.72	13.17	0.688240	0.708681	0.700210	0.475430	0.475430	0.475430	-41.25
Online A (2016/11)	1340	NMT	YES	33.04	33.92	33.34	0.824829	0.829122	0.829067	0.735470	0.735470	0.735470	+32.50
u-tkb 1	1465	NMT	NO	31.80	33.19	32.83	0.819791	0.826055	0.825025	0.706720	0.706720	0.706720	+21.75

Table 29: JPC-JC submissions

SYSTEM ID	ID	METHOD	OTHER	BLEU			RIBES			AMFM			Pair
				juman	kytea	mecab	juman	kytea	mecab	juman	kytea	mecab	
SMT Hiero	430	SMT	NO	39.22	39.52	39.14	0.806058	0.802059	0.804523	0.729370	0.729370	0.729370	—
SMT Phrase	431	SMT	NO	38.34	38.51	38.22	0.782019	0.778921	0.781456	0.723110	0.723110	0.723110	—
SMT T2S	432	SMT	NO	39.39	39.90	39.39	0.814919	0.811350	0.813595	0.725920	0.725920	0.725920	+20.75
Online A (2015)	647	Other	YES	25.80	27.81	26.89	0.712242	0.707264	0.711273	0.693840	0.693840	0.693840	-7.00
Online B (2015)	648	Other	YES	12.33	12.72	12.44	0.648996	0.641255	0.648742	0.588380	0.588380	0.588380	—
RBMT A (2015)	759	RBMT	NO	10.49	10.72	10.35	0.674060	0.664098	0.667349	0.557130	0.557130	0.557130	-39.25
RBMT B	760	RBMT	NO	7.94	8.07	7.73	0.596200	0.581837	0.586941	0.502100	0.502100	0.502100	—
Online A (2016)	1040	Other	YES	25.99	27.91	27.02	0.707739	0.702718	0.706707	0.693720	0.693720	0.693720	-19.75
Online A (2016/11)	1341	NMT	YES	42.66	43.76	42.95	0.845858	0.844918	0.845794	0.747240	0.747240	0.747240	+54.25
EHR 1	1408	NMT	NO	47.08	47.44	46.83	0.859070	0.856376	0.858888	0.756350	0.756350	0.756350	+68.25
EHR 2	1414	NMT	NO	45.52	47.17	46.35	0.859619	0.856784	0.858353	0.761370	0.761370	0.761370	+69.75
JAPIO 1	1447	SMT	YES	50.52	51.25	50.57	0.847793	0.843774	0.846081	0.774660	0.774660	0.774660	+60.50
JAPIO 2	1484	NMT	YES	50.06	50.51	50.00	0.875398	0.873390	0.874822	0.779420	0.779420	0.779420	+80.25
u-tkb 1	1468	NMT	NO	33.79	40.47	38.99	0.832144	0.833610	0.831209	0.729580	0.729580	0.729580	+55.50

Table 30: JPC-CJ submissions

SYSTEM ID	ID	METHOD	OTHER	BLEU			RIBES			AMFM			Pair
				juman	kytea	mecab	juman	kytea	mecab	juman	kytea	mecab	
SMT Phrase	438	SMT	NO	69.22	70.36	69.73	0.941302	0.939729	0.940756	0.856220	0.856220	0.856220	—
SMT Hiero	439	SMT	NO	67.41	68.65	68.00	0.937162	0.935903	0.936570	0.850560	0.850560	0.850560	+2.75
Online B (2015)	651	Other	YES	36.41	38.72	37.01	0.851745	0.852263	0.851945	0.728750	0.728750	0.728750	—
Online A (2015)	652	Other	YES	55.05	56.84	55.46	0.909152	0.909385	0.908838	0.800460	0.800460	0.800460	+38.75
RBMT A (2015)	653	Other	YES	42.00	43.97	42.45	0.876396	0.873734	0.875146	0.712020	0.712020	0.712020	-7.25
RBMT B	654	Other	YES	34.74	37.51	35.54	0.845712	0.849014	0.846228	0.643150	0.643150	0.643150	—
Online A (2015)	963	Other	YES	55.05	56.84	55.46	0.909152	0.909385	0.908838	0.800610	0.800610	0.800610	—
RBMT A (2015)	964	Other	YES	42.00	43.97	42.45	0.876396	0.873734	0.875146	0.712700	0.712700	0.712700	—
Online A (2016)	1039	Other	YES	54.78	56.68	55.14	0.907320	0.907652	0.906743	0.798750	0.798750	0.798750	+8.00
Online A (2016/11)	1344	NMT	NO	44.42	45.14	44.72	0.857642	0.854158	0.857083	0.783850	0.783850	0.783850	-55.75
EHR 1	1416	NMT	NO	71.52	72.34	71.82	0.944516	0.942940	0.944219	0.866060	0.866060	0.866060	+6.25
EHR 2	1417	NMT	NO	71.36	72.26	71.65	0.946126	0.944812	0.945888	0.871110	0.871110	0.871110	+11.25
JAPIO 1	1448	SMT	YES	73.00	73.71	73.23	0.946880	0.945754	0.946645	0.872510	0.872510	0.872510	+48.75
JAPIO 2	1450	SMT	YES	73.00	73.73	73.25	0.946985	0.945841	0.946745	0.873200	0.873200	0.873200	+48.50

Table 31: JPC-KJ submissions

SYSTEM ID	ID	METHOD	OTHER	BLEU	RIBES	AMFM	Pair
Online A (2016)	1031	Other	YES	21.37	0.714537	0.621100	+44.75
Online B (2016)	1048	Other	YES	15.58	0.683214	0.590520	+14.00
SMT Phrase	1054	SMT	NO	10.32	0.638090	0.574850	0.00
XMUNLP 1	1511	NMT	NO	22.44	0.750921	0.629530	+68.25
IITB-MTG 1	1726	NMT	NO	11.55	0.682902	0.557040	+21.00

Table 32: IITB-HE submissions

SYSTEM ID	ID	METHOD	OTHER RESOURCES	BLEU	RIBES	AMFM	Pair
Online A (2016)	1032	Other	YES	18.720000	0.716788	0.670660	+57.25
Online B (2016)	1047	Other	YES	16.970000	0.691298	0.668450	+42.50
SMT Phrase	1252	SMT	NO	10.790000	0.651166	0.660860	—
XMUNLP 1	1576	NMT	NO	21.390000	0.749660	0.688770	+64.50
IITB-MTG 1	1725	NMT	NO	12.230000	0.688606	0.624780	+28.75

Table 33: IITB-EH submissions

SYSTEM ID	ID	METHOD	OTHER	BLEU	RIBES	AMFM	Pair
SMT Phrase	1394	SMT	NO	15.11	0.554550	0.475740	—
SMT Hiero	1396	SMT	NO	15.67	0.558225	0.470610	+10.25
SMT S2T	1398	SMT	NO	14.54	0.556728	0.477170	—
ONLINE-A 1	1523	NMT	NO	8.19	0.529844	0.450850	+70.00
RBMT-A	1525	RBMT	NO	4.36	0.472312	0.391050	—
RBMT-B	1526	RBMT	NO	4.67	0.475760	0.385600	+51.75
NTT 1	1599	NMT	NO	19.44	0.638841	0.476200	+32.00
NTT 2	1677	NMT	NO	20.90	0.648931	0.474360	+26.75
NICT-2 1	1473	NMT	NO	16.52	0.642379	0.459000	+0.25
NICT-2 2	1474	NMT	NO	18.19	0.632638	0.453420	+7.25
XMUNLP 1	1442	NMT	NO	17.95	0.637059	0.465710	+20.75
CUNI 1	1668	SMT	NO	10.67	0.564797	0.432700	-24.00

Table 34: JIJI-JE submissions

SYSTEM ID	ID	METHOD	OTHER	BLEU			RIBES			AMFM			Pair
				juman	kytea	mecab	juman	kytea	mecab	juman	kytea	mecab	
SMT Phrase	1393	SMT	NO	15.77	16.65	15.76	0.580284	0.584892	0.585437	0.545240	0.545240	0.545240	—
SMT Hiero	1395	SMT	NO	16.22	16.95	16.22	0.594923	0.601505	0.602516	0.550260	0.550260	0.550260	+10.25
SMT T2S	1397	SMT	NO	14.95	15.38	14.79	0.594072	0.597791	0.599530	0.530370	0.530370	0.530370	—
RBMT-A	1514	RBMT	NO	5.31	6.68	5.69	0.505227	0.515050	0.513580	0.473940	0.473940	0.473940	+31.25
RBMT-B	1515	RBMT	NO	4.72	5.98	4.97	0.518416	0.531603	0.532079	0.487320	0.487320	0.487320	—
ONLINE-A 1	1518	NMT	NO	11.29	13.12	11.84	0.597473	0.605532	0.603374	0.533120	0.533120	0.533120	+69.75
NTT 1	1603	NMT	NO	19.13	20.47	19.41	0.668517	0.670920	0.676594	0.536970	0.536970	0.536970	+14.50
NTT 2	1679	NMT	NO	20.37	21.82	20.68	0.680598	0.684048	0.688863	0.537800	0.537800	0.537800	+17.75
XMUNLP 1	1443	NMT	NO	19.61	20.72	20.14	0.684120	0.688497	0.691056	0.546360	0.546360	0.546360	+11.75

Table 35: JIJI-EJ submissions

SYSTEM ID	ID	METHOD	OTHER	BLEU	RIBES	AMFM	Pair
RBMT-A	1538	RBMT	NO	11.14	0.484800	0.613950	—
RBMT-B	1539	RBMT	NO	12.52	0.520800	0.607190	-24.75
ONLINE-B 1	1544	NMT	NO	20.33	0.563419	0.656630	-15.50
SMT Phrase	1571	SMT	NO	44.42	0.830105	0.859040	—
XMUNLP 1	1635	NMT	NO	46.98	0.831261	0.854970	+3.50

Table 36: RECIPEING-JE submissions

SYSTEM ID	ID	METHOD	OTHER	BLEU			RIBES			AMFM			Pair
				juman	kytea	mecab	juman	kytea	mecab	juman	kytea	mecab	
RBMT-A	1536	RBMT	NO	4.52	4.74	4.29	0.365913	0.371584	0.355798	0.426550	0.426550	0.426550	—
RBMT-B	1537	RBMT	NO	5.44	4.95	5.07	0.385269	0.363344	0.372793	0.445370	0.445370	0.445370	-48.50
ONLINE-B 1	1542	NMT	NO	15.57	14.89	14.85	0.548026	0.544581	0.537147	0.618010	0.618010	0.618010	-24.25
SMT Phrase	1570	SMT	NO	31.39	30.61	29.60	0.749305	0.740283	0.741249	0.775770	0.775770	0.775770	—
XMUNLP 1	1634	NMT	NO	34.88	34.26	33.19	0.747521	0.742770	0.739909	0.778530	0.778530	0.778530	-3.75

Table 37: RECIPEING-EJ submissions

SYSTEM ID	ID	METHOD	OTHER	BLEU	RIBES	AMFM	Pair
RBMT-A	1547	RBMT	NO	5.37	0.546642	0.315930	—
RBMT-B	1548	RBMT	NO	5.82	0.565086	0.268580	-60.25
ONLINE-A 1	1551	NMT	NO	11.04	0.670484	0.415880	+2.75
SMT Phrase	1569	SMT	NO	22.84	0.705506	0.595290	—
XMUNLP 1	1632	NMT	NO	28.03	0.784235	0.598050	+40.50

Table 38: RECIPESTE-JE submissions

SYSTEM ID	ID	METHOD	OTHER	BLEU			RIBES			AMFM			Pair
				juman	kytea	mecab	juman	kytea	mecab	juman	kytea	mecab	
RBMT-A	1545	RBMT	NO	3.06	4.55	3.43	0.518467	0.533326	0.521713	0.368710	0.368710	0.368710	—
RBMT-B	1546	RBMT	NO	3.30	5.19	4.00	0.525116	0.532919	0.529113	0.441180	0.441180	0.441180	-65.50
ONLINE-A 1	1549	NMT	NO	8.14	11.23	8.97	0.623865	0.635888	0.629012	0.526680	0.526680	0.526680	-29.25
SMT Phrase	1568	SMT	NO	17.60	21.43	18.53	0.694179	0.698499	0.695400	0.626610	0.626610	0.626610	—
XMUNLP 1	1633	NMT	NO	22.55	26.87	24.00	0.776539	0.776469	0.775689	0.645050	0.645050	0.645050	+45.50

Table 39: RECIPESTE-EJ submissions

SYSTEM ID	ID	METHOD	OTHER	BLEU	RIBES	AMFM	Pair
RBMT-A	1530	RBMT	NO	0.53	0.086378	0.433380	—
RBMT-B	1531	RBMT	NO	0.56	0.100899	0.445400	-25.75
ONLINE-A 1	1534	NMT	NO	2.19	0.199338	0.509470	+10.25
SMT Phrase	1567	SMT	NO	9.72	0.451707	0.571230	—
XMUNLP 1	1637	NMT	NO	15.57	0.526993	0.542690	+10.25

Table 40: RECIPETTL-JE submissions

SYSTEM ID	ID	METHOD	OTHER	BLEU			RIBES			AMFM			Pair
				juman	kytea	mecab	juman	kytea	mecab	juman	kytea	mecab	
RBMT-A	1527	RBMT	NO	0.00	0.00	0.00	0.128134	0.137884	0.122371	0.187540	0.187540	0.187540	—
RBMT-B	1528	RBMT	NO	2.57	2.30	2.08	0.299133	0.300578	0.270482	0.402830	0.402830	0.402830	-50.25
ONLINE-B 1	1533	NMT	NO	16.16	15.85	15.40	0.573771	0.559142	0.532130	0.590440	0.590440	0.590440	+3.75
SMT Phrase	1566	SMT	NO	17.16	16.23	16.57	0.600503	0.576617	0.548811	0.571650	0.571650	0.571650	—
XMUNLP 1	1636	NMT	NO	19.4_	18.87	18.78	0.592087	0.573466	0.558997	0.584980	0.584980	0.584980	+23.75

Table 41: RECIPETTL-EJ submissions

References

Rafael E. Banchs, Luis F. D'Haro, and Haizhou Li. 2015. Adequacy-fluency metrics: Evaluating mt in the continuous space model framework. *IEEE/ACM Trans. Audio, Speech and Lang. Proc.*, 23(3):472–482.

Jacob Cohen. 1968. Weighted kappa: Nominal scale agreement with provision for scaled disagreement or partial credit. *Psychological Bulletin*, 70(4):213 – 220.

Fabien Cromieres, Raj Dabre, Toshiaki Nakazawa, and Sadao Kurohashi. 2017. Kyoto university participation to wat 2017. In *Proceedings of the 4th Workshop on Asian Translation (WAT2017)*, pages 146–153, Taipei, Taiwan. Asian Federation of Natural Language Processing.

Terumasa Ehara. 2017. Smt reranked nmt. In *Proceedings of the 4th Workshop on Asian Translation (WAT2017)*, pages 119–126, Taipei, Taiwan. Asian Federation of Natural Language Processing.

J.L. Fleiss et al. 1971. Measuring nominal scale agreement among many raters. *Psychological Bulletin*, 76(5):378–382.

Kenneth Heafield, Ivan Pouzyrevsky, Jonathan H. Clark, and Philipp Koehn. 2013. Scalable modified kneser-ney language model estimation. In *Proceedings of the 51st Annual Meeting of the Association for Computational Linguistics (Volume 2: Short Papers)*, pages 690–696, Sofia, Bulgaria. Association for Computational Linguistics.

Hieu Hoang, Philipp Koehn, and Adam Lopez. 2009. A unified framework for phrase-based, hierarchical, and syntax-based statistical machine translation. In *Proceedings of the International Workshop on Spoken Language Translation*, pages 152–159.

Kenji Imamura and Eiichiro Sumita. 2017. Ensemble and reranking: Using multiple models in the nict-2 neural machine translation system at wat2017. In *Proceedings of the 4th Workshop on Asian Translation (WAT2017)*, pages 127–134, Taipei, Taiwan. Asian Federation of Natural Language Processing.

Hideki Isozaki, Tsutomu Hirao, Kevin Duh, Katsuhito Sudoh, and Hajime Tsukada. 2010. Automatic evaluation of translation quality for distant language pairs. In *Proceedings of the 2010 Conference on Empirical Methods in Natural Language Processing*, EMNLP '10, pages 944–952, Stroudsburg, PA, USA. Association for Computational Linguistics.

Satoshi Kinoshita, Tadaaki Oshio, and Tomoharu Mitsuhashi. 2017. Comparison of smt and nmt trained with large patent corpora: Japio at wat2017. In *Proceedings of the 4th Workshop on Asian Translation (WAT2017)*, pages 140–145, Taipei, Taiwan. Asian Federation of Natural Language Processing.

Tom Kocmi, Dušan Variš, and Ondřej Bojar. 2017. Cuni nmt system for wat 2017 translation tasks. In *Proceedings of the 4th Workshop on Asian Translation (WAT2017)*, pages 154–159, Taipei, Taiwan. Asian Federation of Natural Language Processing.

Philipp Koehn. 2004. Statistical significance tests for machine translation evaluation. In *Proceedings of EMNLP 2004*, pages 388–395, Barcelona, Spain. Association for Computational Linguistics.

Philipp Koehn, Hieu Hoang, Alexandra Birch, Chris Callison-Burch, Marcello Federico, Nicola Bertoldi, Brooke Cowan, Wade Shen, Christine Moran, Richard Zens, Chris Dyer, Ondrej Bojar, Alexandra Constantin, and Evan Herbst. 2007. Moses: Open source toolkit for statistical machine translation. In *Annual Meeting of the Association for Computational Linguistics (ACL), demonstration session*.

T. Kudo. 2005. Mecab : Yet another part-of-speech and morphological analyzer. *http://mecab.sourceforge.net/*.

Sadao Kurohashi, Toshihisa Nakamura, Yuji Matsumoto, and Makoto Nagao. 1994. Improvements of Japanese morphological analyzer JUMAN. In *Proceedings of The International Workshop on Sharable Natural Language*, pages 22–28.

Zi Long, Ryuichiro Kimura, Takehito Utsuro, Tomoharu Mitsuhashi, and Mikio Yamamoto. 2017. Patent nmt integrated with large vocabulary phrase translation by smt at wat 2017. In *Proceedings of the 4th Workshop on Asian Translation (WAT2017)*, pages 110–118, Taipei, Taiwan. Asian Federation of Natural Language Processing.

Yukio Matsumura and Mamoru Komachi. 2017. Tokyo metropolitan university neural machine translation system for wat 2017. In *Proceedings of the 4th Workshop on Asian Translation (WAT2017)*, pages 160–166, Taipei, Taiwan. Asian Federation of Natural Language Processing.

Makoto Morishita, Jun Suzuki, and Masaaki Nagata. 2017. Ntt neural machine translation systems at wat 2017. In *Proceedings of the 4th Workshop on Asian Translation (WAT2017)*, pages 89–94, Taipei, Taiwan. Asian Federation of Natural Language Processing.

Toshiaki Nakazawa, Chenchen Ding, Hideya MINO, Isao Goto, Graham Neubig, and Sadao

Kurohashi. 2016. Overview of the 3rd workshop on asian translation. In *Proceedings of the 3rd Workshop on Asian Translation (WAT2016)*, pages 1–46, Osaka, Japan. The COLING 2016 Organizing Committee.

Toshiaki Nakazawa, Hideya Mino, Isao Goto, Sadao Kurohashi, and Eiichiro Sumita. 2014. Overview of the 1st Workshop on Asian Translation. In *Proceedings of the 1st Workshop on Asian Translation (WAT2014)*, pages 1–19, Tokyo, Japan.

Toshiaki Nakazawa, Hideya Mino, Isao Goto, Graham Neubig, Sadao Kurohashi, and Eiichiro Sumita. 2015. Overview of the 2nd Workshop on Asian Translation. In *Proceedings of the 2nd Workshop on Asian Translation (WAT2015)*, pages 1–28, Kyoto, Japan.

Masato Neishi, Jin Sakuma, Satoshi Tohda, Shonosuke Ishiwatari, Naoki Yoshinaga, and Masashi Toyoda. 2017. A bag of useful tricks for practical neural machine translation: Embedding layer initialization and large batch size. In *Proceedings of the 4th Workshop on Asian Translation (WAT2017)*, pages 99–109, Taipei, Taiwan. Asian Federation of Natural Language Processing.

Graham Neubig, Yosuke Nakata, and Shinsuke Mori. 2011. Pointwise prediction for robust, adaptable japanese morphological analysis. In *Proceedings of the 49th Annual Meeting of the Association for Computational Linguistics: Human Language Technologies: Short Papers - Volume 2*, HLT '11, pages 529–533, Stroudsburg, PA, USA. Association for Computational Linguistics.

Yusuke Oda, Katsuhito Sudoh, Satoshi Nakamura, Masao Utiyama, and Eiichiro Sumita. 2017. A simple and strong baseline: Naist nict neural machine translation system for wat2017 english-japanese translation task. In *Proceedings of the 4th Workshop on Asian Translation (WAT2017)*, pages 135–139, Taipei, Taiwan. Asian Federation of Natural Language Processing.

Kishore Papineni, Salim Roukos, Todd Ward, and Wei-Jing Zhu. 2002. Bleu: a method for automatic evaluation of machine translation. In *ACL*, pages 311–318.

Slav Petrov, Leon Barrett, Romain Thibaux, and Dan Klein. 2006. Learning accurate, compact, and interpretable tree annotation. In *Proceedings of the 21st International Conference on Computational Linguistics and 44th Annual Meeting of the Association for Computational Linguistics*, pages 433–440, Sydney, Australia. Association for Computational Linguistics.

Sandhya Singh, Ritesh Panjwani, Anoop Kunchukuttan, and Pushpak Bhattacharyya.

2017. Comparing recurrent and convolutional architectures for english-hindi neural machine translation. In *Proceedings of the 4th Workshop on Asian Translation (WAT2017)*, pages 167–170, Taipei, Taiwan. Asian Federation of Natural Language Processing.

Huihsin Tseng. 2005. A conditional random field word segmenter. In *In Fourth SIGHAN Workshop on Chinese Language Processing*.

Masao Utiyama and Hitoshi Isahara. 2007. A japanese-english patent parallel corpus. In *MT summit XI*, pages 475–482.

Ashish Vaswani, Noam Shazeer, Niki Parmar, Jakob Uszkoreit, Llion Jones, Aidan N. Gomez, Lukasz Kaiser, and Illia Polosukhin. 2017. Attention is all you need. *CoRR*, abs/1706.03762.

Boli Wang, Zhixing Tan, Jinming Hu, Yidong Chen, and xiaodong shi. 2017. Xmu neural machine translation systems for wat 2017. In *Proceedings of the 4th Workshop on Asian Translation (WAT2017)*, pages 95–98, Taipei, Taiwan. Asian Federation of Natural Language Processing.

Controlling Target Features in Neural Machine Translation via Prefix Constraints

Shunsuke Takeno[†*]　**Masaaki Nagata**[‡]　**Kazuhide Yamamoto**[†]

[†]Nagaoka University of Technology,

1603-1 Kamitomioka, Nagaoka, Niigata, 940-2188 Japan

{takeno, yamamoto}@jnlp.org

[‡]NTT Communication Science Laboratories, NTT Corporation,

2-4 Hikaridai, Seika-cho, Soraku-gun, Kyoto, 619-0237 Japan

nagata.masaaki@labs.ntt.co.jp

Abstract

We propose *prefix constraints*, a novel method to enforce constraints on target sentences in neural machine translation. It places a sequence of special tokens at the beginning of target sentence (target prefix), while side constraints (Sennrich et al., 2016) places a special token at the end of source sentence (source suffix). Prefix constraints can be predicted from source sentence jointly with target sentence, while side constraints must be provided by the user or predicted by some other methods. In both methods, special tokens are designed to encode arbitrary features on target-side or metatextual information. We show that prefix constraints are more flexible than side constraints and can be used to control the behavior of neural machine translation, in terms of output length, bidirectional decoding, domain adaptation, and unaligned target word generation.

1 Introduction

It is difficult to change the behaviors of a current neural machine translation system, because the internal states of the system are represented by vectors of real numbers. There are no symbols to be manipulated and end-to-end optimization makes it impossible to identify the source of poor performance.

Some studies control the output of the encoder-decoder model, through the use of additional information such as target-side information and meta-textual information. Target-side information includes politeness (Sennrich et al., 2016), voice (Yamagishi et al., 2016), sentence length (Kikuchi et al., 2016), and target language (Johnson et al., 2016). Meta-textual information include dialogue act (Wen et al., 2015), user personality (Li et al., 2016), topic (Chen et al., 2016), and domain (Kobus et al., 2016)

Two approaches can be used to provide additional information to the encoder-decoder model, word-level methods and sentence-level methods. Word-level methods encode the additional information as a vector (embedding) that is input together with a word at each time step of either (or both) encoder and decoder (Wen et al., 2015; Li et al., 2016; Kikuchi et al., 2016). Sentence level methods encode the additional information as special tokens. Side constraints are placed at the end of source sentence (Sennrich et al., 2016; Johnson et al., 2016; Yamagishi et al., 2016), while our proposal, prefix constraints, is placed at the beginning of target sentence.

The advantage of sentence-level methods over word-level methods is their simplicity in application. The network structure of the underlying encoder-decoder model does not have to be modified. The problem with side constraints is that, at test time, additional information must be either specified by the user or automatically predicted by some other method. As prefix constraints move the special tokens from source to target, they can be predicted by the network jointly with target sentence. Like side constraints, the user can specify prefix constraints by using prefix-constrained decoding (Wuebker et al., 2016), which can be implemented by a trivial modification of the decoder.

The following sections start by describing the framework of prefix constraints. We then show three simple use cases, namely, length control, bidirectional decoding, and domain adaptation. We then show a more sophisticated usage of prefix constraints: unaligned target word generation.

---

*Currently, Retty Inc.

55

Proceedings of the 4th Workshop on Asian Translation, pages 55–63,
Taipei, Taiwan, November 27, 2017. ©2017 AFNLP

2 Encoder-Decoder Model with Prefix Constraints

2.1 Encoder-Decoder Model

First, we briefly describe the attention-based encoder-decoder model (Bahdanau et al., 2015; Luong et al., 2015), which is the state-of-the-art neural machine translation method and the baseline of this study.

Given input sequence $x = x_1 \ldots x_n$ and model parameters θ, the encoder-decoder model formulates the likelihood of the output sequences $y = y_1 \ldots y_m$ as follows:

$$\log p(\boldsymbol{y}|\boldsymbol{x}) = \sum\nolimits_{j=1}^{m} \log p\left(y_j|\boldsymbol{y}_{<j}, \boldsymbol{x}; \theta\right) \quad (1)$$

The encoder is a recurrent neural network (RNN) which projects input sequence x into a sequence of hidden states $h = h_1 \ldots h_n$ via non-linear transformation. The decoder is another RNN which predicts target words y sequentially, one word at a time. The encoder-decoder model is trained to maximize the conditional likelihood on a parallel corpus by stochastic gradient descent.

$$J = - \sum_{(x,y)\in D} \log p(\boldsymbol{y}|\boldsymbol{x}) \quad (2)$$

Attention-based encoder-decoder models have an additional single-layer feed-forward neural network, called attention layer. It calculates a weight for each source word x_i to predict target word y_j from previous target word y_{j-1} and hidden states of the encoder h_i.

2.2 Side Constraints

Sennrich et al. (2016) proposed a method to control the level of politeness in target sentence in English-to-German translation. They add a T-V distinction tag at the end of the source sentence, so that target sentence is either familiar (Latin *Tu*) or polite (Latin *Vos*).

Are you kidding? [T] $\rightarrow$ Machst du Witze?
Are you kidding? [V] $\rightarrow$ Machen Sie Witze?

In their method, the features that the generated target sentence must satisfy are called *side constraints*. At training time, the correct feature is extracted from the sentence pair. At test time, the special token is assumed to be provided by the user. Automatic prediction of the side constraints from the source sentence at test time is an open problem. Johnson et al. (2016) used the framework for multilingual translation.

2.3 Prefix Constraints

In our proposed method, a sequence of special tokens is placed at the beginning of the target sentence. In other words, they are the prefix to the extended target sentence.

Let a sequence of features extracted from a pair of source sentence x and target sentence y be $c = c_1 \ldots c_k$, and extended target sentence be $\tilde{\boldsymbol{y}} = \boldsymbol{c}\boldsymbol{y}$. The baseline encoder-decoder model Eq. (1) is extended as follows.

$$\log p(\tilde{\boldsymbol{y}}|\boldsymbol{x}) = \log p(\boldsymbol{c}|\boldsymbol{x}) + \log p(\boldsymbol{y}|\boldsymbol{x}, \boldsymbol{c}) \quad (3)$$

$$\log p(\boldsymbol{c}|\boldsymbol{x}) = \sum\nolimits_{j=1}^{k} \log p\left(c_j|\boldsymbol{c}_{<j}, \boldsymbol{x}; \theta\right)$$

$$\log p(\boldsymbol{y}|\boldsymbol{x}, \boldsymbol{c}) = \sum\nolimits_{j=1}^{m} \log p\left(y_j|\boldsymbol{y}_{<j}, \boldsymbol{x}, \boldsymbol{c}; \theta\right)$$

and the objective function becomes

$$J = - \sum_{(x,y)\in D} \log p(\boldsymbol{y}|\boldsymbol{x}, \boldsymbol{c}) + \log p(\boldsymbol{c}|\boldsymbol{x}). \quad (4)$$

Prefix constraints can be either automatically predicted or specified by the user. In the default use of the decoder, both prefix and target sentence are jointly generated (predicted) from source sentence. Prefix can be specified by using *prefix-constrained decoding* (Wuebker et al., 2016), which is a beam search method that constrains the output to match a specified prefix. In the constrained mode, we feed c_j directly to the next time step regardless of the current prediction of the decoder. Once the specified prefix has been utilized, the decoder switches to standard (unconstrained) beam search and the most probable word y_j is passed to the next time step.

3 Basic Examples

3.1 Length Control

The first example encodes the desired length of the target sentence for length control.

京都が好きです $\rightarrow$ #3 I love Kyoto

Length control is extremely be useful when translating headlines, captions, and subtitles. Kikuchi et al. (2016) proposed four methods to control the length of the sentence generated by an encoder-decoder model in a text summarization task; they considered two learning-based methods using length embeddings, namely *LenEmb* and *LenInit*. *LenEmb* method explicitly enters the remaining length to the decoder at each time step, while *LenInit* method enters the desired length once at the initial state of the decoder. They designed a dedicated network structure for each method.

In spirit, our method is similar to the *LenInit* method, but we don't have to modify the underlying network structure. Note that we do not tell the network that '#3' is the length of the target sentence. The network automatically learns the meaning of the symbol from the regularity of the training data and then calculates its embedding.

3.2 Bidirectional Decoding

The second example encodes the decoding direction of target sentence for bidirectional decoding.

京都が好きです → #L2R I love Kyoto
京都が好きです → #R2L Kyoto love I

We make two sentence pairs, one with prefix '#L2R' (left-to-right) and the other with prefix '#R2L' (right-to-left) for each sentence pair, and train a single model. At test time, given an input sentence, the decoder automatically selects optimal decoding direction either '#L2R' or '#R2L' depending on their probabilities.

Liu et al. (2016) proposed a target-bidirectional decoding method that encourages the agreement between left-to-right and right-to-left decoding. Their method requires two separate models, one for left-to-right n-best decoding and the other for right-to-left rescoring, and an additional mechanism for encouraging agreement (rescoring). Our method implements bidirectional decoding in one pass decoding without changing the underlying network structure.

3.3 Domain Adaptation

The third example encodes dataset names of a bilingual text for domain adaptation. Here, IWSLT is a travel expression corpus and KFTT is a corpus of Japanese Wikipedia pages on Kyoto and its English translation.

朝食はいくらですか。
→ #IWSLT How much is the breakfast ?
妙法蓮華経を根本経典とする。
→ #KFTT Its fundamental sutra is lotus sutra .

Kobus et al. (2016) proposed a domain adaptation method using side constraints. They used a separate classifier for predicting the domain of a sentence before translation if it is not known. Li et al. (2016) used Speaker IDs of Twitter to add personality to a conversational agent. Speaker embeddings are learned jointly with word embeddings and entered into the decoder at each time step. Luong and Manning (2015) proposed a domain adaptation method based on fine tuning in which an out-of-domain model is further trained on in-domain data.

Our method can automatically predict domain jointly with target sentence. We don't have to change the underlying network structure and domain embeddings are jointly learned with word embeddings as a part of target vocabulary. One of the potential benefits of our method is that only one model is made and used for all domains. If multiple domains must be supported, the methods based on fine tuning (Luong and Manning, 2015) have to make a model for each domain.

4 Unaligned Target Word Generation

The fourth example encodes information on unaligned target words for generating target sentences. It is significantly more complex than the previous examples. We first describe its motivation and then derive two types of prefix constraints.

4.1 Unaligned Target Words

Given a pair of sentences that are translations of each other, some words in one language cannot be aligned to any words in the other language. We call them *unaligned words*.

Japanese case markers such as が *(ga)*, を *(wo)*, に *(ni)* and English articles such as *a, an, the* do not have counterparts in the other language. Other than these grammatical differences between two languages, unaligned words can be caused by specific linguistic phenomena in one language, such as zero pronouns (dropped subject and object) in Japanese and expletives in English (*there* in there-construction, *do* in interrogative sentence, *it* in formal subject, etc.).

In machine translation, unaligned words in target sentence are problematic because the information required for translation is not explicitly present in the source sentence. There are many works that aim at improving machine translation performance by supplementing unaligned words, but they focus on specific linguistic phenomena such as Japanese case marker (Hisami and Suzuki, 2007), Chinese zero pronoun (empty category) (Chung and Gildea, 2010;

Xiang et al., 2013; Wang et al., 2016), Japanese zero pronoun (Taira et al., 2012; Kudo et al., 2014) and English determiner (Tsvetkov et al., 2013). There are no language independent methods that can cope with unaligned target words.

4.2 Identifying Unaligned Target Words

We first propose a language independent method for automatically identifying unaligned target words. We assume word alignment is given for a bilingual sentence pair, where NULL represents empty word. We define a score $S_u(w)$. It represents the likelihood that a word w in target sentence e aligns to the NULL in source sentence f. The most straightforward way to define $S_u(w)$ is to use the word translation probability obtained from the word alignment in the training corpus,

$$S_u(w) = p(f = NULL | e = w) \quad (5)$$

Our preliminary experiment showed that the scores yielded by Eq. (5) are not reliable for low frequency target words. We therefore use the following equation to filter out low frequency NULL-generated target words.

$$S_u(w) = p(e = w | f = NULL)$$
$$* p(f = NULL | e = w) \quad (6)$$

We use GIZA++ (Och and Ney, 2003) to obtain word alignment for both translation directions. Word alignment is symmetrized by *intersection* heuristics, because the word alignment obtained by *grow-diag-final-and*, is noisy for unaligned words.

Table 1 shows the top 50 unaligned target words as determined by Eq. (6) in the IWSLT-2005 Japanese-to-English translation dataset, which is described in the experiment section. We can see that the automatically extracted unaligned target words include zero pronouns (*i, you, it*), articles (*a, the*), light verbs (*take, get, make*), and expletives (*do, does*).

4.3 Prefix Constraints for Unaligned Target Words

We propose here two types of prefix constraints for improving the translation of unaligned target words: LEX and COUNT.

LEX places a sequence of unaligned target words at the beginning of the target sentence in the same order they appear in the target sentence.

A special token, #GO, is added to delimit the variable length prefix relative to target sentence. In the following examples, words with underline indicate unaligned target words.

赤ワインを頂けますか。
→#i #GO may i have some red wine ?
では当日御待ちして居ります。
→#we #you #GO we are waiting for you that day .

COUNT uses the number of unaligned target words as a prefix. As shown in the following examples, the number of unaligned target words are surrounded by "[" and "]" to distinguish the (fixed length) prefix from target sentence [1].

赤ワインを頂けますか。
→ [1] may i have some red wine ?
では当日御待ちして居ります。
→ [2] we are waiting for you that day .

5 Experiment

5.1 Datasets and Tools

The experiments used five publicly available Japanese-English parallel corpora, namely IWSLT-2005, KFTT, GVOICES, REUTERS, and TATOEBA, as shown in Table 2. IWSLT-2005 is a dataset for Japanese-English Tasks of the International Workshop on Spoken Language Translation (Eck and Hori, 2005). It is available from ALA-GIN[2]. KFTT (Kyoto Free Translation Task) is a Japanese-English translation task on Wikipedia articles related to Kyoto[3]. Parallel Global Voices is a multilingual corpus created from Global Voices websites which translate social media and blogs (Prokopidis et al., 2016). Tatoeba is a collection of multilingual translated example sentences from Tatoeba website. These last two are available from OPUS (Tiedemann, 2012). Reuters are Japanese-English parallel corpus made by aligning Reuters RCV1 RCV2 multilingual text categorization test collection data set (RCV1 for English and RCV2 for other languages) available from NIST (Utiyama and Isahara, 2003)[4].

The unaligned target word generation experiments used two additional proprietary spoken

---

[1]The COUNT feature can be thought of a substitute for the fertility of the IBM model (Brown et al., 1993), or the generative model for NULL-generated target words (Schulz et al., 2016).
[2]http://alagin.jp/
[3]http://www.phontron.com/kftt/index.html
[4]The aligned parallel corpus is available from the homepage of the first author of (Utiyama and Isahara, 2003)

	$S_u(w)$		$S_u(w)$		$S_u(w)$		$S_u(w)$		$S_u(w)$
i	0.263	like	0.119	's	0.090	be	0.070	want	0.060
the	0.233	of	0.118	can	0.090	'll	0.070	that	0.059
a	0.214	me	0.114	'm	0.089	take	0.068	there	0.059
you	0.171	in	0.109	at	0.084	would	0.068	one	0.054
,	0.166	my	0.108	how	0.082	and	0.067	could	0.051
it	0.155	have	0.101	some	0.078	what	0.067	was	0.051
to	0.133	on	0.098	your	0.077	get	0.066	make	0.051
for	0.132	we	0.097	will	0.075	any	0.066	this	0.049
do	0.129	'd	0.094	with	0.074	an	0.064	here	0.049
please	0.126	is	0.091	are	0.074	does	0.063	by	0.048

Table 1: Top 50 unaligned target words in IWSLT2005

Name	Label	Sents.	len.(ja)	len.(en)
IWSLT-2005	train	19,972	9.9	9.4
(Conversation)	dev	506	8.1	7.5
	test	1,000	8.2	7.6
KFTT	train	440,288	27.0	26.3
(Wikipedia)	dev	1,235	27.8	25.1
	test	1,160	24.5	23.5
GVOICES	train	43,488	26.3	19.8
(Blog)	dev	1,000	25.1	18.9
	test	1,000	28.7	21.2
REUTERS	train	54,011	34.3	25.2
(News)	dev	1,000	34.4	25.2
	test	1,000	34.6	25.5
TATOEBA	train	185,426	10.1	9.14
(Examples)	dev	1,000	10.2	9.21
	test	1,000	11.8	9.23
ALL	train	753,185	23.3	21.2
	dev	4,741	23.2	18.6
	test	5,160	22.2	17.5

Table 2: Datasets Statistics

language corpora as the IWSLT-2005 dataset is very small. One is the *Daionsen* parallel sentence database, made by Straightword Inc[5], which is a phrase book for daily conversation. It has 50,709 sentences with 431,258 words in English and 471,677 words in Japanese. The other is the HIT (Harbin Institute of Technology) parallel corpus (Yang et al., 2006) developed for speech translation. It is a collection of 62,727 sentences with 635,809 words in English and 796,200 words in Japanese. We call this dataset IWSLT-2005+EXTRA.

English sentences are tokenized and lower-cased by the scripts used in Moses (Koehn et al., 2007). Japanese sentences are normalized by NFKC (a unicode normalization form) and word segmented by MeCab[6] with UniDic. For neural

machine translation, we used seq2seq-attn[7], which implements an attention-based encoder-decoder (Luong et al., 2015). We used default settings unless otherwise specified. Translation accuracy is measured by BLEU (Papineni et al., 2002).

5.2 Length Control

Table 3 compares side constraints with prefix constraints in terms of length control for IWSLT-2005 dataset. Baseline is a NMT system trained on the parallel corpus without length tag. Side Constraints and Prefix Constraints stand for NMT systems trained on the corpus with length tags placed at the end of source sentence and at the begging of target sentence, respectively. In None, source sentences without length tag are entered into the system at test time. In Oracle, reference length is encoded as length tag and prefix constrained decoding is used in Prefix Constraints. In the training for Side Constraints, we mixed tagged sentences and non-tagged sentences to avoid over-fitting to length tag as described in (Sennrich et al., 2016).

	None	Oracle
Baseline	34.8	-
Side Constraints	33.0	35.4
Prefix Constraints	31.7	**35.7**

Table 3: Comparison between side constraints and prefix constraints on length control

As shown in Table 3, Prefix Constraints are comparable to or better than Side Constraints in controlling the length of the target sentence if the correct length is known and provided as an oracle. It is difficult to predict the length of target sentence from source sentence, which lowered the ac-

[5] http://www.straightword.jp/
[6] http://taku910.github.io/mecab/
[7] https://github.com/harvardnlp/seq2seq-attn

curacy of Prefix Constraints for None. The accuracy of length prediction for short sentences (less than 10 words) is 97.7%, while that for long sentences (more than or equal to 10 words) is 45.7%.

We found that length control for short sentence worked surprisingly well. The following is an example of prefix constrained decoding where length tags were changed from #2 to #9 for the source sentence どういたしまして (You're welcome). All of them are acceptable and have the specified length.

どういたしまして →
#2 anytime .
#3 you welcome .
#4 you 're welcome .
#5 you 're welcome up .
#6 you 're welcome , sir .
#7 you 're welcome . thank you .
#8 you 're welcome . you 're welcome .
#9 it 's all right . you 're welcome .

5.3 Bidirectional Decoding

	IWSLT	KFTT	REUTERS
L2R	34.8	20.9	19.7
R2L	32.8	20.1	19.6
Target-Bidi	**35.8**	21.1	20.2
Predict-Dir	35.6	**21.5**	**20.6**

Table 4: Comparison of target bidirectional method (Liu et al., 2016) and decoding direction prediction using prefix constraints

Table 4 shows a comparison between our implementation of target-bidirectional method (Target-Bidi) (Liu et al., 2016) and decoding direction prediction using prefix constraints (Predict-Dir) on IWSLT-2005, KFTT, and REUTERS datasets. L2R and R2L are baseline NMT system with left-to-right and right-to-left decoding, respectively. For the evaluation of Predict-Dir, sentences with '#R2L' tags are reversed and both '#L2R' and '#R2L' tags are removed. Predict-Dir is comparable to or better than Target-Bidi. Considering the simplicity of the proposed method, it is a viable option for bidirectional decoding.

5.4 Domain adaptation

Table 5 shows BLEU scores for the five datasets for different systems in terms of domain adaptation techniques. In Single, for each domain (dataset), the translation model is trained using only each dataset in isolation. In Join, one translation model is trained using a corpus made by simply concatenating all datasets without domain tags. In Predict and Oracle, one translation model is trained using a corpus made by concatenating all datasets with domain tags as target prefix. In Predict, domain tag is automatically predicted, while in Oracle, the domain tag of the reference is provided and used for prefix constrained decoding.

Comparing Single and Join, Small corpora such as GVOICES and REUTERS benefit most when additional parallel data is used, while the largest corpus KFTT experiences no such benefit. By adding domain tags (Predict and Oracle), all corpora including the largest KFTT can benefit from the combination of data sources. As the difference in accuracy between Predict and Oracle is small, we assume the domain prediction accuracy for the proposed method is high enough for the task.

In order to understand what is happening when domain tags are used as prefix constraints, we randomly selected 100 sentences from each dataset and calculated the hidden states for each reference. We then visualized the hidden state of the last layer of the decoder in the first time step (before domain tag entered) and the second time step (after domain tag entered) using t-SNE in Figure 1.

The figure shows the proximity between domains. In the initial step of the decoder, some domains such as IWSLT-2005 and TATOEBA, or GVOICES and REUTERS are very close each other. After domain tags are entered, all domains are clearly separated. Specifying the domain tag corresponds to moving the point in the figure from one cluster to another.

5.5 Unaligned target word generation

We made two lists of unaligned target words, top 10 and top 50, based on Eq. (6). For each sentence in the training data, unaligned target words were identified and used to make prefix constraints if they are in the list and unaligned in the sentence pair. Table 6 shows translation accuracy when COUNT and LEX are used as prefix constraints, where the candidates of target unaligned words are either top-10 or top-50. Baseline is the attention-based encoder-decoder model without prefix constraints. In Predict, prefix constraints are predicted from source sentence. In Oracle, prefix constraints are specified using reference target sentence and prefix constrained decoding is used.

	Single	Join	Predict	Oracle
GVOICES (43k sents.)	6.31	16.9	17.0	17.1
IWSLT (20k sents.)	34.8	36.8	37.1	37.1
KFTT (440k sents.)	20.9	20.8	21.1	21.1
REUTERS (54k sents.)	19.7	24.6	25.0	25.0
TATOEBA (185k sents.)	36.0	59.4	59.5	59.7

Table 5: BLEU scores for different systems in terms of domain adaptation techniques

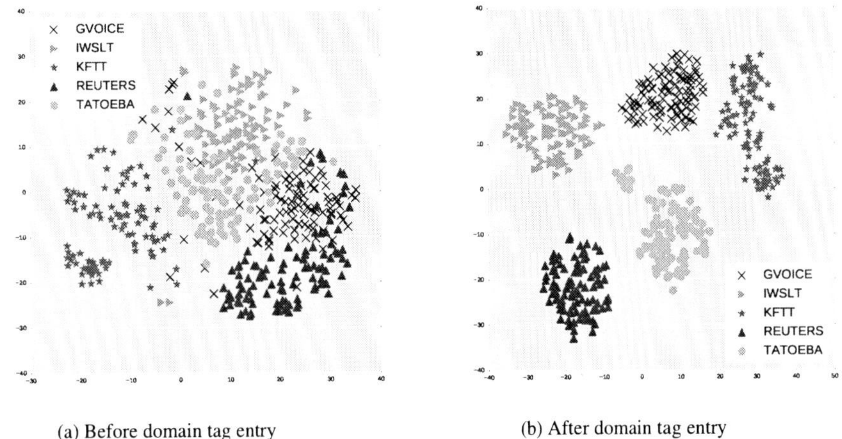

(a) Before domain tag entry   (b) After domain tag entry

Figure 1: t-SNE visualization of the hidden states of the decoder for various domains

		IWSLT-2005+EXTRA	
	#UTW	Predict	Oracle
Baseline		36.5	-
COUNT	10	**37.5**	38.1
	50	36.9	38.0
LEX	10	36.4	41.7
	50	32.4	**46.9**

Table 6: Translation accuracy of prefix constraint prediction and prefix-constrained decoding

	Precision	Recall
i	76	68
you	72	78
it	61	67

Table 7: Precision and recall of pronouns

As for Predict, COUNT is significantly better than Baseline (about 1 BLEU point) when the small list of unaligned words, top-10, is used. It shows that translation accuracy can be improved by predicting prefix constraints and generating target sentence at the same time [8].

The accuracies for Oracle show that translation accuracy can be greatly improved if the user provides some information on unaligned target words.

If the number of unaligned words is provided, translation accuracy can be improved by about 3 BLEU points, and if the correct list of unaligned target words is provided, it can be improved by about 10 points. There is still much room for improvement as regards the problem of unaligned target words.

Table 7 shows precision and recall of unaligned target pronouns when COUNT based on top-10 list is used for prefix constraint prediction and the dataset is IWSLT-2005+EXTRA. We think the accuracies of around 70% are reasonable considering that some pronouns are context dependent.

Table 8 is a real example of the outputs of LEX and COUNT. In fact, it is very difficult to predict the correct set of unaligned words from just the

---

[8]The average numbers of unaligned target words in train, dev, test set of IWSLT-2005+EXTRA are 3.1, 2.5, 2.6, respectively

Input	いつ でも 話し合い に 応じる 準備 は でき て いる から 、ゴー サイン を 送って 下さい 。
Reference	#i #GO i 'm ready to start talks anytime so just say when .
Baseline	you 're always ready to talk to me , so you 'll have to have a thorough signature .
Predict (LEX)	#you #have #to #and #you #GO you 're ready to let us have ready and sent them to you .
Predict (COUNT)	[4] you 're always ready to talk with us . please send us a liqueur .

Table 8: A real example of the outputs of LEX and COUNT

source sentence without context. Leaving aside the errors caused by the unknown Japanese words ゴーサイン (go-ahead, green light, literally "go-sign"), the major challenge here is the Japanese zero subject. It could be "i", "you", "he/she", and depends on the context. In the other words, Oracle (LEX) is significantly better than Baseline because this kind of context dependent information is provided from the outside.

6 Conclusion

In this paper, we showed that prefix constraints can be used as a general framework for controlling the target features commonly needed in neural machine translation, such as length control, bidirectional decoding, domain adaptation, and unaligned target word generation.

There are many issues that must be tackled: For length control, translation accuracy could be improved if we can accurately predict the length of target sentence from source sentence. For domain adaptation, rigorous comparison between prefix constraints with other domain adaptation techniques, such as side constraints (Kobus et al., 2016), fine tuning (Luong and Manning, 2015), and their combination (Chu et al., 2017), are required to realize its full effectiveness. For unaligned target word generation, applying the proposed method to other domains such as news articles and other language pairs such as Chinese-to-English is required to show its generality.

References

Dzmitry Bahdanau, Kyunghyun Cho, and Yoshua Bengio. 2015. Neural Machine Translation by Jointly Learning to Align and Translate. In *Proceedings of the ICLR-2015*.

Peter E. Brown, Stephen A. Della Pietra, Vincent J. Della Pietra, and Robert L. Mercer. 1993. The mathematics of statistical machine translation: Parameter estimation. *Computational Linguistics* 19(2):263–311.

Wenhu Chen, Evgeny Matusov, Shahram Khadivi, and Jan-Thorsten Peter. 2016. Guided Alignment Training for Topic-Aware Neural Machine Translation. In *Proceedings of AMTA-2016*.

Chenhui Chu, Raj Dabre, and Sadao Kurohashi. 2017. An empirical comparison of domain adaptation methods for neural machine translation. In *Proceedings of the ACL-2017*.

Tagyoung Chung and Daniel Gildea. 2010. Effects of Empty Categories on Machine Translation. In *Proceedings of the EMNLP-2010*. pages 636–645.

Matthias Eck and Chiori Hori. 2005. Overview of the iwslt 2005 evaluation campaign. In *Proceedings of the IWSLT-2005*. pages 1–22.

Toutanova Hisami and Kristina Suzuki. 2007. Generating case markers in machine translation. In *Proceedings of the NAACL-HLT-2007*. pages 49–56.

Melvin Johnson, Mike Schuster, Quoc V Le, Maxim Krikun, Yonghui Wu, Zhifeng Chen, Nikhil Thorat, Fernanda Viegas, Martin Wattenberg, Greg Corrado, Macduff Hughes, and Jeffrey Dean. 2016. Google's Multilingual Neural Machine Translation System: Enabling Zero Shot Translation. arXiv preprint arXiv:1611.04558 .

Yuta Kikuchi, Graham Neubig, Ryohei Sasano, Hiroya Takamura, and Manabu Okumura. 2016. Controlling Output Length in Neural Encoder-Decoders. In *Proceedings of the EMNLP-2016*. pages 1328–1338.

Catherine Kobus, Josep Maria Crego, and Jean Senellart. 2016. Domain control for neural machine translation. *arXiv preprint arXiv:1612.06140* .

Philipp Koehn, Hieu Hoang, Alexandra Birch, Chris Callison-Burch, Marcello Federico, Nicola Bertoldi, Brooke Cowan, Wade Shen, Christine Moran, Richard Zens, Chris Dyer, and Ondrej Bojar and. 2007. Moses: Open source toolkit for statistical machine translation. In *Proceedings of the ACL-2007*.

Taku Kudo, Hiroshi Ichikawa, and Hideto Kazawa. 2014. A joint inference of deep case analysis and zero subject generation for Japanese-to-English statistical machine translation. In *Proceedings of the ACL-2014*. pages 557–562.

Jiwei Li, Michel Galley, Chris Brockett, Georgios Spithourakis, Jianfeng Gao, and Bill Dolan. 2016. A Persona-Based Neural Conversation Model. In *Proceedings of the ACL-2016*. pages 994–1003.

Lemao Liu, Masao Utiyama, Andrew Finch, and Eiichiro Sumita. 2016. Agreement on target-bidirectional neural machine translation. In *Proceedings of the NAACL-HLT-2016*. pages 411–416.

Minh-Thang Luong and Christopher D. Manning. 2015. Stanford neural machine translation systems for spoken language domains. In *Proceedings of the IWSLT-2015*.

Minh-Thang Luong, Hieu Pham, and Christopher D Manning. 2015. Effective approaches to attention-based neural machine translation. In *Proceedings of the EMNLP-2015*.

Franz Josef Och and Hermann Ney. 2003. A systematic comparison of various statistical alignment models. *Computational Linguistics* 29(1):19–51.

Kishore Papineni, Salim Roukos, Todd Ward, and Wei-Jing Zhu. 2002. Bleu: a method for automatic evaluation of machine translation. In *Proceedings of the ACL-2002*. pages 311–318.

Prokopis Prokopidis, Vassilis Papavassiliou, and Stelios Piperidis. 2016. Parallel global voices: a collection of multilingual corpora with citizen media stories. In *Proceedings of the LREC-2016*.

Philip Schulz, Wilker Aziz, and Khalil Sima'an. 2016. Word alignment without null words. In *Proceedings of the ACL-2016*.

Rico Sennrich, Barry Haddow, and Alexandra Birch. 2016. Controlling Politeness in Neural Machine Translation via Side Constraints. In *Proceedings of the NAACL-HLT-2016*. pages 35–40.

Hirotoshi Taira, Katsuhito Sudoh, and Masaaki Nagata. 2012. Zero pronoun resolution can improve the quality of je translation. In *Proceedings of the SSST-2012*. pages 111–118.

Jörg Tiedemann. 2012. Parallel data, tools and interfaces in opus. In *Proceedings of LREC-2012*.

Yulia Tsvetkov, Chris Dyer, Lori Levin, and Archna Bhatia. 2013. Generating english determiners in phrase-based translation with synthetic translation options. In *Proceeding of the WMT-2013*. pages 271–280.

Masao Utiyama and Hitoshi Isahara. 2003. Reliable measures for aligning japanese-english news articles and sentences. In *Proceedings of ACL-2003*. pages 72–79.

Longyue Wang, Zhaopeng Tu, Xiaojun Zhang, Hang Li, Andy Way, and Qun Liu. 2016. A Novel Approach to Dropped Pronoun Translation. In *Proceedings of the NAACL-2016*. pages 983–993.

Tsung-Hsien Wen, Milica Gasic, Nikola Mrkšić, Pei-Hao Su, David Vandyke, and Steve Young. 2015. Semantically conditioned lstm-based natural language generation for spoken dialogue systems. In *Proceedings of EMNLP-2015*.

Joern Wuebker, Spence Green, John DeNero, Sasa Hasan, and Minh-Thang Luong. 2016. Models and Inference for Prefix-Constrained Machine Translation. In *Proceedings of the ACL-2016*. pages 66–75.

Bing Xiang, Xiaoqiang Luo, and Bowen Zhou. 2013. Enlisting the ghost: Modeling empty categories for machine translation. In *Proceedings of the ACL-2013*. pages 822–831.

Hayahide Yamagishi, Shin Kanouchi, Takayuki Sato, and Mamoru Komachi. 2016. Controlling the Voice of a Sentence in Japanese-to-English Neural Machine Translation. In *Proceedings of the WAT-2016*. pages 203–210.

Muyun Yang, Hongfei Jiang, Tiejun Zhao, and Sheng Li. 2006. Construct trilingual parallel corpus on demand. In *Chinese Spoken Language Processing*, Springer, pages 760–767.

Improving Japanese-to-English Neural Machine Translation by Paraphrasing the Target Language

Yuuki Sekizawa and **Tomoyuki Kajiwara** and **Mamoru Komachi**
{sekizawa-yuuki, kajiwara-tomoyuki}@ed.tmu.ac.jp, komachi@tmu.ac.jp

Abstract

Neural machine translation (NMT) produces sentences that are more fluent than those produced by statistical machine translation (SMT). However, NMT has a very high computational cost because of the high dimensionality of the output layer. Generally, NMT restricts the size of the vocabulary, which results in infrequent words being treated as out-of-vocabulary (OOV) and degrades the performance of the translation. In order to improve the translation quality regarding words that are OOV in the target language, we propose a preprocessing method that paraphrases infrequent words or phrases expressed as OOV with frequent synonyms from the target side of the training corpus. In an evaluation using Japanese to English translation, we achieved a statistically significant BLEU score improvement of 0.55–0.77 over baselines that included the state-of-the-art method.

1 Introduction

Recently, neural-network-based methods have gained considerable popularity in many natural language processing tasks. In the field of machine translation, neural machine translation (NMT) is actively being researched because of the advantage that it can output sentences that are more fluent compared with statistical machine translation (SMT). However, NMT has a problem of high computational cost because it addresses the output generation task by solving a classification problem in vocabulary dimension. Typically, NMT has to restrict the size of the vocabulary to reduce the computational cost. Therefore, the target language vocabulary includes only high-frequency words (e.g., 30,000 high-frequency words) in training; other words are treated as out-of-vocabulary (OOV) and substituted with a special symbol such as "<unk>" in the output. The symbol has no meaning, so the output has reduced quality.

As a previous work attempting to reduce the OOV rate in NMT, Li et al. (2016), replaced OOV words with a translation table using word similarity in the training and test data. In particular, they replaced each OOV word with an in-vocabulary word using word similarity in a parallel training corpus; they reduced the OOV rate in the output and improved the translation quality. However, they sometimes substituted OOV words with a similar word such as a proper noun. In addition, they deleted OOV words that aligned to null, which can result in a loss of sentence content and reduced translation adequacy.

In this work, we present a preprocessing method for improving translation related to OOV words. We paraphrase low-frequency words treated as OOV in the target corpus with high frequency words while retaining the meaning.

Our main contributions are as follows.

- We propose a paraphrasing-based preprocessing method for Japanese-to-English NMT to improve translation accuracy with regard to OOV words. Our method can be combined with any NMT system.

- We show that our method achieved a statistically significant BLEU (Kishore et al., 2002) score improvement of 0.58 and a METEOR (Lavie and Agarwal, 2007) score improvement of 0.52 over the previous method (Li et al., 2016) and reduced the OOV rate in output sentences by approximately 0.20.

Proceedings of the 4th Workshop on Asian Translation, pages 64–69,
Taipei, Taiwan, November 27, 2017. ©2017 AFNLP

2   Related Work

There have been studies on improving translation accuracy by reducing the OOV rate using pre- and post-processing for machine translation. Luong et al. (2015) proposed a post-processing method that translates OOV words with a corresponding word in the source sentence using a translation dictionary. This method needs to align training sentence pairs before training to learn correspondences between OOV words and their translations. In the method described in this paper, we need no word alignment, and we retain the meaning of the original word by paraphrasing the target side of the training corpus. Jean et al. (2015) proposed another post-processing method that translates each OOV word with the word that has the largest attention weight in the source sentence using a translation dictionary. Their method does not need word alignment, but it still does not necessarily consider the meaning in the target language, unlike our paraphrasing approach. Sennrich et al. (2016) applied byte pair encoding (BPE) to source and target corpora to split OOV words into units of frequent substrings to reduce the OOV rate. Their method splits words greedily without considering their meaning. Since we use lexical paraphrasing in the training data, we hope to reduce the OOV rate in the translation output while retaining the meaning. Additionally, since ours is a preprocessing method, it can be combined with a post-processing method.

On the other hand, there are methods similar to ours that paraphrase corpora as a preprocessing step of machine translation to reduce the complexity of source and/or target sentences. Sanja and Maja (2016) paraphrased source sentence vocabulary with a simple grammar as a preprocessing step for machine translation. We attempt to improve translation quality by reducing the OOV rate in the target language using paraphrasing without simplifying the source input sentences. Li et al. (2016) substituted OOV words in training corpora with a similar in-vocabulary word as pre- and post-processing steps. They replaced OOV words with frequent words using cosine similarity and a language model. They obtained word alignment between an OOV word and its counterpart in training corpora. In addition, they deleted OOV words from the training corpus if they aligned to null. However, this leads to a loss of sentence meaning and degrades the adequacy

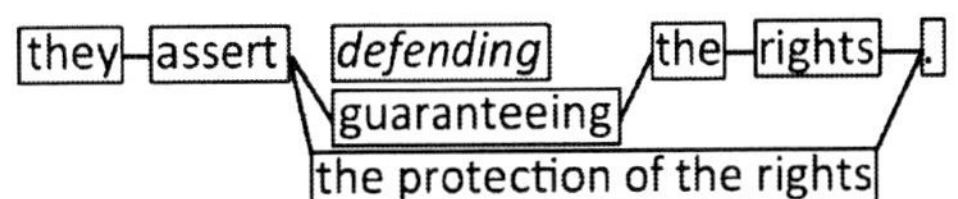

original: the *pedagogues* had *quarrels.*
paraphrase, first round: the educators had discussions.
paraphrase, second round: the teachers had discussions.

Figure 1: Examples of paraphrasing. Original word is shown in italics. Upper: paraphrase lattice; lower: iterative paraphrasing of OOV word.

of the translation. They also might replace OOV words with similar but non-synonymous words since they used distributional similarity. For instance, they replaced "surfing" with "snowboard", which leads to rewriting "internet surfing" as "internet snowboard", resulting in a change of meaning. We use a paraphrase score calculated from bilingual pivoting instead of distributional similarity; therefore, we are not likely to paraphrase OOV words with inappropriate expressions. In the aforementioned example, we paraphrase "surfing" as "browser", which preserves the original meaning to some extent.

3   Proposed Method

In this paper, we propose a preprocessing method that paraphrases infrequent words or phrases with frequent ones on the target side of the training sentences in order to train a better NMT model by reducing the number of OOV words while keeping their original meaning. We paraphrase infrequent words using a paraphrase dictionary that has paraphrase pairs annotated with a paraphrase score. We employ three scores: (1) paraphrase score, (2) language model (LM) score, and (3) a combination of these scores. The paraphrase score is meant to reflect translation adequacy, and the language model score is sensitive to fluency. We combined the paraphrase score and the language model score by linear interpolation[1] as follows:

$$paraphrase\_score =$$
$$\lambda(PPDBscore) + (1 - \lambda)(LMscore)$$

Figure 1 shows an example of paraphrasing with a paraphrase lattice and the Viterbi algorithm. Suppose "defending" is OOV. We can paraphrase the OOV word "defending" with a frequent word,

---

[1] In a preliminary experiment, normalization of these scores was not found to yield any improvements.

method	BLEU	METEOR	OOV
baseline	25.70†	31.06	1,123
Luong et al.	25.87†	31.04	567
Sennrich et al.	25.92*	31.50	0
Li et al.	25.89*	31.10	832
proposed (multi. word + phrase)	**26.47**	**31.62**	668

Table 1: Japanese-to-English translation result of each method. † and * indicate that the proposed method significantly outperformed the other methods at p<0.01 and p<0.05, respectively, using bootstrap resampling.

"guaranteeing", or we can paraphrase the OOV phrase "defending the rights" with another phrase, "the protection of the rights", which has no OOV words. In addition to calculating the paraphrase score, our paraphrase algorithm calculates the 2-gram language model score in "assert guaranteeing the rights .", "assert the", and "rights ." and chooses the highest scoring paraphrase, thus generating "they assert the protection of the rights.". We do not calculate the 2-gram language model score in phrases.[2]

In addition, our method can paraphrase OOV words iteratively until a paraphrase with frequent words is reached. In the lower example in Figure 1, suppose that "pedagogues" and "quarrels" are OOV. The latter word in the original sentence is paraphrased with a frequent word, "discussions", whereas the former is paraphrased with an infrequent word, "educators", in the first round. We can then paraphrase the infrequent word "educators" again, this time with a frequent word, "teachers", in the second round. If we allow only the first round of paraphrasing, the infrequent word "pedagogues" will not be paraphrased with the frequent word "teachers" because the paraphrase dictionary does not have this entry, and the infrequent word "pedagogues" will not be paraphrased with the infrequent word "educators". In this paper, we express one-pass paraphrasing as "single", and iterative paraphrasing as "multi.". In addition, we use "word" when we paraphrase words, and "word + phrase" when paraphrasing words and phrases.

4 Experiment

4.1 Settings

In this study, we used the Japanese–English portion of the Asian Scientific Paper Excerpt Corpus (ASPEC) (Nakazawa et al., 2016). For train-

ing, we used one million sentence pairs ranked by alignment accuracy. We deleted sentence pairs longer than 41 words. The final training corpus contained 827,503 sentence pairs. We followed the official development/test split: 1,790 sentence pairs for development, and 1,812 sentence pairs for testing. We used the development dataset to select the best model and used the test dataset to evaluate BLEU scores.

We used the Moses script as an English tokenizer and MeCab[3] (using IPAdic) as a Japanese tokenizer. We employed KenLM[4] to build a 2-gram language model trained with all sentences from ASPEC. We utilized the XXXL-size PPDB 2.0 (Pavlick et al., 2015) as the English paraphrase dictionary and PPDB:Japanese (Mizukami et al., 2014) as the Japanese paraphrase dictionary. Neither of these dictionaries contains the ASPEC corpus. We paraphrased either the target side of the training corpus only or both the source and target sides of the training corpus to conduct a fair comparison. We experimented with $\lambda = 0.0, 0.25, 0.50, 0.75,$ and 1.0.

We used OpenNMT-py[5] as the NMT system, which is a Python implementation of OpenNMT (Klein et al., 2017). We built a model with settings as described below. We used bi-recurrent-neural-network, batch size 64, epoch 20, embedding size 500, vocabulary size of source and target 30,000, dropout rate 0.3, optimizer SGD with learning rate 1.0, and number of RNN layers 2 with an RNN size of 500. Our baseline was trained with these settings without any paraphrasing. We re-implemented previous methods described in this paper (Luong et al., 2015; Li et al., 2016; Sennrich et al., 2016) using the underlying NMT with the abovementioned settings. We

---

[2]Calculating language model scores of phrases does not improve NMT.

[3]https://github.com/taku910/mecab
[4]http://kheafield.com/code/kenlm/
[5]https://github.com/OpenNMT/OpenNMT-py

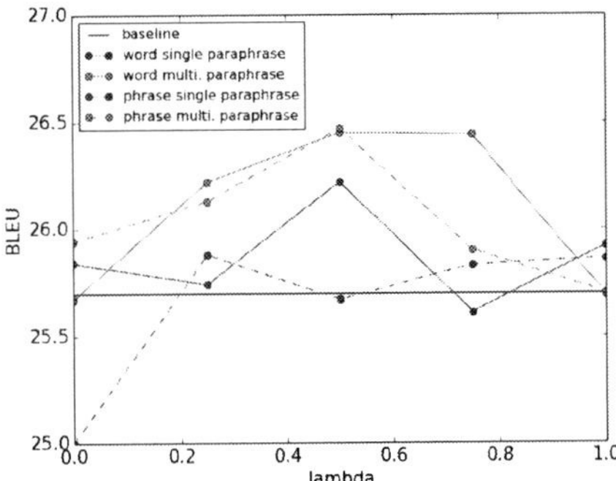

Figure 2: BLEU score of the proposed method in Japanese-to-English translation using various weightings for the paraphrase score and the language model score.

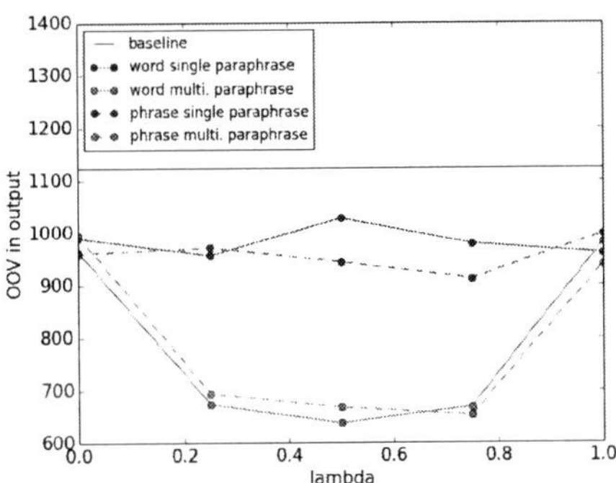

Figure 3: Number of OOV terms in the output of the proposed method in Japanese-to-English translation.

used BLEU (Kishore et al., 2002) and METEOR (Lavie and Agarwal, 2007) for extrinsic evaluation. We also analyzed the number of OOV words in the translated sentences as an intrinsic evaluation.

English PPDB 2.0 achieved higher quality than PPDB 1.0 by using a supervised regression model to estimate paraphrase scores. However, because there are no training data to build a supervised regression model for PPDBs other than in English, the quality of PPDBs in other languages may affect the quality of the proposed method. To investigate whether PPDB quality relates to translation quality, we performed English to Japanese translation by the proposed method using PPDB:Japanese (Mizukami et al., 2014).

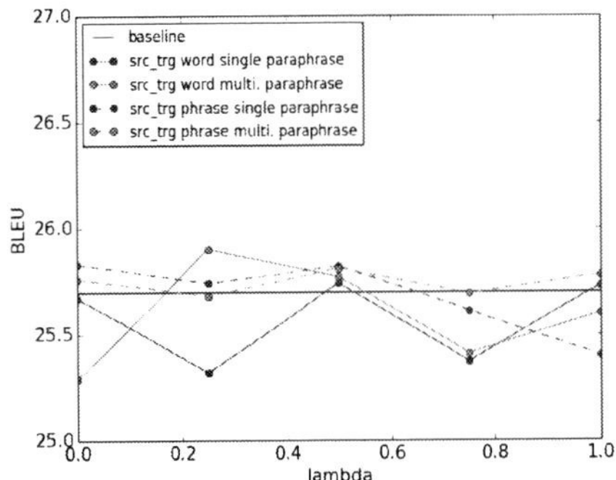

Figure 4: BLEU score in Japanese-to-English translation using source and target paraphrasing.

method	BLEU	OOV
baseline	33.91	1,003
single (word)	33.97	915
multi. (word)	**34.09**	966
single (word + phrase)	33.65	938
multi. (word + phrase)	33.86	**902**

Table 2: English-to-Japanese translation results with variations in the number of paraphrasings and the unit used.

4.2 Results

Table 1 shows the experimental results compared with those in previous work. The proposed method is multi. word + phrase paraphrasing. In the BLEU evaluation, our method significantly outperformed not only the baseline and Luong et al. (p<0.01) but also Sennrich et al. and Li et al. (p<0.05). We improved the BLEU score by 0.77 and the METEOR score by 0.56 as well as reducing the number of OOV words in the output by approximately 40% compared with the baseline.

Figure 2 reports the BLEU score of our method under variations in the linear interpolation coefficient and the number of paraphrasings. Figure 3 shows the number of OOV words in the output. The best BLEU score was achieved by multi-round paraphrasing and $\lambda = 0.50$, which means that the paraphrase score is balanced by the PPDB score and the LM score.

Table 2 shows the BLEU score of the proposed method on English to Japanese translation. The best model improved the BLEU score by 0.18 over the baseline, and the number of OOV words in the output decreased slightly.

In the last experiment, we paraphrased the

method	translation
source	ロックインアンプ を 使用 すれ ば , ノイズ を 著しく 減少 できる こと を 期待 できる 。
reference	with the lock ‐ in amplifier used , significant reduction of the noise is expected .
baseline	it is expected that the noise can be reduced remarkably , if the <unk> is used .
multi. (word)	it is expected that the noise can be remarkably decreased , if the amplifier is used .
multi. (phrase)	it is expected that the noise can be remarkably reduced by using the lock-in amplifier .

Table 3: Translation example in Japanese-to-English translation.

infrequent word	frequent word
megahertz	mhz
deflagration	combustion
cone-shaped	conical
revalued	examined
titrated	measured
teleportation	transport

Table 4: Iterative paraphrasing example of domain-specific words with frequent words.

source and target sides of the training corpora to compare the effect of target-only paraphrasing. Figure 4 shows that the method paraphrasing both source and target sentences does not improve the translation quality over the baseline.

5 Discussion

Figures 2 and 3 show that a multi-round paraphrasing method is better than a single-round paraphrase in terms of BLEU score and OOV rate. In multi-round paraphrasing, however, a paraphrased word does not necessarily retain its original meaning in successive paraphrases. The number of OOV words is negatively correlated with the BLEU score, demonstrating that our hypothesis is correct.

On English-to-Japanese translation, the improvement is not statistically significant; however, we believe that our system does not rely on PPDB quality, although the degree of improvement will depend on the quality of the PPDB.

Table 3 is an example of a translation result. This table indicates that the baseline system outputs "<unk>" instead of "amplifier". In contrast, a paraphrasing system can output "amplifier" because a number of words corresponding to "amplifier" are paraphrased into "amplifier" in the proposed method. As a result, the proposed systems can correctly output the word "amplifier".

Table 4 is an example of iterative paraphrasing on special words in ASPEC. This shows that

we can paraphrase domain-specific words and that these paraphrases can improve the translation. The paraphrases shown in the upper half of the table preserve meaning, whereas those in the lower half lose a little of the original meaning.

6 Conclusion

This paper has proposed a preprocessing method that paraphrases infrequent words with frequent words in a target corpus during training to train a better NMT model by reducing the OOV rate. An evaluation using the Japanese-to-English part of the ASPEC corpus showed a decrease in the OOV rate in the translation result and a significant improvement in the BLEU score over state-of-the-art methods. We expect that our method can be effective not only in NMT but also in other text generation tasks using neural networks, such as abstractive summarization, which solves the classification problem of vocabulary dimension.

References

Dzmitry Bahdanau, Kyunghyun Cho, and Yoshua Bengio. 2015. Neural machine translation by jointly learning to align and translate. In *Proc. of ICLR*.

Sébastien Jean, Orhan Firat, Kyunghyun Cho, Roland Memisevic, and Yoshua Bengio. 2015. Montreal neural machine translation systems for WMT'15. In *Proc. of the Tenth Workshop on Statistical Machine Translation*. pages 134–140.

Papineni Kishore, Roukos Salim, Ward Todd, and Zhu Wei-Jing. 2002. BLEU: a method for automatic evaluation of machine translation. In *Proc. of ACL*. pages 311–318.

Guillaume Klein, Yoon Kim, Yuntian Deng, Jean Senellart, and Alexander M Rush. 2017. OpenNMT: Open-source toolkit for neural machine translation. *arXiv preprint arXiv: 1701.02810*.

Alon Lavie and Abhaya Agarwal. 2007. METEOR: An automatic metric for MT evaluation with high levels of correlation with human judgments. In *Proc. of the Second Workshop on Statistical Machine Translation*. pages 228–231.

Xiaoqing Li, Jiajun Zhang, and Chengqing Zong. 2016.
Towards zero unknown word in neural machine
translation. In *Proc. of IJCAI*. pages 2852–2858.

Minh-Thang Luong, Ilya Sutskever, Quoc Le, Oriol
Vinyals, and Wojciech Zaremba. 2015. Addressing
the rare word problem in neural machine translation.
In *Proc. of ACL-IJCNLP*. pages 11–19.

Masahiro Mizukami, Graham Neubig, Sakriani Sakti,
Tomoki Toda, and Satoshi Nakamura. 2014. Build-
ing a free, general-domain paraphrase database for
Japanese. In *Proc. of O-COCOSDA*. pages 1–4.

Toshiaki Nakazawa, Manabu Yaguchi, Kiyotaka Uchi-
moto, Masao Utiyama, Eiichiro Sumita, Sadao
Kurohashi, and Hitoshi Isahara. 2016. ASPEC:
Asian scientific paper excerpt corpus. In *Proc. of
LREC*. pages 2204–2208.

Ellie Pavlick, Pushpendre Rastogi, Juri Ganitkevitch,
Benjamin Van Durme, and Chris Callison-Burch.
2015. PPDB 2.0: Better paraphrase ranking, fine-
grained entailment relations, word embeddings, and
style classification. In *Proc. of ACL*. pages 425–430.

Štajner Sanja and Popovic Maja. 2016. Can text sim-
plification help machine translation? *Baltic Journal
of Modern Computing* 4(2):230–242.

Rico Sennrich, Barry Haddow, and Alexandra Birch.
2016. Neural machine translation of rare words with
subword units. In *Proc. of ACL*. pages 1715–1725.

Improving Low-Resource Neural Machine Translation
with Filtered Pseudo-parallel Corpus

Aizhan Imankulova and **Takayuki Sato** and **Mamoru Komachi**
Tokyo Metropolitan University
{imankulova-aizhan, sato-takayuki}@ed.tmu.ac.jp,
komachi@tmu.ac.jp

Abstract

Large-scale parallel corpora are indispensable to train highly accurate machine translators. However, manually constructed large-scale parallel corpora are not freely available in many language pairs. In previous studies, training data have been expanded using a pseudo-parallel corpus obtained using machine translation of the monolingual corpus in the target language. However, in low-resource language pairs in which only low-accuracy machine translation systems can be used, translation quality is reduces when a pseudo-parallel corpus is used naively. To improve machine translation performance with low-resource language pairs, we propose a method to expand the training data effectively via filtering the pseudo-parallel corpus using a quality estimation based on back-translation. As a result of experiments with three language pairs using small, medium, and large parallel corpora, language pairs with fewer training data filtered out more sentence pairs and improved BLEU scores more significantly.

1 Introduction

A large-scale parallel corpus is an essential resource for training statistical machine translation (SMT) and neural machine translation (NMT) systems. Creating a high-quality large-scale parallel corpus requires time, money and professionals to translate a large amount of texts. As a result, many of the existing large-scale parallel corpora are limited to specific languages and domains. In contrast, large monolingual corpora are easier to obtain.

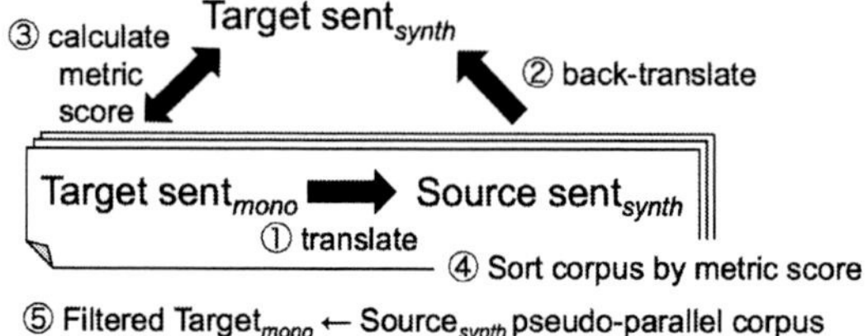

Figure 1: Creating and filtering a pseudo-parallel corpus using back-translation.

Various approaches have been proposed to create a pseudo-parallel corpus from a monolingual corpus. For example, Zhang et al. (2016) proposed a method to generate a pseudo-parallel corpus based on a monolingual corpus of the source language and its automatic translation. Sennrich et al. (2016) obtained substantial improvements by automatically translating a monolingual corpus of the target language into the source language, which they refer to as synthetic, and treating the obtained pseudo-parallel corpus as additional training data. They used monolingual data of the target language to learn the language model more effectively. However, they experimented on language pairs where relatively large-scale parallel corpora are available. Thus, they did not need to fully exploit the training corpus nor care about the quality of the pseudo-parallel corpus.

Therefore, we propose a method to create a pseudo-parallel corpus by back-translating and filtering a monolingual corpus in the target language for low-resource language pairs. If the target sentence and its back-translation are similar, we assume that the synthetic source sentence is appropriate regarding its monolingual target sentence and can be included into the filtered pseudo-parallel corpus. The quality of the pseudo-parallel corpus is especially important because low-quality

70

Proceedings of the 4th Workshop on Asian Translation, pages 70–78,
Taipei, Taiwan, November 27, 2017. ©2017 AFNLP

parallel sentences will degrade NMT performance more than SMT. Our motivation is to filter out low-quality synthetic sentences that might be included in such a pseudo-parallel corpus to obtain a high-quality pseudo-parallel corpus for low-resource language pairs. To the best of our knowledge, this is the first attempt to (1) filter a pseudo-parallel corpus using back-translation and (2) bootstrap NMT.

The main contributions of our research are as follows:

- We filter a pseudo-parallel corpus using sentence-level similarity metric, in our case sentence-level BLEU (Lin and Och, 2004a,b), and obtain a trainable high-quality pseudo-parallel corpus.
- We show that the proposed filtering method is useful for low-resource language pairs, although bootstrapping does not outperform the proposed filtering method significantly.
- We will release the obtained filtered pseudo-parallel corpora[1].

In this study, we used Japanese↔Russian as low-resource language pairs, French→Malagasy as medium-resource language pairs and German→English as high-resource language pairs. We show that a previous state-of-the-art method (Sennrich et al., 2016) is effective for high-resource language pairs; however, in the case of low-resource language pairs, it is more effective to use a filtered pseudo-parallel corpus as additional training data.

The remainder of this paper is organized as follows: Section 2 discusses previous studies related to improving low-resource machine translation systems; Section 3 outlines the proposed method for filtering a pseudo-parallel corpus and bootstrapping NMT; Sections 4 and 5 evaluate the proposed model; and Section 6 discusses the results. Conclusions and suggestions for future work are presented in Section 7.

2 Related Work

To address the data sparsity problem, there are many methods that use source language monolingual data to improve translation quality (Ueffing et al., 2007; Shwenk, 2008; Bertoldi and Federico, 2009; Hsieh et al., 2013; Zhang et al., 2016). Specifically, Bertoldi and Federico

(2009) addressed the problem of domain adaptation by training a translation model from a generated pseudo-parallel corpus created from a monolingual in-domain corpus. Hsieh et al. (2013) create a pseudo-parallel corpus from patterns learned from source and monolingual target in-domain corpora for cross-domain adaptation. They manually conducted filtration of "relatively more accurate" translated sentences and used them to revise the language model. Similarly, we use a pseudo-parallel corpus created by translating a monolingual corpus from the target language rather than the source language; however we apply automatic filtering to the obtained pseudo-parallel corpus.

Data filtering is often used in domain adaptation (Moore and Lewis, 2010; Axelrod et al., 2011) and phrase-based SMT systems. Sentences are extracted from large corpora to optimize the language model and the translation model (Wang et al., 2014; Yıldız et al., 2014). The work most closely related to our work is Yıldız et al. (2014), who build a quality estimator to obtain high-quality parallel sentence pairs and achieve better translation performance and reduce time-complexity with a small high-quality corpus. This method filters data by calculating similarity between source and target sentences. In our work, we calculate similarity between monolingual and synthetic target sentences.

Recently, van der Wees et al. (2017) performed dynamic data selection during training an NMT. To sort and filter the training data, they used language models from the source and target sides of in-domain and out-of-domain data to calculate cross-entropy scores. However, we employ back-translation to filter data considering its meaning.

He et al. (2016) present a dual learning approach. They simultaneously train two models through a reinforcement learning process. They use monolingual data of both source and target languages and generate informative feedback signals to train the translation models. While the dual learning approach is shown to alleviate the issue of noisy data by increasing coverage, we are attempting to remove the noisy data. In addition, they assume a high-recourse language pair to cold start the reinforcement learning process, while we target low-resource language pairs wherein high-quality seed NMT models are difficult to obtain.

---

[1]https://github.com/aizhanti/filtered-pseudo-parallel-corpora

3 Improving Low-resource Neural Machine Translation (NMT) with Filtered Pseudo-parallel Corpus

In this paper, we propose a method of filtering a pseudo-parallel corpus used as additional training data by back-translating a monolingual corpus for low-resource language pairs. Then, we attempt to bootstrap an NMT model by iterating the filtering process until convergence.

3.1 Filtering

As shown in Figure 1, the proposed method has following steps:

1. Translate monolingual target sentences (Target sent$_{mono}$) using a model trained on parallel corpus in target→source direction to produce synthetic source sentences (Source sent$_{synth}$). Here, we obtain an *"Unfiltered"* pseudo-parallel corpus as additional data without a filtration, similar to Sennrich et al. (2016).
2. Back-translate the synthetic source sentences using a model trained on parallel corpus in source→target direction to obtain a synthetic target sentences (Target sent$_{synth}$).
3. Calculate sentence-level similarity metric scores using the monolingual target sentences as reference and the synthetic target sentences as candidates.
4. Sort the monolingual target sentences and the corresponding synthetic source sentences by a descending order of sentence-level similarity metric scores and filter out sentences with low scores. The threshold is determined by the translation quality on the development set.
5. Use the filtered synthetic source sentences as the source side and the monolingual target sentences as the target side of the pseudo-parallel corpus; this is referred to as a *Filtered* pseudo-parallel corpus as additional data.

3.2 Bootstrapping

Bootstrapping involves the following steps:

1. *"Bootstrap 1"*: we use a pseudo-parallel corpus created using the *"Parallel"* model as additional data to train the seed NMT systems.
2. *"Bootstrap 2"*: we select the best model on the development set from *"Bootstrap 1"* and train its target→source model. Here, we use target sentences from the pseudo-parallel cor-

Corpus	Ru↔Ja	Fr→Mg	De→En
Parallel	10,231	106,406	4,535,522
Dev	500	1,000	3,000
Test	500	1,000	3,003
Mono target	75k↔167k	105,570	4,208,439

Table 1: Data statistics.

pus that have been filtered out in the previous iteration to train the best model. If there is no improvement over the previous iteration, terminate the bootstrapping process and return to the *Filtered* pseudo-parallel corpus and the translation model as output. Repeat.

Even if the monolingual target sentences remain the same, the synthetic source sentences are refreshed at each iteration. In other words, the translation quality of both the *"Unfiltered"* and *"Filtered"* pseudo-parallel corpus will be improved via the bootstrapping process until the termination criterion is met.

4 Experiments Using a Filtered Pseudo-parallel Corpus

4.1 Settings

We used the OpenNMT toolkit[2] (Klein et al., 2017) to train all translation models. For the Russian↔Japanese and French→Malagasy experiments, we used the following parameters: the number of recurrent layers of the encoder and decoder was 1, BiLSTM with concatenation, maximum batch size was 32, and the optimization method was Adadelta. For the German→English experiments, OpenNMT default settings were used. The vocabulary size in all experiments was 50,000.

We tokenized and truecased French, English, German, and Russian sentences using Moses' scripts. For Japanese sentences, we used MeCab 0.996 with the IPAdic dictionary[3] for word segmentation. We eliminated duplicated sentences and sentences with more than 50 words for all languages. We report BLEU scores (Papineni et al., 2002) to compare translation results. We used the Travatar toolkit (Neubig, 2013) to calculate the significance of differences between systems using bootstrap resampling ($p < 0.05$).

---

[2] http://opennmt.net/OpenNMT/
[3] http://taku910.github.io/mecab

Threshold	Size	Dev	Test
Baselines			
Parallel Ja-Ru	10,231	10.13	9.53
Parallel Ru-Ja	10,231	17.47	**18.71**
Unfiltered	170,991	16.86	17.05
Filtered			
sent-LM $\geq$ 0.1	168,572	18.65	18.01
sent-LM $\geq$ 0.2	167,340	17.42	16.65
sent-LM $\geq$ 0.3	165,166	18.42	16.85
sent-LM $\geq$ 0.4	160,635	**18.69**	16.23
sent-LM $\geq$ 0.5	150,974	17.82	17.28
sent-LM $\geq$ 0.6	131,402	17.37	16.86
sent-LM $\geq$ 0.7	95,573	17.69	17.54
sent-LM $\geq$ 0.8	40,774	17.56	16.95
sent-LM $\geq$ 0.9	11,542	18.13	17.22
sent-LM $=$ 1.0	10,232	18.38	16.93

(a) Bootstrap 1.

Threshold	Size	Dev	Test
Baselines			
B1 Parallel Ja-Ru	160,635	9.05	8.32
B1 Parallel Ru-Ja	160,635	**18.69**	16.23
B1 Unfiltered	170,991	17.03	17.75
Filtered			
sent-LM $\geq$ 0.1	161,261	16.92	17.63
sent-LM $\geq$ 0.2	160,866	17.75	16.58
sent-LM $\geq$ 0.3	160,704	18.29	18.33
sent-LM $\geq$ 0.4	160,654	18.64	17.37
sent-LM $\geq$ 0.5	160,640	18.29	17.63

(b) Bootstrap 2.

Table 2: Russian→Japanese translation BLEU scores. Sorting was performed using sent-LM score.

4.2 Dataset

The parallel corpora for low-resource Russian↔Japanese[4] and for medium-resource French→Malagasy[5] experiments were downloaded from OPUS. For the medium-resource French-Malagasy language pair, we used the GlobalVoices corpus, which differs from the Tatoeba corpus used in the previous experiments. Note that the GlobalVoices corpus has more available parallel data (106,406 sentence pairs compared to 10,231).

We split the Tatoeba parallel corpus for the

Threshold	Size	Dev	Test
Baselines			
Parallel Ja-Ru	10,231	10.13	9.53
Parallel Ru-Ja	10,231	17.47	18.71
Unfiltered	170,991	16.86	17.05
Filtered			
sent-BLEU $\geq$ 0.1	26,826	19.86⋆†	19.80⋆†
sent-BLEU $\geq$ 0.2	24,794	20.29⋆†	19.53⋆†
sent-BLEU $\geq$ 0.3	19,444	**20.63**⋆†	19.69⋆†
sent-BLEU $\geq$ 0.4	15,438	20.34⋆†	**20.05**⋆†
sent-BLEU $\geq$ 0.5	13,101	20.03⋆†	19.35†
sent-BLEU $\geq$ 0.6	11,904	18.89	19.52†
sent-BLEU $\geq$ 0.7	11,244	18.79	18.81†
sent-BLEU $\geq$ 0.8	10,976	18.19	19.21†
sent-BLEU $\geq$ 0.9	10,867	18.42	17.30
sent-BLEU $=$ 1.0	10,865	18.40	18.45

Table 3: Russian→Japanese translation BLEU scores. Sorting was performed using sent-BLEU score (Bootstrap 1). There is a significant difference: ⋆: against *"Parallel"* baseline; †: against *"Unfiltered"* baseline.

Russian↔Japanese experiments as follows: training set, 10,231 sentences; development set, 500 sentences; and test set, 500 sentences. In addition, to perform Japanese→Russian→Japanese translation for the Russian to Japanese experiment, we sampled an additional 167,600 Japanese monolingual sentences from Tatoeba. We also sampled 75,401 Russian monolingual sentences from Tatoeba for Japanese→Russian translation to facilitate Russian→Japanese→Russian translation.

We performed experiments for the language pair French→Malagasy language pairs using the data from the GlobalVoices corpus. Parallel data were split as follows: training set, 106,406 sentences; development set, 1,000 sentences; and test set, 1,000 sentences. Note that 105,570 Malagasy monolingual sentences from GlobalVoices were used to create a French→Malagasy pseudo-parallel corpus.

For the German→English experiments, we downloaded pre-trained German↔English models and 4,535,522 parallel sentences provided by OpenNMT[6] and used the OpenNMT settings to preprocess all data. We downloaded 4,208,439 German→English sentences from automatically back-translated monolingual data[7] and translated the synthetic German side back to English using

---

[4] http://opus.lingfil.uu.se/Tatoeba.php
[5] http://opus.lingfil.uu.se/GlobalVoices.php
[6] http://opennmt.net/Models/
[7] http://data.statmt.org/rsennrich/wmt16_backtranslations/de-en/

Threshold	Size	Dev	Test
Baselines			
B1 Parallel Ja-Ru	19,444	12.13	9.78
B1 Parallel Ru-Ja	19,444	20.63†	19.69†
B1 Unfiltered	170,991	18.06	16.85
Filtered			
sent-BLEU $\geq$ 0.1	40,567	21.03†	21.01†
sent-BLEU $\geq$ 0.2	37,531	**21.48†**	19.20†
sent-BLEU $\geq$ 0.3	29,533	21.06†	20.69†
sent-BLEU $\geq$ 0.4	24,290	21.16†	21.08†
sent-BLEU $\geq$ 0.5	21,742	20.58†	**21.57⋆†**
sent-BLEU $\geq$ 0.6	20,478	19.93†	20.80†
sent-BLEU $\geq$ 0.7	19,920	20.46†	20.48†
sent-BLEU $\geq$ 0.8	19,726	20.78†	20.60†
sent-BLEU $\geq$ 0.9	19,626	20.38†	21.54⋆†
sent-BLEU $=$ 1.0	19,623	21.23†	21.17⋆†

Table 4: Russian→Japanese translation BLEU scores. Sorting was performed using sent-BLEU score (Bootstrap 2).

Threshold	Size	Dev	Test
Baselines			
B2 Parallel Ja-Ru	37,531	12.35	11.78
B2 Parallel Ru-Ja	37,531	**21.48†**	19.20†
B2 Unfiltered	170,991	18.96	17.20
Filtered			
sent-BLEU $\geq$ 0.1	53,478	21.34†	19.10†
sent-BLEU $\geq$ 0.2	49,833	20.61†	19.99†
sent-BLEU $\geq$ 0.3	43,470	21.32†	20.59†
sent-BLEU $\geq$ 0.4	40,147	20.75†	20.16†
sent-BLEU $\geq$ 0.5	38,687	20.40†	18.65
sent-BLEU $\geq$ 0.6	38,043	20.03	**21.02⋆†**
sent-BLEU $\geq$ 0.7	37,758	20.17†	20.23†
sent-BLEU $\geq$ 0.8	37,639	20.33†	20.61†
sent-BLEU $\geq$ 0.9	37,600	19.75	19.80†
sent-BLEU $=$ 1.0	37,598	20.83†	20.62†

Table 5: Russian→Japanese translation BLEU scores. Sorting was performed using sent-BLEU score (Bootstrap 3).

the pre-trained German→English model to filter this pseudo-parallel corpus. We used newtest2013 (3,000 sentence pairs) as a development set and newtest2014 (3,003 sentence pairs) as a test set. Table 1 shows the data statistics.

4.3 Baselines

Sennrich et al. (2016) obtained additional training data by automatically translating monolingual target sentences into the source language using their *"Parallel"* baseline system. Our process differs from theirs in that we construct *"Parallel"* baseline machine translation systems in both directions using an available parallel corpus to obtain a filtered pseudo-parallel corpus.

Our baseline systems were as follows: 1) *"Parallel"* systems that trained on a parallel corpus in both directions, which were used to create a pseudo-parallel corpus; or *"B{1,2} Parallel"* in case of bootstrapping 2) *"Unfiltered"* system, which was trained on a concatenated parallel corpus with all pseudo-parallel corpora without filtration; or *"B{1,2} Unfiltered"* in case of bootstrapping.

4.4 Sentence-level similarity metric

We used sentence-level BLEU (sent-BLEU) as a sentence-level similarity metric. The sent-BLEU scores were calculated using mteval-sentence of the mteval toolkit[8]. In Russian→Japanese experi-

ments, we compared the sent-BLEU scores, which require back-translation of the target monolingual data for the proposed filtration method, with a language model (sent-LM) that performs filtration by scoring only synthetic source sentences. We used the KenLM Language Model Toolkit[9] to build a 5-gram language model from 23,239,280 sentences from the Russian side of the Russian-English UN corpus (Ziemski et al., 2016).[10] We also applied Kneser-Ney smoothing. To extract the scores, we normalized the language model log probability of the sentence to be between [0, 1] as in sent-BLEU using a feature scaling method.

Translation performance increases as the number of parallel sentences increases (Koehn, 2002). For a pseudo-parallel corpus, however, translation performance does not necessarily increase with the number of sentences. To determine the effects of the quantity and quality of the pseudo-parallel corpus in machine translation, we set thresholds with increment steps of 0.1. Thus, pseudo-parallel sentences included as additional data have sentence-level similarity scores greater or equal to some threshold (e.g., sentence-level BLEU$\geq$ 0.1,..., sentence-level BLEU$\geq$ 0.9, ...). Sentences scored and filtered by sentence-level similarity were used to train *"Filtered"* models. For example, sentences with sentence-level sim-

---

[8] https://github.com/odashi/mteval

[9] https://kheafield.com/code/kenlm/
[10] https://conferences.unite.un.org/ UNCorpus/en/DownloadOverview

Threshold	Size	Dev	Test
Baselines			
Parallel Ru-Ja	10,231	17.47	18.71
Parallel Ja-Ru	10,231	10.13	9.53
Unfiltered	85,632	10.40	9.01
Filtered			
sent-BLEU $\geq$ 0.1	12,686	12.86$\star$†	12.81$\star$†
sent-BLEU $\geq$ 0.2	12,613	12.82$\star$†	13.60$\star$†
sent-BLEU $\geq$ 0.3	12,325	**14.08**$\star$†	13.34$\star$†
sent-BLEU $\geq$ 0.4	11,860	13.14$\star$†	**14.08**$\star$†
sent-BLEU $\geq$ 0.5	11,462	11.95$\star$†	13.86$\star$†
sent-BLEU $\geq$ 0.6	11,114	11.92$\star$†	11.50$\star$†
sent-BLEU $\geq$ 0.7	10,965	12.34$\star$†	12.73$\star$†
sent-BLEU $\geq$ 0.8	10,903	12.30$\star$†	11.81$\star$†
sent-BLEU $=$ 1.0	10,880	11.69$\star$	11.52$\star$†

Table 6: Japanese→Russian translation BLEU scores. Sorting was performed using sent-BLEU score.

Threshold	Size	Dev	Test
Baselines			
Parallel Mg-Fr	106,406	13.29	12.74
Parallel Fr-Mg	106,406	16.79	15.15
Unfiltered	211,976	16.39	14.80
Filtered			
sent-BLEU $\geq$ 0.1	152,578	**17.31**	**16.27**$\star$†
sent-BLEU $\geq$ 0.2	135,179	17.08	15.33
sent-BLEU $\geq$ 0.3	121,376	17.11	15.00
sent-BLEU $\geq$ 0.4	114,391	16.62	15.81
sent-BLEU $\geq$ 0.5	110,944	16.65	14.84
sent-BLEU $\geq$ 0.6	109,186	16.38	14.05
sent-BLEU $\geq$ 0.7	108,252	16.48	15.19
sent-BLEU $\geq$ 0.8	107,801	16.29	14.53
sent-BLEU $\geq$ 0.9	107,537	16.42	15.24
sent-BLEU $=$ 1.0	107,515	16.38	15.26

Table 7: French→Malagasy translation BLEU scores. Sorting was performed using sent-BLEU score.

ilarity scores (e.g., sent-BLEU) greater than or equal to 0.1 were used to train the *"sent-BLEU $\geq$ 0.1"* model. We trained the NMT system using different thresholds and compared the performance using development and test sets.

5 Results

5.1 Bootstrapping the NMT: Russian→Japanese

For the data shown in Tables 2 and 3, we used the parallel 10,231 sentence pairs (Section 4.2) to train the first *"Parallel"* models in both directions. Then, we used these models to create a pseudo-parallel corpus by translating 160,760 Japanese monolingual sentences (Section 3). A concatenation of parallel and pseudo-parallel sentences was used to train the *"Unfiltered"* model. The results obtained using the *"Unfiltered"* model demonstrate that using all pseudo-parallel data as additional data results in reduced BLEU scores (16.86 BLEU compared to 17.47 BLEU). Generally, these results suggest that unfiltered data contain many incorrect sentence pairs, which leads to reduced machine translation accuracy.

Tables 2a and 3 show the *"Bootstrap 1"* results. Here, the same pseudo-parallel corpus was used as additional data with different filtration scoring metrics. Even though the models trained using data sorted by a language model metric outperformed the baselines on the development set, none of the sent-LM models achieved better results

than sent-BLEU. In contrast, using sent-BLEU increased performance even when much less data were used for training. The *"sent-BLEU $\geq$ 0.3"* model outperformed the *"Unfiltered"* model by +3.77 and +2.64 points on the development and test sets, respectively. A sent-LM model resulted in lower BLEU scores compared to sent-BLEU because it assigned high scores to very short but grammatically correct synthetic sentences. For example, a sent-LM assigned a score of 0.94 to the synthetic Russian sentence "д а . *(yes .)*", even though its corresponding monolingual sentence was "歌える 。 *(I can sing .)*". In contrast, sent-BLEU assigned this pseudo-parallel sentence a score of 0.00, because the back-translation resulted in "はい 。 *(yes .)*". Furthermore, for a sent-LM, the bootstrapping attempt using the best *"sent-LM $\geq$ 0.4"* model of *"Bootstrap 1"* failed according to the results shown in Table 2b. None of the *"Filtered"* models could outperform the *"Bootstrap 1"* and *"Bootstrap 2"* baseline models.

Table 4 shows the *"Bootstrap 2"* results. We used the best model, i.e., *"sent-BLEU $\geq$ 0.3"* from *"Bootstrap 1"* (referred to as *"B1 Parallel"*), to create a pseudo-parallel corpus by translating the filtered out Japanese monolingual sentences (with sent-BLEU $<$ 0.3). The resulting 151,547 pseudo-parallel sentences were added to the 37,531 *"B1 Parallel"* sentences to train the *"B1 Unfiltered"* model. The filtered *"sent-BLEU $\geq$ 0.2"* model

Threshold	Size	Dev	Test
Baselines			
Parallel En-De	4,535,522	19.51	18.55
Parallel De-En	4,535,522	22.33	20.58
Unfiltered	8,743,961	**25.09★**	**24.86★**
Filtered			
sent-BLEU $\geq$ 0.1	7,681,105	24.84★	24.52★
sent-BLEU $\geq$ 0.2	7,345,367	24.87★	24.13★
sent-BLEU $\geq$ 0.3	6,598,845	23.06★	22.65★
sent-BLEU $\geq$ 0.4	5,808,701	24.13★	22.84★
sent-BLEU $\geq$ 0.5	5,216,440	23.73★	22.28★
sent-BLEU $\geq$ 0.6	7,345,367	23.50★	21.85★
sent-BLEU $\geq$ 0.7	6,598,845	23.07★	21.30★
sent-BLEU $\geq$ 0.8	5,808,701	22.80★	20.90★
sent-BLEU $\geq$ 0.9	5,216,440	22.60★	20.49
sent-BLEU $=$ 1.0	4,585,655	22.13	20.33

Table 8: German→English translation BLEU scores. Sorting was performed using sent-BLEU score.

was the best model in *"Bootstrap 2"*. This model achieved a 21.48 BLEU score on the development set, thereby outperforming the *"B1 Parallel"* model by +0.85 BLEU points.

The *"Bootstrap 3"* results are shown in Table 5. In the third iteration, no *"Filtered"* models obtained higher scores than the *"B2 Parallel"* model. However, in the Russian→Japanese experiments, all *"Filtered"* models outperformed the *"Unfiltered"* models on the development and test sets in each *"Bootstrap"* step for sentence-level BLEU scoring, demonstrating a maximum improvement of +3.77 BLEU points on the development set and +4.72 BLEU points on the test set.

5.2 Filtering

5.2.1 Japanese→Russian

We examined the effect of the proposed filtering method on Japanese to Russian translations. The results are shown in Table 6. Here, we used a Russian monolingual corpus to create a Japanese→Russian parallel corpus rather than using the Japanese monolingual corpus.

The *"sent-BLEU $\geq$ 0.3"* model outperformed the *"Parallel"* and *"Unfiltered"* models in terms of BLEU scores on the development set by +3.95 and +3.68 points, respectively. All filtered models were significantly better than the unfiltered model, except for *"sent-BLEU = 1.0"*.

Threshold	Ja-Ru	Ru-Ja	Fr-Mg	En-De
sent-BLEU $\geq$ 0.1	3.26%	10.32%	43.73%	74.74%
sent-BLEU $\geq$ 0.2	3.16%	9.06%	27.25%	66.77%
sent-BLEU $\geq$ 0.3	2.78%	5.73%	14.18%	43.09%
sent-BLEU $\geq$ 0.4	2.16%	3.24%	7.56%	30.25%
sent-BLEU $\geq$ 0.5	1.63%	1.79%	4.30%	16.18%
sent-BLEU $\geq$ 0.6	1.17%	1.04%	2.63%	7.88%
sent-BLEU $\geq$ 0.7	0.97%	0.63%	1.75%	3.85%
sent-BLEU $\geq$ 0.8	0.89%	0.46%	1.32%	1.98%
sent-BLEU $\geq$ 0.9	0.89%	0.40%	1.07%	1.25%
sent-BLEU $=$ 1.0	0.86%	0.39%	1.05%	1.19%

Table 9: The percentage of used pseudo-parallel corpora for each language pair.

5.2.2 French→Malagasy

The results are shown in Table 7. In these experiments, we used the Malagasy monolingual corpus comprising 105,570 sentences to create a French-Malagasy pseudo-parallel corpus using the proposed filtering method. The *"sent-BLEU $\geq$ 0.1"* model yielded better results over the baselines of up to +0.92 BLEU points on the development set and +1.47 BLEU points on the test set (statistically significant).

5.2.3 German→English

Table 8 shows the BLEU scores of German→English experiments. None of the filtered models outperformed the *"Unfiltered"* baseline on the development and test sets.

6 Discussion

The results showed that rather than using all additional pseudo-parallel data, the proposed filtering method improved translation performance in nearly all experiments conducted for low-resource language pairs.

The threshold results (Section 4.4) in Tables 2-8 demonstrate that filtered models outperform the baselines with larger margin for low-resource language pairs than high-resource language pair and in the most cases, overfiltering (e.g., sent-BLEU = 1.0) leads to no or negligible improvement over the baselines.

Sennrich et al. (2016) showed that using a pseudo-parallel corpus as additional data greatly improves the performance over the *"Parallel"* baseline. The experiments showed that a better *"Parallel"* system results in the creation of a better pseudo-parallel corpus. This fact is also demonstrated in Table 9, in which the percentages of used pseudo-parallel corpora for each language

Boot	Synthetic Russian sentence	Synthetic Japanese sentence	sent-BLEU
Example 1 - Japanese monolingual sentence: あなた は その ニュース を 聞き まし た か 。 (have you heard the news ?)			
B1	ты видели эту по-английски ? (did you see this in English ?)	君 は 英語 を 英語 を 見 まし た か 。 (have you seen English in English ?)	0.25
B2	Вы получили эту радио ? (did you get this radio ?)	その ニュース を 借り た の です か 。 (did you borrow the news ?)	0.00
B3	Вы получили эту новости ? (did you receive this news ?)	その ニュース を 聞き まし た か 。 (have you heard the news ?)	0.77
Example 2 - Japanese monolingual sentence: 僕 は 終電車 に 乗り遅れ た 。 (I missed the last train .)			
B1	я опоздал на поезд . (I missed the train .)	私 は 列車 に 遅刻 し た 。 (I was late for the train .)	0.00
B2	я опоздал на поезд . (I missed the train .)	私 は 列車 に 遅れ た 。 (I was late for the train .)	0.00
B3	я опоздал на последний поезд . (I missed the last train .)	私 は 終電車 に 乗り遅れ た 。 (I missed the last train .)	0.80
Example 3 - Japanese monolingual sentence: なぜ 遅刻 し た の です か 。 (why were you late .)			
B1	почему ты сделал ? (why did you do it ?)	どうして やった の ? (why did it ?)	0.00
B2	почему ты опоздал ? (why are you late ?)	なぜ そんな 遅れ た の ? (why was such a delay?)	0.00
B3	почему ты сделал ? (why did you do it ?)	なぜ そんな こと を し た の です か 。 (why did a such thing ?)	0.53

Table 10: Examples from Russian→Japanese pseudo-parallel corpus used on every bootstrapping step.

pair are shown. The size of the usable pseudo-parallel corpus for low-resource language pairs is very small, which indicates that filtering out very noisy data (e.g., approximately 96%-98% data for Japanese→Russian) results in higher accuracy of the NMT system trained using a filtered pseudo-parallel corpus. The size of very noisy data for a high-resource language pair (e.g. approximately 25% of the data for German→English) is small and does not significantly degrade the accuracy of the NMT system compared to low-resource cases. In other words, the weaker the *"Parallel"* system is the more effective is the proposed filtration method.

Example 1 in the Table 10 shows the steps required to create a better Russian-Japanese pseudo-parallel sentence. As the synthetic Russian sentence from *"Bootstrap 1"* which was significantly incorrect relative to the correct translation of the Japanese monolingual sentences, eventually became a good translation, we can say that the Japanese→Russian and Russian→Japanese models used to create a pseudo-parallel corpus improved with each bootstrapping step. Example 2 in Table 10 shows good translations of the original sentence; however, due to surface mismatching of the synthetic and monolingual target sentences, the sentence-level BLEU scores were 0.00. Nonetheless, with *"Bootstrap 3"*, the Japanese→Russian and Russian→Japanese models produced translations that were the closest to the original sentence. Regarding Example 3, the sentence in *"Bootstrap 2"* was not used to train the best model due to surface mismatching of target sentences despite the fact that it was correctly translated to Russian. As a result, *"Bootstrap 3"* used an incorrect translation of the original sentence.

The experimental results show that bootstrapping over several iterations improves the NMT without significant difference and eventually stops improving over the previous step. We hypothesize that the reason for this is that the *"Parallel"* system used to create a new pseudo-parallel corpus becomes weaker in each iteration.

We used sent-BLEU to calculate the similarity of the synthetic and monolingual target sentences. However, word embedding-based sentence similarity measures, such as those employed by Song and Roth (2015), can be used to further improve the corpus filtering because sentence-level BLEU is sensitive to surface mismatch.

7 Conclusion

The models trained using the filtered pseudo-parallel corpus as additional data showed better translation performance than the baselines for low-resource language pairs. We have also shown that we can further improve translation performance by bootstrapping, although bootstrapping has its limitations. These results suggest that translation accuracy depends on both data size and quality.

Further experimental investigations are required to estimate the limitations of the proposed filtration method. We plan to investigate the other sentence similarity metrics described in Song and Roth (2015), such as average alignment and maximum alignment sentence-level word2vec scores. Sentence-level BLEU calculates the similarity of the synthetic and monolingual target sentences based solely on surface information, whereas word2vec uses a distributed representation of the sentences.

To further our research we plan to improve our filtering method by detecting good and bad synthetic translations using reinforcement learning.

References

Amittai Axelrod, Xiaodong He, and Jianfeng Gao. 2011. Domain adaptation via pseudo in-domain data selection. In *Proceedings of the conference on empirical methods in natural language processing*. Association for Computational Linguistics, pages 355–362.

Nicola Bertoldi and Marcello Federico. 2009. Domain adaptation for statistical machine translation with monolingual resources. In *Proceedings of the Fourth Workshop on Statistical Machine Translation*. pages 182–189.

Di He, Yingce Xia, Tao Qin, Liwei Wang, Nenghai Yu, Tieyan Liu, and Wei-Ying Ma. 2016. Dual learning for machine translation. In *Advances in Neural Information Processing Systems*. pages 820–828.

An-Chang Hsieh, Hen-Hsen Huang, and Hsin-Hsi Chen. 2013. Uses of monolingual in-domain corpora for cross-domain adaptation with hybrid MT approaches. In *Proceedings of the Second Workshop on Hybrid Approaches to Translation*. pages 117–122.

Guillaume Klein, Yoon Kim, Yuntian Deng, Jean Senellart, and Alexander M. Rush. 2017. Open-NMT: Open-Source Toolkit for Neural Machine Translation. *arXiv preprint arXiv:1701.02810* .

Philipp Koehn. 2002. Europarl: A multilingual corpus for evaluation of machine translation.

Chin-Yew Lin and Franz Josef Och. 2004a. Automatic evaluation of machine translation quality using longest common subsequence and skip-bigram statistics. In *Proceedings of the 42nd Annual Meeting on Association for Computational Linguistics*. pages 605–612.

Chin-Yew Lin and Franz Josef Och. 2004b. Orange: a method for evaluating automatic evaluation metrics for machine translation. In *Proceedings of*

the 20th International Conference on Computational Linguistics. pages 501–507.

Robert C Moore and William Lewis. 2010. Intelligent selection of language model training data. In *Proceedings of the ACL 2010 conference short papers*. Association for Computational Linguistics, pages 220–224.

Graham Neubig. 2013. Travatar: A Forest-to-String Machine Translation Engine based on Tree Transducers. In *the 51st Annual Meeting of the Association for Computational Linguistics: System Demonstrations*. pages 91–96.

Kishore Papineni, Salim Roukos, Todd Ward, and Wei-Jing Zhu. 2002. BLEU: a method for automatic evaluation of machine translation. Proceedings of the 40th Annual Meeting on Association for Computational Linguistics, pages 311–318.

Rico Sennrich, Barry Haddow, and Alexandra Birch. 2016. Improving neural machine translation models with monolingual data. In *Proceedings of the 54th Annual Meeting of the Association for Computational Linguistics (Volume 1: Long Papers)*. pages 86–96.

Yangqiu Song and Dan Roth. 2015. Unsupervised sparse vector densification for short text similarity. In *Proceedings of the 2015 Conference of the North American Chapter of the Association for Computational Linguistics: Human Language Technologies*. pages 1275–1280.

Marlies van der Wees, Arianna Bisazza, and Christof Monz. 2017. Dynamic data selection for neural machine translation. *arXiv preprint arXiv:1708.00712. Accepted at EMNLP2017* .

Longyue Wang, Derek F Wong, Lidia S Chao, Yi Lu, and Junwen Xing. 2014. A systematic comparison of data selection criteria for SMT domain adaptation. *The Scientific World Journal* 2014.

Eray Yıldız, Ahmed Cüneyd Tantuğ, and Banu Diri. 2014. The effect of parallel corpus quality vs size in English-to-Turkish SMT. In *Proceedings of the Sixth International Conference on Web services and Semantic Technology (WeST 2014)*. pages 21–30.

Jiajun Zhang and Chengqing Zong. 2016. Exploiting source-side monolingual data in neural machine translation. In *Proceedings of the 2016 Conference on Empirical Methods in Natural Language Processing*. pages 1535–1545.

Michal Ziemski, Marcin Junczys-Dowmunt, and Bruno Pouliquen. 2016. The United Nations parallel corpus v1. 0. In *Proceedings of the Tenth International Conference on Language Resources and Evaluation*. pages 3530–3534.

Japanese to English/Chinese/Korean Datasets
for Translation Quality Estimation and Automatic Post-Editing

Atsushi Fujita and **Eiichiro Sumita**

National Institute of Information and Communications Technology
3-5 Hikaridai, Seika-cho, Soraku-gun, Kyoto, 619-0289, Japan
firstname.lastname@nict.go.jp

Abstract

Aiming at facilitating the research on quality estimation (QE) and automatic post-editing (APE) of machine translation (MT) outputs, especially for those among Asian languages, we have created new datasets for Japanese to English, Chinese, and Korean translations. As the source text, actual utterances in Japanese were extracted from the log data of our speech translation service. MT outputs were then given by phrase-based statistical MT systems. Finally, human evaluators were employed to grade the quality of MT outputs and to post-edit them. This paper describes the characteristics of the created datasets and reports on our benchmarking experiments on word-level QE, sentence-level QE, and APE conducted using the created datasets.

1 Introduction

Technologies of machine translation (MT) have been dramatically improved in the last decades; however, the strict requirements for high-quality translations in real-world applications (Hutchins and Somers, 1992) have not yet fulfilled by MT systems alone.[1] Thus, in practice, techniques of computer-aided translation (CAT) have been widely used to provide satisfiable translations for such requirements. For instance, manual post-editing of MT outputs has become a prevalent translation work-flow in translation services (ISO/TC27, 2017). Quality estimation (QE) of MT outputs also plays a critical role in CAT to reduce human effort, thereby increasing productivity (Specia et al., 2010).

To facilitate and encourage the research on QE tasks concerning several different levels of granularity, i.e., word, phrase, sentence, and document levels, and automatic post-editing (APE), WMT workshops and conferences (henceforth, WMT) have created datasets specialized for these tasks (Bojar et al., 2014, 2015, 2016, 2017), mainly focusing on European languages.[2] As a result, they have successfully led to the rapid enhancement of QE/APE technologies.

However, to the best of our knowledge, such a resource for Asian languages have never emerged, and QE/APE for Asian languages have been less studied. Aiming at facilitating this line of research, we have created new datasets[3] consisting of the 5-tuples shown in Figure 1. While the tuples of first two elements, i.e., source text and human translation, compose ordinary parallel corpus used to train (data-driven) MT systems, the remaining three are specific to this kind of QE/APE datasets. So far, we have regarded Japanese (Ja) as the source language, and English (En), Chinese (Zh), and Korean (Ko) as the target languages. In addition to cover these new language pairs, we also aim to improve our speech translation service[4] with QE/APE technologies. To this end, we have used actual utterances for the source texts, accumulated by the speech translation service, with our best effort to clean and anonymize the data.

In the remainder of this paper, we first describe the procedure of creating our QE/APE datasets for Ja→En, Ja→Zh, and Ja→Ko translation tasks in Section 2. Then, in Section 3, we present statistics of the created datasets, observations, and remaining issues. Section 4 describes our benchmarking

---

[1] Bar-Hillel (1951) even mentioned that the fully automatic high-quality translation is not only unrealistic, but also theoretically impossible.

[2] Only the exception is Chinese-to-English in 2017 (Bojar et al., 2017).

[3] NICT QE/APE Dataset, `http://att-astrec.nict.go.jp/en/product/`

[4] VoiceTra, `http://voicetra.nict.go.jp/en/`

Proceedings of the 4th Workshop on Asian Translation, pages 79–88,
Taipei, Taiwan, November 27, 2017. ©2017 AFNLP

Component	Example
src: Source segment in Japanese	片道だけで買えますか。
ref: Human translation	May I get it for one way?
hyp: MT output	Can I buy just one way?
grade: Quality grade of MT output	B ($\in \{$S, A, B, C, D$\}$)
pe: Manually post-edited MT output	Can I just buy a one way ticket?

Figure 1: Example record in our QE/APE datasets (see Section 2.4 for the definition of *grade*).

experiments on word-level QE, sentence-level QE, and APE conducted using the created datasets. Finally, Section 5 summarizes this paper.

2 Procedure of Corpus Construction

We have created our QE/APE datasets, regarding Japanese as the source language. We have so far regarded English, Chinese, and Korean as the target languages, considering that the speakers of these languages hold the largest proportion of visitors to Japan (Japan National Tourism Organization, 2017). Following the procedure in previous studies (Snover et al., 2006; Potet et al., 2012) and practices in WMT (Bojar et al., 2014, 2015, 2016), we determined the following five-step process.

1. Collecting Japanese utterances (*src*)

2. Generation of MT outputs (*hyp*)

3. Manual translation (*ref*)

4. Manual grading of MT output (*grade*)

5. Manual post-editing of MT output (*pe*)

For the latter three tasks (detailed in Sections 2.3, 2.4 and 2.5, respectively), we allocated adult native speakers of the target language who also understand Japanese.

2.1 Collecting Japanese utterances (*src*)

First, we collected the following two sets of utterances in Japanese that have been used with our speech translation service.

Travel-related utterances (*travel*): From the log data that our speech translation service accumulates, we randomly sampled 20,000 identical transcribed segments[5] that were identified as Japanese by its automatic speech recognition (ASR) module. Most segments were spoken language and related to travel and tourism, even though we had no restriction to the input of our users.

---

[5]In this paper, we refer to each utterance as "segment," as one utterance may contain more than one sentence.

Utterances in hospital (*hospital*): We employed the role-play dialogs of health care providers, such as doctors and nurses, and patients, containing 2,225 identical segments of utterances. They were surely spoken language, although they were manually written and more formal than those in the *travel* domain.

We have been examining the installation of our speech translation service into several practical situations where such system helps cross-lingual communication between humans. For this purpose, we have manually created role-play dialogs between Japanese and non-Japanese speakers. The *hospital* data is one of them.

The extracted segments, especially those in the *travel* domain, include ungrammatical ones, non-understandable ones, and those containing inappropriate expressions with respect to social standards. We therefore asked a native Japanese speaker to filter out such segments. As a result, 8,783 and 1,676 segments in the *travel* and *hospital* domains were retained, respectively.

Many segments do not have an explicit subject, as Japanese is a pro-drop language; even obligatory arguments can be missing. For instance, in the *src* segment in Figure 1, both the subject "I" and the direct object "ticket" are omitted. However, we cannot recover them as our speech translation service does not record any discourse elements of individual utterances.

2.2 Generation of MT outputs (*hyp*)

The collected Japanese segments (*src*) were then translated by our in-house MT systems, which implement a phrase-based statistical MT (Koehn, 2009). The Ja→En translations were obtained in 2013, with the system trained on 736k sentence pairs. The Ja→Zh and Ja→Ko translations were generated later in 2016, with the systems trained on 1.44M and 1.40M sentence pairs, respectively.

Table 1 summarizes the statistics of *src* and *hyp*. These segments are relatively shorter than sentences in written texts, such as news articles and patent documents.

Table 1: Statistics of the Japanese *src* and *hyp* in each target language.

Partition	Unit	*travel* (8,783 segments)				*hospital* (1,676 segments)			
		Total	Min	Avg.	Max	Total	Min	Avg.	Max
Japanese *src*	character	105,606	2	12.0	49	33,979	5	20.3	71
English *hyp*	word	44,604	1	5.1	28	14,844	1	8.9	29
Chinese *hyp*	character	65,710	2	7.5	30	21,974	3	13.1	41
Korean *hyp*	character	94,578	2	10.8	48	30,283	3	18.1	60

Table 2: Grading criterion for human evaluators.

Grade	Summary	Description
S	Perfect	Information of the source text has been completely translated. There are no grammatical errors in the target text. Lexical choice and phrasing are natural even from a native speaker point-of-view.
A	Good	The information of the source text has been completely translated and there are no grammatical errors in the target text, but lexical choice and phrasing are slightly unnatural.
B	Fair	There are some minor errors in the target text of less important textual information, but the meaning of the source text can be easily understood.
C	Acceptable	Important parts of the source text are omitted or could not be translated correctly, but the meaning of the source text can still be understood with some efforts.
D	Incorrect	The meaning of the source text is incomprehensible from target text.

2.3 Manual translation (*ref*)

Reference translations were manually given, referring only to the source segments (*src*). As each *src* was not attributed with its specific context, we asked the translators to imagine some context as long as it is reasonable considering the domain. On the contrary, we also asked to avoid adding too much contents that cannot be specified only from the *src*. For the *src* which has more than one interpretation, only one translation is given rather than enumerating all the possible interpretations.

2.4 Manual grading of MT output (*grade*)

The quality of MT output (*hyp*) with respect to its source (*src*) was graded according to a standard presented in Table 2, which is compatible[6] with the "Acceptability" criterion in Goto et al. (2013). In case the evaluator cannot understand the meaning of *src*, she/he is allowed to refer to the corresponding reference translation (*ref*), with an advice that it is not only the correct translation.

2.5 Manual post-editing of MT output (*pe*)

Human workers were asked to post-edit MT outputs (*hyp*), i.e., to produce *pe*, under the following guidance.

(1) Refer only to *src* and *hyp* basically. Refer also to *ref* if necessary.

(2) Make each *hyp* grammatical and semantically appropriate with respect to its *src*, i.e., the quality of *pe* must be "A" or "S" in Table 2.

(3) Perform minimal edits, as we use *pe* for the reference of computing HTER (Snover et al., 2006).

The workers were also informed that we consider the following four edit operations equally.

Deletion of a word: Delete an unnecessary word: e.g., "the an" → "the"

Insertion of a word: Insert a missing but necessary word: e.g., "We will stay at hotel." → "We will stay at the hotel."

Substitution of a word: Substitute a word with another word. Change of inflection and conjugation is also regarded as this operation: e.g., "Can you teach me the way to the station?" → "Can you tell me the way to the station?"

Shift of a word or a phrase: Change the word order by moving a single word or a sequence of consecutive words: e.g., "I'll send a card my friend." → "I'll send my friend a card."[7]

2.6 Consistency check

Note that the last two tasks, i.e., grading and post-editing of MT outputs, were performed completely separately. Now, discrepancies between *grade* and *pe* were resolved in this final step. When both *grade* and *pe* for the same pair of *src* and *hyp* were registered, we assessed them according to the following three criteria.

---

[6]Their "AA" and "F" correspond to our "S" and "D," respectively.

[7]One can edit this *hyp* to "I'll send a card to my friend." In this case, the operation is considered as an "Insertion of a word (to)."

Table 3: Distribution of segments according to their grade.

| Grade | travel (8,783 segments) | | | | | | hospital (1,676 segments) | | | | | |
| | Ja→En | | Ja→Zh | | Ja→Ko | | Ja→En | | Ja→Zh | | Ja→Ko | |
	#seg	%	#seg	%	#seg	%	#seg	%	#seg	%	#seg	%
S	1,961	22.3%	2,827	32.2%	3,466	39.5%	95	5.7%	708	42.2%	903	53.9%
A	1,462	16.6%	1,874	21.3%	2,326	26.5%	107	6.4%	514	30.7%	482	28.8%
B	1,269	14.4%	1,275	14.5%	1,360	15.5%	181	10.8%	172	10.3%	166	9.9%
C	1,067	12.1%	899	10.2%	724	8.2%	333	19.9%	107	6.4%	97	5.8%
D	3,024	34.4%	1,908	21.7%	907	10.3%	960	57.3%	175	10.4%	28	1.7%

Table 4: Proximity between translations obtained through different ways.

| Domain | Translations compared | BLEU (↑) | | | TER (↓) | | |
		Ja→En	Ja→Zh	Ja→Ko	Ja→En	Ja→Zh	Ja→Ko
travel	(a) *hyp* against *ref*	21.52	26.18	38.85	57.95	50.81	43.43
	(b) *hyp* against *pe*	51.97	69.44	81.98	35.14	19.20	12.25
	(c) *pe* against *ref*	49.00	39.73	49.11	34.46	38.79	34.75
hospital	(a) *hyp* against *ref*	9.19	30.38	51.01	75.35	48.54	32.44
	(b) *hyp* against *pe*	18.95	86.45	93.52	66.03	8.63	4.12
	(c) *pe* against *ref*	65.15	34.29	54.16	24.69	43.78	30.00

- If the *grade* is either "S" or "A" but *pe* is not identical to the given *hyp*, both grading and post-editing are performed again.

- If the *grade* is either "B," "C," or "D" but *pe* is identical to *hyp*, both grading and post-editing are performed again.

- If *hyp* is closer to *ref* than to *pe*, i.e., TER(hyp, pe) > TER(hyp, ref), the number of edits is not minimal;[8] so post-editing is performed again.[9]

As there could be a variety of translation options, seeking the complete minimality does not seem feasible. Nevertheless, we introduced the last constraint, because we need less-edited translations as *pe*. To compute TER scores using TERCOM,[10] we tokenized *hyp*, *ref*, and *pe*, using the tool in Moses[11] for English MeCab[12] with mecab-ko-dic[13] for Korean. For Chinese, we regarded each character as one token.

3 Analyses of the Created Datasets

This section describes characteristics of the created datasets, observations, and remaining issues.

First, the results of manual grading are summarized in Table 3. While MT outputs for the *travel* domain were much better than the *hospital* domain in the Ja→En task, the segments in the *hospital* domain were better translated by the Ja→Zh and Ja→Ko MT systems.

Table 4 shows proximity in terms of BLEU (Papineni et al., 2002) and TER (Snover et al., 2006), between translations obtained through different ways. (a) "*hyp* against *ref*" presents what is measured in standard evaluation of MT outputs. The scores in these rows reflect the distribution of MT outputs shown in Table 3. On the other hand, (b) "*hyp* against *pe*" gauges the amount of post-edits. As we asked to perform only necessary edits to assure at least grade "A," the scores in these rows should be good in general. Only the exception is the *hospital* domain in the Ja→En task. As most of the MT outputs were of low quality, the workers tended to abandon them rather than correcting them. Finally, (c) "*pe* against *ref*" rows demonstrate that these two types of translations were not necessarily highly similar. Nevertheless, *pe* were certainly better than *hyp* with respect to *ref*. Again, *pe* in the *hospital* domain in the Ja→En task show exceptionally good scores. We plan to make an in-depth analysis with this respect.

The human judgment and the quantity of post-edits (HTER) evaluate the translation quality from different aspects. Indeed, as illustrated in Figure 2, many *hyp* that got grade "B" did not have smaller HTER score than those of grade "D." Figure 3 exemplifies some discrepancies between *grade* and HTER score observed in the Ja→En dataset. The

---

⁸This constraint can easily be satisfied by just copying *ref* to *pe*, but we prohibited this.

⁹We asked to restart from *hyp*, because resuming from the submitted *pe* would make the total number of edits unclear.

¹⁰http://www.cs.umd.edu/~snover/tercom/, version 0.7.25

¹¹http://statmt.org/moses/, RELEASE-2.1.1

¹²https://github.com/taku910/mecab/, version 0.996

¹³https://bitbucket.org/eunjeon/mecab-ko-dic/, version 2.0.1-20150920

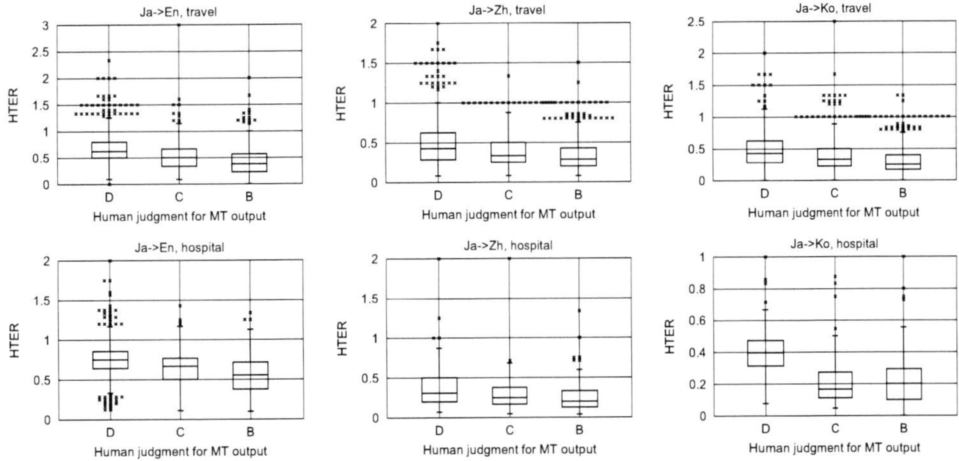

Figure 2: Distribution of sentence-wise HTER score with regard to each human judgment.

	src	多額の現金は持ってこないでください。
	ref	Please don't bring a lot of cash.
#1	hyp	Please bring a lot of cash.
	grade	D
	pe	Please don't bring a lot of cash.
	HTER	0.22
	src	首が痛くありませんか。
	ref	Doesn't your neck hurt?
#2	hyp	Do you have pain in my neck?
	grade	D
	pe	Do you have pain in your neck?
	HTER	0.13
	src	素晴らしい景色だね
	ref	It's a wonderful view, isn't it?
#3	hyp	It's beautiful scenery.
	grade	B
	pe	The scenery's beautiful, isn't it?
	HTER	0.78

Figure 3: Examples from the Ja→En dataset.

hyp in the first two examples were graded "D," while they were only slightly edited. The *hyp* in #1 failed to appropriately convey the meaning of negation. On the other hand, considering that the segment #2 is given by a health care provider, the possessor of "首 (neck)" must not be him/her (the utterer), but the patient (the hearer). In both cases, the error in *hyp* is critical, even though it can be corrected with a small number of edits. This suggests that sentence-level QE systems should be optimized according to appropriate criteria, depending on their application.

There were also several examples that were graded "B" but were post-edited significantly. For instance, the *hyp* in #3 could be corrected by simply replacing the full stop with a tag question, i.e.,

Table 5: Number of segments in each partition.

Partition	*travel*	*hospital*	Merger
train	7,083	1,376	8,459
dev	850	150	1,000
test	850	150	1,000

"isn't it?" with a HTER score of 0.56. However, the worker also changed the syntactic structure of the main clause, increasing the HTER score. To avoid this kind of over-editing, the instruction in Section 2.5 should be improved.

4 Benchmarking

Using the created datasets, we conducted benchmarking experiments on word-level QE, sentence-level QE, and APE.

4.1 Common Settings

First, each of the *travel* and *hospital* datasets was randomly partitioned into training, development, and test sets as shown in Table 5. Although we believe that our datasets are useful for examining domain adaptation methods, in this paper, we report on experiments using the merger of data in the two domains. Table 6 summarizes the statistics of each partition in each task.[14] "BAD%-WQE" indicates the percentages of "BAD" tags for word-level QE (see Section 4.2 for details), while "BAD%-SQE" indicates the ratio of *hyp* that need post-editing, i.e., those graded either "B," "C," or "D."

---

[14] We tokenized them with our in-house tokenizer, which is also used in our speech translation service.

Table 6: Statistics of the training, development, and test partitions of the datasets.

Task	Partition	#seg	Tokens			Types			BAD%	
			src	*hyp*	*pe*	*src*	*hyp*	*pe*	WQE	SQE
Ja→En	train	8,459	65,855	59,377	63,970	5,739	3,772	4,475	29.0	65.2
	dev	1,000	7,657	7,004	7,526	1,680	1,201	1,365	28.9	66.9
	test	1,000	7,700	7,002	7,544	1,726	1,231	1,439	29.2	65.1
Ja→Zh	train	8,459	65,855	50,482	51,735	5,739	4,907	5,139	9.0	43.3
	dev	1,000	7,657	5,883	5,993	1,680	1,483	1,530	9.6	42.3
	test	1,000	7,700	5,915	6,042	1,726	1,516	1,562	9.9	44.9
Ja→Ko	train	8,459	65,844	65,520	66,550	5,739	5,103	5,213	7.6	31.3
	dev	1,000	7,657	7,674	7,791	1,680	1,598	1,632	8.3	32.2
	test	1,000	7,700	7,614	7,740	1,726	1,632	1,680	7.3	30.9

Table 7: Statistics of the DLC corpus.

Partition	#seg	Tokens				Types			
		Ja	En	Zh	Ko	Ja	En	Zh	Ko
train	1.57M	25.1M	22.3M	20.1M	24.0M	274,746	227,033	236,410	264,328
dev	14k	224k	200k	179k	215k	14,388	12,492	12,552	11,966

For the QE/APE tasks, due to the scarcity of training data, even baseline approaches have employed external resources, such as parallel and monolingual corpora, in addition to the task-specific training data. However, there is no publicly available parallel and monolingual data of spoken language in the language pairs of our concern. Therefore, we reluctantly employed an in-house parallel corpus of daily life conversations (DLC). Its statistics are shown in Table 7.

4.2 Word-level QE (WQE)

Given a pair of source text (*src*) and MT output (*hyp*), the task of word-level QE is to predict a sequence of tags with the same length as *hyp*, where each tag indicates how good the corresponding word in *hyp* is. While some previous studies, such as Bach et al. (2011), addressed to gauge the quality of each word with a real-valued score, WMT adopted a coarse-grained binary tag, i.e., {OK, BAD}, presumably because this form of tags can be automatically generated as the by-product of computing HTER score by comparing *hyp* with its post-edited version (*pe*) (Bojar et al., 2015). Following the recent convention in WMT, we automatically generated a sequence of binary tags for each pair of *src* and *hyp* using TERCOM. As the evaluation metrics, we used F_1 score of detecting "OK" tags (F_1-OK), that for "BAD" tags (F_1-BAD), and their product (F_1-mult) as in Bojar et al. (2016).

As a system for WQE, we adopted an implementation[15] based on a feed-forward neural net-

[15] https://github.com/lemaoliu/qenn/

Table 8: Pseudo data for the WQE task.

Task	Tokens	BAD%
Ja→En	10,945,486	50.3
Ja→Zh	9,867,440	39.4
Ja→Ko	11,891,369	30.6

work with its default setting. Following the investigation in Liu et al. (2017), we also generated a set of pseudo training data using the DLC corpus as follows.

Step 1. Phrase-based statistical MT systems for Ja→∗ translation tasks were built from the first half of the DLC corpus using Moses.

Step 2. Japanese sentences in the remaining half of the DLC corpus were decoded by the MT systems.

Step 3. Tag sequences for the MT outputs were given in the same manner as the manually created data, except that we regarded reference translations in the second half of the DLC corpus as post-edited MT outputs.

As presented in Table 8, we generated much larger data than the manually created training data in Table 6, although the pseudo training data tended to contain more "BAD" tags than the manually created data due to the independence between *hyp* and *ref*.

Our experimental results are presented in Table 9. The results for the Ja→En and Ja→Zh tasks are consistent to the observations in Liu et al. (2017), i.e., pseudo training data improve F_1-BAD scores. However, introduction of such data do not improve F_1-BAD in the Ja→Ko task.

Table 9: Results for the WQE task.

System	F_1-mult ($\uparrow$)			F_1-BAD ($\uparrow$)			F_1-OK ($\uparrow$)		
	Ja→En	Ja→Zh	Ja→Ko	Ja→En	Ja→Zh	Ja→Ko	Ja→En	Ja→Zh	Ja→Ko
All BAD	-	-	-	0.452	0.181	0.136	-	-	-
All OK	-	-	-	-	-	-	0.829	0.948	0.962
FNN-manual	0.345	0.205	0.295	0.469	0.229	0.313	0.736	0.896	0.942
FNN-pseudo	0.315	0.195	0.181	0.477	0.247	0.220	0.660	0.790	0.827
FNN-both	0.341	0.211	0.196	0.487	0.256	0.232	0.701	0.825	0.846

Table 10: Results for the SQE prediction task ("#f" indicates the number of features).

System	#f	Pearson's r ($\uparrow$)			MAE ($\downarrow$)			RMSE ($\downarrow$)		
		Ja→En	Ja→Zh	Ja→Ko	Ja→En	Ja→Zh	Ja→Ko	Ja→En	Ja→Zh	Ja→Ko
Avg. of train	-	-	-	-	0.306	0.198	0.158	0.347	0.238	0.205
QuEst17	17	0.427	0.125	0.239	0.255	0.185	0.159	0.325	0.242	0.201
QuEst17+SntEmb	617	0.516	0.301	0.413	0.239	0.184	0.153	0.298	0.228	0.192

4.3 Sentence-level QE (SQE)

Given a pair of source text (*src*) and MT output (*hyp*), the task of sentence-level QE is to predict how good the entire *hyp* is, with respect to *src*. We conducted experiments on both of the HTER prediction and binary classification tasks.

4.3.1 Prediction of HTER

In WMT, this task is to predict the HTER score, directly from (*src*, *hyp*) pair (Specia et al., 2015), or indirectly through predicting the necessary edits in a similar manner to WQE (Kim and Lee, 2016).

We implemented a tool to extract a set of 17 features[16] of QuEst++ (Specia et al., 2015), which is regarded as the baseline of this task. To compute the features based on language models, we used the corresponding part of the DLC corpus. To estimate the translation-related features, such as the number of translations per word in *src*, we trained a phrase-table on the DLC corpus using Moses. Following the findings in Shah et al. (2016), we also incorporated the distributed representations of *src* and *hyp*. First, word embeddings with 300 dimensions were learned from each part of the DLC corpus using word2vec[17] with its default parameters. Then, the embedding for a given segment is computed by averaging the embeddings of its constituent words, assuming the additive compositionality (Mikolov et al., 2013). During the computation, unknown words were mapped to a zero vector. Finally, values for each of 300 dimensions were regarded as additional features.

The extracted features were used to train support vector regression (SVR) models with a radial basis function (RBF) kernel.[18] Hyper-parameters were optimized with respect to the development set, through a grid search to maximize the Pearson's correlation coefficient r between the predicted HTER and the gold HTER.

Table 10 justifies that sentence embeddings obtained by such a naive way[19] can improve the performance of predicting HTER score, irrespective of the evaluation metrics: Pearson's correlation coefficient r, mean average error (MAE), and root mean squared error (RMSE).

4.3.2 Binary Classification

We assume that users of speech translation services are usually not competent in the target language. Thus, when we consider directly delivering the MT outputs to such users, their quality in terms of our *grade* seems more intuitive than HTER.

We evaluated how well the same feature sets in Section 4.3.1 can predict the grade, using support vector classifier (SVC) instead of SVR. Hyper-parameters were optimized so that they maximize F_1-mult on the development set. The systems (feature sets) were evaluated with the same metrics as in WQE.

As presented in Table 11, we obtained consistent results that baseline systems with QuEst++ features can be improved by incorporating the distributed representations of *src* and *hyp*.

---

[16] http://www.quest.dcs.shef.ac.uk/ quest_files/features_blackbox_baseline_ 17

[17] https://github.com/tmikolov/word2vec/

[18] http://chasen.org/~taku/software/ TinySVM/

[19] As a more advanced alternative, one can train a neural MT system and retrieve annotations from RNN's hidden states as proposed in (Kim and Lee, 2016).

Table 11: Results for the SQE classification task ("#f" indicates the number of features).

System	#f	F_1-mult (↑)			F_1-BAD (↑)			F_1-OK (↑)		
		Ja→En	Ja→Zh	Ja→Ko	Ja→En	Ja→Zh	Ja→Ko	Ja→En	Ja→Zh	Ja→Ko
All BAD	-	-	-	-	0.789	0.620	0.472	-	-	-
All OK	-	-	-	-	-	-	-	0.517	0.711	0.817
QuEst17	17	0.335	0.295	0.310	0.765	0.442	0.403	0.438	0.667	0.770
QuEst17+SntEmb	617	0.450	0.410	0.396	0.798	0.584	0.480	0.563	0.702	0.825

Table 12: Results for the APE task.

Method	BLEU (↑)			TER (↓)		
	Ja→En	Ja→Zh	Ja→Ko	Ja→En	Ja→Zh	Ja→Ko
Raw MT output	43.74	73.14	85.52	42.21	16.98	9.87
(a) APE w/ gold data only	43.38	72.28	84.87	42.33	17.53	10.31
(b) (a) + bitext back-off	44.00	73.01	85.53	41.87	17.05	9.87
(c) (b) + pseudo training data	43.90	73.15	85.57	41.95	16.97	9.82

4.4 APE

The task of APE is to automatically post-edit MT outputs (*hyp*). Although there are a number of methods that also refer to *src* (Béchara et al., 2011; Junczys-Dowmunt and Grundkiewicz, 2016), we have so far examined only classic baseline methods based on phrase-based statistical MT.

The first system (a) was trained only on the gold data (Simard et al., 2007a) using Moses. However, this system tended to deteriorate the translation quality in terms of BLUE and TER, presumably due to the scarcity of training data. Then, our second model (b) introduced identical pairs of sentences in the target side of our DLC corpus in order to conservatively retain grammatical fragment within *hyp*. By (re-)decoding the *hyp* using the multiple decoding path ability of Moses,[20] this model significantly improved the naive baseline system (a), but the translation quality was not consistently better depending on the language pair.

Finally, we introduced in the third system (c) yet another phrase table learned from pseudo training data as proposed by Simard et al. (2007b). Our pseudo training data were obtained in the same manner as those for WQE (see Section 4.2); we coupled each of the decoded result to its corresponding reference translation in the DLC corpus. As summarized in Table 12, this model led to a slight but consistent improvement on both metrics in the all tasks.

5 Conclusion

Aiming to promote the research on quality estimation (QE) and automatic post-editing (APE) of MT outputs, especially for those among Asian languages, we have created new datasets for the Japanese to English, Chinese, and Korean translation tasks. This paper described the process of corpus creation and observations from the created datasets. We also presented our benchmarking experiments using the created datasets, for all of the tasks in our concern: word-level QE, two variants of sentence-level QE, and APE. Although the methods examined in this paper could be far from the state-of-the-art, we confirmed that the performance of these tasks can be improved by introducing features and pseudo training data that had been proven useful in the literature.

Following the emergence of neural MT, we are now working on extending the datasets with translations of such systems. We are planning to further improve the performance on the QE/APE tasks, and to investigate applications of the technologies, including enhancing the functionality of our speech translation service, and filtering automatically harvested parallel sentences (Sennrich et al., 2016; Marie and Fujita, 2017).

Acknowledgments

We are deeply grateful to the anonymous reviewers for their thorough and constructive comments. This work was conducted under the program "Promotion of Global Communications Plan: Research, Development, and Social Demonstration of Multilingual Speech Translation Technology" of the Ministry of Internal Affairs and Communications (MIC), Japan.

---

[20]We used the "either" strategy. If a phrase pair appears in more than one phrase table, different decoding paths are generated and each considers only the corresponding features for scoring.

References

Nguyen Bach, Fei Huang, and Yaser Al-Onaizan. 2011. Goodness: A method for measuring machine translation confidence. In *Proceedings of the 49th Annual Meeting of the Association for Computational Linguistics (ACL)*, pages 211–219.

Yehosua Bar-Hillel. 1951. The present state of research on mechanical translation. *American Documentation*, 2(4):229–237.

Hanna Béchara, Yanjun Ma, and Josef van Genabith. 2011. Statistical post-editing for a statistical MT system. In *Proceedings of the 13th Machine Translation Summit (MT Summit XIII)*, pages 308–315.

Ondřej Bojar, Christian Buck, Christian Federmann, Barry Haddow, Philipp Koehn, Johannes Leveling, Christof Monz, Pavel Pecina, Matt Post, Herve Saint-Amand, Radu Soricut, Lucia Specia, and Aleš Tamchyna. 2014. Findings of the 2014 workshop on statistical machine translation. In *Proceedings of the 9th Workshop on Statistical Machine Translation (WMT)*, pages 12–58.

Ondřej Bojar, Rajen Chatterjee, Christian Federmann, Barry Haddow, Matthias Huck, Chris Hokamp, Philipp Koehn, Varvara Logacheva, Christof Monz, Matteo Negri, Matt Post, Carolina Scarton, Lucia Specia, and Marco Turchi. 2015. Findings of the 2015 workshop on statistical machine translation. In *Proceedings of the 10th Workshop on Statistical Machine Translation (WMT)*, pages 1–46.

Ondřej Bojar, Rajen Chatterjee, Christian Federmann, Yvette Graham, Barry Haddow, Matthias Huck, Antonio Jimeno Yepes, Philipp Koehn, Varvara Logacheva, Christof Monz, Matteo Negri, Aurelie Neveol, Mariana Neves, Martin Popel, Matt Post, Raphael Rubino, Carolina Scarton, Lucia Specia, Marco Turchi, Karin Verspoor, and Marcos Zampieri. 2016. Findings of the 2016 conference on machine translation. In *Proceedings of the 1st Conference on Machine Translation (WMT)*, pages 131–198.

Ondřej Bojar, Rajen Chatterjee, Christian Federmann, Yvette Graham, Barry Haddow, Matthias Huck, Philipp Koehn, Varvara Logacheva, Christof Monz, Matteo Negri, Matt Post, Raphael Rubino, Lucia Specia, and Marco Turchi. 2017. Findings of the 2017 conference on machine translation. In *Proceedings of the 2nd Conference on Machine Translation (WMT)*.

Isao Goto, Ka Po Chow, Bin Lu, Eiichiro Sumita, and Benjamin K. Tsou. 2013. Overview of the patent machine translation task at the NTCIR-10 workshop. In *Proceedings of NTCIR-10 Workshop Meeting*, pages 260–286.

W. John Hutchins and Harold L. Somers. 1992. *An Introduction to Machine Translation*. Academic Press.

ISO/TC27. 2017. ISO 18587:2017 translation services: Post-editing of machine translation output: Requirements.

Japan National Tourism Organization. 2017. Foreign visitors & Japanese departures. https://www.jnto.go.jp/eng/ttp/sta/.

Marcin Junczys-Dowmunt and Roman Grundkiewicz. 2016. Log-linear combinations of monolingual and bilingual neural machine translation models for automatic post-editing. In *Proceedings of the 1st Conference on Machine Translation (WMT)*, pages 751–758.

Hyun Kim and Jong-Hyeok Lee. 2016. A recurrent neural networks approach for estimating the quality of machine translation output. In *Proceedings of Human Language Technologies: The 2016 Annual Conference of the North American Chapter of the Association for Computational Linguistics (NAACL-HLT)*, pages 494–498.

Philipp Koehn. 2009. *Statistical Machine Translation*. Cambridge University Press.

Lemao Liu, Atsushi Fujita, Masao Utiyama, Andrew Finch, and Eiichiro Sumita. 2017. Translation quality estimation using only bilingual corpora. *IEEE/ACM Transactions on Audio, Speech, and Language Processing (TASLP)*, 25(9):1458–1468.

Benjamin Marie and Atsushi Fujita. 2017. Efficient extraction of pseudo-parallel sentences from raw monolingual data using word embeddings. In *Proceedings of the 55nd Annual Meeting of the Association for Computational Linguistics (ACL)*, pages 392–398.

Tomas Mikolov, Ilya Sutskever, Kai Chen, Greg Corrado, and Jeffrey Dean. 2013. Distributed representations of words and phrases and their compositionality. In *Proceedings of the 26th Annual Conference on Neural Information Processing Systems (NIPS)*, pages 3111–3119.

Kishore Papineni, Salim Roukos, Todd Ward, and Wei-Jing Zhu. 2002. BLEU: A method for automatic evaluation of machine translation. In *Proceedings of the 40th Annual Meeting of the Association for Computational Linguistics (ACL)*, pages 311–318.

Marion Potet, Emmanuelle Esperança-Rodier, Laurent Besacier, and Hervé Blanchon. 2012. Collection of a large database of French–English SMT output corrections. In *Proceedings of the 8th International Conference on Language Resources and Evaluation (LREC)*.

Rico Sennrich, Barry Haddow, and Alexandra Birch. 2016. Improving neural machine translation models with monolingual data. In *Proceedings of the 54nd Annual Meeting of the Association for Computational Linguistics (ACL)*, pages 86–96.

Kashif Shah, Fethi Bougares, Loïc Barrault, and Lucia Specia. 2016. SHEF-LIUM-NN: Sentence-level quality estimation with neural network features. In *Proceedings of the 1st Conference on Machine Translation (WMT)*, pages 838–842.

Michel Simard, Cyril Goutte, and Pierre Isabelle. 2007a. Statistical phrase-based post-editing. In *Proceedings of Human Language Technologies 2007: The Conference of the North American Chapter of the Association for Computational Linguistics (NAACL-HLT)*, pages 508–515.

Michel Simard, Nicola Ueffing, Pierre Isabelle, and Roland Kuhn. 2007b. Rule-based translation with statistical phrase-basd post-editing. In *Proceedings of the 2nd Workshop on Statistical Machine Translation (WMT)*, pages 203–206.

Matthew Snover, Bonnie Dorr, Richard Schwartz, Linnea Micciulla, and John Makhoul. 2006. A study of translation edit rate with targeted human annotation. In *Proceedings of the 7th Biennial Conference of the Association for Machine Translation in the Americas (AMTA)*, pages 223–231.

Lucia Specia, Gustavo Paetzold, and Carolina Scarton. 2015. Multi-level translation quality prediction with QuEst++. In *Proceedings of ACL-IJCNLP 2015 System Demonstrations*, pages 115–120.

Lucia Specia, Dhwaj Raj, and Marco Turchi. 2010. Machine translation evaluation versus quality estimation. *Machine Translation*, 24(1):39–50.

NTT Neural Machine Translation Systems at WAT 2017

Makoto Morishita, Jun Suzuki and **Masaaki Nagata**
NTT Communication Science Laboratories, NTT Corporation
2-4 Hikaridai, Seika-cho, Soraku-gun, Kyoto, 619-0237, Japan
{morishita.makoto,suzuki.jun,nagata.masaaki}@lab.ntt.co.jp

Abstract

In this year, we participated in four translation subtasks at WAT 2017. Our model structure is quite simple but we used it with well-tuned hyper-parameters, leading to a significant improvement compared to the previous state-of-the-art system. We also tried to make use of the unreliable part of the provided parallel corpus by back-translating and making a synthetic corpus. Our submitted system achieved the new state-of-the-art performance in terms of the BLEU score, as well as human evaluation.

1 Introduction

In this paper, we describe our systems submitted to this year's translation shared tasks at WAT 2017 (Nakazawa et al., 2017). For this year, we focused on scientific paper (ASPEC Japanese-English, English-Japanese) and newspaper (JIJI Corpus Japanese-English, English-Japanese) translation subtasks.

We use a simple Neural Machine Translation (NMT) model with an attention mechanism (Luong et al., 2015). In addition, for ASPEC, we made a synthetic corpus for the unreliable part of the provided corpus, in a way similar to that reported by Sennrich et al. (Sennrich et al., 2016a). This technique and the well-tuned hyper-parameters led to new state-of-the-art results in all the subtasks in which we participated.

2 Common Settings

2.1 Model Structure

Our model is based on the encoder-decoder with a global attention model proposed by Luong et al. (2015), with a general scoring function and input feeding. The original model uses a uni-directional encoder, but we changed it to a bi-directional one proposed by Bahdanau et al. (2015). After running the bi-directional encoder, we simply added each state and used it for a decoder.

We implemented this model with Chainer toolkit (Tokui et al., 2015), and the implementation is now open for further experiments[1].

2.2 Data Preprocessing

First, we tokenize the provided corpus using KyTea (Neubig et al., 2011) for the Japanese side, and Moses tokenizer[2] for the English side. We remove the sentences over 60 words to clean the corpus. Then we further split it into sub-words using joint byte pair encoding (joint-BPE) (Sennrich et al., 2016c) with applying 16,000 merge operations.

For ASPEC subtasks, though the provided training data contained over 3.0M sentences, we only used the first 2.0M sentences, in the same way as the previous participants (Neubig, 2014). AS-PEC was collected by aligning parallel sentences automatically and sorting them on the basis of the alignment confidence score (Nakazawa et al., 2016). This means that the latter side of the corpus may contain noisy parallel sentences, which would have a negative impact on training. We used the latter 1.0M sentences as a monolingual corpus and made a synthetic corpus (see section 3.1.1 for details).

2.3 Training

Table 1 shows the settings of hyper-parameters we used and tested. We tried several combinations

---

[1] https://github.com/nttcslab-nlp/wat2017
[2] https://github.com/moses-smt/mosesdecoder/blob/master/scripts/tokenizer/tokenizer.perl

Proceedings of the 4th Workshop on Asian Translation, pages 89–94,
Taipei, Taiwan, November 27, 2017. ©2017 AFNLP

Hyper-parameter	Used	Tested
Vocabulary size	16,000	1,000, 5,000
Embedding dimension	512	—
Hidden dimension	512	—
Attention dimension	512	—
Encoder layer	2	4, 1
Decoder layer	2	4, 1
Optimizer	SGD	—
Initial learning rate	1.0	0.5
Gradient clipping	5.0	6.0
Dropout rate	0.3	0.2, 0.0
Mini-batch size	128 sent	64, 256

Table 1: Hyper-parameter settings

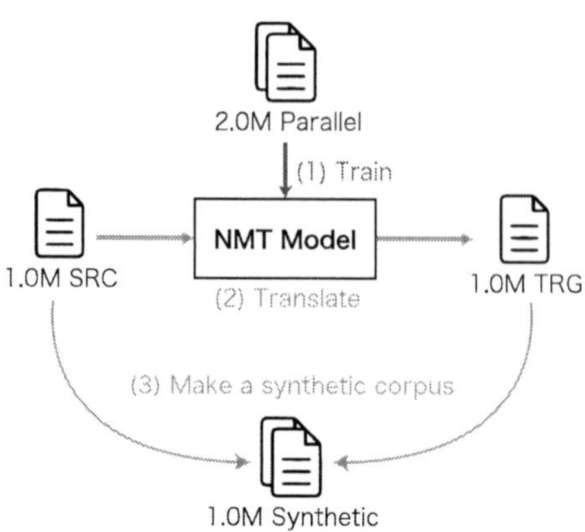

Figure 1: Overview of making a synthetic corpus. First, we make an NMT model with a reliable parallel corpus, then translate the unreliable part of the corpus to make a synthetic parallel corpus.

and we found that these settings were the best. For the vocabulary, we only included the most frequent 16,000 sub-words in the training set[3]. After 13 epochs, we multiplied the learning rate by 0.7 for every epoch, then continued training till 20 epochs.

2.4 Testing

2.4.1 Length Normalized Re-ranking

Naive beam searches with a large beam size may tend to output shorter sentences, leading to a drop in performance (Tu et al., 2017). To reduce this negative effect, we re-ranked the candidate output sentences t by using the following score function once we finished the beam search (Cromieres et al., 2016):

$$\hat{t} = \arg\max_{t \in \mathbf{t}} \left\{ \frac{p(t)}{|t|} \right\}, \tag{1}$$

where $p(t)$ is the predicted log-probability of a candidate output sentence t and $|t|$ is the length of t.

With this length normalized re-ranking, we can use a large beam size without taking the above explained negative effect into account. Through preliminary experiments, we found that a beam size of 20 was sufficient.

2.4.2 Ensembling

It has been reported that ensembling several different models together significantly improves performance. In an ensembling process, several models are run at each time step and an arithmetic mean of predicted probability is obtained, which is used to determine the next word. In our settings, we trained eight models independently and used them for the ensemble.

3 Task-Specific Settings

3.1 ASPEC

3.1.1 Synthetic Corpus

As we mentioned in section 2.2, ASPEC contains some unreliable sentence pairs. For SMT, we can use these sentences as monolingual data to train a language model. However in the current NMT model architecture, the model cannot be trained with monolingual data, so the previous participants with NMT models simply ignored these parts of the data (Neubig, 2016; Eriguchi et al., 2016).

In a way similar to that reported by Sennrich et al. Sennrich et al. (2016b), we tried to use the unreliable part of the corpus by making a synthetic corpus. Figure 1 illustrates the overview of how we made the synthetic corpus. First, we made an NMT model with the reliable part of the provided data (in our case, the first 2.0M sentences), then translated the unreliable part of the corpus by using it to make a synthetic corpus. Finally, we made a corpus of 3.0M sentences by concatenating this

---

[3]Applying joint-BPE with 16,000 merge operations should make the vocabulary size under 16,000 sub-words, but for Japanese, it may contain some unknown characters (kanji). The actual vocabulary size for each corpus was the following: ASPEC Ja:11271, En:10942, JIJI Ja:16000, En:15795

synthetic corpus and the reliable part of the data. With this corpus, we continued the training of the model for a further 10 epochs.

It should be noted that the target side of the synthetic corpus should be the original sentences (not those generated by the NMT model). This is because an NMT model includes a target side language model and uses it to generating a natural sentence, so it would be better to keep the target side original to train an NMT model effectively. Thus, the synthetic corpus used for Japanese-English training is made with an English-Japanese NMT model, and vice versa.

3.2 JIJI

3.2.1 Model Fine-tuning

We thought the JIJI corpus was too small to train an NMT model, so we tried to train the model with other large parallel corpora and then fine-tune it with the JIJI corpus (Luong and Manning, 2015). In our settings, we first trained the model with AS-PEC (2.0M) and Japan Patent Office Patent Corpus (JPC) (1.0M). We learned BPE codes with the JIJI corpus and applied them to ASPEC and JPC. We trained the model with ASPEC and JPC for 20 epochs, then continued training with the JIJI corpus for a further 20 epochs.

4 Official Results

Tables 2 and 3 show the official results of our submissions[4]. Our system achieved the best BLEU scores and adequacy for all the subtasks in which we participated. For pairwise crowdsourcing evaluations, our system also obtained the best evaluations except for the ASPEC Ja-En subtask. Even in this case, it obtained the second best evaluation.

5 Analysis

5.1 Synthetic Corpus

From Table 2, we can see that the synthetic corpus has a positive impact on the performance, especially for the En-Ja subtask, and contributes to achieving better performance. We also tried to use the original 3.0M corpus for training, but could not see any improvements over the model that uses only the first 2.0M sentences.

Manually comparing the synthetic corpus and the originally provided corpus, we found that the

quality of the synthetic corpus was much better than the original one. The original corpus often includes noisy pairs where the contents are different on each side. Table 4 shows an example sentence of the original parallel corpus and our synthetic corpus. The original Japanese sentence does not contain the words for "*a nonlinear least squares method*" and "*the method of steepest decent*", but the synthetic sentence contains these words and improves the quality of the parallel corpus. Using a synthetic corpus makes it possible to alleviate the noisy sentences and helps to achieve better performance.

5.2 Model Fine-tuning

We thought that training with a larger amount of data would enable the model to use more sentences and that this would be beneficial for further training. However, as is clear from Table 3, we couldn't find any improvements over fine-tuning. We suspect that the parallel corpus used to initialize the model is quite out-of-domain, so the model couldn't get any benefits from it.

5.3 JIJI Corpus Quality

In the JIJI corpus subtasks, we were only able to see a small correlation between BLEU scores and human evaluation. To find out the reason for this, we manually looked into the JIJI corpus. In doing so, we found that it was too noisy for efficient learning. It contained a lot of parallel sentences with different content, which can be noise for NMT training. The JIJI corpus originally comes from Japanese news articles that were translated into English. During this process, translators often add or remove the content of the article to make it easy to understand for English readers. However, this makes it hard to find clean one-by-one sentence alignment and leads to make the parallel corpus dirty. As a result, the trained model learns to generate a sentence with a different meaning, and it leads to a higher BLEU score but lower human evaluations. To deal with this problem, it would be better to consider how to train a cleaner model from a noisy parallel corpus.

5.4 BLEU Scores and Tokenizer

After the evaluation period finished, we found that our BLEU scores tended to be better with KyTea tokenizer. In the English-Japanese subtasks, participants de-tokenize system outputs and the submission system will re-tokenize them with JU-

---

[4]In these tables, we exclude the organizer's submissions for ranking.

	System	BLEU	Rank	Pairwise	Rank	Adequacy	Rank
En-Ja	Single (3.0M)	37.15	—	—	—	—	—
	Single (2.0M)	37.90	7/14	—	—	—	—
	Single (2.0M + 1.0M Synthetic)	38.87	4/14	—	—	—	—
	8 Ensemble (2.0M)	39.80	3/14	72.250	3/11	—	—
	8 Ensemble (2.0M + 1.0M Synthetic)	**40.32**	**1/14**	**75.750**	**1/11**	**4.41**	**1/4**
Ja-En	Single (3.0M)	26.07	—	—	—	—	
	Single (2.0M)	27.43	6/13	75.000	4/10	—	—
	Single (2.0M + 1.0M Synthetic)	27.62	4/13	—	—	—	—
	8 Ensemble (2.0M)	**28.36**	**1/13**	**77.250**	**2/10**	**4.14**	**1/2**
	8 Ensemble (2.0M + 1.0M Synthetic)	28.15	2/13	—	—	—	—

Table 2: Official results of our submitted systems for ASPEC subtasks. For the En-Ja subtask, we show the BLEU scores with JUMAN tokenizer.

	System	BLEU	Rank	Pairwise	Rank	Adequacy	Rank
En-Ja	Single	19.13	3/4	14.500	2/3	—	—
	8 Ensemble	**20.37**	**1/4**	**17.750**	**1/3**	**2.03**	**1/2**
Ja-En	Single	19.44	2/8	**32.000**	**1/6**	**2.05**	**1/2**
	Fine-Tuning	15.77	7/8	—	—	—	—
	8 Ensemble	**20.90**	**1/8**	26.750	2/6	—	—

Table 3: Official results of our submitted systems for JIJI corpus subtasks. For En-Ja subtasks, we show the BLEU scores with JUMAN tokenizer.

MAN, KyTea or MeCab tokenizers, then calculate the BLEU scores. In our experiments, we first pre-tokenized sentences with KyTea tokenizer, and then further split them into sub-words by applying BPE. Therefore, we suspect that our systems are likely to be optimized with KyTea, so we carried out experiments using JUMAN as a pre-tokenizer. Table 5 shows the BLEU scores of our systems pre-tokenized with KyTea or JUMAN. From the results, we found that if we used JUMAN as a pre-tokenizer, we achieved better BLEU scores calculated with JUMAN tokenizer.

5.5 Beam Size and Length Normalized Re-ranking

Figure 2 shows the BLEU score changes in terms of increasing the beam size with the length normalized re-ranking described in section 2.4.1 (w/ LN), and without it (w/o LN). In the case of w/ LN, the BLEU score tends to gradually get better by increasing the beam size. In contrast, the BLEU score dropped as we enlarge the beam size from the highest score at the beam size of 3 in the case of w/o LN.

The reason behind these observations is that the BLEU score is strongly penalized if the length of

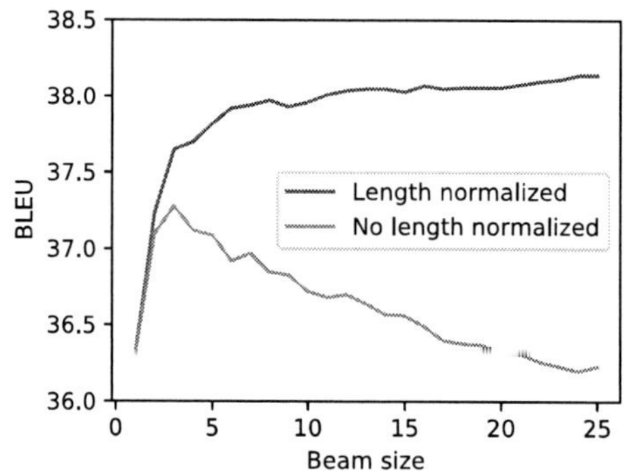

Figure 2: Relations between beam size and BLEU score on ASPEC En-Ja. With length normalization, we achieved better BLEU scores as the beam size became larger.

the hypothesis sentence is shorter than the corresponding reference sentence. This penalty is referred to as "Brevity Penalty (BP)". Figures 3 (a) and (b) respectively show the BP and the "raw BLEU score" (BLEU score while discarding the BP term) changes in w/ LN and w/o LN in terms of increasing the beam size. Clearly, the BP in-

Source	The search procedure utilizes a nonlinear least squares method coupled with the method of steepest descent.
Original	また，具体的な探索の手順を示した。 (We also show the specific search procedure.)
Synthetic	探索手順は最急降下法と結合した非線形最小二乗法を用いた。 (The search procedure utilizes a nonlinear least squares method coupled with the method of steepest descent.)

Table 4: An example sentence pair in the original and synthetic corpus.

	System	BLEU (JUMAN)	BLEU (KyTea)	BLEU (MeCab)
En-Ja	Single (KyTea pre-tokenized)	37.90	**40.48**	38.61
	Single (JUMAN pre-tokenized)	**38.12**	40.22	**38.80**

Table 5: Experimental results of ASPEC En-Ja subtask with different pre-tokenziers.

creasingly penalized the raw BLEU scores as the beam size increased in the case of w/o LN, while for w/ LN it maintained the BP. This observation reveals that the length normalized re-ranking (w/ LN) effectively works to keep the length of the best hypothesis sentences even if we enlarge the beam size. This is basically good behavior for actual use since we do not need to pay much attention to tuning the beam size.

5.6 Ensemble

Figure 4 shows the relation between the number of model ensembles and the BLEU score[5]. As we increased the number of models used, the BLEU scores improved but the impact gradually decreased. We only ensembled eight models for our submissions due to time and computational cost limitations but it would be more effective to ensemble more models.

6 Conclusion

In this paper, we described the systems we submitted to WAT 2017 shared translation tasks. We tried to make a synthetic corpus for an unreliable part of the provided corpus, and found it effectively improves the translation performance. Even though we achieved the highest BLEU score on JIJI corpus subtasks, the human evaluation of our system was worse than we had expected. We suspect that this is due to the noise on the JIJI corpus, so for future work, it would be beneficial to find out how to train the model with the noisy parallel corpus.

---

[5]In this figure, we simply ensembled the models in random order. However, it may be more effective to fix the order in accordance with the BLEU score on the dev set .

References

Dzmitry Bahdanau, Kyunghyun Cho, and Yoshua Bengio. 2015. Neural machine translation by jointly learning to align and translate. In *Proceedings of the 3rd International Conference on Learning Representations (ICLR)*.

Fabien Cromieres, Chenhui Chu, Toshiaki Nakazawa, and Sadao Kurohashi. 2016. Kyoto university participation to WAT 2016. In *Proceedings of the 3rd Workshop on Asian Translation (WAT)*, pages 166–174.

Akiko Eriguchi, Kazuma Hashimoto, and Yoshimasa Tsuruoka. 2016. Character-based decoding in tree-to-sequence attention-based neural machine translation. In *Proceedings of the 3rd Workshop on Asian Translation (WAT)*, pages 175–183.

Minh-Thang Luong and Christopher D. Manning. 2015. Stanford neural machine translation systems for spoken language domain. In *Proceedings of the International Workshop on Spoken Language Translation (IWSLT)*, pages 76–79.

Minh-Thang Luong, Hieu Pham, and Christopher D. Manning. 2015. Effective approaches to attention-based neural machine translation. In *Proceedings of the Conference on Empirical Methods in Natural Language Processing (EMNLP)*.

Toshiaki Nakazawa, Shohei Higashiyama, Chenchen Ding, Hideya Mino, Isao Goto, Graham Neubig, Hideto Kazawa, Yusuke Oda, Jun Harashima, and Sadao Kurohashi. 2017. Overview of the 4th Workshop on Asian Translation. In *Proceedings of the 4th Workshop on Asian Translation (WAT)*.

Toshiaki Nakazawa, Manabu Yaguchi, Kiyotaka Uchimoto, Masao Utiyama, Eiichiro Sumita, Sadao Kurohashi, and Hitoshi Isahara. 2016. ASPEC: Asian scientific paper excerpt corpus. In *Proceedings of the 10th International Conference on Language Resources and Evaluation (LREC)*.

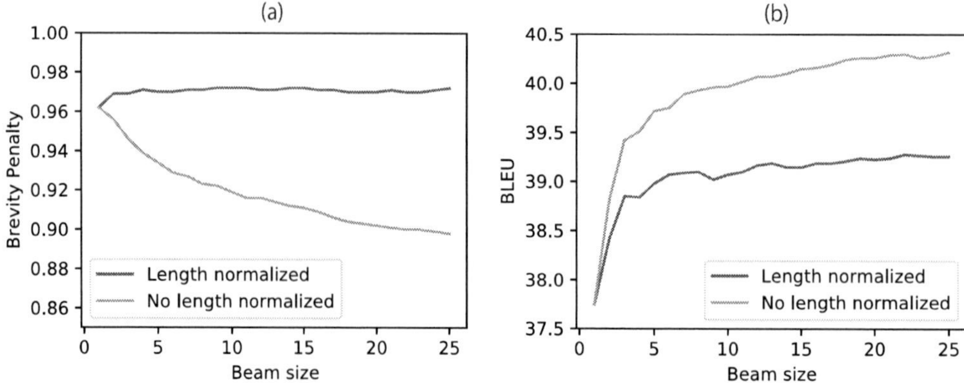

Figure 3: Experimental results on ASPEC En-Ja. (a) Relations between beam size and Brevity Penalty (BP). (b) Relations between beam size and BLEU score without BP. BP penalizes the score if the length of the hypothesis is shorter than the reference. BLEU score gets worse as BP goes down.

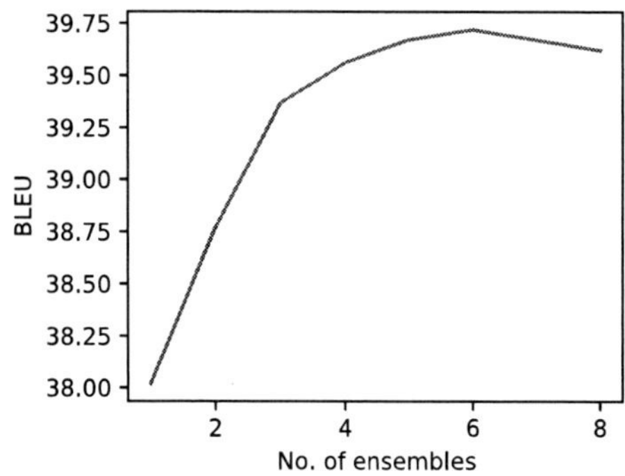

Figure 4: Relation between number of model ensembles and BLEU score on ASPEC En-Ja.

Graham Neubig. 2014. Forest-to-string SMT for asian language translation: NAIST at WAT2014. In *Proceedings of the 1st Workshop on Asian Translation (WAT)*, pages 20–25.

Graham Neubig. 2016. Lexicons and minimum risk training for neural machine translation: NAIST-CMU at WAT2016. In *Proceedings of the 3rd Workshop on Asian Translation (WAT)*, pages 119–125.

Graham Neubig, Yosuke Nakata, and Shinsuke Mori. 2011. Pointwise prediction for robust, adaptable Japanese morphological analysis. In *Proceedings of the 49th Annual Meeting of the Association for Computational Linguistics (ACL)*.

Rico Sennrich, Barry Haddow, and Alexandra Birch. 2016a. Edinburgh neural machine translation systems for WMT 16. In *Proceedings of the 1st Conference on Machine Translation (WMT)*, pages 371–376.

Rico Sennrich, Barry Haddow, and Alexandra Birch. 2016b. Improving neural machine translation models with monolingual data. In *Proceedings of the 54th Annual Meeting of the Association for Computational Linguistics (ACL)*, pages 86–96.

Rico Sennrich, Barry Haddow, and Alexandra Birch. 2016c. Neural Machine Translation of Rare Words with Subword Units. In *Proceedings of the 54th Annual Meeting of the Association for Computational Linguistics (ACL)*, pages 1715–1725.

Seiya Tokui, Kenta Oono, Shohei Hido, and Justin Clayton. 2015. Chainer: a next-generation open source framework for deep learning. In *Proceedings of Workshop on Machine Learning Systems (LearningSys) in The Twenty-ninth Annual Conference on Neural Information Processing Systems (NIPS)*.

Zhaopeng Tu, Yang Liu, Lifeng Shang, Xiaohua Liu, and Hang Li. 2017. Neural machine translation with reconstruction. In *Proceedings of the 31st AAAI Conference on Artificial Intelligence (AAAI)*, pages 3097–3103.

XMU Neural Machine Translation Systems for WAT 2017

Boli Wang, Zhixing Tan, Jinming Hu, Yidong Chen and **Xiaodong Shi**[*]
School of Information Science and Engineering, Xiamen University, Fujian, China
{boliwang, playinf, todtom}@stu.xmu.edu.cn
{ydchen, mandel}@xmu.edu.cn

Abstract

This paper describes the Neural Machine Translation systems of Xiamen University for the shared translation tasks of WAT 2017. Our systems are based on the Encoder-Decoder framework with attention. We participated in three subtasks. We experimented subword segmentation, synthetic training data and model ensembling. Experiments show that all these methods can give substantial improvements.

1 Introduction

Neural Machine Translation (NMT) (Bahdanau et al., 2015; Cho et al., 2014; Sutskever et al., 2014) has achieved great success in recent years and outperforms traditional statistical machine translation (SMT) on various language pairs (Sennrich et al., 2016a; Wu et al., 2016; Zhou et al., 2016). This paper describes the NMT systems of Xiamen University (XMU) for the WAT 2017 evaluation (Nakazawa et al., 2017). We participated in three translation subtasks: JIJI Japanese↔English newswire subtask, IITB Hindi↔English mixed domain subtasks, and Cookpad Japanese↔English recipe subtask.

In all three subtasks, we use our reimplementation of dl4mt-tutorial[1] with minor changes. We use both Byte Pair Encoding (BPE) (Sennrich et al., 2016c) and mixed word/character segmentation (Wu et al., 2016) to achieve open-vocabulary translation. We apply back-translation method (Sennrich et al., 2016b) to make use of monolingual data. We use ensemble (Sutskever et al., 2014) of multiple models to further improve the translation quality.

The remainder of this paper is organized as follows: Section 2 describes our NMT system, including the training details. Section 3 describes the processing of the data. Section 4 describes all experimental features. Section 5 shows the results of our experiments. Finally, we conclude in section 6.

2 Baseline System

Our NMT system is a reimplementation of dl4mt-tutorial model. We import some minor changes and new features such as dropout (Srivastava et al., 2014).

For all three subtasks, we train our models with almost the same settings of hyper-parameters. We use word embeddings of size 620 and hidden layers of size 1000. We use mini-batches of size 128 and adopt Adam (Kingma and Ba, 2015) ($\beta_1 = 0.9$, $\beta_2 = 0.999$ and $\epsilon = 1 \times 10^{-8}$) as the optimizer. The initial learning rate is set to 5×10^{-4}. We gradually halve the learning rate during the training process. As a common way to train RNN models, we clip the norm of gradients to a predefined value 1.0 (Pascanu et al., 2013). We use dropout to avoid over-fitting with a keep probability of 0.8. For ensembling, we train multiple models with different random initialization of parameters and different data shuffling.

In Decoding, we employ beam search strategy with a beam size of 10. We use a modified version of AmuNMT C++ decoder[2] for parallel decoding. We use the same ensembling method as (Sutskever et al., 2014) with uniform weights for different models.

---

[*]Corresponding author.
[1]https://github.com/nyu-dl/
dl4mt-tutorial

[2]https://github.com/emjotde/amunmt

Proceedings of the 4th Workshop on Asian Translation, pages 95–98,
Taipei, Taiwan, November 27, 2017. ©2017 AFNLP

3 Data Processing

We use all training data provided by JIJI, IITB, and Cookpad corpora[3]. For JIJI and Cookpad corpora, Moses[4] tokenizer and truecaser are applied on the English side. On the Japanese side, the full-width ASCII variants are first converted into their half-width form and the `mecab`[5] segmenter is used to segment the sentences. For IITB corpus, we directly use the tokenized data and truecase the English sentences with Moses truecaser.

For all three corpora, we remove duplications and filter out bad sentence pairs according to the word alignment scores obtained by `fast-align` toolkit[6]. For IITB corpus, we also filter out sentence pairs which are not in English-Hindi according to the range of Devanagari characters' Unicode, as well as a language identification toolkit `langid`[7].

4 Experimental Features

4.1 Subword Segmentation

To enable open-vocabulary, we apply subword-based translation approaches. In our preliminary experiments, we found that BPE and mixed word/character segmentation works better than UNK replacement techniques.

In JIJI and IITB tasks, we apply BPE[8] with 20K operations to English sentences and Hindi sentences separately. We use mixed word/character model in the Japanese sides of JIJI task. We keep 20K most frequent Japanese words and split other words into characters. Unlike (Wu et al., 2016), we do not add any extra prefixes or suffixes to the segmented Japanese characters. In the post-processing step, we simply remove all spaces in Japanese sentences.

Similarly, in Cookpad task, we also use BPE segmentation in English side, but with 10K operations, since the vocabulary size is much smaller. Correspondingly, mixed word/character model with a shortlist of 10K words is applied to the Japanese sentences.

4.2 Synthetic Training Data

To utilize the monolingual data in IITB corpus, we employ the back-translation method. We use `srilm`[9] to train a 5-gram KN language model on the monolingual data and select monolingual sentences according to their perplexity. By this way, 2.5M English sentences are selected from IITB's monolingual data. We use one single EN-HI NMT baseline model to translate the selected English monolingual sentences back to Hindi. The synthetic sentence pairs are used to train HI-EN NMT models.

Similarly, we also select 2.5M Hindi monolingual sentences and use one single HI-EN NMT baseline model to translate them back to English. The synthetic sentence pairs are used to train EN-HI NMT models.

In preliminary experiments, we found that training or tuning on the synthetic data alone could not significantly improve the performance of NMT models. Therefore, we mix up the synthetic data with a comparable amount of bilingual pairs over sampled from IITB's parallel data and train NMT models on the mixture data. A similar method is also used in (Sennrich et al., 2017).

5 Results

In this section, we report the automatic evaluation results (word-level BLEU score[10]) and human evaluation results on test sets. We compare our NMT systems with the best SMT systems provided by the organizer.

5.1 Results on JIJI Subtask

System	EN-JA		JA-EN	
	BLEU	Human	BLEU	Human
HPBMT	16.22	10.25	15.67	10.25
Baseline	17.92	– –	15.77	– –
+Ensemble	**20.14**	**11.75**	**17.95**	**20.75**

Table 1: Automatic evaluation and human evaluation results on JIJI subtask.

Table 1 shows the results of JIJI subtask. We apply subword segmentation on the parallel data and train 4 English-Japanese NMT models and 4

---

[3]For Cookpad corpus, we extract parallel pairs from six fields: *step, history, ingredient, title, advice,* and *description.*
[4]`http://statmt.org/moses/`
[5]`https://taku910.github.io/mecab/`
[6]`https://github.com/clab/fast_align`
[7]`https://pypi.python.org/pypi/langid`
[8]`https://github.com/rsennrich/subword-nmt`

[9]`http://www.speech.sri.com/projects/srilm/`
[10]The references and translations are tokenized by Moses English tokenizer, Mecab Japanese word segmenter and Indic Hindi tokenizer respectively.

Japanese-English models. We found that both in EN-JP and JP-EN, one single NMT model can outperform the traditional SMT systems, such as a hierarchical phrase-based model. Ensembles of 4 NMT models can further improve the results by more than +2.0 BLEU scores.

5.2 Results on IITB Subtask

System	EN-HI		HI-EN	
	BLEU	Human	BLEU	Human
PBMT	10.79	– –	10.32	– –
Baseline	13.69	– –	13.30	– –
+Synthetic	19.79	– –	20.61	– –
+Ensemble	**21.39**	**64.50**	**22.44**	**68.25**

Table 2: Automatic evaluation and human evaluation results on IITB subtask.

In IITB subtask, we first train an English-Hindi and a Hindi-English baseline NMT models on the parallel data with subword segmentation. Then we select monolingual sentences and synthesize larger training data using the backward baseline NMT models. As shown in Table 2, both in EN-HI and HI-EN, training on synthetic data is effective to improve the BLEU score (more than +6.0). When ensembling 4 models, we further gain more than +1.6 BLEU scores.

5.3 Results on Cookpad Subtask

In Cookpad subtask, we hope one single NMT model has the robustness to translate different types of text. So we directly train NMT models on all training data without any extra data separation or labelling. And we use the same models for four test sets. The results are shown in Table 3. Our single NMT baselines beat phrase-based SMTs in almost all test sets, except for JA-EN *ingredient*. When ensembling 4 models, we further gain +1.3 to +3.1 BLEU scores in all test sets and outperform SMTs by +2.2 to +5.8 BLEU scores. For human evaluation results, we found that NMT models achieve good results in *title* and *step* sets, but not in *ingredient* sets. It's reasonable because NMT models are good at fluency, instead of adequacy. And for *title* and *step*, human readers usually focus on fluency. But for *ingredient*, human readers care more about adequacy.

System	EN-JA		JA-EN	
	BLEU	Human	BLEU	Human
all				
PBMT	19.10	– –	23.87	– –
Baseline	22.47	– –	27.04	– –
+Ensemble	**24.44**	– –	**28.83**	– –
title				
PBMT	16.57	– –	9.72	– –
Baseline	16.90	– –	14.25	– –
+Ensemble	**18.78**	**23.75**	**15.57**	**10.25**
step				
PBMT	18.53	– –	22.84	– –
Baseline	22.01	– –	26.31	– –
+Ensemble	**24.00**	**45.50**	**28.03**	**40.50**
ingredient				
PBMT	29.60	– –	44.42	– –
Baseline	30.90	– –	43.89	– –
+Ensemble	**33.19**	**-3.75**	**46.98**	**3.50**

Table 3: Automatic evaluation and human evaluation results on Cookpad subtask.

6 Conclusion

We describe XMU's neural machine translation systems for the WAT 2017 shared translation tasks. Our models perform quite well and proved to be effective enough to outperform traditional SMT systems in all tasks, even with limited training data. Experiments also show the effectiveness of all features we used, including subword segmentation, synthetic training data, and multi-model ensemble.

Acknowledgments

This work was supported by the Natural Science Foundation of China (Grant No. 61573294), the Ph.D. Programs Foundation of Ministry of Education of China (Grant No. 20130121110040), the Foundation of the State Language Commission of China (Grant No. WT135-10) and the National High-Tech R&D Program of China (Grant No. 2012BAH14F03).

References

Dzmitry Bahdanau, KyungHyun Cho, and Yoshua Bengio. 2015. Neural machine translation by jointly learning to align and translate. In *Proceedings of ICLR*.

Kyunghyun Cho, Bart van Merrienboer, Caglar Gulcehre, Dzmitry Bahdanau, Fethi Bougares, Holger

Schwenk, and Yoshua Bengio. 2014. Learning phrase representations using rnn encoder–decoder for statistical machine translation. In *Proceedings of EMNLP*, pages 1724–1734.

Diederik Kingma and Jimmy Ba. 2015. Adam: A method for stochastic optimization. In *Proceedings of ICLR*.

Toshiaki Nakazawa, Shohei Higashiyama, Chenchen Ding, Hideya Mino, Isao Goto, Graham Neubig, Hideto Kazawa, Yusuke Oda, Jun Harashima, and Sadao Kurohashi. 2017. Overview of the 4th Workshop on Asian Translation. In *Proceedings of the 4th Workshop on Asian Translation (WAT2017)*, Taipei, Taiwan.

Razvan Pascanu, Tomas Mikolov, and Yoshua Bengio. 2013. On the difficulty of training recurrent neural networks. In *Proceedings of ICML*, pages 1310–1318.

Rico Sennrich, Alexandra Birch, Anna Currey, Ulrich Germann, Barry Haddow, Kenneth Heafield, Antonio Valerio Miceli Barone, and Philip Williams. 2017. The University of Edinburgh's Neural MT Systems for WMT17. *arXiv preprint arXiv:1708.00726*.

Rico Sennrich, Barry Haddow, and Alexandra Birch. 2016a. Edinburgh neural machine translation systems for wmt 16. *arXiv preprint arXiv:1606.02891*.

Rico Sennrich, Barry Haddow, and Alexandra Birch. 2016b. Improving neural machine translation models with monolingual data. In *Proceddings of ACL*, pages 86–96.

Rico Sennrich, Barry Haddow, and Alexandra Birch. 2016c. Neural machine translation of rare words with subword units. In *Proceedings of ACL*, pages 1715–1725.

Nitish Srivastava, Geoffrey Hinton, Alex Krizhevsky, Ilya Sutskever, and Ruslan Salakhutdinov. 2014. Dropout: A simple way to prevent neural networks from overfitting. *The Journal of Machine Learning Research*, 15(1):1929–1958.

Ilya Sutskever, Oriol Vinyals, and Quoc V Le. 2014. Sequence to sequence learning with neural networks. In *Advances in neural information processing systems*, pages 3104–3112.

Yonghui Wu, Mike Schuster, Zhifeng Chen, Quoc V Le, Mohammad Norouzi, Wolfgang Macherey, Maxim Krikun, Yuan Cao, Qin Gao, Klaus Macherey, et al. 2016. Google's neural machine translation system: Bridging the gap between human and machine translation. *arXiv preprint arXiv:1609.08144*.

Jie Zhou, Ying Cao, Xuguang Wang, Peng Li, and Wei Xu. 2016. Deep recurrent models with fast-forward connections for neural machine translation. *Transactions of the Association for Computational Linguistics*, 4:371–383.

A Bag of Useful Tricks for Practical Neural Machine Translation: Embedding Layer Initialization and Large Batch Size

Masato Neishi[*] and **Jin Sakuma**[*] and **Satoshi Tohda**[*] and **Shonosuke Ishiwatari**
The University of Tokyo
{neishi, jsakuma, tohda, ishiwatari}@tkl.iis.u-tokyo.ac.jp

Naoki Yoshinaga and **Masashi Toyoda**
Institute of Industrial Science, the University of Tokyo
{ynaga, toyoda}@iis.u-tokyo.ac.jp

Abstract

In this paper, we describe the team UT-IIS's system and results for the WAT 2017 translation tasks. We further investigated several tricks including a novel technique for initializing embedding layers using only the parallel corpus, which increased the BLEU score by 1.28, found a practical large batch size of 256, and gained insights regarding hyperparameter settings. Ultimately, our system obtained a better result than the state-of-the-art system of WAT 2016. Our code is available on https://github.com/nem6ishi/wat17.

1 Introduction

The advent of neural networks in machine translation has contributed greatly to the translation quality. Since proposed in (Cho et al., 2014; Sutskever et al., 2014), the sequence-to-sequence (SEQ2SEQ) model has been achieving the state-of-the-art performance when combined with the attention mechanism (Bahdanau et al., 2015). Many studies have focused on modifying the SEQ2SEQ network structure, including modifying the encoder (Eriguchi et al., 2016; Gehring et al., 2017; Li et al., 2017; Chen et al., 2017), or the decoder (Ishiwatari et al., 2017; Eriguchi et al., 2017; Aharoni and Goldberg, 2017; Wu et al., 2017).

While these network structure modifications have been found to improve the translation quality, many systems, including the best system from WAT 2016 (Cromieres et al., 2016), still depend on the vanilla SEQ2SEQ model, the model with the attention mechanism. Denkowski and Neubig (2017) confirmed the large impact of common techniques such as training algorithms, subwords (Sennrich et al., 2016) and model ensem-

bles upon this vanilla SEQ2SEQ model. This suggests that there may be some unexplored tricks we may apply to the vanilla model to significantly improve the translation quality.

This paper describes the system that we have built for the ASPEC (Nakazawa et al., 2016) en-ja translation subtask for WAT 2017 (Nakazawa et al., 2017), which incorporates a novel trick, embedding layer initialization. This trick improves upon the vanilla SEQ2SEQ model by initializing the word embedding layers of both the encoder and the decoder with word embeddings that are pretrained on the parallel corpus. Our system involves generating multiple models using SEQ2SEQ with embedding layer initialization, exhaustively searching for a combination of models with the highest ensemble score, and finally, conducting a beam search on the best ensemble. We achieved a BLEU score of 38.93 on the ASPEC en-ja translation task as the team UT-IIS, which outperforms the state-of-the-art system of WAT 2016.

Furthermore, we have provided insight on NMT by detailing experiments on the tricks used in our system. This includes testing embedding layer initialization with multiple word embedding methods (§ 5.3.1), a thorough investigation of the point where increasing the batch size ceases to be beneficial (§ 5.3.2), finding the optimal learning rate (§ 5.3.3), and investigating the relation between the number of models used in the ensemble and translation performance (§ 5.3.4). We believe that these findings, particularly regarding embedding layer initialization and practical batch size, can serve as useful tricks for future neural machine translation (NMT) systems.

The structure of this paper is as follows. In § 2, we review related work, and in § 3, we present an overview of NMT. We describe our system in § 4 and show the official evaluation result and further investigations in § 5. We conclude our work in § 6.

---

[*]Authors contributed equally.

99

2   Related Work

In this section, we will survey existing techniques used in NMT systems. We first focus on pretraining, for which we have proposed a new method, and then batch size, of which we have confirmed the effect.

2.1   Pretraining

Training deep neural networks with a relatively small amount of training data risks creating a model that performs poorly. One technique used to minimize this drawback is pretraining of the model (Hinton et al., 2006; Bengio et al., 2007), which initializes (part of) the parameters of the model using parameters of another model.

Pretraining has led to promising results in NLP tasks using SEQ2SEQ models. In languages with a small amount of supervised data, it has been found that NMT results can be improved by transferring parameters from a high-resource language pair to a low-resource one (Zoph et al., 2016). Gülçehre et al. (2015) proposed a method using a combination of the output probabilities of a language model trained on large monolingual corpora and a SEQ2SEQ NMT model, which are both trained separately. Venugopalan et al. (2016) studied different types of systems combined with a language model under the video description generation task and also introduced a method to initialize the embedding layer and the RNN layer of the decoder of the SEQ2SEQ based model with pretrained parameters of the language model. They additionally proposed a method to initialize the embedding layer of the decoder with pretrained GloVe (Pennington et al., 2014) embeddings. Ramachandran et al. (2017) initializes both the encoder and decoder of the SEQ2SEQ model with attention using language models trained on monolingual, unlabeled corpus of the source and target domains, respectively. This led to a significant improvement over the baseline.

The aforementioned studies, however, demand a large computational cost for pretraining a complex language model on large external data. Although Ramachandran et al. (2017) has provided a comparison of a system initialized using a language model trained only on the parallel corpus (in addition to their proposed method) to a baseline system without initialization, the translation performance did not improve but rather degraded with this setting.

Our work investigates the effect of initializing only the embedding layer using embeddings pretrained at low cost from the parallel corpus. We will later confirm that this initialization leads to a BLEU score increase of 1.28 (§ 5.3.1).

2.2   Batch Size

Batch size is the number of data points in a mini-batch, which is a representative portion of the training data from which the gradient is calculated at each step in the stochastic gradient descent (SGD) optimizer (or its variants). In general, the batch size chosen for deep neural networks ranges from 32 to 512. It is known that a batch size that is too large leads to performance degradation in deep neural networks (Keskar et al., 2017).

Recent studies in NMT have used values such as 64 (Rush et al., 2015) or 128 (Wu et al., 2016). While Britz et al. (2017) conducted a thorough investigation of hyperparameters in NMT, they fixed batch size to 128. The specific effect of batch size on NMT was studied by Morishita et al. (2017), who found that, for batch sizes of 8 to 64, a larger batch size has a positive impact on model performance.

In this study, we seek to empirically clarify the point where increasing the batch size no longer improves NMT performance. Our work expands upon Morishita et al. (2017) and further investigates how NMT performance varies with larger batch sizes, up to 512.

3   The Vanilla SEQ2SEQ Model

The SEQ2SEQ (or encoder-decoder) model have been achieving the state-of-the-art in machine translation (Kalchbrenner and Blunsom, 2013; Sutskever et al., 2014; Cho et al., 2014). Bahdanau et al. (2015) further improved this model by proposing the attention mechanism.

This neural machine translation (NMT) approach involves an RNN-based encoder that converts the source sentence into vector representations which are then converted into the output sentence by an RNN-based decoder.

While there are several variations in encoder implementation, including long-short term memory (LSTM) (Hochreiter and Schmidhuber, 1997), gated recurrent unit (GRU) (Cho et al., 2014), and convolutional neural network (CNN) (Gehring et al., 2017), our system implements a two-layer bidirectional LSTM for the encoder. A bidirec-

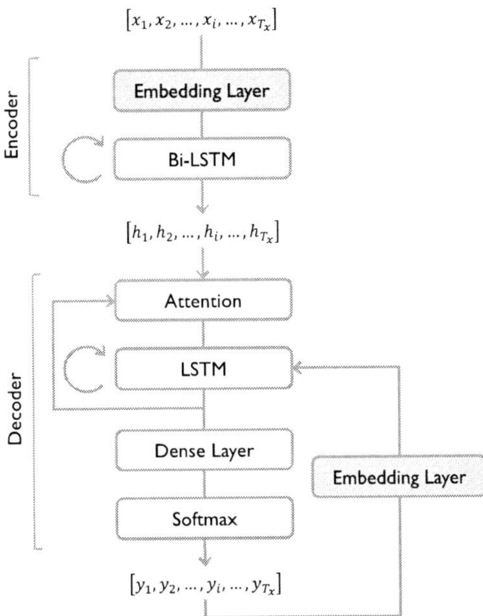

$$[x_1, x_2, ..., x_i, ..., x_{T_x}]$$

$$[h_1, h_2, ..., h_i, ..., h_{T_x}]$$

$$[y_1, y_2, ..., y_i, ..., y_{T_x}]$$

Figure 1: Basic structure of our system.

tional LSTM consists of a forward LSTM and a backward LSTM that move from left to right and right to left respectively to update their hidden states. The hidden states of the last layer are the outputs of the encoder which is then fed into the decoder.

Given the encoder output, the decoder generates an output sequence. Following Sutskever et al. (2014) and Bahdanau et al. (2015), we decided to use a multi-layer LSTM decoder with an attention mechanism. At each step, an attention mechanism computes a weighted average of vectors in the encoder output, called an attention context vector. A weight of a hidden state vector is computed using both itself and the hidden state of the decoder at that step. In addition to the attention context vector, the decoder also receives an embedding vector of the previous output token in order to retain the information of tokens it has already generated. These two vectors, an attention context vector and an embedding vector of the previous output token, are concatenated and given to the decoder LSTM, which then generates tokens and updates its state.

4 System Description

Our system implemented two tricks on a vanilla SEQ2SEQ model implemented by Google (Britz

et al., 2017)[1] on Tensorflow[2] (ver. 1.0). The tricks are embedding layer initialization (§ 4.2) and batch size expansion (§ 4.3).

In what follows, we explain our system in detail. The basic structure of our system is depicted in Figure 1. The configuration and the default parameters used in our experiments are described in § 5.1 and in Appendix.

4.1 Preprocessing

As for the preprocessing, we basically followed the description of WAT 2017 Baseline Systems Data preparation.[3] We used scripts included in Moses toolkit[4] (ver. 2.2.1) (Koehn et al., 2007) for English tokenization and truecasing, and KyTea[5] (ver. 0.4.2) (Neubig et al., 2011) for Japanese segmentations.

After the above basic preprocessing, we applied SentencePiece,[6] which is an unsupervised text tokenizer and detokenizer, to the corpus. SentencePiece decides token boundaries using raw sentences (a white space is treated as a character) based on statistical models like character n-grams. This alleviates the problem of unknown tokens in a similar manner as using subword units. For this model, we picked unigram which is a default setting in the given implementation.

4.2 Embedding Layer Initialization

Because of the nature of the neural network model, each layer in the NMT model can only handle fixed-length inputs and outputs. Since our model is an end-to-end NMT model, both the first encoder layer and the decoder layer which feeds the previous output into the decoder accepts a vocabulary-size-length one-hot vector. In this regard, both layers are embedding layers which convert a one-hot vector into a word embedding vector.

Usually, all the layers, including embedding layers, are initialized randomly and trained in the exact same way. We attempted pretraining of these embedding layers, initializing them with word embeddings from an unsupervised neural language model trained on the training datasets in the source

---

[1] https://google.github.io/seq2seq/
[2] https://www.tensorflow.org/
[3] http://lotus.kuee.kyoto-u.ac.jp/WAT/WAT2017/baseline/dataPreparationJE.html
[4] http://www.statmt.org/moses/
[5] http://www.phontron.com/kytea/
[6] https://github.com/google/sentencepiece

and target languages. It is expected that these word embeddings improve the translation performance as well as speeding up convergence.

In addition to the original vocabulary, there are three special tokens in our system, "SEQUENCE_START," "SEQUENCE_END," and "UNK." The embeddings for the first two tokens were trained by adding them into the training dataset before the pretraining procedure. On the other hand, the embedding for "UNK" was generated by averaging all the out-of-vocabulary token embeddings.

Our proposed embedding layer initialization is a quick and simple trick, but effective on NMT systems (§ 5.3.1).

4.3 Using Large Batch Size

Gradient descent (GD) computes a gradient of parameters based on the entire dataset to update the parameters at each step. While this gives the most accurate gradient, it is computationally inefficient, as all data points need to be evaluated.

To overcome this issue, stochastic gradient descent (SGD) and its variants computes a gradient using a small portion of the dataset, called a mini-batch. We may consider the gradient computed in SGD as an expectation of the gradient which is inaccurate. However, as SGD is faster than GD, we can execute more steps which leads to better training in the same amount of time.

The accuracy of a gradient at each step depends on batch size, the number of samples in a mini-batch. A larger batch size leads to a more accurate gradient. The impact of large batch size on the translation quality will be investigated in § 5.3.2, in which we found that large batch size improves the translation significantly up to 256.

4.4 Ensemble

Ensemble of models is a widely used technique that improves the translation quality. After training several models, the decoders' outputs are combined to get the ensemble output. The effectiveness of ensemble was investigated in Denkowski and Neubig (2017).

For our system, we implemented a simple averaging ensemble. Let N be the number of models to ensemble, $X = \{x_1, x_2, \cdots, x_{T_x}\}$ and $Y = \{y_1, y_2, \cdots, y_{T_y}\}$ be the source and target sequences respectively, and $p_n(w|X, Y_{:j-1})$ be the probability of word w of the nth model at step j, where $Y_{:j-1}$ denotes the first $j-1$ tokens in the

sequence Y. Then, the probability of word w is determined by taking the average of all models.

$$p(w|X, Y_{:j-1}) = \frac{1}{N} \sum_{n=1}^{N} p_n(w|X, Y_{:j-1})$$

Each model is independently trained in the training phase and the decoders' outputs are combined in the prediction phase. This simple technique gave us a significant BLEU score boost (§ 5.3.4).

4.5 Beam Search

Another technique to improve the translation quality is a beam search. The objective of translation system is

$$\hat{Y} = \arg\max_{Y \in \mathcal{Y}} p(Y|X)$$

where $\mathcal{Y}$ is the set of all possible translations and X is the input sequence. However, $\mathcal{Y}$ is such a huge set that computing $p(Y|X)$ for all $Y \in \mathcal{Y}$ is not realistic. A simple solution to this problem is to decide y_j to be

$$y_j = \arg\max_{w \in V} p(w|X, Y_{:j-1}).$$

This algorithm is called a greedy search. A greedy search algorithm is fast but may miss the best output sequence if the early portion of the sequence has a low probability.

The beam search algorithm addresses this issue by keeping multiple possible hypotheses, which are incomplete output sequences (Boulanger-Lewandowski et al., 2013). At each step, the top l hypotheses with the highest scores are kept for the next step. When every hypothesis terminates with an EOS token, the hypothesis with the highest score is chosen as the final result.

The beam search algorithm favors shorter sequences on average because a longer sequence tends to have a lower probability, $p(Y|X)$.

To overcome this problem, Wu et al. (2017) proposed a length penalty which gives advantages to longer sentences. With a length penalty, the score of a sequence Y given a source sequence X is computed by

$$score(Y|X) = \frac{\log(P(Y|X))}{lp(Y)}$$

$$lp(Y) = \frac{(5 + |Y|)^\alpha}{(5 + 1)^\alpha}$$

where α is a hyperparameter.

	Train		Dev		Test	
	en	ja	en	ja	en	ja
# sentences	1,783,817		1790		1812	
Ave. # tokens	31.08	33.13	31.06	34.58	30.69	34.03

Table 1: Details of corpus after preprocessing.

5 Evaluation

In this section, we report the default configuration of our system (§ 5.1) and the official evaluation result of our system for ASPEC English to Japanese translation subtask (§ 5.2). Furthermore, we report several other experiments that aim to show the effects of our tricks (§ 5.3).

5.1 Setup

The following settings are used as our default configuration in the experiments and the final system, unless otherwise noted. We use a two-layer bidirectional LSTM with dropout on input with $p = 0.8$ for the encoder, and a four-layer LSTM with the same dropout settings for the decoder. The number of units in hidden layers and the embedding dimension are set to 512. Adam (Kingma and Ba, 2015) is used for the optimizer, with a learning rate of 0.0001 and batch size is set to 256.

The vocabulary size after SentencePiece preprocessing is 16,000. The number of sentences and the average number of tokens after preprocessing in a single sentence are shown in Table 1.

As the default embedding method for embedding layer initializaion, we use Continuous Bag of Words (CBOW) (Mikolov et al., 2013) with window size of 5. We use word2vec (ver. 1.0)[7] with default parameters, except for the embedding dimension which was changed to 512. We train the word embeddings using only the preprocessed training dataset, in which both languages are concatenated to share the source and target vocabulary. All other layers were initialized randomly using uniform distribution.

We train the model for 200,000 steps, and at every 2000 steps during training, the current model is saved as a "checkpoint." When the training is done, all the checkpoints are evaluated using a greedy search algorithm on the development corpus. Only the checkpoint with the highest BLEU score is used for all of the following experiments and our final translation system. If the checkpoint with the highest BLEU score is at or near 200,000

---

[7]https://github.com/svn2github/
word2vec

ID	Hyperparameters			Dev		Test	
	batch size	hidden layer	learning rate	greedy	beam	greedy	beam
1	256	256	0.0001	34.22	35.65	34.40	35.54
2	256	384	0.0001	**35.32**	**36.74**	34.85	36.28
3	256	512	0.0001	35.22	36.48	34.81	36.29
4	256	512	0.0002	35.19	36.43	34.29	35.60
5	256	512	0.0005	34.40	36.08	34.19	35.57
6	256	768	0.0001	34.78	36.37	34.70	35.92
7	256	768	0.0002	34.97	36.46	**34.88**	**36.43**
8*	512	512	0.0001	34.62	36.61	34.68	36.35
9*	512	768	0.0001	34.31	36.42	34.28	35.97
10*	800	512	0.0001	30.05	33.73	29.35	33.36
Average				34.31	36.10	34.04	35.73
Best ensemble							
(2, 3, 4, 5, 6, 8, 9, 10)				38.00	39.03	37.40	38.93

Table 2: List of models trained for use in ensemble (* 200k steps unattained due to time constraints).

steps (we define this as larger than 190,000 steps), we regard this model as not having converged, and will be identified as such in the results.

For all evaluations, KyTea segmentation was used to compute the BLEU score. For a prediction with the beam search algorithm, we used beam width of 128 except in our final system, which we used 256. For length penalty, we choose $\alpha = 1$ after parameter turning. Detailed settings are provided in the Appendix.

5.2 Official Evaluation Result

This section briefly explains how we built our final system and its result for the ASPEC English to Japanese translation subtask. We trained ten models with different hyperparameters which are listed in Table 2. For these models, we evaluated every possible ensemble combination using greedy search on the development corpus.[8] We chose the ensemble combination with the highest BLEU score to make prediction on the test corpus using a beam search algorithm. Consequently, we chose an ensemble of eight models, which achieved a BLEU score of 38.93 and an official human evaluation score of 68.000.

5.3 Further Investigations

In addition to the official evaluation, we conducted several other experiments. This section reports results and analyses of these experiments. We first confirm the impact of the embedding layer initialization, and then compare several word embedding methods (§ 5.3.1). Next, we investigate the

---

[8]Due to GPU memory limitations, three combinations are not evaluated: (2, 3, 4, 5, 6, 7, 8, 9, 10), (1, 3, 4, 5, 6, 7, 8, 9, 10), and (1, 2, 3, 4, 5, 6, 7, 8, 9, 10).

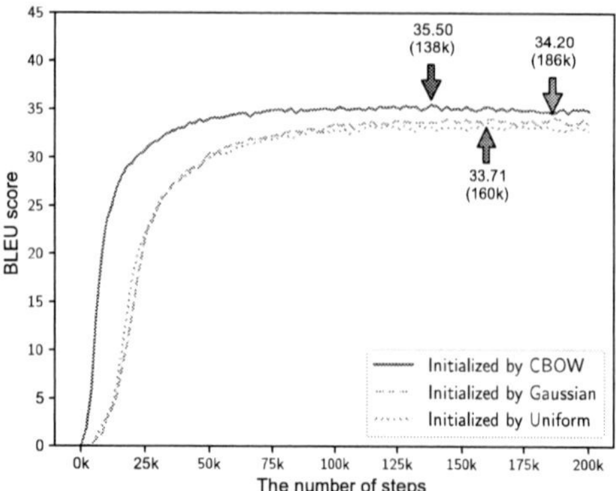

Figure 2: Training curve for models with different initialization methods. Arrows indicate the steps that achieved the best BLEU score on development data.

Initialization	Window	Greedy	Beam	Δ
Random (Gaussian)	-	34.20	35.57	-
Random (Uniform)	-	33.71	35.02	−0.55
CBOW	2	34.97	36.38	+0.81
	5	**35.50**	**36.85**	+1.28
	10	35.25	36.57	+1.00
Skip-gram	2	34.17	35.90	+0.33
	5	34.44	36.04	+0.47
	10	34.38	36.00	+0.43
SI-Skip-gram	2	34.04	35.16	−0.41
	5	34.44	35.91	+0.34
	10	34.33	35.69	+0.12
GloVe	2	34.50	36.01	+0.44
	5	34.58	35.86	+0.29
	10	33.98	35.39	−0.18
	15	34.35	36.00	+0.43

Table 3: Translation performance by embedding methods and window size. Evaluation is done on development dataset.

effect of batch size (§ 5.3.2). We then conduct experiments to discover the optimal learning rate when our initialization trick is employed (§ 5.3.3). Lastly, we examine the relation between the number of models used in the ensemble and translation performance (§ 5.3.4).

5.3.1 Impact of Embedding Layer Initialization

We first investigated the impact of our embedding layer initialization. The embeddings for the initialization are trained only on the training dataset of ASPEC using word2vec with CBOW and window size of 5. The question here is whether or not initialization with those word embeddings which were trained without any external data, by a task-independent, unsupervised method, improves the NMT model. In these experiments, the greedy search algorithm was used in order to obtain the training curve, as there are too many checkpoints to be evaluated by a beam search.

Figure 2 shows the training curve of three models, one initialized using CBOW, and the rest initialized randomly, with one using a Gaussian distribution, and the other a uniform distribution. The best score of the model with the CBOW initialization is 35.50 at step 138,000, and the best score of the model with random initialization is 34.20 with the Gaussian distribution at step 186,000. We observed that embedding layer initialization improves both the translation performance and the convergence time, increasing the former and decreasing the latter. Along with the following batch

size experiment in § 5.3.2, the same experiment was done (using the greedy search algorithm) with batch sizes of 32, 64, 128, and 512, and this effect was observed across all batch sizes.

The results indicate that embedding layer initialization works in our NMT model, even though the embeddings are generated by CBOW, which is a totally task-irrelevant method.

Since we confirmed the effectiveness of our embedding layer initialization, we then investigate the effect of different embedding methods on translation performance. There are various methods other than CBOW to create word embeddings. Mikolov et al. (2013) proposed Skip-gram. Pennington et al. (2014) proposed another method called GloVe. Bojanowski et al. (2017) proposed Subword Information Skip-gram (SI-Skip-gram) that utilizes morphological information by including character n-grams of words in the model.

These methods train word embeddings using windows that obtain co-occurrences of neighboring words. It is known that a smaller window size leads to more syntactic embeddings and a larger one leads to more semantic embeddings (Lin and Wu, 2009; Levy and Goldberg, 2014).

The question is: which embedding method and window size yield the best results for the translation task when used to initialize the embedding layer? To answer this question, we trained 13 models using CBOW, Skip-gram, Subword Information Skip-gram (SI-Skip-gram), and GloVe, with window sizes of 2, 5, and 10, as well as a window size of 15 with GloVe, as this was its default value. For implementations of CBOW and Skip-

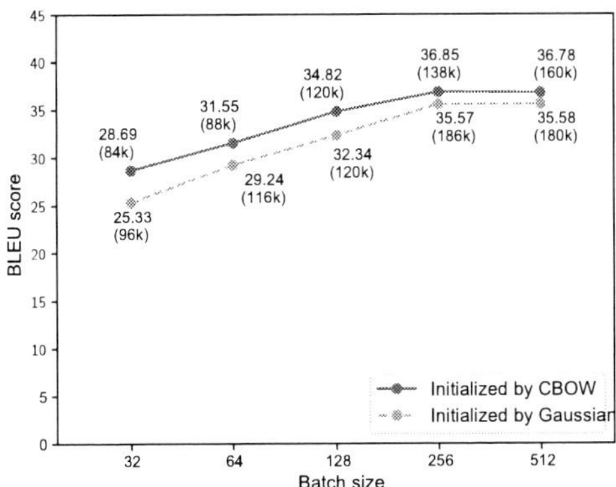

Figure 3: Translation performance by initialization and batch size. The values in the parentheses indicate the step that resulted in the best BLEU score on development data.

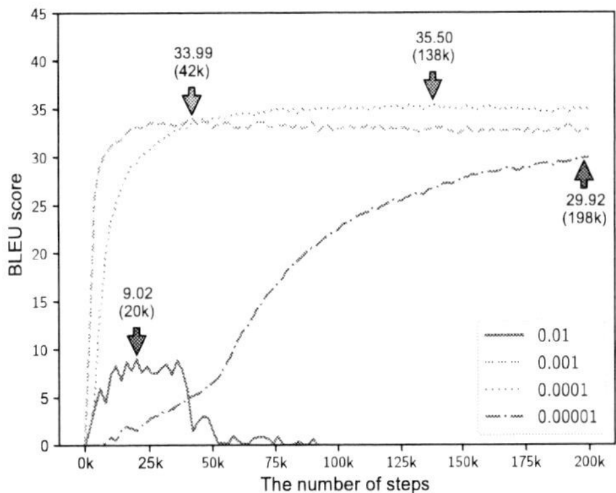

Figure 4: Training curve for different learning rates. Arrows indicate the steps that achieved the best BLEU score on development data.

gram, we used word2vec (ver. 1.0). For GloVe and SI-Skip-gram, we used GloVe (ver 1.2)[9] and fasttext (ver. 1.0),[10] respectively.

The results are shown in Table 3. Most of the embedding methods outperformed random initialization by Gaussian distribution. This confirms the effectiveness of embedding layer initialization. Among those embedding methods, CBOW yields the best BLEU score of 35.50 for greedy search and 36.85 for beam search. For the window sizes, we found that each method has a different window size that yields the best result. Given this result, we decided to use CBOW with window size of 5 as our default setting.

5.3.2 Impact of Large Batch Size

We used the mini-batch method to train the network. While Morishita et al. (2017) investigated the effect of large batch size up to 64, it is unclear how an even larger batch size will impact translation performance. To evaluate this, we conducted experiments with different batch sizes.

Figure 3 confirms our idea and shows that, up until 256,[11] a larger batch size results in a better BLEU score, indicating that batch size has a significant impact on translation performance. The

significance of the results are surprising, given the trick's simplicity.

When using this trick in NMT systems, it is important to recognize the tradeoff between translation performance and the memory and time required. In terms of the required memory, we were able to conduct the experiments up to a batch size of 256 on a server with 12GB of GPU memory, but a server with 24GB of GPU memory was required for experiments with a batch size of 512. Also, when we compared the time required to reach 200,000 steps when trained with batch sizes of 128 and 256, which were both trained on the same server, the larger batch size took 1.57 times as much time. The steps needed to reach the maximum BLEU score on development set became larger as the batch size increases, which indicates slower convergence with the larger batch size.

With the above factors taken into consideration, a batch size of 256 is a practical choice, and we can also expect an additive effect in translation quality by the use of CBOW initialization.

5.3.3 Impact of Learning Rate

An improperly large learning rate changes the values of each layers in a neural network drastically. Since we hypothesize that the pretrained embeddings have well-adjusted values, a drastic change in these values would spoil the effect of embedding layer initialization. To confirm this hypothesis, we compared four different learning rates of [0.01, 0.001, 0.0001, 0.00001] with the same configuration including initialization method.

Figure 4 shows the training curve of these four

---

[9]https://github.com/stanfordnlp/GloVe

[10]https://github.com/facebookresearch/fastText

[11]Initialized randomly by uniform distribution, the models achieved BLEU scores of 35.02 and 36.15 for batch sizes 256 and 512 respectively, and are seemingly still improving. However, we think this is within fluctuation range caused by random initialization.

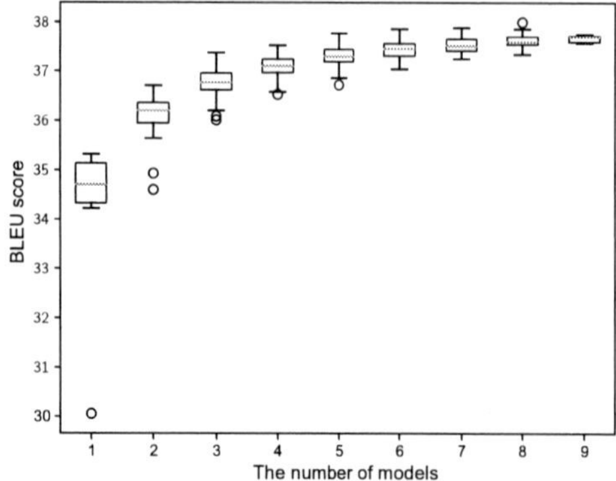

Figure 5: Performance of ensemble. As a beam search is costly, a greedy search was used.

different models. A learning rate of 0.01 performed abysmally, not only in terms of the worst best score but also in terms of the unstable training curve. The neural network could not be successfully trained at this learning rate. With the learning rate less than or equal to 0.001, the training curve becomes stable and the best score marks a reasonable value. A learning rate of 0.001 resulted in the best score of 33.99 at step 42,000, which is good and fast enough. As expected, a learning rate of 0.0001 raised the best score to 35.50 at step 138,000, which is 1.51 higher than the score with a learning rate of 0.001, but at a much later step. The best score for learning rate of 0.00001 was 29.92 at step 198,000, but the model did not converge.

It is difficult to confirm our hypothesis that smaller learning rate is always better for keeping the well-adjusted values by the initialization, with the above results. However, considering the fact that the time spent on training is limited, we believe 0.0001 to be the most practical learning rate among them, because it marked a score almost 1.0 higher than the second best one.

5.3.4 Ensemble Strategy

It is known that ensemble technique improves translation (Denkowski and Neubig, 2017). The intuition is that the larger the number of models is, the better the translation will be. To test this hypothesis, we exhaustively compared the results of ensembles with a different number of models.

The ten models from Table 2 were used for this experiment. We evaluated ensembles of all possible combinations. As mentioned in the footnote in § 5.2, three combinations are omitted because of the memory limitation, which yielded 1,020 combinations in total.

The result is reported in Figure 5. We can see the positive correlation between number of models used in the ensemble and the performance. However, as the number of models gets bigger, the effect of adding models gets smaller; the difference between a single model and two model ensemble is significant, but the difference between an eight model ensemble and a nine model ensemble is not so evident.

6 Conclusion

We have described the translation system, experiments, and the results of the team UT-IIS. As for the result of our system on the ASPEC En-Ja task, we were able to achieve a BLEU score of 38.93, which is higher than the score for the state-of-the-art system of WAT 2016. This reflects the effectiveness of our word embedding layer initialization technique, when combined with model ensemble and a beam search on the vanilla SEQ2SEQ model. Our findings are as follows:

- Embedding layer initialization technique using only the parallel corpus improves translation quality (§ 5.3.1).

- Embedding layer initialization trick with CBOW works the best (§ 5.3.1).

- Benefits of a larger batch size reached saturation at 256, and we believe this to be the practical setting (§ 5.3.2).

- A learning rate of 0.0001 is both good and fast enough to be practical with the initialization trick (§ 5.3.3).

- Ensemble of many models improves translation quality significantly (§ 5.3.4).

We believe that the embedding layer initialization technique, as well as the insights gained from our experiments, will contribute to the improvement of NMT when used in combination with other novel techniques.

We have published our code on `https://github.com/nem6ishi/wat17`.

Acknowledgements This work was partially supported by JSPS KAKENHI Grant Number 16K16109 and 16H02905.

model	AttentionSeq2Seq
model_params	
attention.class	seq2seq.decoders.attention.AttentionLayerBahdanau
attention.params	
num_units	512
bridge.class	seq2seq.models.bridges.ZeroBridge
embedding.dim	512
encoder.class	seq2seq.encoders.BidirectionalRNNEncoder
encoder.params	
rnn_cell	
cell_class	LSTMCell
cell_params	
num_units	512
dropout_input_keep_prob	0.8
dropout_output_keep_prob	1.0
num_layers	2
decoder.class	seq2seq.decoders.AttentionDecoder
decoder.params	
rnn_cell	
cell_class	LSTMCell
cell_params	
num_units	512
dropout_input_keep_prob	0.8
dropout_output_keep_prob	1.0
num_layers	4
optimizer.name	Adam
optimizer.params	
epsilon	0.0000008
optimizer.learning_rate	0.0001
source.max_seq_len	50
source.reverse	false
target.max_seq_len	50

Table 4: Configuration of seq2seq model.

A   Hyperparameters and configuration

Table 4 lists the default hyperparameters and configuration for our system, which is built based on Google's implementation of the SEQ2SEQ model (Britz et al., 2017).

References

Roee Aharoni and Yoav Goldberg. 2017. Towards string-to-tree neural machine translation. In *Proceedings of the 55th Annual Meeting of the Association for Computational Linguistics (ACL), Short Papers*, pages 132–140.

Dzmitry Bahdanau, Kyunghyun Cho, and Yoshua Bengio. 2015. Neural machine translation by jointly learning to align and translate. In *Proceedings of the Third International Conference on Learning Representations (ICLR)*.

Yoshua Bengio, Pascal Lamblin, Dan Popovici, and Hugo Larochelle. 2007. Greedy layer-wise training of deep networks. In *Advances in Neural Information Processing Systems (NIPS) 19*, pages 153–160.

Piotr Bojanowski, Edouard Grave, Armand Joulin, and Tomas Mikolov. 2017. Enriching word vectors with subword information. *Transactions of the Association of Computational Linguistics*, 5:135–146.

Nicolas Boulanger-Lewandowski, Yoshua Bengio, and Pascal Vincent. 2013. Audio chord recognition with recurrent neural networks. In *Proceedings of the 14th International Society for Music Information Retrieval Conference (ISMIR)*, pages 335–340.

Denny Britz, Anna Goldie, Minh-Thang Luong, and Quoc V. Le. 2017. Massive exploration of neural machine translation architectures. *arXiv preprint arXiv: 1703.03906*.

Huadong Chen, Shujian Huang, David Chiang, and Jiajun Chen. 2017. Improved neural machine translation with a syntax-aware encoder and decoder. In *Proceedings of the 55th Annual Meeting of the Association for Computational Linguistics (ACL)*, pages 1936–1945.

Kyunghyun Cho, Bart van Merriënboer, Caglar Gulcehre, Dzmitry Bahdanau, Fethi Bougares, Holger Schwenk, and Yoshua Bengio. 2014. Learning phrase representations using RNN encoder–decoder for statistical machine translation. In *Proceedings of the 2014 Conference on Empirical Methods in Natural Language Processing (EMNLP)*, pages 1724–1734.

Fabien Cromieres, Chenhui Chu, Toshiaki Nakazawa, and Sadao Kurohashi. 2016. Kyoto university participation to WAT 2016. In *Proceedings of the Third Workshop on Asian Translation (WAT)*, pages 166–174.

Michael Denkowski and Graham Neubig. 2017. Stronger baselines for trustable results in neural machine translation. In *Proceedings of the First Workshop on Neural Machine Translation (WNMT)*, pages 18–27.

Akiko Eriguchi, Kazuma Hashimoto, and Yoshimasa Tsuruoka. 2016. Tree-to-sequence attentional neural machine translation. In *Proceedings of the 54th Annual Meeting of the Association for Computational Linguistics (ACL)*, pages 823–833.

Akiko Eriguchi, Yoshimasa Tsuruoka, and Kyunghyun Cho. 2017. Learning to parse and translate improves neural machine translation. In *Proceedings of the 55th Annual Meeting of the Association for Computational Linguistics (ACL), Short Papers*, pages 72–78.

Jonas Gehring, Michael Auli, David Grangier, and Yann Dauphin. 2017. A convolutional encoder model for neural machine translation. In *Proceedings of the 55th Annual Meeting of the Association for Computational Linguistics (ACL)*, pages 123–135.

Çaglar Gülçehre, Orhan Firat, Kelvin Xu, Kyunghyun Cho, Loïc Barrault, Huei-Chi Lin, Fethi Bougares, Holger Schwenk, and Yoshua Bengio. 2015. On using monolingual corpora in neural machine translation. *arXiv preprint arXiv: 1503.03535.*

Geoffrey E. Hinton, Simon Osindero, and Yee-Whye Teh. 2006. A fast learning algorithm for deep belief nets. *Neural Computation*, 18(7):1527–1554.

Sepp Hochreiter and Jürgen Schmidhuber. 1997. Long short-term memory. *Neural Computation*, 9(8):1735–1780.

Shonosuke Ishiwatari, Jingtao Yao, Shujie Liu, Mu Li, Ming Zhou, Naoki Yoshinaga, Masaru Kitsuregawa, and Weijia Jia. 2017. Chunk-based decoder for neural machine translation. In *Proceedings of the 55th Annual Meeting of the Association for Computational Linguistics (ACL)*, pages 1901–1912.

Nal Kalchbrenner and Phil Blunsom. 2013. Recurrent continuous translation models. In *Proceedings of the 2013 Conference on Empirical Methods in Natural Language Processing (EMNLP)*, pages 1700–1709.

Nitish Shirish Keskar, Dheevatsa Mudigere, Jorge Nocedal, Mikhail Smelyanskiy, and Ping Tak Peter Tang. 2017. On large-batch training for deep learning: Generalization gap and sharp minima. In *Proceedings of 5th International Conference on Learning Representations (ICLR)*.

Diederik P. Kingma and Jimmy Ba. 2015. Adam: A method for stochastic optimization. In *Proceedings of the third International Conference on Learning Representations (ICLR)*.

Philipp Koehn, Hieu Hoang, Alexandra Birch, Chris Callison-Burch, Marcello Federico, Nicola Bertoldi, Brooke Cowan, Wade Shen, Christine Moran, Richard Zens, Chris Dyer, Ondrej Bojar, Alexandra Constantin, and Evan Herbst. 2007. Moses: Open source toolkit for statistical machine translation. In *Proceedings of the 45th Annual Meeting of the Association for Computational Linguistics (ACL), Demo and Poster Sessions*, pages 177–180.

Omer Levy and Yoav Goldberg. 2014. Dependency-based word embeddings. In *Proceedings of the 52nd Annual Meeting of the Association for Computational Linguistics (ACL), Short Papers*, pages 302–308.

Junhui Li, Deyi Xiong, Zhaopeng Tu, Muhua Zhu, Min Zhang, and Guodong Zhou. 2017. Modeling source syntax for neural machine translation. In *Proceedings of the 55th Annual Meeting of the Association for Computational Linguistics (ACL)*, pages 688–697.

Dekang Lin and Xiaoyun Wu. 2009. Phrase clustering for discriminative learning. In *Proceedings of the Joint Conference of the 47th Annual Meeting of the ACL and the 4th International Joint Conference on Natural Language Processing (ACL-IJCNLP)*, pages 1030–1038.

Tomas Mikolov, Kai Chen, Greg Corrado, and Jeffrey Dean. 2013. Efficient estimation of word representations in vector space. In *Proceedings of the First International Conference on Learning Representations (ICLR)*.

Makoto Morishita, Yusuke Oda, Graham Neubig, Koichiro Yoshino, Katsuhito Sudoh, and Satoshi Nakamura. 2017. An empirical study of mini-batch creation strategies for neural machine translation. In *Proceedings of the First Workshop on Neural Machine Translation*, pages 61–68.

Toshiaki Nakazawa, Shohei Higashiyama, Chenchen Ding, Hideya Mino, Isao Goto, Graham Neubig, Hideto Kazawa, Yusuke Oda, Jun Harashima, and Sadao Kurohashi. 2017. Overview of the 4th Workshop on Asian Translation. In *Proceedings of the 4th Workshop on Asian Translation (WAT2017)*, Taipei, Taiwan.

Toshiaki Nakazawa, Manabu Yaguchi, Kiyotaka Uchimoto, Masao Utiyama, Eiichiro Sumita, Sadao Kurohashi, and Hitoshi Isahara. 2016. ASPEC: Asian scientific paper excerpt corpus. In *Proceedings of the Ninth International Conference on Language Resources and Evaluation (LREC 2016)*, pages 2204–2208.

Graham Neubig, Yosuke Nakata, and Shinsuke Mori. 2011. Pointwise prediction for robust, adaptable Japanese morphological analysis. In *Proceedings of the 49th Annual Meeting of the Association for Computational Linguistics: Human Language Technologies (ACL-HLT), Short Papers*, pages 529–533.

Jeffrey Pennington, Richard Socher, and Christopher D. Manning. 2014. Glove: Global vectors for word representation. In *Proceedings of the 2014 Conference on Empirical Methods in Natural Language Processing (EMNLP)*, pages 1532–1543.

Prajit Ramachandran, Peter Liu, and Quoc Le. 2017. Unsupervised pretraining for sequence to sequence learning. In *Proceedings of the 2017 Conference on Empirical Methods in Natural Language Processing*, pages 383–391.

Alexander M. Rush, Sumit Chopra, and Jason Weston. 2015. A neural attention model for abstractive sentence summarization. In *Proceedings of the 2015 Conference on Empirical Methods in Natural Language Processing (EMNLP)*, pages 379–389.

Rico Sennrich, Barry Haddow, and Alexandra Birch. 2016. Neural machine translation of rare words with subword units. In *Proceedings of the 54th Annual Meeting of the Association for Computational Linguistics (ACL)*, pages 1715–1725.

Ilya Sutskever, Oriol Vinyals, and Quoc V. Le. 2014. Sequence to sequence learning with neural networks. In *Advances in Neural Information Processing Systems (NIPS) 27*, pages 3104–3112.

Subhashini Venugopalan, Lisa Anne Hendricks, Raymond Mooney, and Kate Saenko. 2016. Improving LSTM-based video description with linguistic knowledge mined from text. In *Proceedings of the 2016 Conference on Empirical Methods in Natural Language Processing (EMNLP)*, pages 1961–1966.

Shuangzhi Wu, Dongdong Zhang, Nan Yang, Mu Li, and Ming Zhou. 2017. Sequence-to-dependency neural machine translation. In *Proceedings of the 55th Annual Meeting of the Association for Computational Linguistics (ACL)*, pages 698–707.

Yonghui Wu, Mike Schuster, Zhifeng Chen, Quoc V. Le, Mohammad Norouzi, Wolfgang Macherey, Maxim Krikun, Yuan Cao, Qin Gao, Klaus Macherey, Jeff Klingner, Apurva Shah, Melvin Johnson, Xiaobing Liu, Lukasz Kaiser, Stephan Gouws, Yoshikiyo Kato, Taku Kudo, Hideto Kazawa, Keith Stevens, George Kurian, Nishant Patil, Wei Wang, Cliff Young, Jason Smith, Jason Riesa, Alex Rudnick, Oriol Vinyals, Greg Corrado, Macduff Hughes, and Jeffrey Dean. 2016. Google's neural machine translation system: Bridging the gap between human and machine translation. *arXiv preprint arXiv: 1609.08144*.

Barret Zoph, Deniz Yuret, Jonathan May, and Kevin Knight. 2016. Transfer learning for low-resource neural machine translation. In *Proceedings of the 2016 Conference on Empirical Methods in Natural Language Processing (EMNLP)*, pages 1568–1575.

Patent NMT integrated with
Large Vocabulary Phrase Translation by SMT
at WAT 2017

Zi Long
Ryuichiro Kimura
Takehito Utsuro
Grad. Sc. Sys. & Inf. Eng.,
University of Tsukuba,
Tsukuba, 305-8573, Japan

Tomoharu Mitsuhashi
Japan Patent
Information Organization,
4-1-7, Tokyo, Koto-ku,
Tokyo, 135-0016, Japan

Mikio Yamamoto
Grad. Sc. Sys. & Inf. Eng.,
University of Tsukuba,
Tsukuba, 305-8573, Japan

Abstract

Neural machine translation (NMT) cannot handle a larger vocabulary because the training complexity and decoding complexity proportionally increase with the number of target words. This problem becomes even more serious when translating patent documents, which contain many technical terms that are observed infrequently. Long et al. (2017) proposed to select phrases that contain out-of-vocabulary words using the statistical approach of branching entropy. The selected phrases are then replaced with tokens during training and post-translated by the phrase translation table of SMT. In this paper, we apply the method proposed by Long et al. (2017) to the WAT 2017 Japanese-Chinese and Japanese-English patent datasets. Evaluation on Japanese-to-Chinese, Chinese-to-Japanese, Japanese-to-English and English-to-Japanese patent sentence translation proved the effectiveness of phrases selected with branching entropy, where the NMT model of Long et al. (2017) achieves a substantial improvement over a baseline NMT model without the technique proposed by Long et al. (2017).

1 Introduction

Neural machine translation (NMT), a new approach to solving machine translation, has achieved promising results (Bahdanau et al., 2015; Cho et al., 2014; Jean et al., 2014; Kalchbrenner and Blunsom, 2013; Luong et al., 2015a,b; Sutskever et al., 2014). An NMT system builds a simple large neural network that reads the entire input source sentence and generates an output translation. The entire neural network is jointly trained to maximize the conditional probability of the correct translation of a source sentence with a bilingual corpus. Although NMT offers many advantages over traditional phrase-based approaches, such as a small memory footprint and simple decoder implementation, conventional NMT is limited when it comes to larger vocabularies. This is because the training complexity and decoding complexity proportionally increase with the number of target words. Words that are out of vocabulary are represented by a single "$\langle unk \rangle$" token in translations, as illustrated in Figure 1. The problem becomes more serious when translating patent documents, which contain several newly introduced technical terms.

There have been a number of related studies that address the vocabulary limitation of NMT systems. Jean et al. (2014) provided an efficient approximation to the softmax function to accommodate a very large vocabulary in an NMT system. Luong et al. (2015b) proposed annotating the occurrences of the out-of-vocabulary token in the target sentence with positional information to track its alignments, after which they replace the tokens with their translations using simple word dictionary lookup or identity copy. Li et al. (2016) proposed replacing out-of-vocabulary words with similar in-vocabulary words based on a similarity model learnt from monolingual data. Sennrich et al. (2016) introduced an effective approach based on encoding rare and out-of-vocabulary words as sequences of subword units. Luong and Manning (2016) provided a character-level and word-level hybrid NMT model to achieve an open vocabulary, and Costa-jussà and Fonollosa (2016) proposed an NMT system that uses character-based embeddings.

Proceedings of the 4th Workshop on Asian Translation, pages 110–118,
Taipei, Taiwan, November 27, 2017. ©2017 AFNLP

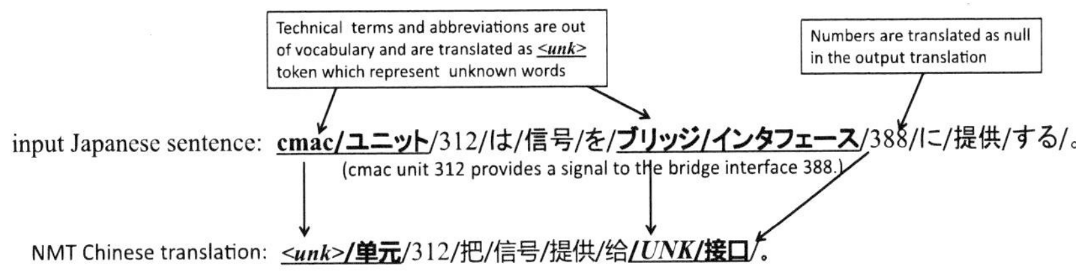

Figure 1: Example of translation errors when translating patent sentences with technical terms using NMT

However, these previous approaches have limitations when translating patent sentences. This is because their methods only focus on addressing the problem of out-of-vocabulary words even though the words are parts of technical terms. It is obvious that a technical term should be considered as one word that comprises components that always have different meanings and translations when they are used alone. An example is shown in Figure 1, where the Japanese word "ブリッジ"(bridge) should be translated to Chinese word "桥架" when included in technical term "bridge interface"; however, it is always translated as "桥".

To address this problem, Long et al. (2016) proposed extracting compound nouns as technical terms and replacing them with tokens. Long et al. (2017) proposed to select phrase pairs using the statistical approach of branching entropy; this allows the proposed technique to be applied to the translation task on any language pair without needing specific language knowledge to formulate the rules for technical term identification. In this paper, we apply the method proposed by Long et al. (2017) to the WAT 2017 Japanese-Chinese and Japanese-English patent datasets. On the WAT 2017 Japanese-Chinese JPO patent dataset, the NMT model of Long et al. (2017) achieves an improvement of 1.4 BLEU points over a baseline NMT model when translating Japanese sentences into Chinese, and an improvement of 0.8 BLEU points when translating Chinese sentences into Japanese. On the WAT 2017 Japanese-English JPO patent dataset, the NMT model of Long et al. (2017) achieves an improvement of 0.8 BLEU points over a baseline NMT model when translating Japanese sentences into English, and an improvement of 0.7 BLEU points when translating English sentences into Japanese. More-over, the number of translation error of under-translations[1] by PosUnk model proposed by Luong et al. (2015b) reduces to around 30% by the NMT model of Long et al. (2017).

2 Neural Machine Translation

NMT uses a single neural network trained jointly to maximize the translation performance (Bahdanau et al., 2015; Cho et al., 2014; Kalchbrenner and Blunsom, 2013; Luong et al., 2015a; Sutskever et al., 2014). Given a source sentence $x = (x_1, \ldots, x_N)$ and target sentence $y = (y_1, \ldots, y_M)$, an NMT model uses a neural network to parameterize the conditional distributions

$$p(y_z \mid y_{<z}, x)$$

for $1 \leq z \leq M$. Consequently, it becomes possible to compute and maximize the log probability of the target sentence given the source sentence as

$$\log p(y \mid x) = \sum_{l=1}^{M} \log p(y_z | y_{<z}, x)$$

In this paper, we use an NMT model similar to that used by Bahdanau et al. (2015), which consists of an encoder of a bidirectional long short-term memory (LSTM) (Hochreiter and Schmidhuber, 1997) and another LSTM as decoder. In the model of Bahdanau et al. (2015), the encoder consists of forward and backward LSTMs. The forward LSTM reads the source sentence as it is ordered (from x_1 to x_N) and calculates a sequence of forward hidden states, while the backward LSTM reads the source sentence in the reverse order

---

[1] It is known that NMT models tend to have the problem of the under-translation. Tu el al. (2016) proposed coverage-based NMT which considers the problem of the under-translation.

(from x_N to x_1), resulting in a sequence of backward hidden states. The decoder then predicts target words using not only a recurrent hidden state and the previously predicted word but also a context vector as followings:

$$p(y_z \mid y_{<z}, \boldsymbol{x}) = g(y_{z-1}, s_{z-1}, c_z)$$

where s_{z-1} is an LSTM hidden state of decoder, and c_z is a context vector computed from both of the forward hidden states and backward hidden states, for $1 \leq z \leq M$.

3 Phrase Pair Selection using Branching Entropy

Branching entropy has been applied to the procedure of text segmentation (e.g., (Jin and Tanaka-Ishii, 2006)) and key phrases extraction (e.g., (Chen et al., 2010)). In this work, we use the left/right branching entropy to detect the boundaries of phrases, and thus select phrase pairs automatically.

3.1 Branching Entropy

The left branching entropy and right branching entropy of a phrase $\boldsymbol{w}$ are respectively defined as

$$H_l(\boldsymbol{w}) = - \sum_{v \in V_l^{\boldsymbol{w}}} p_l(v) \log_2 p_l(v)$$

$$H_r(\boldsymbol{w}) = - \sum_{v \in V_r^{\boldsymbol{w}}} p_r(v) \log_2 p_r(v)$$

where $\boldsymbol{w}$ is the phrase of interest (e.g., "ブリッジ/インターフェース" in the Japanese sentence shown in Figure 1, which means "bridge interface"), $V_l^{\boldsymbol{w}}$ is a set of words that are adjacent to the left of $\boldsymbol{w}$ (e.g., "を" in Figure 1, which is a Japanese particle) and $V_r^{\boldsymbol{w}}$ is a set of words that are adjacent to the right of $\boldsymbol{w}$ (e.g., "388" in Figure 1). The probabilities $p_l(v)$ and $p_r(v)$ are respectively computed as

$$p_l(v) = \frac{f_{v,\boldsymbol{w}}}{f_{\boldsymbol{w}}} \qquad p_r(v) = \frac{f_{\boldsymbol{w},v}}{f_{\boldsymbol{w}}} \qquad (1)$$

where $f_{\boldsymbol{w}}$ is the frequency count of phrase $\boldsymbol{w}$, and $f_{v,\boldsymbol{w}}$ and $f_{\boldsymbol{w},v}$ are the frequency counts of sequence "$v,\boldsymbol{w}$" and sequence "$\boldsymbol{w},v$" respectively. According to the definition of branching entropy, when a phrase $\boldsymbol{w}$ is a technical term that is always used as a compound word, both its left branching entropy $H_l(\boldsymbol{w})$ and right branching entropy $H_r(\boldsymbol{w})$ have high values because many different

words, such as particles and numbers, can be adjacent to the phrase. However, the left/right branching entropy of substrings of $\boldsymbol{w}$ have low values because words contained in $\boldsymbol{w}$ are always adjacent to each other.

3.2 Selecting Phrase Pairs

Given a parallel sentence pair $\langle S_s, S_t \rangle$, all n-grams phrases of source sentence S_s and target sentence S_t are extracted and aligned using phrase translation table and word alignment of SMT according to the approaches described in Long et al. (2016). Next, phrase translation pair $\langle t_s, t_t \rangle$ obtained from $\langle S_s, S_t \rangle$ that satisfies all the following conditions is selected as a phrase pair and is extracted:

(1) Either t_s or t_t contains at least one out-of-vocabulary word.

(2) Neither t_s nor t_t contains predetermined stop words.

(3) Entropies $H_l(t_s)$, $H_l(t_t)$, $H_r(t_s)$ and $H_r(t_t)$ are larger than a lower bound, while the left/right branching entropy of the substrings of t_s and t_t are lower than or equal to the lower bound.

Here, the maximum length of a phrase as well as the lower bound of the branching entropy are tuned with the validation set.[2] All the selected source-target phrase pairs are then used in the next section as phrase pairs.

4 NMT with a Large Phrase Vocabulary

In this work, the NMT model is trained on a bilingual corpus in which phrase pairs are replaced with tokens. The NMT system is then used as a decoder to translate the source sentences and replace the tokens with phrases translated using SMT.

____

[2] Throughout the evaluations on patent translation of both language pairs of Japanese-Chinese and Japanese-English, the maximum length of the extracted phrases is tuned as 7. The lower bounds of the branching entropy are tuned as 5 for patent translation of the language pair of Japanese-Chinese, and 8 for patent translation of the language pair of Japanese-English. We also tune the number of stop words using the validation set, and use the 200 most-frequent Japanese morphemes and Chinese words as stop words for the language pair of Japanese-Chinese, use the 100 most-frequent Japanese morphemes and English words as stop words for the language pair of Japanese-English.

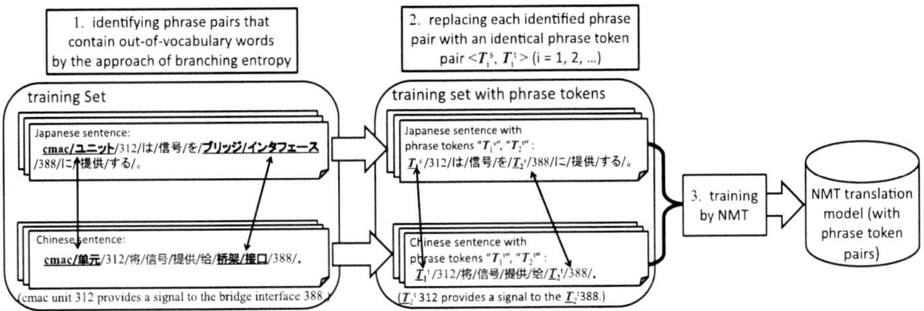

Figure 2: NMT training after replacing phrase pairs with token pairs $\langle T_i^s, T_i^t \rangle$ $(i = 1, 2, \ldots)$

4.1 NMT Training after Replacing Phrase Pairs with Tokens

Figure 2 illustrates the procedure for training the model with parallel patent sentence pairs in which phrase pairs are replaced with phrase token pairs $\langle T_1^s, T_1^t \rangle$, $\langle T_2^s, T_2^t \rangle$, and so on.

In the step 1 of Figure 2, source-target phrase pairs that contain at least one out-of-vocabulary word are selected from the training set using the branching entropy approach described in Section 3.2. As shown in the step 2 of Figure 2, in each of the parallel patent sentence pairs, occurrences of phrase pairs $\langle t_1^s, t_1^t \rangle$, $\langle t_2^s, t_2^t \rangle$, $\ldots$, $\langle t_k^s, t_k^t \rangle$ are then replaced with token pairs $\langle T_1^s, T_1^t \rangle$, $\langle T_2^s, T_2^t \rangle$, $\ldots$, $\langle T_k^s, T_k^t \rangle$. Phrase pairs $\langle t_1^s, t_1^t \rangle$, $\langle t_2^s, t_2^t \rangle$, $\ldots$, $\langle t_k^s, t_k^t \rangle$ are numbered in the order of occurrence of the source phrases t_i^s $(i = 1, 2, \ldots, k)$ in each source sentence S_s. Here note that in all the parallel sentence pairs $\langle S_s, S_t \rangle$, the tokens pairs $\langle T_1^s, T_1^t \rangle$, $\langle T_2^s, T_2^t \rangle$, $\ldots$ that are identical throughout all the parallel sentence pairs are used in this procedure. Therefore, for example, in all the source patent sentences S_s, the phrase t_1^s which appears earlier than other phrases in S_s is replaced with T_1^s. We then train the NMT model on a bilingual corpus, in which the phrase pairs are replaced by token pairs $\langle T_i^s, T_i^t \rangle$ $(i = 1, 2, \ldots)$, and obtain an NMT model in which the phrases are represented as tokens.

4.2 NMT Decoding and SMT Phrase Translation

Figure 3 illustrates the procedure for producing target translations by decoding the input source sentence using the NMT model of Long et al. (2017).

In the step 1 of Figure 3, when given an input source sentence, we first generate its transla-

Table 1: Statistics of datasets

	training set	validation set	test set
ja ↔ ch	998,054	2,000	2,000
ja ↔ en	999,636	2,000	2,000

tion by decoding of SMT translation model. Next, as shown in the step 2 of Figure 3, we automatically extract the phrase pairs by branching entropy according to the procedure of Section 3.2, where the input sentence and its SMT translation are considered as a pair of parallel sentence. Phrase pairs that contains at least one out-of-vocabulary word are extracted and are replaced with phrase token pairs $\langle T_i^s, T_i^t \rangle$ $(i = 1, 2, \ldots)$. Consequently, we have an input sentence in which the tokens "T_i^s" $(i = 1, 2, \ldots)$ represent the positions of the phrases and a list of SMT phrase translations of extracted Japanese phrases. Next, as shown in the step 3 of Figure 3, the source Japanese sentence with tokens is translated using the NMT model trained according to the procedure described in Section 4.1. Finally, in the step 4, we replace the tokens "T_i^t" $(i = 1, 2, \ldots)$ of the target sentence translation with the phrase translations of the SMT.

5 Evaluation

5.1 DataSets

We evaluated the effectiveness of the NMT model of Long et al. (2017) on the WAT 2017 Japanese-Chinese and Japanese-English JPO dataset.[3] Out of the training set of the WAT 2017 Japanese-Chinese JPO dataset, we used 998,954 patent sentence pairs, whose Japanese sentences contain

---

[3] http://lotus.kuee.kyoto-u.ac.jp/WAT/patent/index.html

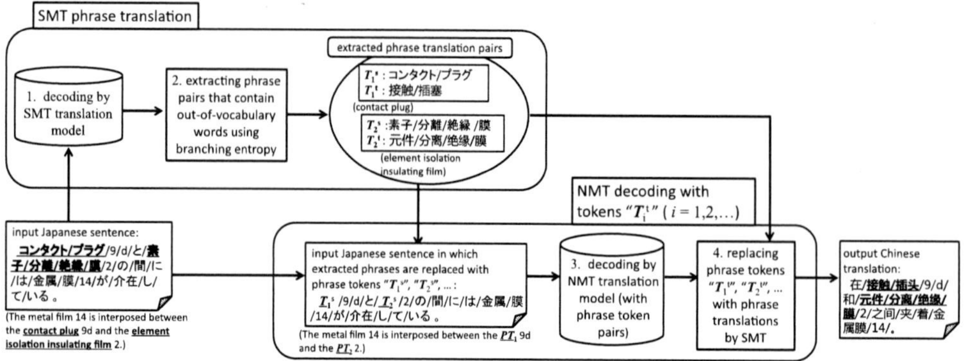

Figure 3: NMT decoding with tokens "T_i^s" ($i = 1, 2, \ldots$) and the SMT phrase translation

fewer than 100 morphemes, Chinese sentences contain fewer than 100 words. Out of the training set of the WAT 2017 Japanese-English JPO dataset, we used 999,636 sentence pairs whose Japanese sentences contain fewer than 100 morphemes and English sentences contain fewer than 100 words. In both cases, we used all of the sentence pairs contained in the development sets of the WAT 2017 JPO datasets as development sets, and we used all of the sentence pairs contained in the test sets of the WAT 2017 JPO datasets as test sets. Table 1 show the statistics of the dataset.

According to the procedure of Section 3.2, from the Japanese-Chinese sentence pairs of the training set, we collected 102,630 occurrences of Japanese-Chinese phrase pairs, which are 69,387 types of phrase pairs with 52,786 unique types of Japanese phrases and 67,456 unique types of Chinese phrases. Within the total 2,000 Japanese patent sentences in the Japanese-Chinese test set, 266 occurrences of Japanese phrases were extracted, which correspond to 247 types. With the total 2,000 Chinese patent sentences in the Japanese-Chinese test set, 417 occurrences of Chinese phrases were extracted, which correspond to 382 types.

From the Japanese-English sentence pairs of the training set, we collected 38,457 occurrences of Japanese-English phrase pairs, which are 35,544 types of phrase pairs with unique 34,569 types of Japanese phrases and 35,087 unique types of English phrases. Within the total 2,000 Japanese patent sentences in the Japanese-English test set, 249 occurrences of Japanese phrases were extracted, which correspond to 221 types. With the total 2,000 English patent sentences in the

Japanese-English test set, 246 occurrences of English phrases were extracted, which correspond to 230 types.

5.2 Training Details

For the training of the SMT model, including the word alignment and the phrase translation table, we used Moses (Koehn et al., 2007), a toolkit for phrase-based SMT models. We trained the SMT model on the training set and tuned it with the validation set.

For the training of the NMT model, our training procedure and hyperparameter choices were similar to those of Bahdanau et al. (2015). The encoder consists of forward and backward deep LSTM neural networks each consisting of three layers, with 512 cells in each layer. The decoder is a three-layer deep LSTM with 512 cells in each layer. Both the source vocabulary and the target vocabulary are limited to the 40K most-frequently used morphemes / words in the training set. The size of the word embedding was set to 512. We ensured that all sentences in a minibatch were roughly the same length. Further training details are given below: (1) We set the size of a minibatch to 128. (2) All of the LSTM's parameter were initialized with a uniform distribution ranging between -0.06 and 0.06. (3) We used the stochastic gradient descent, beginning at a fixed learning rate of 1. We trained our model for a total of 10 epochs, and we began to halve the learning rate every epoch after the first seven epochs. (4) Similar to Sutskever et al.(2014), we rescaled the normalized gradient to ensure that its norm does not exceed 5. We trained the NMT model on the training set. The training time was around two days when using the described parameters on a 1-GPU

Table 2: Automatic evaluation results (BLEU)

System	ja → ch	ch → ja	ja → en	en → ja
Baseline SMT (Koehn et al., 2007)	30.0	36.2	28.0	29.4
Baseline NMT	34.2	40.8	43.1	41.8
NMT with PosUnk model (Luong et al., 2015b)	34.5	41.0	43.5	42.0
NMT with phrase translation by SMT (Long et al., 2017)	**35.6**	**41.6**	**43.9**	**42.5**

Table 3: Human evaluation results of pairwise evaluation

System	ja → ch	ch → ja	ja → en	en → ja
NMT with PosUnk model (Luong et al., 2015b)	13	12.5	9.5	14.5
NMT with phrase translation by SMT (Long et al., 2017)	**23.5**	**22.5**	**15.5**	**19**

machine.

We compute the branching entropy using the frequency statistics from the training set.

5.3 Evaluation Results

In this work, we calculated automatic evaluation scores for the translation results using a popular metrics called BLEU (Papineni et al., 2002). As shown in Table 2, we report the evaluation scores, using the translations by Moses (Koehn et al., 2007) as the baseline SMT and the scores using the translations produced by the baseline NMT system without the approach proposed by Long et al. (2017) as the baseline NMT. As shown in Table 2, the BLEU score obtained by the NMT model of Long et al. (2017) is clearly higher than those of the baselines. Here, as described in Section 3, the lower bounds of branching entropy for phrase pair selection are tuned as 5 throughout the evaluation of language pair of Japanese-Chinese, and tuned as 8 throughout the evaluation of language pair of Japanese-English, respectively. On the WAT 2017 Japanese-Chinese JPO patent dataset, when compared with the baseline SMT, the performance gains of the NMT model of Long et al. (2017) are approximately 5.6 BLEU points when translating Japanese into Chinese and 5.4 BLEU when translating Chinese into Japanese. On the WAT 2017 Japanese-English JPO patent dataset, when compared with the baseline SMT, the performance gains of the NMT model of Long et al. (2017) are approximately 15.9 BLEU points when translating Japanese into English and 13.1 BLEU when translating English into Japanese.

When compared with the result of the baseline NMT, the NMT model of Long et al. (2017) achieved performance gains of 1.4 BLEU points on the task of translating Japanese into Chinese and 0.8 BLEU points on the task of translating Chinese into Japanese. When compared with the result of the baseline NMT, the NMT model of Long et al. (2017) achieved performance gains of 0.8 BLEU points on the task of translating Japanese into English and 1.4 BLEU points on the task of translating English into Japanese.

Furthermore, we quantitatively compared our study with the work of Luong et al. (2015b). Table 2 compares the NMT model with the PosUnk model, which is the best model proposed by Luong et al. (2015b) The NMT model of Long et al. (2017) achieves performance gains of 0.9 BLEU points when translating Japanese into Chinese, and performance gains of 0.6 BLEU points when translating Chinese into Japanese. The NMT model of Long et al. (2017) achieves performance gains of 0.4 BLEU points when translating Japanese into English, and performance gains of 0.5 BLEU points when translating English into Japanese

In this study, we also conducted two types of human evaluations according to the work of Nakazawa et al. (2015): pairwise evaluation and JPO adequacy evaluation. In the pairwise evaluation, we compared each translation produced by the baseline NMT with that produced by the NMT model of Long et al. (2017) as well as the NMT model with PosUnk model, and judged which translation is better or whether they have

Table 4: Human evaluation results of JPO adequacy evaluation

System	ja → ch	ch → ja	ja → en	en → ja
Baseline SMT (Koehn et al., 2007)	3.1	3.2	2.9	3.0
Baseline NMT	3.6	3.6	3.7	3.7
NMT with PosUnk model (Luong et al., 2015b)	3.8	3.9	3.9	3.9
NMT with phrase translation by SMT (Long et al., 2017)	**4.1**	**4.1**	**4.2**	**4.1**

Table 5: Evaluation results from WAT 2017

Evaluation	System	ja → ch	ch → ja	ja → en	en → ja
Automatic evaluation (BLEU)	Baseline (PBSMT)	32.1	38.5	30.8	34.3
	NMT with phrase translation by SMT (Long et al., 2017)	**33.2**	**40.5**	**37.3**	**41.1**
Pairwise evaluation	NMT with phrase translation by SMT (Long et al., 2017)	21.8	40.1	51.5	49.5
JPO adequacy evaluation	NMT with phrase translation by SMT (Long et al., 2017)	4.1	3.9	4.2	4.3

comparable quality. In contrast to the study conducted by Nakazawa et al. (2015), we randomly selected 200 sentence pairs from the test set for human evaluation, and both human evaluations were conducted using only one judgement. Table 3 and Table 4 show the results of the human evaluation for the baseline SMT, baseline NMT, NMT model with PosUnk model, and the NMT model of Long et al. (2017). We observe that the NMT model of Long et al. (2017) achieves the best performance for both the pairwise and JPO adequacy evaluations when we replace the tokens with SMT phrase translations after decoding the source sentence with the tokens.

Moreover, Table 5 shows the results of automatic evaluation, pairwise evaluation and JPO adequacy evaluation from the WAT 2017 (Nakazawa et al., 2017).[4] We observe that the NMT model of Long et al. (2017) achieves a substantial improvement over the WAT 2017 baseline.

For the test sets, we also counted the numbers of the untranslated words of input sentences. As shown in Table 6, the number of untranslated words by the baseline NMT reduced to around 65% by the NMT model of Long et al. (2017). This is mainly because part of untranslated source words are out-of-vocabulary, and thus are untrans-

lated by the baseline NMT. The NMT model of Long et al. (2017) extracts those out-of-vocabulary words as a part of phrases and replaces those phrases with tokens before the decoding of NMT. Those phrases are then translated by SMT and inserted in the output translation, which ensures that those out-of-vocabulary words are translated.

Figure 4 compares an example of correct translation produced by the NMT model of Long et al. (2017) with one produced by the baseline NMT. In this example, the translation is a translation error because the Japanese word "焼入れ (quenching)" is an out-of-vocabulary word and is erroneously translated into the "$\langle unk \rangle$" token. The NMT model of Long et al. (2017) correctly translated the Japanese sentence into Chinese, where the out-of-vocabulary word "焼入れ" is correctly selected by the approach of branching entropy as a part of the Japanese phrase "焼入れ剤 (quenching agent)". The selected Japanese phrase is then translated by the phrase translation table of SMT. Figure 5 shows another example of correct translation produced by the NMT model of Long et al. (2017) with one produced by the baseline NMT. As shown in Figure 5, the translation produced by baseline NMT is a translation error because the out-of-vocabulary English words "eukaryotic" and "promoters" are untranslated words and their translations are not contained in the output translation of the baseline NMT. The NMT model of

[4] http://lotus.kuee.kyoto-u.ac.jp/WAT/evaluation/

Table 6: Numbers of untranslated morphemes / words of input sentences

System	ja → ch	ch → ja	ja → en	en → ja
NMT with PosUnk model (Luong et al., 2015b)	1,112	846	1,031	794
NMT with phrase translation by SMT (Long et al., 2017)	736	581	655	571

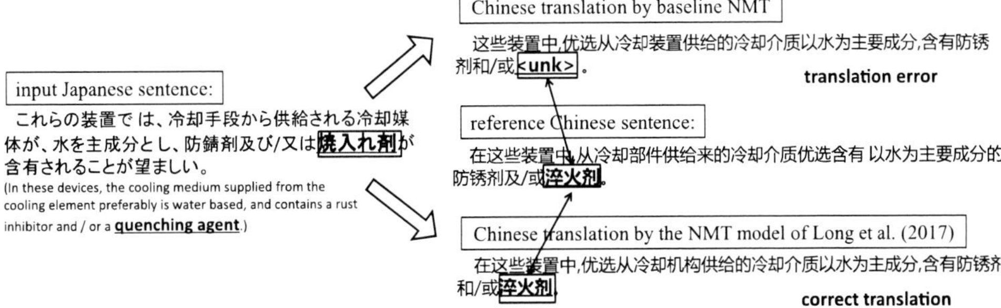

Figure 4: An example of correct translations produced by the NMT model of Long et al. (2017) when addressing the problem of out-of-vocabulary words (Japanese-to-Chinese)

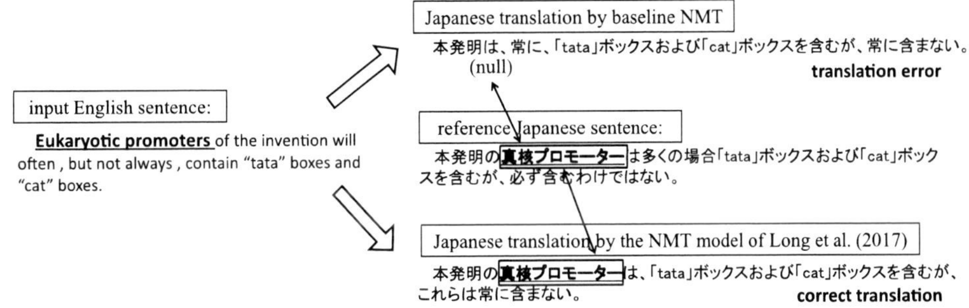

Figure 5: An example of correct translations produced by the NMT model of Long et al. (2017) when addressing the problem of under-translation (English-to-Japanese)

Long et al. (2017) correctly translated those English words into Japanese because those English words "eukaryotic" and "promoters" are selected as an English phrase "Eukaryotic promoters" with branching entropy and then are translated by SMT.

6 Conclusion

Long et al. (2017) proposed selecting phrases that contain out-of-vocabulary words using the branching entropy. These selected phrases are then replaced with tokens and post-translated using an SMT phrase translation. In this paper, we apply the method proposed by Long et al. (2017) to the WAT 2017 Japanese-Chinese and Japanese-English patent datasets. We observed that the NMT model of Long et al. (2017) performed much better than the baseline NMT system in all of the language pairs: Japanese-to-Chinese/Chinese-to-Japanese and Japanese-to-English/English-to-Japanese. One of our important future tasks is to compare the translation performance of the NMT model of Long et al. (2017) with that based on subword units (e.g. (Sennrich et al., 2016)). Another future work is to integrate the reranking framework for minimizing untranslated content (Goto and Tanaka, 2017) into the NMT model of Long et al. (2017), which is expected to further reduce the number of untranslated words. This future work is roughly based on the observation reported in Kimura et al. (2017), where the NMT model of Long et al. (2017) is not only effective in reducing the untranslated content without any specific framework of minimizing the untranslated content, but also successfully reduced the estimated volumes of the untranslated content, which was proposed by Goto and Tanaka (2017).

References

D. Bahdanau, K. Cho, and Y. Bengio. 2015. Neural machine translation by jointly learning to align and translate. In *Proc. 3rd ICLR*.

Y. Chen, Y. Huang, S. Kong, and L. Lee. 2010. Automatic key term extraction from spoken course lectures using branching entropy and prosodic/semantic features. In *Proc. 2010 IEEE SLT Workshop*, pages 265–270.

K. Cho, B. van Merriënboer, C. Gulcehre, F. Bougares, H. Schwenk, and Y. Bengio. 2014. Learning phrase representations using RNN encoder-decoder for statistical machine translation. In *Proc. EMNLP*, pages 1724–1734.

M. R. Costa-Jussà and J. A. R. Fonollosa. 2016. Character-based neural machine translation. In *Proc. 54th ACL*, pages 357–361.

I. Goto and H. Tanaka. 2017. Detecting untranslated content for neural machine translation. In *Proc. 1st NMT*, pages 47–55.

S. Hochreiter and J. Schmidhuber. 1997. Long short-term memory. *Neural Computation*, 9(8):1735–1780.

S. Jean, K. Cho, Y. Bengio, and R. Memisevic. 2014. On using very large target vocabulary for neural machine translation. In *Proc. 28th NIPS*, pages 1–10.

Z. Jin and K. Tanaka-Ishii. 2006. Unsupervised segmentation of Chinese text by use of branching entropy. In *Proc. COLING/ACL 2006*, pages 428–435.

N. Kalchbrenner and P. Blunsom. 2013. Recurrent continuous translation models. In *Proc. EMNLP*, pages 1700–1709.

R. Kimura, Z. Long, T. Utsuro, T. Mitsuhashi, and M. Yamamoto. 2017. Effect on reducing untranslated content by neural machine translation with a large vocabulary of technical terms. In *Proc. 7th PSLT*, pages 9–20.

P. Koehn, H. Hoang, A. Birch, C. Callison-Burch, M. Federico, N. Bertoldi, B. Cowan, W. Shen, C. Moran, R. Zens, C. Dyer, O. Bojar, A. Constantin, and E. Herbst. 2007. Moses: Open source toolkit for statistical machine translation. In *Proc. 45th ACL, Companion Volume*, pages 177–180.

X. Li, J. Zhang, and C. Zong. 2016. Towards zero unknown word in neural machine translation. In *Proc. 25th IJCAI*, pages 2852–2858.

Z. Long, R. Kimura, T. Utsuro, T. Mitsuhashi, and M. Yamamoto. 2017. Neural machine translation model with a large vocabulary selected by branching entropy. In *Proc. MT Summit XVI*, pages 227–240.

Z. Long, T. Utsuro, T. Mitsuhashi, and M. Yamamoto. 2016. Translation of patent sentences with a large vocabulary of technical terms using neural machine translation. In *Proc. 3rd WAT*, pages 47–57.

M. Luong and C. D. Manning. 2016. Achieving open vocabulary neural machine translation with hybrid word-character models. In *Proc. 54th ACL*, pages 1054–1063.

M. Luong, H. Pham, and C. D. Manning. 2015a. Effective approaches to attention-based neural machine translation. In *Proc. EMNLP*, pages 1412–1421.

M. Luong, I. Sutskever, O. Vinyals, Q. V. Le, and W. Zaremba. 2015b. Addressing the rare word problem in neural machine translation. In *Proc. 53rd ACL*, pages 11–19.

T. Nakazawa, S. Higashiyama, C. Ding, H. Mino, I. Goto, G. Neubig, H. Kazawa, Y. Oda, J. Harashima, and S. Kurohashi. 2017. Overview of the 4th workshop on Asian translation. In *Proc. 4th WAT*.

T. Nakazawa, H. Mino, I. Goto, G. Neubig, S. Kurohashi, and E. Sumita. 2015. Overview of the 2nd workshop on Asian translation. In *Proc. 2nd WAT*, pages 1–28.

K. Papineni, S. Roukos, T. Ward, and W.-J. Zhu. 2002. BLEU: a method for automatic evaluation of machine translation. In *Proc. 40th ACL*, pages 311–318.

R. Sennrich, B. Haddow, and A. Birch. 2016. Neural machine translation of rare words with subword units. In *Proc. 54th ACL*, pages 1715–1725.

I. Sutskever, O. Vinyals, and Q. V. Le. 2014. Sequence to sequence learning with neural machine translation. In *Proc. 27th NIPS*, pages 3104–3112.

Z. Tu, Z. Lu, Y. Liu, X. Liu, and H. Li. 2016. Modeling coverage for neural machine translation. In *Proc. ACL 2016*, pages 76–85.

SMT reranked NMT

Terumasa EHARA

Ehara NLP Research Laboratory
Seijo, Setagaya, Tokyo, JAPAN

eharate @ gmail . com

Abstract

System architecture, experimental settings and experimental results of the EHR team for the WAT2017 tasks are described. We participate in three tasks: JPCen-ja, JPCzh-ja and JPCko-ja. Although the basic architecture of our system is NMT, reranking technique is conducted using SMT results. One of the major drawback of NMT is under-translation and over-translation. On the other hand, SMT infrequently makes such translations. So, using reranking of n-best NMT outputs by the SMT output, discarding such translations can be expected. We can improve BLEU score from 46.03 to 47.08 by this technique in JPCzh-ja task.

1 Introduction

Rapidly progressing of NMT techniques make paradigm change in machine translation not only for the research purpose but for the practical field. Although the NMT provides high quality and fluent translations, it has several drawbacks. One of them is under- and over-translation which is infrequent in a SMT output.

We propose a reranking method for n-best NMT outputs using a SMT output. We compare n-best NMT outputs with a SMT output by the measure of IMPACT (Echizen-ya and Araki, 2007) which is one of the automatic evaluation measure of machine translation results. The NMT output which has the highest IMPACT score referring to SMT output is selected as the system output.

In the following sections, we describe system architecture and experimental settings in section 2, experimental results and discussions in section 3 and conclusion in section 4.

2 System architecture and experimental settings

2.1 Overall system architecture

Our system architecture is shown in Figure 1. An input source sentence is fed to the NMT part and also to the SMT part. NMT part outputs n-best translations ("NMT translation 1" to "NMT translation n") and SMT part outputs another translation ("SMT translation"). Reranking part compares NMT translations with SMT translation and reranks them. The best reranked "NMT translation i" is outputted.

2.2 NMT part

We use OpenNMT (Minh-Thang Luong et al., 2015) in NMT part.

Segmentation of English sentences is sub word based. The English segmenter segments each non-alphabetical characters (characters except for A to Z and a to z) as separate words. Segmentation of Chinese sentences and Korean sentences are both word based and character based. Word segmentation policy for these languages are described in the previous paper (Ehara, 2016). Japanese segmentation is word based, sub word based and character based. For JPCzh-ja task and JPCko-ja task, word based and character based Japanese segmenters are used. The word based Japanese segmenters are described in the previous paper (Ehara, 2016). For JPCen-ja task, we use sub word based Japanese segmenter which segments each special characters (characters except for Hiragana, Kanji, Katakana and Roman characters) as separate words, in addition to Juman's word segmentation (Kurohashi et al., 1994).

Option settings for OpenNMT are as follows: Source sequence length (-src_seq_len): 100 (word based), 120 (sub word based), 250 (character based); Target sequence length (-tgt_seq_len):

Proceedings of the 4th Workshop on Asian Translation, pages 119–126,
Taipei, Taiwan, November 27, 2017. ©2017 AFNLP

100 (word based), 120 (sub word based), 250 (character based); Encoder type (-encoder_type): brnn (bidirectional recurrent NN); Replace unknown word (-replace_unk): yes; Unknown word dictionary (-phrase_table): yes (see 2.3); Beam size (-beam_size): 50; N-best size (-n_best): 50.

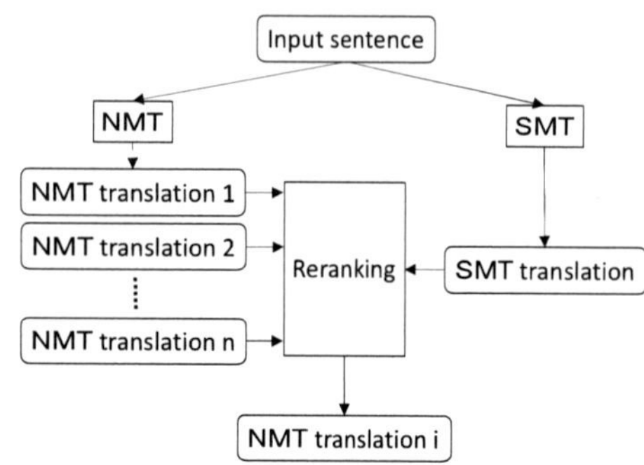

Figure 1: System architecture

2.3 SMT part

Our SMT system is phrase-based SMT by Moses v.3 (Koehn et al., 2003) with default option settings. For JPCen-ja task and JPCzh-ja task, preordering is applied. The preordering system is same as described in the previous papers (Ehara, 2015; Ehara, 2016).

We use unknown dictionary for NMT part. It is made from the phrase-table of Moses. For every source word, we select the target phrase which has the highest translation probability for the source word. And the unknown word dictionary is constructed as the source word and target phrase pairs.

2.4 Reranking part

For reranking of n-best outputs of NMT part, we use automatic evaluation measure IMPACT (Echizen-ya and Araki, 2007). For the preliminary study, we compared BLEU, RIBES and IMPACT with human evaluation score JPO adequacy by the WAT2016's evaluation results (Nakazawa et al., 2016). As the results, we found IMPACT was the best correlated score with JPO adequacy. Then we use IMPACT as the reranking measure. Reranking part calculates IMPACT score for NMT's n-best translations with SMT translation as the reference. And the best translation which has the highest IMPACT score is outputted as the system output.

3 Experimental results and discussions

The official evaluation results of our submissions are shown in Table 1 (Nakazawa et al., 2017). In the Table 1, "Original system" means the NMT without reranking and "SMT" means SMT part of our system.

For JPCen-ja task, reranking decreases BLEU, RIBES and AMFM scores and also HUMAN score. Although the overall evaluation result doesn't show the effectiveness of the reranking, several improvements are observed. Examples are listed in Table 2. Original translation of the example 1 has under-translation. Only the first two words (The oldest) and the punctuation mark (.) are translated in the original translation. Original translations of example 2 has also under-translation. None of words "(ACT , READ , PRE) , GBSTB , GBSTT , FXb 2 , PUMP , FXB , FXT , SWL , and RFX" is translated. On the other hand, reranking system does not make such under-translations. Original translation of example 3 has over translation. "異 な る (differ)" occurs two times. But the reranked translation has no over-translation.

Task	Data ID	System	Segment.	BLEU	RIBES	AMFM	HUMAN	JPO adeq.
JPCen–ja	1406	Reranking	Subword	44.44	0.8610	0.7471	58.250	-----
	1407	Original	Subword	44.63	0.8667	0.7478	60.000	4.63
	----	SMT	Word	36.20	0.8128	0.7237	-----	-----
JPCzh–ja	1408	Reranking	Word	47.08	0.8591	0.7564	68.250	-----
	1415	Original	Word	46.03	0.8586	0.7559	-----	-----
	1414	Reranking	Character	46.52	0.8596	0.7614	69.750	4.31
	1409	Original	Character	45.27	0.8544	0.7571	-----	-----
	----	SMT	Word	40.79	0.8270	0.7384	-----	-----
JPCko–ja	1416	Reranking	Word	71.52	0.9445	0.8661	6.250	-----
	1418	Original	Word	70.23	0.9432	0.8623	-----	-----
	1417	Reranking	Character	71.36	0.9461	0.8711	11.250	4.81
	1419	Original	Character	69.42	0.9364	0.8605	-----	-----
	----	SMT	Word	71.08	0.9440	0.8645	-----	-----

Table 1: Official evaluation results (Japanese segmenter is Juman)

1	source	The oldest is the capacitive divider bridge , one arm of which consists of a reference capacitance and the other of the capacitance to be measured .
	reference	最も 古い もの は 容量 分圧 器 ブリッジ であり 、その 1 つの アーム は 基準 静 電 容量 から 成り 、その他 の 静 電 容量 が 測定 される 。
	reranking	最も 古い もの は 容量 分圧 ブリッジ であり 、その 1 つの アーム は 、測定 される べき 基準 キャパシタンス と 他の キャパシタンス と から 成る 。
	original	最も 古い 。
	SMT	最も古いものは、容量性ディバイダブリッジ、基準キャパシタンスと測定されるべきキャパシタンスの他の1つを構成するアームである。
2	source	FIG . 5 shows a portion of waveforms of a simulation result of the circuit in FIG . 4 , and commands (ACT , READ , PRE) , GBSTB , GBSTT , FXb 2 , PUMP , FXB , FXT , SWL , and RFX are shown as signals .
	reference	図 5 に は 、図 4 の 回路 の シミュレーション 結果 の 波形 が 一部 示され て おり 、信号 として 、コマンド (ACT 、READ 、PRE) 、GBSTB 、GBSTT 、FXb 2 、PUMP 、FXB 、FXT 、SWL 、RFX が 示されて い る 。
	reranking	図 5 は 、図 4 の 回路 の シミュレーション 結果 の 一部 を 示す もの であり 、コマンド (ACT 、READ 、PRE) 、GBSTB 、GBSTT 、FXb 2 、P UMP 、FXB 、SWL 、RFX を 信号 として 示す 。
	original	図 4 の 回路 の シミュレーション 結果 の 一部 と 、図 4 の 回路 の シミュレーション 結果 の 一部 を 示す 図 である 。
	SMT	図5は、図4の回路のシミュレーション結果の波形の一部を示す、及びコマンド（ACT、READ、PRE）、GBSTB、GBSTT、FXb 2、PUMP、FXB、FXT RF X SWLとは、信号として示されている。
3	source	However, specifications sometimes differ from one image forming apparatus to another.
	reference	しかし、画像形成装置ごとにスペックが異なる場合がある。
	reranking	しかし、ある仕様は、時々、1つの画像形成装置とは異なる。
	original	しかし、時々、1つの画像形成装置とは異なる仕様が異なる。
	SMT	しかし、仕様は、装置を形成する1つの画像から別の画像へ時には異なる。

Table 2: JPCen-ja task's examples having effectiveness of reranking (recover of under-translation: example 1 and 2; recover of over-translation: example 3)

For JPCen-ja task, comparing our submission of data ID 1407 (EHR) and another submission (OTHER), BLEU score of the EHR is 44.63 and it is less than the OTHER's score (50.27). On the other hand, HUMAN score of the EHR is 60.00 and it is greater than the OTHER's score (56.25). There are 20 data that the BLEU[1] score of EHR is less than the OTHER's score but the HUMAN score of EHR is greater than the OTHER's score[2].

We examine these data and find that several data have the differences between the source expression and the reference expression. Table 3 shows examples of source, reference, EHR output and OTHER output. Example 1 has the voice change (the source is passive and the reference is active). Example 2 has the topic change (the topic of the source is "valve" and the topic of the reference is "経路 (passage)". Example 3 has the additive translation[3] (the source "GELD" corresponds the reference "有機 EL ディスプレー（ＯＥＬ Ｄ，ｏｒｇａｎｉｃｅｌｅｃｔｒｏ－ｌｕｍｉ ｎｅｓｃｅｎｔｄｉｓｐｌａｙ）"). Example 4 has the subtractive translation[4] (the source has

---

[1] Sentence level BLEU is calculated by mteval-v13a.pl in the Moses package.

[2] For the BLEU score, "less" means "less or equal -10" and "greater" means "greater or equal 10". If the difference of BLEU is between -10 to 10, it is considered "tie".

[3] We distinguish between "additive translation" and "over-translation". The former means the translation including

complemental information and the latter means the translation including needless information.

[4] We distinguish between "subtractive translation" and "under-translation". The former means the translation omitting complemental information and the latter means the translation omitting needful information.

"given within this range" and the reference has no such expression).

Comparing JPO adequacy score of EHR and OTHER, the EHR's score 4.63 is less than the OTHER's score 4.75. Although HUMAN and JPO adequacy are both human evaluation, they have a contradiction. One possible reason is that the evaluators of HUMAN score do not look at the reference translations but the evaluators of JPO adequacy score can look at the reference translations.

1	source	In FIG. 6 , the same symbols are used to the same elements as the elements shown in FIGS. 1-5
	reference	図 6 において 、 図 1 〜 図 5 に 示す 要素 と 同じ 要素 には 同じ 符号 を 付して ある 。
	EHR	図 6 では 、 同じ 記号 が 、 図 1 〜 5 に 示される 要素 と 同じ 要素 に 使用 される 。
	OTHER	図 6 において 、 図 1 〜 図 5 と 同じ 要素 には 同じ 符号 を 付 して いる 。
2	source	A sixth on-off valve 202 is disposed on the fourth bypass passage 204 .
	reference	第 4 バイパス 経路 204 には 第 6 開閉 弁 202 が 設け られて いる 。
	EHR	第 6 の オン オフ 弁 202 は 、 第 4 バイパス 通路 204 上 に 配置 される 。
	OTHER	第 4 の バイパス 通路 204 には 、 第 6 の 開閉 弁 202 が 配 置 されて いる 。
3	source	The display device 4 is, for example, an LCD and an GELD.
	reference	表示 装置 4 は 、 例えば 、 液晶 ディスプレイ (LCD , liquidcry staldisplay) や 有機 EL ディスプレイ (OELD , organicelectr o − luminescentdisplay) 等 である 。
	EHR	表示 装置 4 は 、 例えば LCD および GELD である 。
	OTHER	表示 装置 4 は 、 例えば LCD や OELD (OELD , organicele ctro − luminescentdisplay) 等 である 。
4	source	In this case, the proportion of the additive given within this range corresponds to 3% or lower.
	reference	この 場合 の 添加 剤 の 添加 量 は 3 % 以下 である 。
	EHR	この 場合 、 この 範囲 内 に 与え られる 添加 剤 の 割合 は 、 3 % 以下 に 相当 する 。
	OTHER	この 場合 、 添加 剤 の 割合 は 、 3 % 以下 である 。

Table 3: Different expressions between sources and references (example 1: voice change; example 2: topic change; example 3: additive translation; example 4: subtractive translation)

For JPCzh-ja and JPCko-ja tasks, reranking increases BLEU, RIBES and AMFM scores. However, we don't have a HUMAN scores comparing the reranking and the original for these tasks. Examples having the effectiveness of the reranking for these tasks are shown in Table 4 and Table 5.

Example 1 and 2 of Table 4 have under-translation in original translation. Example 3 of Table 4 has over-translation in original translation. Example 1 and 2 of Table 5 have under-translation in original translation.

1	source	图 3（A）是 对 进行 2 次 通过 间隙 的 处理 的 高分子 组合物 的 制造 装置 从 上面 透视 装置 内部 时 的 概略 透视图，图 3（B）是 图 3（A）的 装置 的 P－Q 截面 上 的 概略 截面 图 。
	reference	図 3（Ａ）は 、 間隙 通過 処理 を 2 回 行う 高 分子 組成 物 の 製造 装置 に ついて 上 面 から 装置 内部 を 透視 した とき の 概略 透視 図 であり 、 図 3（Ｂ）は 、 図 3（Ａ）の 装置 の Ｐ－Ｑ 断面 に おける 概略 断面 図 である 。
	reranking	図 3（Ａ）は 、 ギャップ を 2 回 行う 処理 を 行う 高 分子 組成 物 の 製造 装置 を 上 面 透視 装置 内部 から 見た 場合 の 概略 透視 図 であり 、 図 3（Ｂ）は 、 図 3（Ａ）の 装置 の Ｐ－Ｑ 断面 に おける 概略 断面 図 である 。
	original	図 3（Ａ）は 、 図 3（Ａ）の 装置 の Ｐ－Ｑ 断面 上 の 概略 的な 断面 図 である 。
	SMT	図3(A)については、2次ギャップの処理によって高分子組成物の製造装置を上面から装置内部透視時の概略斜視図であり、図3(B)は、図3(A)の装置のP－Q断面における概略断面図である。
2	source	此外，根据 元素 的话， 一 个 元素 有 可能 形成 不同 化合价 的 氧化物 。
	reference	また 、 元素 に よって は 、 1 つ の 元素 が 異なる 価 数 の 酸化 物 を 形 成 する こと が 可能である 。
	reranking	また 、 元素 に よって は 、 1 つ の 元素 が 異なる 種類 の 酸化 物 を 形成 する こと が できる 。
	original	また 、 元素 に よって は 、 異なる 元素 を 形成 する こと が できる 。
	SMT	また、元素とによれば、異なる原子価元素の酸化物を形成することができる。
3	source	实施例 14
	reference	【 実施 例 14 】
	reranking	実施 例 14 :
	original	（ 実施 例 14 ） 実施 例 14 に ついて 説明 する 。
	SMT	実施例14

Table 4: JPCzh-ja task's examples having effectiveness of reranking (recover of under-translation: example 1 and 2; recover of over-translation: example 3)

1	source	이어서 , 용매 로서 DINP (디 이소노 닐 프탈 레이트) 183 질 량부 를 첨가 하 였 다 .
	reference	次いで 、 溶媒 として DINP (ジイソノニルフタレート) 183 質量 部 を 添加 した 。
	reranking	次いで 、 溶媒 として DINP (ジメチルホルムアミド) 183 質量 部 を 添加 した 。
	original	次に 、 溶媒 として DINP (、) 183 質量 部 を 添加 した 。
	SMT	次いで、溶媒としてDINP（記述이소노アニールフタレート）183質量部を添加した。
2	source	저장 장치 (70) 는 다음 을 포함 할 수 있 다 (도 15 및 도 16) : - 하나 혹 은 그 이상 의 전기 배터리 (81) ; 또는 - 하이브리드 배터리 (82) 및 , 상 기 하이브리드 배터리 (82) 와 유효 하 게 연결 된 내연 기관 (83) .
	reference	貯蔵 装置 70 は 下記 を 備える ことが できる (図 15 と 16) ： 一　1 台 または 2 台 以上 の 電気 バッテリ 81 ；または 、 一　ハイブリッド バッテリ 82 と 、 前記 ハイブリッド バッテリ 82 に 接続 されて いる 内燃機 関 83 。
	reranking	記憶 装置 70 は 、 以下 を 含む ことが できる (図 15 及び 図 16) : 1 つ または それ 以上 の 電気 バッテリー 81 、 又は ハイブリッド バッテリー 82 、 及び 、 ハイブリッド バッテリ 82 と 有効に 連結 された 内燃機 関 83 。
	original	記憶 装置 70 は 、 以下 を 含む ことが できる (図 15 および 図 16) 。
	SMT	記憶装置70は以下を含むことができる（図15及び図16:－1つあるいはそれ以上の電気バッテリ81；又は－ハイブリッドバッテリ82及び、上記ハイブリッドバッテリ82と有効に連結された内燃機関（83）。

Table 5: JPCko-ja task's examples having effectiveness of reranking (recover of under-translation: example 1 and 2)

For JPCzh-ja and JPCko-ja tasks, the word based translations have higher BLEU, RIBES and AMFM compared with the character based translations. However, HUMAN score of the word based translations are lower than the score of the character based translations.

For JPCzh-ja task, there are 7 data that the BLEU score of the word based translation is greater than the character based translation's score but the HUMAN score of the word based translation is less than the character based translation's score. Examples of such translations are listed in Table 6. Example 1 has an under-translation in the word based translation ("滴度"). Example 2 also has an under-translation in the word based translation ("実行される(进行的)"). Example 3 has miss translations both in the character based translation and the word based translation. In the character based translation, "取付面図" is used instead of "実装面図(安装面図)". And in the word based translation, "分波器モジュール" is used instead of "デュプレクサモジュール(双工器模块)". However, the latter miss translation is more significant than the former. Example 4 has another different translations. Character based translation uses "が良い(好)", and word based translation uses "に優れる".

For JPCko-ja task, there are 3 data that the BLEU score of the word based translation is greater than the character based translation's score and the HUMAN score of the word based translation is less than the character based translation's score. Examples of such translations are listed in Table 7. Example 1 has a different translation. Literal translation of "연 결" is "連結" and non-literal translation is "接続". Example 2 shows the effectiveness of the unknown word translation in the character based translation. The expression

"디 펜 타 에 리 트 리 톨 펜 타 아 크 릴 레 이 트 와

디 펜 타 에 리 트 리 톨" does not be translated in the word based translation. Example 3 has different translations. Character based translation uses "ブレーキ(브 레 이 크)", and word based translation uses "ブレーク".

1	source	这进一步提示高估了CAZ028单价散装液滴度。
	reference	このことは、CAZ028一価バルクの力価が高く見積もられていることをさらに示唆する。
	char. based	これはさらに、CAZ028単価の分散液の滴度を高めることを示唆する。
	word based	これにより、CAZ028の一価ばら積みをさらに示唆する。
2	source	图9示出了电台110为释放额外的无线资源所进行的处理过程900的设计。
	reference	図9は、余分な無線リソースを放棄するために局110によって実行される方法900の設計を示す。
	char. based	図9は、局110が、追加の無線リソースを解放するために行われる処理プロセス900の設計を示す。
	word based	図9は、追加の無線リソースを解放するために局110が処理プロセス900の設計を示す。
3	source	图4(A)是双工器模块的简要等效电路图，图4(B)是双工器模块的安装面图。
	reference	図4(A)はデュプレクサモジュールの概略の等価回路図であり、図4(B)はデュプレクサモジュールの実装面図である。
	char. based	図4(A)は、デュプレクサモジュールの概略等価回路図であり、図4(B)は、デュプレクサモジュールの取付面図である。
	word based	図4(A)はデュプレクサモジュールの概略的な等価回路図であり、図4(B)は分波器モジュールの実装面図である。
4	source	另一方面，如果大于4.2倍，则虽然耐水解性好，但基材层(B)的凝聚强度降低，因此不理想。
	reference	他方、4．2倍を超えると耐加水分解性は良いが基材層（B）の凝集強度が低くなり好ましくない。
	char. based	一方、4．2倍を超えると、耐加水分解性が良いが、基材層（B）の凝集強度が低下するため好ましくない。
	word based	一方、4．2倍を超えると耐加水分解性に優れるが、基材層（B）の凝集強度が低下するため好ましくない。

Table 6: JPCzh-ja task's examples having BLEU and HUMAN scores contradiction (under-translation in word based: example 1 and 2; different translation: example 3 and 4)

1	source	이러한 경우, 수신기는 S707단계로 진행하여 2차 장치가 연결되었는지 판단한다.
	reference	この場合、受信機は、S707段階において、2次装置が接続しているか否か判断する。
	char. based	このような場合、受信機は、S707段階に進行して二次装置が連結されたか否かを判断する。
	word based	このような場合、受信機は、S707段階に進行して二次装置が接続されたか否かを判断する。
2	source	[B] 중합성 화합물은, 디펜타에리트리톨펜타아크릴레이트와 디펜타에리트리톨헥사아크릴레이트의 혼합물인 것이 바람직하다.
	reference	[B]重合性化合物は、ジペンタエリスリトールペンタアクリレートとジペンタエリスリトールヘキサアクリレートとの混合物であることが好ましい。
	char. based	[B]重合性化合物は、ディペンタエリトリトールペンタアクリレートとディペンターにリトリトールヘキサアクリレートの混合物であることが好ましい。
	word based	[B]重合性化合物は、ペンタエリトリトールとペンタエリトリトールヘキサレートの混合物であることが好ましい。
3	source	이렇게 하면 브레이크한 부분에서 머더 기판을 단위 기판으로 분단할 수 있다.
	reference	こうすればブレイクした部分でマザー基板を単位基板に分断することができる。
	char. based	こうすればブレーキした部分でマザー基板を単位基板に分断することができる。
	word based	こうすればブレイクした部分でマザー基板を単位基板に分断することができる。

Table 7: JPCko-ja task's examples having BLEU and HUMAN scores contradiction (different translation: example 1 and 3; un-translation in word based: example 2)

4   Conclusion

System descriptions, experimental settings and experimental results of the EHR team are described. We participate in the 3 tasks and submitted 10 systems' outputs. We can observe our re-ranking technique is effective to remove under-translation and over-translation which are in NMT outputs sometimes.

References

Hiroshi Echizen-ya and Kenji Araki. 2007. Automatic Evaluation of Machine Translation based on Recursive Acquisition of an Intuitive Common Parts Continuum, *Proceedings of the Eleventh Machine Translation Summit (MT SUMMIT XI)*, Page.151-158.

Terumasa Ehara. 2015. System Combination of RBMT plus SPE and Preordering plus SMT. *Proceedings of the 2nd Workshop on Asian Translation (WAT2015)*, pages 29–34.

Terumasa Ehara. 2016. Translation systems and experimental results of the EHR group for WAT2016 tasks. *Proceedings of the 3rd Workshop on Asian Translation (WAT2016)*, pages 111-118.

Philipp Koehn, Franz J. Och and Daniel Marcu. 2003. Statistical Phrase-Based Translation. *Proceedings of HLTNAACL 2003*, pages 48-54.

Sadao Kurohashi, Toshihisa Nakamura, Yuji Matsumoto and Makoto Nagao. 1994. Improvements of Japanese morphological analyzer JUMAN. *Proceedings of The International Workshop on Sharable Natural Language Resources*, pages 22-28.

Minh-Thang Luong, Hieu Pham and Christopher D. Manning. 2015. Effective Approaches to Attention-based Neural Machine Translation, *Proceedings of the 2015 Conference on Empirical Methods in Natural Language Processing*, pages 1412–1421.

Toshiaki Nakazawa, Chenchen Ding, Hideya Mino, Isao Goto, Graham Neubig and Sadao Kurohashi. 2016. Overview of the 3rd Workshop on Asian Translation. *Proceedings of the 3rd Workshop on Asian Translation (WAT2016)*, pages 1-46.

Toshiaki Nakazawa, Shohei Higashiyama, Chenchen Ding, Hideya Mino, Isao Goto, Graham Neubig, Hideto Kazawa, Yusuke Oda, Jun Harashima and Sadao Kurohashi. 2017. Overview of the 4th Workshop on Asian Translation. *Proceedings of the 4th Workshop on Asian Translation (WAT2017)*, pages ??-??.

Ensemble and Reranking: Using Multiple Models
in the NICT-2 Neural Machine Translation System at WAT2017

Kenji Imamura and **Eiichiro Sumita**

National Institute of Information and Communications Technology,
3-5 Hikaridai, Seika-cho, Soraku-gun, Kyoto 619-0289, Japan
{kenji.imamura, eiichiro.sumita}@nict.go.jp

Abstract

In this paper, we describe the NICT-2 neural machine translation system evaluated at WAT2017. This system uses multiple models as an ensemble and combines models with opposite decoding directions by reranking (called bi-directional reranking).

In our experimental results on small data sets, the translation quality improved when the number of models was increased to 32 in total and did not saturate. In the experiments on large data sets, improvements of 1.59–3.32 BLEU points were achieved when six-model ensembles were combined by the bi-directional reranking.

1 Introduction

This paper presents the NICT-2 machine translation system evaluated at WAT2017 (Nakazawa et al., 2017). This system is a basic encoder-decoder with an attention mechanism (Sutskever et al., 2014; Bahdanau et al., 2015). This methodology is known to achieve high translation quality, even when using a single model. It is also known that better quality can be achieved by utilizing multiple models. In this paper, we use as many models as possible and attempt to improve the translation quality.

There are two major approaches that use multiple models: ensemble (Hansen and Salamon, 1990) and reranking (e.g., (Och et al., 2004)). The ensemble approach independently encodes and decodes input sentences by multiple models and averages the word distributions output from the decoder (c.f., Sec. 2.1). The reranking approach first creates an n-best list of translations using a model A, rescores it using another model B, and selects the highest scoring translation (c.f., Sec. 2.2).

	Pros	Cons
Ensemble		
	• All hypotheses in the search space are candidates for translation.	• Models that have different output layers in the decoders cannot be incorporated (from the viewpoints of vocabulary and decoding direction).
	• It is possible to speed up the computations by parallel processing.	• All models should be loaded on graphics processing units (GPUs) at the same time.
Reranking		
	• Arbitrary models can be combined if the language pairs are the same.	• The system cannot select candidates that are not in the n-best list.
	• The models for the generation and rescoring of the n-best candidates have to be loaded separately on GPUs.	• The n-best generation and rescoring processes are sequential.

Table 1: Pros and Cons of Ensemble and Reranking

Both methods have pros and cons, as shown in Table 1. The aim of this paper is to use as many models as possible, based on these characteristics.

In this paper, we first obtain the following information on small data sets and then apply the ensemble and reranking methods on large data sets.

- How many models contribute to the translation quality?

- If both methods use the same number of models, which method is better? In this paper, we only evaluate the translation quality and ignore the translation speed.

The rest of this paper is organized as follows. Sec. 2 describes in detail the ensemble and reranking methods and their combination used at WAT2017. Sec. 3 evaluates characteristics of the

Proceedings of the 4th Workshop on Asian Translation, pages 127–134,
Taipei, Taiwan, November 27, 2017. ©2017 AFNLP

ensemble and reranking methods using small data sets (the JIJI Corpus and the MED Corpus, which was developed in-house). In Sec. 4, we evaluate the NICT-2 system using ASPEC (Asian Scientific Paper Excepts Corpus; (Nakazawa et al., 2016b)) data sets, and the paper is concluded in Sec. 5.

Note that we only evaluate Japanese-English (Ja-En) and Japanese-Chinese (Ja-Zh) pairs. Thus, additional investigation of whether the conclusions are valid for other language pairs is necessary. However, we believe that the results in this paper are valuable as a case study.

2   Ensemble and Reranking

2.1   Ensemble

The ensemble approach is a method for neural networks that trains multiple models using the same data sets and applies them to test data while averaging the outputs (Hansen and Salamon, 1990). In the case of neural machine translation, an input sentence is encoded and decoded using multiple models. Then, the word distributions output from the decoder (i.e., vectors of the target vocabulary size) are averaged. A beam search is applied to this averaged distribution. Note that each model is independently trained in the same way as the training of a single model.

If we represent the output word selection for a single model by Eq. (1), the selection for an ensemble is represented by Eq. (2). In this case, we use the geometric mean.

$$\hat{y}_t = \arg\max \log Pr(y_t | y_1^{t-1}, \mathbf{x}; M) \tag{1}$$

$$\hat{y}_t = \arg\max \frac{1}{J} \sum_{j=1}^{J} \log Pr(y_t | y_1^{t-1}, \mathbf{x}; M_j) \tag{2}$$

where y_t denotes the tth output word, y_1^{t-1} denotes the history of the output words from the beginning of the sentence to the $(t-1)$th position, $\mathbf{x}$ denotes the input word sequence, M denotes the model (M_j denotes the jth model), and J denotes the number of ensemble models.

The ensemble approach has some restrictions. Firstly, it has to use identical target vocabularies for all models because it averages the output vectors. Secondly, the decoding direction (from the beginning to the end of a sentence or from the end to the beginning) has to be consistent over all models because the beam search is applied after averaging. In this paper, we call the directions from the beginning to the end and from the end to the

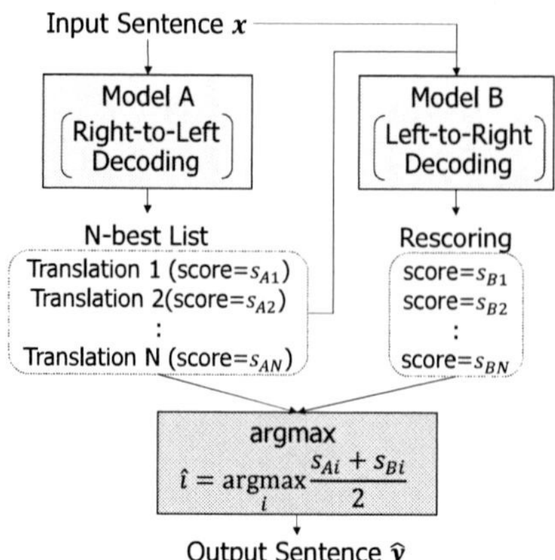

Figure 1: Structure of Bi-directional Reranking

beginning the left-to-right and right-to-left directions, respectively.

2.2   Reranking

The reranking method for machine translation (Och et al., 2004) comprises two steps. Firstly, an input sentence is translated using a model A, and an n-best list is generated. Then, the translations in the n-best list are rescored using another model B. Finally, the translation that has the highest score is selected/output (Figure 1). The models A and B are independently trained as single models.

The final translations are influenced by the rescoring method. In this paper, we use the arithmetic mean of the log-likelihoods of the models A and B.

The reranking method has the advantage that arbitrary models can be used if the target languages are the same. In addition, the reranking method consumes less memory than the ensemble method because only one model is used at each step in the reranking method, even though it uses two models in total. However, it has the disadvantage that the translation quality cannot be improved if good translation hypotheses are not included in the n-best list.

2.3   Combination of Ensemble and Reranking

The pros and cons of the ensemble and reranking methods are shown in Table 1. To combine both methodologies while retaining as many advantages as possible, we employ reranking as the general methodology. The ensemble method is used for the n-best list generation and rescoring

Corpus	Language Pair	#Sentences		#Sub-word Types		Remarks
ASPEC	Ja ↔ En	Train:	2,977,320	Ja:	49,656	Scientific paper excerpts
		Dev.:	1,790	En:	49,776	Sentences in which the number of sub-words is
		Test.:	1,812			equal to or less than 80
	Ja ↔ Zh	Train:	656,635	Ja:	49,654	Scientific paper excerpts
		Dev.:	2,090	Zh:	49,385	Sentences in which the number of sub-words is
		Test.:	2,107			equal to or less than 80
JIJI	Ja → En	Train:	199,905	Ja:	35,009	Newswire
		Dev.:	2,000	En:	33,934	Sentences in which the number of sub-words is
		DevTest.:	2,000			equal to or less than 80
		Test.:	2,000			
MED	Ja → En	Train:	238,214	Ja:	20,327	Pseudo-dialogues at hospitals
		Dev.:	1,000	En:	21,043	Sentences in which the number of sub-words is
		Test.:	1,000			equal to or less than 80

Table 2: Corpus Statistics

to combine multiple models. We can combine many models using this architecture because the reranking method can combine twice the number of models without consuming extra memory.

We use an identical vocabulary set among all models so that the ensemble method can be applied. In addition, the models used here have the same structure for simplicity. The only difference is that each model is learned using a different random seed.

For the generation and rescoring of the n-best translations in the reranking, we use models with opposite decoding directions, which are impossible to combine with the ensemble method. In this paper, we call this bi-directional reranking. More precisely, the n-best list is generated by right-to-left decoding (i.e., from the end to the beginning of a sentence). Then, the hypotheses in the list are rescored by left-to-right decoding (i.e., from the beginning to the end of the sentence). Finally, the translation likelihoods for both directions are averaged, and the hypothesis with the highest likelihood is output.

The bi-directional reranking approach realizes Liu et al. (2016)'s method, which uses bi-directional decoding, by reranking. In the bi-directional reranking approach, the target word sequence is inverted during training and translation. Therefore, small changes are required in the training and translation programs.

3 Experiments Using Small Data Sets

We perform Japanese-English translation experiments using small data (with approximately 200k sentences) to clarify characteristics of the ensemble and the bi-directional reranking approaches.

3.1 Experimental Settings

Corpora: Table 2 shows the list of corpora that were used here. We used two corpora as small data sets. The first is the JIJI Corpus, which consists of newswires. Japanese and English articles were automatically aligned sentence by sentence. Note that the translations are sometimes not literal because the original articles were not translated sentence by sentence.

The second is the corpus of pseudo-dialogues at hospitals (MED Corpus). This corpus is a collection of conversations between patients and hospital staffs, which were created by writers (developed in-house). The pseudo-dialogues were first written in Japanese and then translated into English.

The byte-pair encoding (Sennrich et al., 2016) rules were acquired from a training set of each corpus, and they were applied to the training, development, and test sets. The number of sub-word types is 34–35k in the JIJI Corpus and 20–21k in the MED Corpus. We used sentences with 80 or fewer sub-words for training.

Preprocessing, Postprocessing: Table 3 shows a summary of our system. As shown in the table, we used the same preprocessing and postprocessing steps as the WAT baseline systems (Nakazawa et al., 2016a).

Translation System: We used OpenNMT (Klein et al., 2017)[1] as the base translation system. The encoder comprises a two-layer bi-directional LSTM (long short-term memory), in which the number of units is 500 each. The decoder comprises a two-layer LSTM (1000

---

[1] http://opennmt.net/

		Japanese	English	Chinese
Preprocessing	Character Normalization	NFKC Normalization of Unicode		
	Tokenizer	MeCab (Kudo et al., 2004)	Moses Toolkit	Stanford Segmenter (CTB)
	TrueCaser	–	Moses Toolkit	–
	Byte Pair Encoding	In-house Encoder		
Training and Translation	System	OpenNMT (modified for right-to-left decoding and the ensemble method)		
	Encoder	Word embedding: 500 units, two-layer Bi-LSTM (500 + 500 units)		
	Decoder	Word embedding: 500 units, two-layer LSTM (1,000 units)		
	Attention	Global Attention		
	Training	Mini Batch Size:64, SGD Optimization (10+6 epochs), Dropout:0.3		
	Translation	Beam Width:5 (c.f., Sec. 3.2)		
Postprocessing	DeTrueCaser	–	Moses Toolkit	–
	DeTokenizer	WAT Official's	Moses Toolkit	WAT Official's

Table 3: Summary of the NICT-2 NMT System

units). Global Attention (Luong et al., 2015) was utilized.

We used the stochastic gradient descent (SGD) method for the optimization. The learning rate was 1.0 for the first ten epochs, and then annealing was performed for six epochs while decreasing the learning rate by half.

To implement the methods described in Section 2.3, we modified OpenNMT as follows.

- We enabled the ensemble in the translator.
- We enabled right-to-left decoding in the trainer and translator.

The n-best size for the reranking was determined by the experiment in Section 3.2.

Evaluation: Of the WAT official evaluation metrics, we employ BLEU (Papineni et al., 2002) for the evaluation. WAT official scores are changed by word segmenters. In this paper, we use JUMAN (Kurohashi et al., 1994) for Japanese, Moses tokenizer (Koehn et al., 2007) for English, and Stanford Word Segmenter (Chinese Penn Treebank Model) (Chang et al., 2008) for Chinese evaluation.

3.2 Optimal Size of N-best List

To output n-best translations using the beam search, beam width is better to set equal or more than n. In our experiments, we set the beam width equal to the size of the n-best list.

Figure 2 shows the BLEU scores of various n-best sizes on the DevTest set of the JIJI Corpus. It contains the scores obtained by left-to-right and right-to-left decoding and bi-directional reranking. A single model is used here, i.e., an ensemble is not used in this experiment.

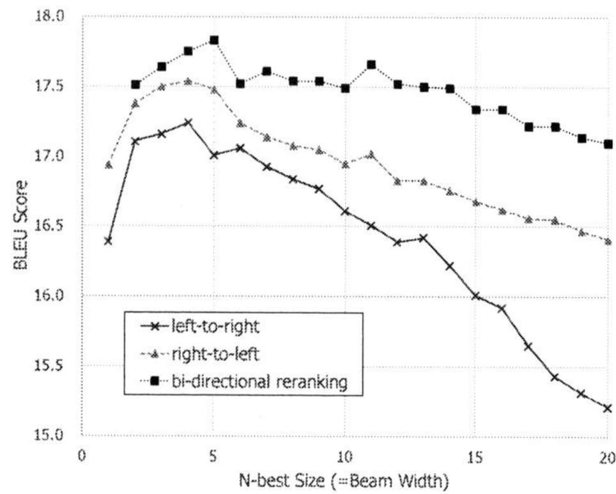

Figure 2: BLEU Scores According to N-best Size

In all methods, the BLEU scores changed according to the size of the n-best list. For left-to-right and right-to-left decoding, the BLEU scores were highest when the n-best size was 4, and the scores decreased when the n-best size increased above 4. After the bi-directional reranking, the BLEU score was the highest when the n-best size was 5, and slowly decreased when the size increased above 5.

In general, large n-best size is expected in reranking to include good hypotheses. However, in our NMT system, the peak score was achieved with a small n-best size when a single model was used, and similarly, a small n-best size was the best in the reranking. This is because decreasing the accuracy of the single model had greater influence than improving the coverage of n-best sizes. Based on the above observation, we use 5 as the n-best size hereafter.

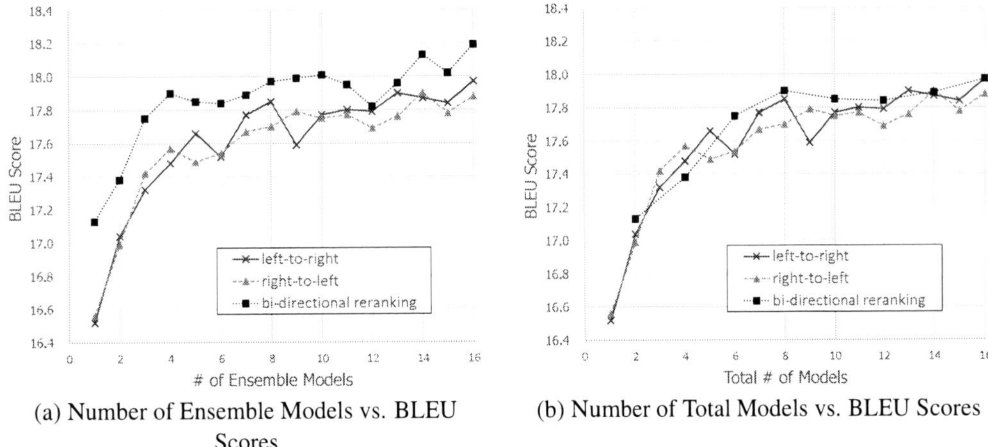

(a) Number of Ensemble Models vs. BLEU Scores

(b) Number of Total Models vs. BLEU Scores

Figure 3: Results of Multiple Model Combination on the JIJI Corpus
In the bi-directional reranking, the total number of models in (b) is equal to twice the number of ensemble models in (a).

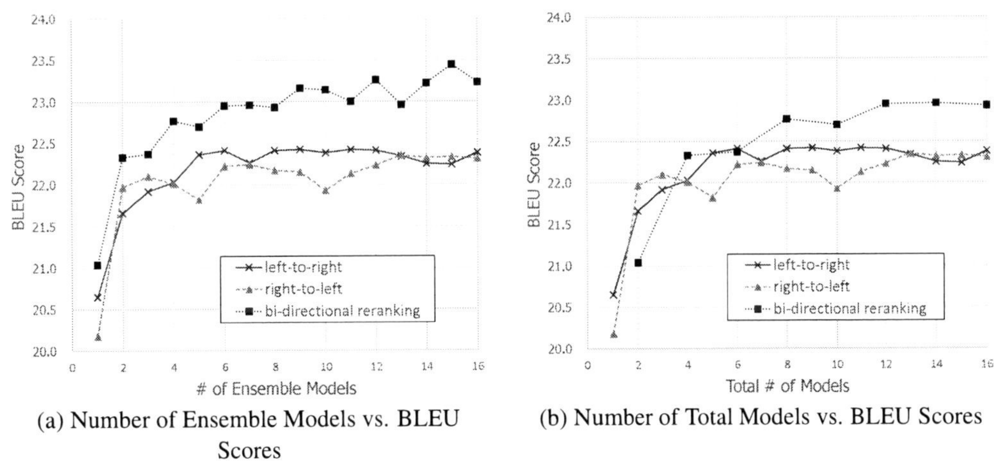

(a) Number of Ensemble Models vs. BLEU Scores

(b) Number of Total Models vs. BLEU Scores

Figure 4: Results of Multiple Model Combination on the MED Corpus
In the bi-directional reranking, the total number of models in (b) is equal to twice the number of ensemble models in (a).

3.3 Effects of Multiple Models

Figures 3 and 4 show the results of the left-to-right and right-to-left decodings, which use the simple ensemble, and the bi-directional reranking on the JIJI and MED corpora, respectively. Note that the number of models used in the reranking is double of that used by the ensemble model. Therefore, we show two graphs: (a) a graph based on the number of ensemble models and (b) a graph based on the total number of models. We increased the number of models incrementally, i.e., models are added one at a time. Therefore, the settings for many models must be compatible with the settings of fewer models.

We firstly focus on the number of models and the translation quality. The BLEU scores tend to increase with the number of models for the all methods in the graphs. However, the rates of increase become slower as the number of models increases. On the JIJI Corpus, the BLEU scores are still increasing slightly with the 16-model ensemble. On the MED Corpus, the BLEU scores almost saturate with two- to six-model ensembles but do not saturate in the bi-directional reranking.

Zhou et al. (2002) indicated that the ensemble

131

is more effective when models are selected, rather than using all models. However, in our experiment, degradation of the translation quality was not observed when all the models were used. The BLEU score improved by 1.67 points in the bi-directional reranking with 16 ensembles (32 models in total) on the JIJI Corpus compared with a single model in the left-to-right decoding. On the MED Corpus, the BLEU score improved by 2.58 points.

Secondly, we focus on the left-to-right and right-to-left decodings of the ensemble. On MED Corpus, the BLEU scores of the right-to-left decoding are higher than those of the left-to-right decoding. In contrast, the BLEU scores of the both decoding directions are almost the same on JIJI Corpus. We expected that the results would depend on the data sets and language pairs. However, these results show that the translation quality changed according to the decoding direction.

Thirdly, focusing on the graphs in (a), the scores of the reranking almost always surpass those of the simple ensembles (left-to-right and right-to-left decodings). From these results, we make the following observations.

- The model combination using the reranking favorably affects the translation quality.

- Bi-directional reranking can improve the translation quality from different aspects than the ensemble.

Since we combined models with opposite decoding directions, effects similar to those of bi-directional decoding (Liu et al., 2016) were realized.

The graphs in (b) show that the total number of models is double the number of ensemble models in the reranking. As shown in the graphs, the BLEU scores of the reranking almost always surpass those of the ensembles. In our experiments, bi-directional reranking was more effective than the ensembles if the number of models was the same.

4 Experiments Using Large Data Sets

In this section, we show the results of Ja-En, En-Ja, Ja-Zh, and Zh-Ja translation of the ASPEC task.

4.1 Experimental Settings

Corpora: The corpora used here are the ASPEC data sets listed in Table 2. From these training sets, we acquired the byte-pair encoding rules, which generate approximately 50k sub-word types per language, and used sentences in which the number of sub-words is equal to or less than 80.

Translation System: The other settings such as the translation system, preprocessing, and post-processing are the same as those in Section 3. Table 3 shows a summary of the settings.

4.2 Results

The results of the Ja-En and En-Ja translations are shown in Table 4, and those of the Ja-Zh and Zh-Ja translations are shown in Table 5.

We tested up to six ensembles due to resource limitations; however, the results have the same tendency as those of the small data sets. Namely, the BLEU scores increased with the number of models in both the cases, ensembles and reranking. The best BLEU scores were obtained in the bi-directional reranking with six-model ensembles in all language pairs, except En-Ja.

The improvements from the left-to-right single model to the bi-directional reranking with six-model ensemble were +1.97, +3.32, +1.59, and +2.58 points in the Ja-En, En-Ja, Ja-Zh, and Zh-Ja translations, respectively.

5 Conclusion

In this paper, we presented the NICT-2 neural machine translation system evaluated at WAT2017. The main characteristics of this system are that multiple models are used by the ensemble, and moreover, double models are used by the bi-directional reranking.

In the experiments on small data sets, we increased the number of models in the ensemble to 16. However, the translation quality did not saturate and can be further improved on some data sets.

We confirmed that the decoding direction influences the translation quality. In addition, the reranking can combine models with different properties from the ensemble. Using this feature, we combined models with opposite decoding directions in the reranking. By incorporating the ensemble and bi-directional reranking, we achieved higher translation quality than with the ensemble alone. In our experiments using ASPEC data

# of Ensemble Models	Ja-En			En-Ja		
	Ensemble (left-to-right)	Ensemble (right-to-left)	Reranking	Ensemble (left-to-right)	Ensemble (right-to-left)	Reranking
1	24.79	24.72	25.34	36.85	38.20	39.10
2	25.60	25.40	25.89	38.37	38.69	39.41
3	26.17	25.62	26.08	38.95	39.23	39.87
4	25.89	25.77	26.26	38.97	39.37	40.03
5	25.94	26.06	26.37	39.19	39.55	**40.23**
6	26.21	26.29	**26.76**	39.13	39.26	40.17

Table 4: WAT2017 Official Scores (Ja-En Pair of ASPEC).
Note: The Japanese scores are based on the JUMAN segmenter.

# of Ensemble Models	Ja-Zh			Zh-Ja		
	Ensemble (left-to-right)	Ensemble (right-to-left)	Reranking	Ensemble (left-to-right)	Ensemble (right-to-left)	Reranking
1	33.64	33.60	34.10	44.26	44.13	45.10
2	34.67	34.22	34.77	45.59	45.52	46.20
3	34.75	34.64	34.98	45.88	45.93	46.53
4	34.75	34.64	34.98	46.13	46.10	46.55
5	35.02	34.81	35.18	46.27	46.36	46.69
6	35.27	34.95	**35.23**	46.55	46.31	**46.84**

Table 5: WAT2017 Official Scores (Ja-Zh Pair of ASPEC).
Note: The Japanese and Chinese scores are based on the JUMAN and Stanford (CTB Model) segmenters, respectively.

sets, the BLEU scores improved from 1.59 to 3.32 points compared with the single model.

Both the ensemble and reranking can further improve the translation quality if the quality of a single model can be improved. Therefore, we will tackle the improvement of single models. At the time, we should evaluate the qualities of single and multiple models separately.

Currently, the ensemble approach might not be practical due to restrictions on the number and memory of GPUs. However, we assume that advances in hardware will decrease these restrictions.

Acknowledgments

This work was supported by "Promotion of Global Communications Plan — Research and Development and Social Demonstration of Multilingual Speech Translation Technology," a program of Ministry of Internal Affairs and Communications, Japan.

References

Dzmitry Bahdanau, KyungHyun Cho, and Yoshua Bengio. 2015. Neural machine translation by jointly learning to align and translate. In *Proceedings of International Conference on Learning Representations (ICLR 2015)*.

Pi-Chuan Chang, Michel Galley, and Christopher D. Manning. 2008. Optimizing Chinese word segmentation for machine translation performance. In *Proceedings of the Third Workshop on Statistical Machine Translation*, pages 224–232, Columbus, Ohio.

Lars Kai Hansen and Peter Salamon. 1990. Neural network ensembles. *IEEE Transactions on Pattern Analysis and Machine Intelligence*, 12(10):993–1001.

Guillaume Klein, Yoon Kim, Yuntian Deng, Jean Senellart, and Alexander M. Rush. 2017. OpenNMT: Open-source toolkit for neural machine translation. In *Proceedings of ACL 2017, System Demonstrations*, pages 67–72, Vancouver, Canada.

Philipp Koehn, Hieu Hoang, Alexandra Birch, Chris Callison-Burch, Marcello Federico, Nicola Bertoldi, Brooke Cowan, Wade Shen, Christine Moran, Richard Zens, Chris Dyer, Ondrej Bojar, Alexandra Constantin, and Evan Herbst. 2007. Moses: Open source toolkit for statistical machine translation. In *Proceedings of the 45th Annual Meeting of the Association for Computational Linguistics Companion Volume Proceedings of the Demo and Poster Sessions*, pages 177–180, Prague, Czech Republic.

Taku Kudo, Kaoru Yamamoto, and Yuji Matsumoto. 2004. Applying conditional random fields to Japanese morphological analysis. In *Proceedings of EMNLP 2004*, pages 230–237, Barcelona, Spain.

Sadao Kurohashi, Toshihisa Nakamura, Yuji Matsumoto, and Makoto Nagao. 1994. Improvements of

Japanese morphological analyzer JUMAN. In *Proceedings of the International Workshop on Sharable Natural Language*, pages 22–28.

Lemao Liu, Masao Utiyama, Andrew Finch, and Eiichiro Sumita. 2016. Agreement on target-bidirectional neural machine translation. In *Proceedings of the 2016 Conference of the North American Chapter of the Association for Computational Linguistics: Human Language Technologies*, pages 411–416, San Diego, California.

Thang Luong, Hieu Pham, and D. Christopher Manning. 2015. Effective approaches to attention-based neural machine translation. In *Proceedings of the 2015 Conference on Empirical Methods in Natural Language Processing*, pages 1412–1421, Lisbon, Portugal.

Toshiaki Nakazawa, Shohei Higashiyama, Chenchen Ding, Hideya Mino, Isao Goto, Graham Neubig, Hideto Kazawa, Yusuke Oda, Jun Harashima, and Sadao Kurohashi. 2017. Overview of the 4th Workshop on Asian Translation. In *Proceedings of the 4th Workshop on Asian Translation (WAT2017)*, Taipei, Taiwan.

Toshiaki Nakazawa, Hideya Mino, Chenchen Ding, Isao Goto, Graham Neubig, Sadao Kurohashi, and Eiichiro Sumita. 2016a. Overview of the 3rd workshop on Asian translation. In *Proceedings of the 3rd Workshop on Asian Translation (WAT2016)*, Osaka, Japan.

Toshiaki Nakazawa, Manabu Yaguchi, Kiyotaka Uchimoto, Masao Utiyama, Eiichiro Sumita, Sadao Kurohashi, and Hitoshi Isahara. 2016b. ASEPC: Asian scientific paper excerpt corpus. In *Proceedings of the Tenth Edition of the Language Resources and Evaluation Conference (LREC-2016)*, Portoroz, Slovenia.

Franz Josef Och, Daniel Gildea, Sanjeev Khudanpur, Anoop Sarkar, Kenji Yamada, Alex Fraser, Shankar Kumar, Libin Shen, David Smith, Katherine Eng, Viren Jain, Zhen Jin, and Dragomir Radev. 2004. A smorgasbord of features for statistical machine translation. In *HLT-NAACL 2004: Main Proceedings*, pages 161–168, Boston, Massachusetts, USA.

Kishore Papineni, Salim Roukos, Todd Ward, and Wei-Jing Zhu. 2002. Bleu: a method for automatic evaluation of machine translation. In *Proceedings of the 40th Annual Meeting of the Association for Computational Linguistics (ACL)*, pages 311–318, Philadelphia, Pennsylvania, USA.

Rico Sennrich, Barry Haddow, and Alexandra Birch. 2016. Neural machine translation of rare words with subword units. In *Proceedings of the 54th Annual Meeting of the Association for Computational Linguistics (Volume 1: Long Papers)*, pages 1715–1725, Berlin, Germany.

Ilya Sutskever, Oriol Vinyals, and Quoc V. Le. 2014. Sequence to sequence learning with neural networks. In *Proceedings of Advances in Neural Information Processing Systems 27 (NIPS 2014)*, pages 3104–3112.

Zhi-Hua Zhou, Jianxin Wu, and Wei Tang. 2002. Ensembling neural networks: Many could be better than all. *Artificial Intelligence*, 137(1-2):239–263.

A Simple and Strong Baseline: NAIST-NICT Neural Machine Translation System for WAT2017 English-Japanese Translation Task

Yusuke Oda[†‡]   Katsuhito Sudoh[†]   Satoshi Nakamura[†]
Masao Utiyama[‡]   Eiichiro Sumita[‡]
† Nara Institute of Science and Technology
8916-5 Takayama-cho, Ikoma-shi, Nara 630-0192, Japan
‡ National Institute of Information and Communications Technology
3-5 Hikaridai, Seika-cho, Kyoto 619-0289, Japan

Abstract

This paper describes the details about the NAIST-NICT machine translation system for WAT2017 English-Japanese Scientific Paper Translation Task. The system consists of a language-independent tokenizer and an attentional encoder-decoder style neural machine translation model. According to the official results, our system achieves higher translation accuracy than any systems submitted previous campaigns despite simple model architecture.

1 Introduction

Neural machine translation (NMT) methods became one of the main-stream techniques in current machine translation studies. Previous WAT campaign showed that NMT methods can achieve higher translation accuracy in spite of simple model configurations (Nakazawa et al., 2016a). In this year, we chose the NMT architecture as our translation systems submitted for WAT2017 English-Japanese Scientific Paper Translation Task (Nakazawa et al., 2017). The main translation model is constructed by an encoder-decoder model (Sutskever et al., 2014) enforced by an attention mechanism (Bahdanau et al., 2014; Luong et al., 2015). This paper describes the details of our system, including whole model architecture, training criteria, decoding strategy, and data preparation. Results show that our system achieves higher translation accuracy than any systems submitted in previous WAT campaigns.

2 Architecture of the System

2.1 Model formulation

Our translation model is built by an attentional encoder-decoder network implemented in NMTKit [1]. Overall model structure is based on the combination of Bahdanau et al. (2014) and Luong et al. (2015). This translation model represents a conditional probability $\Pr(e|f)$, where $e := [e_1, e_2, \cdots, e_E]$ and $f := [f_1, f_2, \cdots, f_F]$ are sequences of target/source words, and E, F are the numbers of the target/source words. Encoder-decoder style NMT models behaves a sequential word generators, which yields target words one-by-one along the time step. Formally, the whole translation model is separated into the product of token-wise conditional probabilities:

$$\Pr(e|f) = \prod_{t=1}^{E} \Pr(e_t|e_{<t}, f), \qquad (1)$$

where $e_{<t} := [e_1, \cdots, e_t]$ is the history of generated target words. In each time step t, the condition $\langle e_{<t}, f \rangle$ is represented as a *condition* vector η_t and each conditional probability in Equation (1) is calculated by the softmax function as follows:

$$
\begin{aligned}
\Pr(e_t|e_{<t}, f) &:= \Pr(e_t|\eta_t) & (2) \\
&:= \mathrm{softmax}(\mathbf{W}_e \eta_t + b_e). & (3)
\end{aligned}
$$

where $\mathbf{W}_e$ and b_e are the parameters to be trained: weight matrix and bias vector respectively. We calculate the condition vector η_t using three submodels: *encoder*, *decoder* and *attention* described in the following sections.

2.1.1 Encoder

The *encoder* converts given source sequence f to a set of vectors $R := [r_1, r_2, \cdots, r_F]$. Each vector at the position i is calculated as follows:

$$
\begin{aligned}
r_i &:= \mathrm{concat}(\overrightarrow{r}_i, \overleftarrow{r}_i), & (4) \\
\overrightarrow{r}_i &:= \mathrm{RNN}(\mathrm{emb}(f_i), \overrightarrow{r}_{i-1}) & (5) \\
\overleftarrow{r}_i &:= \mathrm{RNN}(\mathrm{emb}(f_i), \overleftarrow{r}_{i+1}), & (6)
\end{aligned}
$$

---

[1] https://github.com/odashi/nmtkit

Proceedings of the 4th Workshop on Asian Translation, pages 135–139,
Taipei, Taiwan, November 27, 2017. ©2017 AFNLP

where $\text{concat}(\cdots)$ represents the concatenation of given vectors, $\text{emb}(w)$ represents the lookup of embedding vectors corresponding to the token w, and $\text{RNN}(\cdot, \cdot)$ represents an independent recurrent unit. We use the long short-term memory units (Gers et al., 2000) with input/forget/output gates to all recurrent units. We also introduce the *n-stacked encoder* to represent richer source information as follows:

$$
\begin{aligned}
\boldsymbol{r}_i &:= \text{concat}(\overrightarrow{\boldsymbol{r}}_i^{(n)}, \overleftarrow{\boldsymbol{r}}_i^{(n)}), & (7) \\
\overrightarrow{\boldsymbol{r}}_i^{(n)} &:= \text{RNN}(\overrightarrow{\boldsymbol{r}}_i^{(n-1)}, \overrightarrow{\boldsymbol{r}}_{i-1}^{(n)}), & (8) \\
\overleftarrow{\boldsymbol{r}}_i^{(n)} &:= \text{RNN}(\overleftarrow{\boldsymbol{r}}_i^{(n-1)}, \overleftarrow{\boldsymbol{r}}_{i+1}^{(n)}), & (9) \\
\overrightarrow{\boldsymbol{r}}_i^{(0)} &:= \text{emb}(f_i), & (10) \\
\overleftarrow{\boldsymbol{r}}_i^{(0)} &:= \text{emb}(f_i). & (11)
\end{aligned}
$$

We set all initial recurrent states $\overrightarrow{\boldsymbol{r}}_0^{(n)}$ and $\overleftarrow{\boldsymbol{r}}_{F+1}^{(n)}$ to $\boldsymbol{0}$.

2.1.2 Decoder and attention

The *decoder* calculates the condition vector $\boldsymbol{\eta}_t$ as follows:

$$
\boldsymbol{\eta}_t := \tanh(\mathbf{W}_\eta \text{concat}(\boldsymbol{c}_t, \boldsymbol{h}_t) + \boldsymbol{b}_\eta), \quad (12)
$$

where $\mathbf{W}_\eta$ and $\boldsymbol{b}_\eta$ are the parameters. $\boldsymbol{h}_t$ is the current decoder's state calculated by a uni-directional recurrent unit:

$$
\boldsymbol{h}_t := \text{RNN}(\text{concat}(\text{emb}(e_{t-1}), \boldsymbol{\eta}_{t-1}), \boldsymbol{h}_{t-1})),
\tag{13}
$$

and we extend this formulation to the *n-stacked* version with the notation $\boldsymbol{h}_t^{(n)}$ by the similar modification to that of the encoder. In this calculation, we also introduce the previous condition vector $\boldsymbol{\eta}_{t-1}$ as an additional input of the recurrent unit. This is called as the *input feeding* (Luong et al., 2015), allows to propagate previous decision of the decoder with keeping differentiability of the network. $\boldsymbol{c}_t$ is the *context* vector calculated from $\boldsymbol{R}$ using an *attention* mechanism:

$$
\boldsymbol{c}_t := \mathbf{R}\boldsymbol{a}_t, \quad (14)
$$

where $\mathbf{R}$ is a matrix created by substituting all vectors $\boldsymbol{r}_i$ to the i-th columns. $\boldsymbol{a}_t$ represents the weight of each vector $\boldsymbol{r}_i$ at the time t, which is calculated by an arbitrary *score* function $\boldsymbol{\alpha}$:

$$
\boldsymbol{a}_t := \text{softmax}(\boldsymbol{\alpha}(\mathbf{R}, \boldsymbol{h}_t)). \quad (15)
$$

We follow the multi-layer perceptron based score function proposed by Bahdanau et al. (2014):

$$
\alpha_i(\mathbf{R}, \boldsymbol{h}_t) := \boldsymbol{v}_\alpha^\top \tanh(\mathbf{W}_\alpha \text{concat}(\boldsymbol{r}_i, \boldsymbol{h}_t)), \quad (16)
$$

where α_i represents the i-th element of $\boldsymbol{\alpha}$, $\boldsymbol{v}_\alpha$ and $\mathbf{W}_\alpha$ are the parameters.

For the initial values $\boldsymbol{h}_0^{(n)}$, we use the *dense bridge* connection from the encoder units as follows:

$$
\begin{aligned}
\boldsymbol{h}_0^{(n)} &:= \tanh(\boldsymbol{s}_{\boldsymbol{h},0}^{(n)}), & (17) \\
\boldsymbol{s}_{\boldsymbol{h},0}^{(n)} &:= \mathbf{U}^{(n)} \boldsymbol{s}_{\overrightarrow{\boldsymbol{r}},F}^{(n)} + \mathbf{V}^{(n)} \boldsymbol{s}_{\overleftarrow{\boldsymbol{r}},1}^{(n)} + \boldsymbol{b}_{h0}^{(n)},
\end{aligned}
$$
$$
\tag{18}
$$

where $\mathbf{U}^{(n)}$, $\mathbf{V}^{(n)}$ and $\boldsymbol{b}_{h0}^{(n)}$ are the parameters, and $\boldsymbol{s}_{\boldsymbol{x},t}^{(n)}$ denotes the internal states of the LSTMs corresponding to the outputs $\boldsymbol{x}_t^{(n)}$.

2.1.3 Hyper-parameters

The translation model described in previous sections has several hyper-parameters: number of units in source/target embeddings $\text{emb}(\cdot)$, RNN states $\overrightarrow{\boldsymbol{r}}$, $\overleftarrow{\boldsymbol{r}}$ and $\boldsymbol{h}$, the hidden layer in the attention network, and the condition vector $\boldsymbol{\eta}$. We constrained all these numbers same to prevent increasing combination of hyper-parameters. In addition, each recurrent unit also has the depth of stack as an additional hyper-parameter. We also constrained these numbers same due to the Equations (17) and (18). Eventually, we varied the number of units from 256 to 1024 and depth of the recurrent stack from 1 to 4 to construct models that have a different power of model expressiveness and finally selected 512 as the former and 2 as the latter hyper-parameter respectively.

2.2 Model Training

To find an optimal parameters in the model described in the previous sections, we minimize the cross-entropy loss function:

$$
\mathcal{L}(\theta) := -\sum_m \sum_t \log \mathcal{P}_{m,t}(\theta), \quad (19)
$$

$$
\mathcal{P}_{m,t}(\theta) := \Pr(e_t = e_t^{(m)} | \boldsymbol{e}_{<t} = \boldsymbol{e}_{<t}^{(m)}, \boldsymbol{f} = \boldsymbol{f}^{(m)}; \theta),
\tag{20}
$$

where $\boldsymbol{f}^{(m)}$ and $\boldsymbol{e}^{(m)}$ represents the m-th parallel corpora, and θ represents the set of all parameters in a translation model.

To achieve this optimization problem, we use the Adam optimizer (Kingma and Ba, 2014) for all training settings.

Hyper-parameters Since Adam has several hyper-parameters that may directly affect convergence speed and model quality, we tried to train our models with various combination of hyper-parameters, and finally chose as follows: $\alpha = 0.0001$ (default/10), $\beta_1 = 0.9$ (default), $\beta_2 = 0.999$ (default), and $\epsilon = 10^{-8}$ (default).

2.3 Tokenization

Tokenization is one of the worrisome problems of machine translation systems. Since there are no linguistically unified criteria about separating words from original sentences, we often have to choose tokenization methods carefully according to selected languages. In contrast, we use the SentencePiece tokenizer[2] instead of some language-dependent tokenization methods. This tokenizer basically requires only an *untokenized* training corpora to acquire actual tokenization strategies and frees us from selecting actual tokenizers. In our system, all raw sentences are tokenized using the SentencePiece tokenizer trained by the corpus used to train translation models, and resulting tokens generated by the translation models are detokenized by simply removing boundary markers in the concatenated strings. Through the whole process of our translation systems, we never use any other pre/post-processing methods.

Hyper-parameters SentencePiece requires the vocabulary size V as the hyper-parameter. We tried to use $V = 4096, 8192, 16384, 32768$, and finally chose $V = 16384$ for each language.

2.4 Decoding

In decoding actual target sentences, we performed greedy n-best beam search method with the *word penalty* heuristic, which simply multiplies the constant $\exp(WP)$ to all word probabilities in each time. The word penalty introduces an exponential distribution as a prior knowledge about the length of the target sentence. If we set the penalty factor $WP > 0$, then the system penalizes shorter sentences, and tends to generate longer sentences. Note that if the beam width is 1, there is no effect from word penalty, because the translation system can generate only 1-best results.

Hyper-parameters In our decoding strategy, We have 2 hyper-parameters: beam width BW and word penalty factor WP. We varied BW from 1 to 128, and WP from 0 to 1.5, and finally chose $BW = 16$ and $WP = 0.75$.

---

[2]https://github.com/google/sentencepiece

Table 1: Official evaluation results of our systems.

System	BLEU	Place (All / Single)
One-best	36.47	11 / 6
Adjusted	**38.25**	8 / 3
(last-year)	36.19	— / —

System	RIBES	Place (All / Single)
One-best	0.821989	13 / 6
Adjusted	**0.834492**	5 / 2
(last-year)	0.819836	— / —

System	AM-FM	Place (All / Single)
One-best	0.763310	5 / 4
Adjusted	**0.770480**	1 / 1
(last-year)	0.758740	— / —

System	Human	Place (All / Single)
One-best	63.500	8 / 3
Adjusted	**70.000**	4 / 1
(last-year)	—	— / —

2.5 Model Ensembling

Although the model ensembling techniques improve the translation accuracy, they also impose a great deal of computation back-ends (e.g., if a single model requires a full resource of one GPU, the N-ensemble system basically occupies N GPUs while executing it) and this behavior is typically not fit to the most situations of real production systems. Because of this issue, we did not introduce any model ensembling techniques while decoding test inputs.

3 Results

We trained all translation systems varied by model/training/tokenization hyper-parameters described in previous sections, and performed a grid search to find an optimal set of hyper-parameters for this task. For the training data, we used top 2M sentences in ASPEC corpus (Nakazawa et al., 2016b) provided by the organizer. We chose the optimal model that achieves the best BLEU (Papineni et al., 2002) score over the *dev* corpus. For the optimal model, we also performed a grid search about decoding-time hyper-parameters. All the optimal hyper-parameters described in previous sections are found as the results of these searches.

We submitted two results generated from the same optimal model: *one-best* results, i.e., the results with fixing $BW = 1$, and *adjusted* results, i.e., the results with optimal BW and WP de-

Table 2: JPO adequacy results.

System	Ensemble	Scores				
		1	2	3	4	5
(this-year)	8 models	0.25	1.75	8.25	36.50	53.25
Adjusted	Single	0.25	1.75	17.50	37.75	42.75
(last-year)	3 models	2.00	2.75	19.25	43.50	32.50

scribed in Section 2.4.

Table 1 shows the official evaluation scores of our systems, including BLEU, RIBES (Isozaki et al., 2010), AM-FM (Banchs and Li, 2011), and the human evaluation. The rows labeled *last-year* shows the best system in all previous WAT campaigns. We can see that our *one-best* system already achieves higher translation accuracy in all automatic evaluation metrics than *last-year* systems. In addition, *adjusted* system achieves further better scores than *one-best*, which means applying better decoding strategy can improve translation accuracy even using the same model.

Table 1 also shows the place of our systems in this year. Because official results do not separate scores of single (no-ensemble) models and ensemble models, we also calculated the place of our systems out of only single models for fair comparison. In AM-FM and human evaluation, we can see that our *adjusted* model marks the 1st place of this year's campaign.

Table 2 shows the results of the JPO pairwise adequacy evaluation provided by the organizer. We also showed the *this-year* system, the 1st place system (by NTT team) of the same task in this year's campaign, as well as the *Adjusted* and the *last-year* systems. By comparing with *Adjusted* and *last-year*, we can see that our system clearly increases the number of the highest (5) score and reduces all other (1 to 4) scores. In particular, our system reduces the number of lower-range (1 or 2) scores by the same level of the *this-year* system although we did not use model ensembling. However, there is still room for improvement about higher-range (3 to 5) scores.

4 Conclusion

This paper described the details of the NAIST-NICT neural machine translation systems submitted to WAT2017 English-Japanese Scientific Paper Translation Task. Although the model structure is not new, our model achieved higher translation accuracy compared with past systems in this language pair. In addition, we also tried to use SentencePiece, an unsupervised tokenizer to avoid complicated tokenization problems, and also confirmed that the resulting translation systems can perform with no accuracy reduction.

Acknowledgement

Part of this work was supported by JSPS KAKENHI Grant Numbers JP17H06101 and JP16H05873.

References

Dzmitry Bahdanau, Kyunghyun Cho, and Yoshua Bengio. 2014. Neural machine translation by jointly learning to align and translate. *arXiv preprint arXiv:1409.0473*.

Rafael E. Banchs and Haizhou Li. 2011. Am-fm: A semantic framework for translation quality assessment. In *Proceedings of the 49th Annual Meeting of the Association for Computational Linguistics: Human Language Technologies*, pages 153–158, Portland, Oregon, USA. Association for Computational Linguistics.

Felix A Gers, Jürgen Schmidhuber, and Fred Cummins. 2000. Learning to forget: Continual prediction with LSTM. *Neural computation*, 12(10):2451–2471.

Hideki Isozaki, Tsutomu Hirao, Kevin Duh, Katsuhito Sudoh, and Hajime Tsukada. 2010. Automatic evaluation of translation quality for distant language pairs. In *Proceedings of the 2010 Conference on Empirical Methods in Natural Language Processing*, pages 944–952. Association for Computational Linguistics.

Diederik Kingma and Jimmy Ba. 2014. Adam: A method for stochastic optimization. *arXiv preprint arXiv:1412.6980*.

Thang Luong, Hieu Pham, and Christopher D. Manning. 2015. Effective approaches to attention-based neural machine translation. In *Proceedings of the 2015 Conference on Empirical Methods in Natural Language Processing*, pages 1412–1421, Lisbon, Portugal. Association for Computational Linguistics.

Toshiaki Nakazawa, Chenchen Ding, Hideya MINO, Isao Goto, Graham Neubig, and Sadao Kurohashi. 2016a. Overview of the 3rd workshop on asian translation. In *Proceedings of the 3rd Workshop on Asian Translation (WAT2016)*, pages 1–46, Osaka, Japan. The COLING 2016 Organizing Committee.

Toshiaki Nakazawa, Shohei Higashiyama, Chenchen Ding, Hideya Mino, Isao Goto, Graham Neubig, Hideto Kazawa, Yusuke Oda, Jun Harashima, and Sadao Kurohashi. 2017. Overview of the 4th Workshop on Asian Translation. In *Proceedings of the 4th Workshop on Asian Translation (WAT2017)*, Taipei, Taiwan.

Toshiaki Nakazawa, Manabu Yaguchi, Kiyotaka Uchimoto, Masao Utiyama, Eiichiro Sumita, Sadao Kurohashi, and Hitoshi Isahara. 2016b. Aspec: Asian scientific paper excerpt corpus. In *Proceedings of the Ninth International Conference on Language Resources and Evaluation (LREC 2016)*, pages 2204–2208, Portoro, Slovenia. European Language Resources Association (ELRA).

Kishore Papineni, Salim Roukos, Todd Ward, and Wei-Jing Zhu. 2002. Bleu: a method for automatic evaluation of machine translation. In *Proceedings of 40th Annual Meeting of the Association for Computational Linguistics*, pages 311–318, Philadelphia, Pennsylvania, USA. Association for Computational Linguistics.

Ilya Sutskever, Oriol Vinyals, and Quoc V Le. 2014. Sequence to sequence learning with neural networks. In *Advances in neural information processing systems*, pages 3104–3112.

Comparison of SMT and NMT trained with large Patent Corpora:
Japio at WAT2017

Satoshi Kinoshita   Tadaaki Oshio   Tomoharu Mitsuhashi

Japan Patent Information Organization
{satoshi_kinoshita, t_oshio, t_mitsuhashi} @ japio.or.jp

Abstract

Japan Patent Information Organization (Japio) participates in patent subtasks (JPC-EJ/JE/CJ/KJ) with phrase-based statistical machine translation (SMT) and neural machine translation (NMT) systems which are trained with its own patent corpora in addition to the subtask corpora provided by organizers of WAT2017. In EJ and CJ subtasks, SMT and NMT systems whose sizes of training corpora are about 50 million and 10 million sentence pairs respectively achieved comparable scores for automatic evaluations, but NMT systems were superior to SMT systems for both official and in-house human evaluations.

1   Introduction

Japan Patent Information Organization (Japio) provides a patent information service named GPG/FX[1], which enables users to do cross-lingual information retrieval (CLIR) on patent documents by translating English and Chinese patents into Japanese and storing the translations in a full-text search engine.

For this purpose, we use a phrase-based statistical machine translation (SMT) system for Chinese-to-Japanese translation, and are preparing to change an English-to-Japanese translation system from a rule-based machine translation (RBMT) system to an SMT system. To improve translation quality, we have been building technical term dictionaries and parallel corpora, and the current corpora sizes are 300 million sentence pairs for English-Japanese (EJ) and 100 million for Chinese-

Japanese (CJ). We have also built a Korean-Japanese (KJ) corpus which contains about 13 million sentence pairs for adding Korean-to-Japanese translation to enable searching Korean patents as well.

Our current concern is neural machine translation (NMT), which has been used practically in the field of patent translation since last year (WIPO, 2016). The new approach has been reported to produce better translations than SMT by training with a smaller corpus than SMT. Our translation results in the 4th Workshop on Asian Translation (WAT2017) (Nakazawa et al., 2017) show the same conclusion.

2   Systems

2.1   Base Systems

We used three MT tools to produce translations for the workshop; two are SMTs and the rest is an NMT. The SMT tools are a phrase-based SMT toolkit licensed by NICT (Utiyama and Sumita, 2014), and Moses (Koehn et al., 2007). The former is used for EJ and CJ translation because it includes a pre-ordering module, which changes word order of English and Chinese source sentences into a head-final manner to improve translation into Japanese. The latter is used for KJ translation where pre-ordering is not necessary because of linguistic similarities between Korean and Japanese. We used morphological analyzers mecab-ko[2] and juman version 7.0 (Kurohashi et al., 1994) for tokenizing Korean and Japanese respectively.

A toolkit we used for NMT is OpenNMT[3], whose default setting provides an attention-based NMT model which consists of a 2-layer LSTM with 500 hidden units.

---

[1] http://www.japio.or.jp/service/service05.html

[2] https://bitbucket.org/eunjeon/mecab-ko/
[3] http://opennmt.net/

Proceedings of the 4th Workshop on Asian Translation, pages 140–145,
Taipei, Taiwan, November 27, 2017. ©2017 AFNLP

Two major difference between its default and our experimental settings are: 1) a deep bidirectional recurrent neural network (DBRNN) is used instead of a standard recurrent neural network (RNN). 2) The value 100,000 is used as a vocabulary size if a size of training corpus is equal or more than 3 million sentence pairs whereas 50,000, a default value, is used for a smaller training corpus than that. For tokenizing corpus texts, Moses tokenizer, juman and kytea[4] are used to tokenize English, Japanese and Chinese, respectively.

2.2 Treatment of Out of Vocabulary

One of major problems to use an NMT system for translating patent documents, which include a large number of technical terms, is a limited number of vocabulary size. To solve the problem, various approaches have been proposed, such as using a model based on not words but characters or subwords, and a method to replace technical terms in a training corpus and source sentences with technical term tokens (Sennrich et al., 2015; Long et al., 2016).

We propose a method to extract out of vocabulary (OOV) words by the attention mechanism of OpenNMT and translate them with another NMT which has a character-based model. For EJ/JE/CJ NMT systems, such character-based models are trained by using a size of 1 million technical terms extracted from our technical term dictionaries. Japanese and Chinese words of the extracted dictionary entries are tokenized on a character basis while English words are divided by byte pair encoding. In translation, OpenNMT can output source tokens for unknown words instead of <unk> symbols by using attention weights[5]. They are translated by the above-mentioned character-based NMT systems and replaced with their translations.

2.3 Pre- and Post-processing

We include the following pre- and post-editing functions depending on translation systems and directions:
- Recovering lowercased out-of-vocabularies (OOVs) to their original spellings (EJ-SMT)
- Balancing unbalanced parentheses (KJ)
- Splitting long sentences into shorter ones (CJ-NMT)

3 Corpora and Training of SMT

Our patent parallel corpora, hereafter Japio corpora, are built automatically from pairs of patent specifications called "patent families," which typically consist of an original document in one language and its translations in other languages. Sentence alignment is performed by 2 alignment tools: one is a tool licensed by NICT (Utiyama and Isahara, 2007), and the other is E_align[6].

In patent subtask of WAT2016, we achieved the highest BLEU score 58.66 in JPC-CJ with an SMT system trained with about 49 million sentence pairs. However, we found that about 55% of sentences in the test sets were involved in the training corpus[7]. Although we built our corpora independently from those of Japan Patent Office corpora (JPC), methodological similarity to use patent-family documents may have led the situation. In order to make our submission to WAT more meaningful, we determined that we would publish its automatic evaluation result, but submitted another translation which was produced by an SMT which was trained by using a corpus of 4 million sentence pairs with no sentence in the test set. This year, we trained an SMT with a corpus of the 49 million sentence pairs where test set sentences are removed from the original corpus by using publication numbers embedded as data IDs in the JPC corpora. To train NMTs, we used the JPC-CJ corpus as a baseline, and added up to 9 million sentence pairs extracted from the above corpus.

Corpus for EJ translation was prepared as in the case for CJ. A corpus that we used for training an SMT for our service contained 24% of test set sentences. Therefore, we published the result, but did not request human evaluation. What we asked for human evaluation was a result which was translated by an SMT that was trained with a corpus without sentences in the test set. Similarly, to train NMTs, we used the JPC-EJ corpus as a baseline, and added up to 11 million sentence pairs from the corpus prepared for the above SMT.

In the case of KJ patent subtask, we used 8 million sentences pairs from our corpus in addition to

---

[4] http://www.phontron.com/kytea/
[5] To distinguish unknown words in target tokens, we modified source codes of OpenNMT to add a tag to them. The latest version of OpenNMT has a similar function.

[6] http://www.gsk.or.jp/catalog/gsk2017-a/
[7] JPC training sets contain 1.1%, 2.3% and 1.0% of sentences of EJ, CJ and KJ test sets respectively.

Subtask	#	DataID	System	Corpus Size (million)	Use official corpus	Automatic			Human	
						BLEU	RIBES	AMFM	pairwise	JPO adq.
JPC-EJ	1-1	1330*	SMT (PBSMT with preordering)	1	Yes	38.59	0.839141	0.733020	—	—
	1-2	1445	SMT (PBSMT with preordering)	100**	No	55.55	0.875667	0.802260	—	—
	1-3	1462	SMT (PBSMT with preordering)	50	No	**51.79**	0.864038	**0.781150**	41.000	—
	1-4	1451	NMT	1	Yes	44.69	0.864568	0.746720	—	—
	1-5	1453	NMT	5	Yes	48.39	0.880215	0.767720	—	—
	1-6	1454	NMT (Combination of 4 NMTs)	12	Yes	50.27	**0.886403**	0.776790	**56.250**	4.75
JPC-JE	2-1	1455	NMT	1	Yes	44.07	0.863385	0.699930	—	—
	2-2	1578	NMT	5	Yes	48.08	0.873093	0.715560	67.000	—
	2-3	1574	NMT (Combination of 3 NMTs)	11	Yes	**49.00**	**0.878298**	**0.724710**	**68.500**	4.79
JPC-CJ	3-1	1329*	SMT (PBSMT with preordering)	1	Yes	39.29	0.820339	0.733300	—	—
	3-2	1161*	SMT (PBSMT with preordering)	49**	No	58.66	0.868027	0.808090	—	—
	3-3	1447	SMT (PBSMT with preordering)	49	No	**50.52**	0.847793	0.774660	60.500	—
	3-4	1458	NMT	1	Yes	45.07	0.859883	0.754970	—	—
	3-5	1482	NMT	5	Yes	49.51	0.872625	0.777460	—	—
	3-6	1484	NMT (Combination of 3 NMTs)	10	Yes	50.06	**0.875398**	**0.779420**	**80.250**	4.46
JPC-KJ	4-1	1331*	SMT (Character-based PBSMT)	1	Yes	69.10	0.940367	0.859790	—	—
	4-2	1448	SMT (Word-based PBSMT)	9	Yes	**73.00**	0.946880	0.872510	**48.750**	4.84
	4-3	1449	SMT (Character-based PBSMT)	9	Yes	71.97	0.944435	0.868170	—	—
	4-4	1450	SMT (Combination of 2 SMTs)	9	Yes	**73.00**	**0.946985**	**0.873200**	48.500	—

* Submissions with '*' of their DataID are those submitted for WAT2016

** Traing data whose size are given '**' include some sentences of test set.

Table 1: Official Evaluation Results

DataID	Team	Method	Other Resources	Automatic			Human	
				BLEU	RIBES	AMFM	pairwise	JPO adq.
1407	Team-A	NMT	No	44.63	0.866722	0.747770	**60.000**	4.63
1406	Team-A	NMT	No	44.44	0.860998	0.747050	58.250	—
1454	Japio	NMT	Yes	50.27	**0.886403**	0.776790	56.250	**4.75**
1470	Team-B	NMT	No	38.91	0.845815	0.734010	49.500	4.40
1339	Team-C	NMT	Yes	50.60	0.879382	0.770480	48.500	—
1462	Japio	SMT	Yes	**51.79**	0.864038	**0.781150**	41.000	—

Table 2: Official Human Evaluation Results for JPC-EJ subtask

JPC-KJ corpus. By using 9 million sentence corpus, we trained two types of SMTs: one trained with a corpus that is tokenized on a character-basis, while the other with a corpus that is tokenized by mecab-ko.

4 System Combination

It was reported that an NMT system achieved better translation by ensembling multiple models (Sennrich et al., 2016). Because OpenNMT, which we use for our NMT systems, does not provide the function, we combined translations from multiple NMT systems as follows, in addition to using character-based NMTs to resolve OOVs.

(1) Combinations of NMTs that are trained for technical domains

For JPC-EJ, we trained 4 NMTs by using corpora whose data are selected based on its domain label, namely C, E, M and P, which are also given to test set sentences. They are used in addition to JPC-EJ corpus. In translating test set sentences, an appropriate NMT is used according to the domain.

(2) Usage of scores by OpenNMT

For JPC-JE and CJ, we could not complete training which was needed to make 4 domain models as we did for JPC-EJ by the submission deadline. Instead, we used scores which are given to each translation by OpenNMT, and selected a translation with the highest score.

In JPC-KJ, we chose a translation by a character-based SMT when a translation by a word-based SMT contains an OOV with at least one Hangul character.

Subtask	DataID	System	Corpus size (million)	BLEU
JPC-EJ	1462	SMT (PBSMT with preordering)	50	51.79
	1454	NMT (Combination of 4 NMTs)	12	50.27
JPC-CJ	1447	SMT (PBSMT with preordering)	49	50.52
	1484	NMT (Combination of 3 NMTs)	10	50.06

Table 3: Translations for in-house evaluations

	EJ	CJ
SMT is better	24	32
NMT is better	32	68
comparable	144	100

Table 4: Result of pairwise evaluations

Error Type	EJ		CJ	
	SMT	NMT	SMT	NMT
Insertion	10	2	8	4
Deletion	21	6	14	21
Mistranslation	26	31	29	54
Others	19	6	75	13
Total	76	45	126	92

Table 5: Errors of SMT and NMT for JPC-EJ/CJ

5   Results

Table 1 shows official evaluation results for our submissions[8]. In JPC-EJ and CJ, translations by SMTs trained with about 50 million sentence pairs are given comparable scores for automatic evaluation with those by NMTs trained with about 10 million sentence pairs. Human pairwise evaluation, however, gives much higher scores to translations by NMTs than those by SMTs.

Table 2 shows evaluation results for high-ranked submissions of JPC-EJ this year[9]. What is the most interesting for us is that a translation by an SMT which is given the highest scores for BLEU and AMFM is given a lower human evaluation score than those by NMTs trained with only 1 million sentence pairs. Furthermore, comparing results between NMT systems, a result whose DataID is 1339 and is given the highest BLEU score and a result whose DataID is 1454 and is given the highest RIBES and AMFM scores are given lower pairwise evaluation scores than those of Team-A, which are apparently given lower BLEU

and AMFM scores than the formers. These results support previous findings that there is no correlation between automatic and human evaluations.

6   Discussion

To recognize a difference of translation quality between SMT and NMT systems, we conducted two kinds of human evaluations independently from the official evaluation: one is pairwise evaluation, and the other is an error analysis. We used the same sentences used for JPO adequacy evaluation in WAT2017, and one evaluator conducted both evaluations. Table 3 shows translations used for the in-house evaluation.

6.1   Pairwise Evaluation

We conducted pairwise evaluation based on adequacy. When evaluating a translation, which translation is better is determined based on how much of the meaning of a source sentence is expressed in its translation. Taking JPO adequacy into account, insertion and deletion of conjunctions which are considered not to convey important information are ignored if translations are grammatical. Fluency is also ignored.

Table 4 shows the result. In both EJ and CJ, NMTs are evaluated to produce more better translations than SMTs. The tendency is remarkable in

---

[8] Scores of BLEU, RIBES and AMFM for JPC-EJ/CJ/KJ are those calculated with tokens segmented by juman.
[9] A translation result whose DataID is 1339 was not evaluated last year because it was submitted after the deadline for human evaluation.

CJ, which is consistent with the official evaluation result shown in Table 1.

6.2 Error Analysis

In the error analysis, translation errors are categorized into the following 4 categories:

- Insertion
- Deletion
- Mistranslation
- Others (such as grammatical errors)

Note that insertions and deletions which are ignored in the pairwise evaluation are counted in this analysis.

Table 5 shows the result. On the whole, number of errors of the SMT translations is larger than that of NMT in both EJ and CJ. This is consistent with the results of official and in-house pairwise evaluations.

Number of mistranslations of NMT translations is however larger than that of SMT in both EJ and CJ. The reason we think is that technical terms of low frequencies are not properly translated by the following two reasons:

- A corpus that was used for training NMTs is much smaller than that for SMTs.
- In training NMTs, a vocabulary is limited by a pre-defined vocabulary size or vocabulary set, and words out of the involved vocabulary cannot be translated.

A character-based NMT which is used to resolve the OOV problem does not work as we expected. In addition, deletion errors of NMT are smaller than SMT in EJ, but are larger in CJ.

What is the most characteristic in the error analysis is that about 60% of errors of CJ SMT are categorized as "Others." This might be caused by low precision of preordering due to the difficulty of Chinese syntactic analysis.

7 Conclusion

In this paper, we described systems and corpora of Team Japio for submitting translations to WAT2017. To show potential of SMT and NMT in patent translation, we participated in patent subtasks (JPC-EJ/JE/CJ/KJ) with systems which are trained with its own patent corpora in addition to the corpora provided by organizers of WAT2017. The result shows that SMT and NMT systems whose sizes of training corpora are about 50 million and 10 million sentence pairs respectively achieved comparable scores for automatic evaluations in EJ and CJ subtasks. NMT systems were,

however, superior to SMT systems for both official and in-house human evaluations.

References

Satoshi Kinoshita, Tadaaki Oshio, Tomoharu Mitsuhashi, Terumasa Ehara. 2016. Translation Using JAPIO Patent Corpora: JAPIO at WAT2016. In *Proceedings of the 3rd Workshop on Asian Translation (WAT2016)*, pages 133-138.

Philipp Koehn, Hieu Hoang, Alexandra Birch, Chris Callison-Burch, Marcello Federico, Nicola Bertoldi, Brooke Cowan, Wade Shen, Christine Moran, Richard Zens, Chris Dyer, Ondrej Bojar, Alexandra Constantin, and Evan Herbst. 2007. Moses: Open source toolkit for statistical machine translation. In *Annual Meeting of the Association for Computational Linguistics (ACL)*, demonstration session.

Sadao Kurohashi, Toshihisa Nakamura, Yuji Matsumoto, and Makoto Nagao. 1994. Improvements of Japanese morphological analyzer JUMAN. In *Proceedings of the International Workshop on Sharable Natural Language*, pages 22–28.

Zi Long, Takehito Utsuro, Tomoharu Mitsuhashi and Mikio Yamamoto. 2016. Translation of Patent Sentences with a Large Vocabulary of Technical Terms Using Neural Machine Translation. In *Proceedings of the 3rd Workshop on Asian Translation (WAT2016)*, pages 47-57.

Toshiaki Nakazawa, Hideya Mino, Chenchen Ding, Isao Goto, Graham Neubig, Sadao Kurohashi and Eiichiro Sumita. 2016a. Overview of the 3rd Workshop on Asian Translation. In *Proceedings of the 3rd Workshop on Asian Translation (WAT2016)*, pages 1-46.

Toshiaki Nakazawa, Shohei Higashiyama, Chenchen Ding, Hideya Mino, Isao Goto, Graham Neubig, Hideto Kazawa, Yusuke Oda, Jun Harashima and Sadao Kurohashi. 2017. Overview of the 4th Workshop on Asian Translation. In *Proceedings of the 4th Workshop on Asian Translation (WAT2017)*.

Toshiaki Nakazawa, Manabu Yaguchi, Kiyotaka Uchimoto, Masao Utiyama, Eiichiro Sumita, Sadao Kurohashi and Hitoshi Isahara. 2016b. ASPEC: Asian Scientific Paper Excerpt Corpus. In *Proceedings of the 10th Conference on International Language Resources and Evaluation (LREC2016)*.

Rico Sennrich, Barry Haddow and Alexandra Birch. 2015. Neural machine translation of rare words with subword units. In *Proceedings of 54th ACL*, pages 1715-1725.

Rico Sennrich, Barry Haddow and Alexandra Birch. 2016. Edinburgh Neural Machine Translation Systems for WMT 16. In *Proceedings of the First*

Conference on Machine Translation, Volume 2: Shared Task Papers, pages 371–376.

Masao Utiyama and Hiroshi Isahara. 2007. A Japanese-English Patent Parallel Corpus. In *MT summit XI*, pages 475-482.

Masao Utiyama and Eiichiro Sumita. 2014. AAMT Nagao Award Memorial lecture. http://www2.nict.go.jp/astrec-att/member/mutiyama/pdf/AAMT2014.pdf

WIPO. 2016. WIPO Develops Cutting-Edge Translation Tool For Patent Documents. http://www.wipo.int/pressroom/en/articles/2016/article_0014.html

Kyoto University Participation to WAT 2017

Fabien Cromieres
Japan Science and Technology Agency
5-3, Yonbancho, Chiyoda-ku,
Tokyo, 102-8666, Japan
fabien@pa.jst.jp

Raj Dabre
Kyoto University
Yoshida-honmachi, Sakyo-ku,
Kyoto, 606-8501, Japan
prajdabre@gmail.com

Toshiaki Nakazawa
Japan Science and Technology Agency
5-3, Yonbancho, Chiyoda-ku,
Tokyo, 102-8666, Japan
nakazawa@pa.jst.jp

Sadao Kurohashi
Kyoto University
Yoshida-honmachi, Sakyo-ku,
Kyoto, 606-8501, Japan
kuro@i.kyoto-u.ac.jp

Abstract

We describe here our approaches and results on the WAT 2017 shared translation tasks. Motivated by the good results we obtained with Neural Machine Translation in the previous shared task, we continued to explore this approach this year, with incremental improvements in models and training methods. We focused on the ASPEC dataset and could improve the state-of-the-art results for Chinese-to-Japanese and Japanese-to-Chinese translations.

1 Introduction

This paper describes our experiments for the WAT 2017 shared translation task. For more details refer to the overview paper (Nakazawa et al., 2017). This translation task contains several subtasks, but we focused on the ASPEC dataset, for the Japanese-English and Japanese-Chinese language pairs. Following up on our findings during WAT 2016 (Nakazawa et al., 2016) that our Neural Machine Translation system yielded significantly better results than our Example-Based Machine Translation system, we only experimented with NMT this year.

Our improvements are actually quite incremental, with only small changes in the model architectures, model sizes, training and decoding approaches. Together, these small changes, however, allow us to improve over our past year's results by several BLEU points, leading to the best official results for the Japanese-Chinese pair. In terms of pairwise human evaluation scores we have the best official results for all language directions except for English to Japanese. Our JPO adequacy scores are also within 1% of the best score for these language directions.

2 The Kyoto-NMT system

Following its success in the past few years, Neural Machine Translation has become the new major approach to Machine Translation. In particular, the sequence-to-sequence with attention mechanism model, first proposed in (Bahdanau et al., 2015) was proven to be very powerful and has become the de facto baseline for NMT.

Our Kyoto-NMT system largely relies on an implementation of this model, with small modifications. Kyoto-NMT is implemented using the Chainer[1] toolkit (Tokui et al., 2015). We make this implementation available under a GPL license.[2]

2.1 Overview of NMT

We describe here, briefly, our implementation based on the (Bahdanau et al., 2015) model. As shown in Figure 1, an input sentence is first converted into a sequence of vector through an embedding layer; these vectors are then fed to two LSTM layers (one going forward, the other going backward) to give a new sequence of vectors that encode the input sentence. On the decoding part of the model, a target-side sentence is generated with what is conceptually a recurrent neural network language model: an LSTM is sequentially fed the embedding of the previously generated word, and its output is sent through a deep softmax layer to produce the probability of the next word. This decoding LSTM is also fed a context vector, which is

---

[1] http://chainer.org/
[2] https://github.com/fabiencro/knmt . See also (Cromieres, 2016)

146

Proceedings of the 4th Workshop on Asian Translation, pages 146–153,
Taipei, Taiwan, November 27, 2017. ©2017 AFNLP

a weighted sum of the vectors encoding the input sentence, provided by the attention mechanism.

As is a common practice, we stack several layers of LSTMs for both the encoder and the decoder. When using deeper stacks of LSTMs, we can optionally add residual connections (He et al., 2016) to make the training easier. Furthermore, we also added layer normalization (He et al., 2016) to the LSTMs, which is supposed to also help training as well as regularization. However, we did not actually notice improvements when using layer normalization.

2.2 Direct connection from previous word to attention model

There is an interesting flaw in the original architecture of the model (as well as in the model described in (Bahdanau et al., 2015)). This is briefly mentioned[3] in (Goto and Tanaka, 2017), but we will expand on the details a bit more here.

The attention mechanism computes the current context using only the previous decoder state as input. But the previous decoder state has been itself computed before the previously generated target word was selected. Therefore, when computing the current context, the attention mechanism is totally unaware of the previously generated word. Intuitively, this seems wrong: the attention should certainly depend on the previously generated word.

Therefore, we add another input to the attention model: the previous word embedding. To be precise, re-using the notations from (Bahdanau et al., 2015)), the original attention is computed with this equation:

$$e_{ij} = v_a^T \tanh(W_a \cdot s_{i-1} + U_a \cdot h_j) \quad (1)$$

where e_{ij} is the unnormalized attention coefficient on source word j when decoding target word at step i, s_{i-1} is the decoder state at step $i - 1$, and h_j is the encoding of source word j. The matrices W_a and U_a, and the vector v_a are the parameters of the alignment model. We replace this equation with:

$$e_{ij} = v_a^T \tanh(W_a \cdot s_{i-1} + U_a \cdot h_j + X_a \cdot E_{y-1}) \quad (2)$$

---

[3] The author had previously mentioned this to us in private communications.

where E_{y-1} is the embedding of the previously generated target word. This increases the number of parameters by $E_o \cdot H_o$ (ie. the size of the matrix X_a), where E_o is the size of target embeddings, and H_o is the size of the decoder state.

This change appeared to be remarkably efficient, giving a +1 to +2 BLEU improvement at the cost of about 1% increase in the size of the model.

2.3 Feed-Forward model

Aside from this implementation relying on LSTMs, we also implemented a model without recurrent unit but with self-attention layers, based on the model proposed in (Vaswani et al., 2017a). This model obtained state-of-the-art results on some European languages. And the code released by the author of the original paper was used as one of the organizer's baseline of WAT2017. This baseline ended up being unbeaten (in term of BLEU) by participants for the English-to-Japanese direction[4], but was inferior to other participant's submissions (including ours) in the other directions.

Our experiences with our own implementation of a feed-forward self-attention model led to results slightly inferior to the ones we obtained using a more classic LSTM-based architecture. Which is why all results presented in this paper are related to the LSTM-based model. Such feed-forward models probably have high potentials for the future, as they are more computationally efficient and do obtain state-of-the-art results on certain language directions. But, currently, we do not find that they should be necessarily preferred to recurrent architectures.

3 Models hyperparameters and pre-processing

We describe here the general settings we used for the hyperparameters of our models, as well as the pre-processing we applied to the data.

3.1 Preprocessing

As a first preprocessing step, English sentences were tokenized and lowercased. Both Japanese sentences and Chinese sentences were automatically segmented, respectively with JUMAN[5] (Kurohashi, 1994) and SKP (Shen et al., 2016).

---

[4] but see section 4.2.1 for our attempt at system combination

[5] http://nlp.ist.i.kyoto-u.ac.jp/EN/index.php?JUMAN

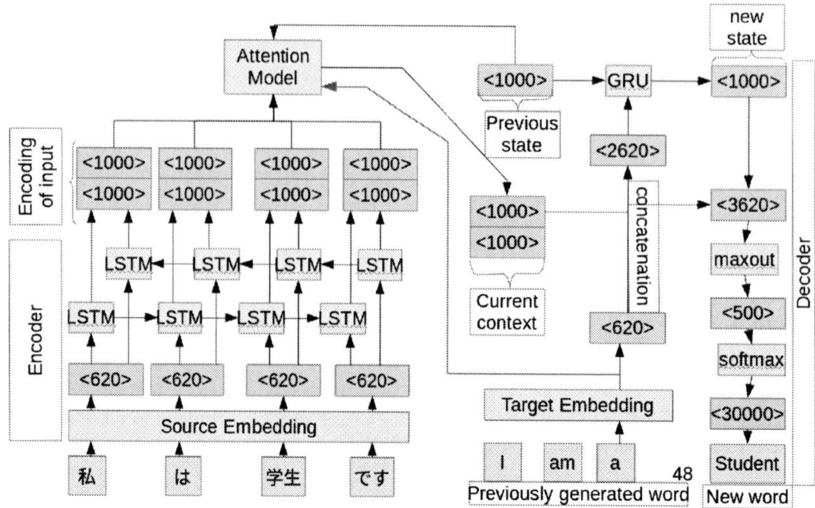

Figure 1: The structure of a NMT system with attention, as described in (Bahdanau et al., 2015) (but with LSTMs instead of GRUs). The notation "<1000>" means a vector of size 1000. The vector sizes shown here are the ones suggested in the original paper. We use this general architecture for our model, but the single LSTMs are replaced by stacks of LSTMs. We also add a connection from the target embedding to the attention model, as suggested by (Goto and Tanaka, 2017), which was not in the original model (see section 2.2)

We used subword segmentation for all target languages, so as to reduce the target vocabulary size. This makes the translation process more efficient memory-wise and computation-wise, while mostly avoiding the need for unknown-word replacement tricks such as in (Luong et al., 2015). The subword segmentation was done using the BPE algorithm (Sennrich et al., 2015) [6].

For the Japanese-Chinese language pair, we learned a joint segmentation (as suggested in (Sennrich et al., 2015)). We used a character equivalence map (Chu et al., 2013) to maximize the number of common characters between Japanese and Chinese when learning the joint segmentation. The joint segmentation was aimed at producing a vocabulary size of about 40,000 words for both the source and target vocabulary.

For the Japanese-English language pair, we did not use a joint segmentation. We created a BPE model of about 40,000 words for the target language, and about 100,000 words for the source vocabulary. Indeed, a large source vocabulary has less impact on performance than a large target vocabulary, and we expected the larger amount of

data available for this language pair would let us correctly train a larger amount of embeddings.

3.2 Model hyper-parameters

For all experiments, we have used the following basic settings:

- Source and target-side embeddings of size 1024

- Source and target-side hidden states of size 1024

- Attention mechanism hidden states of size 1024

- Deep softmax output with a 2-maxout layer of size 512

We used LSTMs (Hochreiter and Schmidhuber, 1997) as the recurrent units for both the encoder and the decoder. We empirically found them to give better results than GRUs (Chung et al., 2014) in the previous shared task.

We considered stacks of 2 and 3 layers of LSTMs. Some preliminary experiments had convinced us that 4 layers or more did not lead to significant improvements, at least in the case of the

---

[6]using the BPE segmentation code at https://github.com/rsennrich/subword-nmt

Japanese-Chinese dataset. Adding residual connections proved to be helpful in accelerating training in the case of a 3-layers encoder-decoder[7]. They are not necessary when we stack only 2 layers of LSTMs.

We also experimented with inter-layer dropout regularization (Srivastava et al., 2014), as first suggested by (Zaremba et al., 2014).

3.3 Training Settings

Our training settings were mostly the same as those reported for WAT2016. We used ADAM (Kingma and Ba, 2014) as the training algorithm.

We also tried to do some annealing after the ADAM training. That is, we first ran ADAM until the dev loss stabilized. Then we switched to a simple stochastic gradient descent with a small learning rate ranging from 0.1 to 0.01. This process did lead to an significant further decrease of dev loss and increase of greedy dev BLEU. However, somehow surprisingly, this did not lead to a BLEU improvement when translating with the beam-search algorithm.

We used a dropout rate of 20% for the inter-layer dropout. We used L2 regularization through a weight decay factor of 1e-6. We also used an early stopping scheme: every 200 training iterations, we computed the perplexity of the development part of the ASPEC data. We also computed a BLEU score by translating this development data with a "greedy search."[8] We kept track of the parameters that gave the best development BLEU and the best development perplexity so far.

We used dynamically-sized minibatches. Minibatches were created by grouping training sentences of similar size until a threshold on the total number of words was met. The threshold was chosen so as to fill the memory of the GPU and could differ depending on the dataset and the model trained. This threshold was usually between 4000 and 8000 words per minibatch. We found these dynamically-sized minibatches to allow for faster training than the fixed-size minibatches we had used previously. We also discarded training sentences longer than 90 words.

As we had described in (Cromières et al., 2016), we added some additional noise to the target embeddings in the hope to make the decoder rely more on the source context than on the previously generated word when generating the next word.

3.4 Beam Search

In general, greedy decoding (that lets the decoder always select the next word with highest probability given the previously generated words) gives sub-optimal translation results. It is therefore common to use a beam-search approach to decoding, keeping a beam of translation hypotheses instead of just the greediest one.

Implementations of such a beam-search decoding can vary. We detail here the way our decoding work, which differs in some ways with, for example, the one originally provided by the LISA lab of Université de Montréal.[9] It is an algorithm we had already used for the WAT2016 shared task and found to give good results. This time, we optionally added some more complex scoring and pruning inspired from the beam-search algorithm in (Wu et al., 2016).

We detail our basic beam search procedure in Algorithm 1. Given an input sentence i of length L_i, we first estimate the maximum length of the translation L_{mt}. L_{mt} is estimated by $L_{mt} = r \cdot L_i$, where r is a language dependent ratio. We empirically found the following values to work well : $r = 1.2$ for Japanese-to-English, $r = 2$ for English-to-Japanese, and $r = 1.5$ for Japanese-to-Chinese and Chinese-to-Japanese. At the end, we found it beneficial to rank the generated translations by their log-probability divided by their length.

Instead of our simple pruning and normalized scores, we also considered pruning and scoring functions such as the ones proposed in (Wu et al., 2016). In particular, the equation 14 of this paper describes a more complex parameterized scoring function that takes into account both the length of the translation and the coverage of the attention. We did not take the time to select the three hyper-parameters of this scoring function and just used the default ones given in the paper. As a result we could only observe benefits from this more complex scoring function for the Japanese-to-English direction (improving the results by only about 0.2 BLEU). For the three other directions, our basic

---

[7]In our participation to WAT2016, we had reported having disappointing results with 3-layers encoder-decoders. We can now confirm that better results can be obtained either by a much longer training or by adding residual connections.

[8]i.e., we did not use the beam search procedure described in section 3.4, but simply translated with the most likely word at each step. Using a beam search is to slow when we need to do frequent BLEU evaluations.

[9]https://github.com/lisa-groundhog/

algorithm gavw slightly better results. It could be that the better results could be obtained by tuning each hyperparameter to each dataset and language direction.

3.5 Averaging and Ensembling

It is well known that using an ensemble of several independently trained models can boost NMT performances by several BLEU points. We did this in the same way as was described in (Cromières et al., 2016).

On top of ensembling independently trained models, we had found it useful to also make an ensemble with the parameters of the same model corresponding respectively to the best loss, best dev BLEU and last obtained during the training process (a practice which we will call here self-ensemble). Following (Junczys-Dowmunt et al., 2016), we tried to compute averaged parameters instead of ensembling models. We found this to work surprisingly well. We observed only non-significant BLEU drops (by about 0.1 BLEU). But with the benefit that the averaged model has the same time and space complexity as a single model, while an ensemble of N models has N times the time and space complexity of a single model. We therefore switched to this averaging approach instead of the self-ensemble approach[10].

4 Results

4.1 Details for each submission

In general, all experiments were run following the methodology and hyperparameters described in section 3. We detail here the specific settings for each submissions.

Ja → En Submission 1 and 2 correspond to an ensemble of 4 models, two of them having 2 layers for encoders and decoders, and two of them having 3 layers. In submission 2, we decode using the scoring function from (Wu et al., 2016) (see section 3.4), while submission 1 uses our normal scoring function.

En → Ja Submission 1 corresponds to an ensemble of 4 models, two of them having 2 layers for encoders and decoders, and two of them having 3 layers.

---

[10]Of course, this is only expected to work when averaging parameters from the same training run. Ensembling remains the only option to combine independently trained models.

Ja → Zh Submission 2 corresponds to an ensemble of 5 models, three of them having 2 layers for encoders and decoders, and two of them having 3 layers. Submission 1 adds 2 additional models to the ensemble, having 3 layers on the encoder and 2 on the decoder.

Zh → Ja Submission 1 corresponds to an ensemble of 5 models, three of them having 2 layers for encoders and decoders, and two of them having 3 layers. Submission 2 does things a bit differently. It is an ensemble of 6 models using a keyword replacement method similar to (Li et al., 2016).

4.2 Official Evaluation Results

Table 1 shows the official automatic and human evaluation results of the ASPEC subtasks that we participated in. "Rank" shows the ranking of our submissions among all the submissions for each subtask.

From the point of view of human pairwise evaluation, our system achieved the best translation quality for all the subtasks except for En → Ja.

From the point of view of automatic BLEU evaluation, we obtained the best results for the two directions of the Japanese-Chinese dataset, but not for the Japanese-English dataset. In the case of JPO Adequacy scores we rank 2nd for the three language directions for which we had ranked first in term of pairwise evaluation. But because the difference in adequacy score with respect to the first system is by less than 1%, it might not be statistcially significant. For Japanese to Chinese we noticed that we had a higher percentage of translations which were rated as perfect compared to the other systems.In general the number of translations with the lowest scores (with a rating of 1) are much lower when compared to last years results which is a clear indication of progress.

It is interesting to note that these results reveal a certain discrepancy between BLEU and human evaluation. In particular, for Japanese-to-English, although our submission was significantly below some other submissions in term of BLEU, it ended up being given a higher score by human evaluation.

It somehow confirms that BLEU is not always a clear indicator of translation quality, maybe especially for a language like Japanese that has free word order. Moreover, there are questions on the reliability of BLEU when the BLEU scores are

Algorithm 1 Beam Search

1: Input: decoder dec conditionalized on input sentence i, beam width B
2: $L_{mt} \leftarrow r \cdot |i|$ ▷ L_{mt}: Maximum translation length, r: Language-dependent length ratio
3: $finished \leftarrow []$ ▷ list of finished translations (log-prob, translation)
4: $beam \leftarrow$ array of L_{mt} item lists ▷ an $item$: (log-probability, decoder state, partial translation)
5: $beam[0] \leftarrow [(0, st_i, ")]$ ▷ st_i: initial decoder state
6: **for** $n \leftarrow 1$ to L_{mt} **do**
7:    **for** $(lp, st, t) \in beam[n-1]$ **do**
8:       $prob, st' \leftarrow dec(st, t[-1])$ ▷ dec return the probability of next words, and the next state
9:       **for** $w, p_w \in top_B(prob)$ **do** ▷ top_B return the B words with highest probability
10:          **if** $w = EOS$ **then**
11:             add $(lp + log(p_w), t)$ to $finished$
12:          **else**
13:             add $(lp + log(p_w), st', t + w)$ to $beam[n]$
14:          **end if**
15:       **end for**
16:    **end for**
17:    prune $beam[n]$
18: **end for**
19: Sort $(lp, t) \in finished$ according to $lp/|t|$
20: **return** t s.t. $lp/|t|$ is maximum

| Subtask | Ja $\rightarrow$ En | | En $\rightarrow$ Ja | Ja $\rightarrow$ Zh | | Zh $\rightarrow$ Ja | |
Submission	1	2	1	1	2	1	2
BLEU	27.55	27.66	38.72	35.31	**35.67**	48.34	**48.43**
Rank(BLEU)	7/10	4/10	6/11	2/6	**1/6**	2/5	**1/5**
Adequacy (JPO)	4.10	-	4.26	3.95	-	4.30	-
Rank(Adequacy)	2/10*	-	4/11	2/6*	-	2/5*	-
RIBES	0.7614	0.7654	0.8324	0.8501	0.8494	**0.8842**	0.8834
AM-FM	0.5855	0.5911	0.7542	0.7854	0.7794	**0.7998**	0.7995
Human (Pairwise)	**77.75**	74.50	69.75	**72.50**	71.50	**82.75**	79.50
Rank(Human)	**1/10**	5/10	5/11	**1/6**	2/6	**1/5**	2/5

Table 1: Official automatic and human evaluation results of our NMT systems for the ASPEC subtasks. The scores in bold are the best compared to the scores of the other systems. For JPO adequacy, rank marked by a * indicates the score was within 1% of the best and therefore the difference might not be statistically significant.

very high. This hints that it might not be a good idea to use training procedures that directly optimize BLEU, something that was already mentioned in (Wu et al., 2016).

We also performed additional experiments for En $\rightarrow$ Ja after the official submission deadline which we describe in the following subsection.

4.2.1 System Combination

Considering that English-to-Japanese was the one direction where we were behind other submissions, we tried to see if we could at least get an improvement by system combination. This experience was done after the shared task results were published and is not part of the official results of WAT2017's shared task.

Tensor2Tensor's Transformer[11] (Vaswani et al., 2017b) achieved the best performance in term of BLEU (organizer's result; also the state-of-the-art) for En $\rightarrow$ Ja and we decided to combine it with our system using MEMT (Heafield and Lavie, 2010). MEMT relies on computing a lattice with various features[12] by aligning the translations at the sentence level and then using a n-gram language model for generating and ranking a n-best list. We used MEMT with the default settings which requires the following:

---

[11] https://github.com/tensorflow/tensor2tensor
[12] These features include paraphrases, synonyms using wordnets and common subwords using a stemmer

System	Google's Transformer	KNMT	MEMT (System Combination)
BLEU	40.79	38.74	**41.53**
RIBES	**0.8448**	0.8318	0.8410
AM-FM	0.7686	0.7565	**0.7710**

Table 2: Automatic evaluation results of system combination for English to Japanese. These results represent the SOTA in terms of BLEU and AM-FM.

- Dev set translations for both systems.

- Test set translations for both systems.

- Dev set reference sentences.

- N-gram Language Model using KenLM (We used a 6 gram model) (Heafield, 2011).

Table 2 shows the results for system combination for En $\rightarrow$ Ja. Although the Transformer model is about 2 BLEU points better than ours system combination still manages to give an increment of 0.74 BLEU which is statistically significant ($p < 0.01$).This indicates that the two models give results that are complementary. In the future we will explore methods to determine the best settings for system combination in order to further improve the translation quality.

5 Conclusion

We have detailed our methods and experimental process for our participation to the WAT2017 translation shared task. We could improve the state-of-the-art for the Japanese-Chinese dataset in term of both BLEU and pairwise human evaluation. We also obtained the best pairwise human evaluation score for Japanese-to-English translation. However, our improvements over our last year's participation were incremental and evolutionary rather than revolutionary. Small improvements across the models, training process and decoding process added up to bring a +2 to +4 BLEU improvements in the results.

In the future, we intend to do experiments with more recent evolutions of the translation models, in particular those that use more linguistic information.

Acknowledgments

This work is funded by the Japan Science and Technology Agency. We are especially grateful to Professor Isao Goto for his insightful comments on the attention model.

References

Dzmitry Bahdanau, Kyunghyun Cho, and Yoshua Bengio. 2015. Neural machine translation by jointly learning to align and translate. In *ICLR 2015*.

Chenhui Chu, Toshiaki Nakazawa, Daisuke Kawahara, and Sadao Kurohashi. 2013. Chinese-japanese machine translation exploiting chinese characters. *ACM Transactions on Asian Language Information Processing (TALIP)*, 12(4):16:1–16:25.

Junyoung Chung, Caglar Gulcehre, KyungHyun Cho, and Yoshua Bengio. 2014. Empirical evaluation of gated recurrent neural networks on sequence modeling. *arXiv preprint arXiv:1412.3555*.

Fabien Cromieres. 2016. Kyoto-NMT: a neural machine translation implementation in Chainer. In *Coling 2016 System Demonstration*.

Fabien Cromières, Chenhui Chu, Toshiaki Nakazawa, and Sadao Kurohashi. 2016. Kyoto university participation to wat 2016. In *Third Workshop on Asian Translation (WAT2016)*.

Isao Goto and Hideki Tanaka. 2017. Detecting untranslated content for neural machine translation. In *Proceedings of the First Workshop on Neural Machine Translation*, pages 47–55, Vancouver. Association for Computational Linguistics.

Kaiming He, Xiangyu Zhang, Shaoqing Ren, and Jian Sun. 2016. Deep residual learning for image recognition. In *Proceedings of the IEEE conference on computer vision and pattern recognition*, pages 770–778.

Kenneth Heafield. 2011. KenLM: faster and smaller language model queries. In *Proceedings of the EMNLP 2011 Sixth Workshop on Statistical Machine Translation*, pages 187–197, Edinburgh, Scotland, United Kingdom.

Kenneth Heafield and Alon Lavie. 2010. Combining machine translation output with open source: The Carnegie Mellon multi-engine machine translation scheme. *The Prague Bulletin of Mathematical Linguistics*, 93:27–36.

Sepp Hochreiter and Jürgen Schmidhuber. 1997. Long short-term memory. *Neural computation*, 9(8):1735–1780.

Marcin Junczys-Dowmunt, Tomasz Dwojak, and Rico Sennrich. 2016. The AMU-UEDIN submission to the WMT16 news translation task: Attention-based NMT models as feature functions in phrase-based SMT. In *Proceedings of the First Conference on Machine Translation, WMT 2016, colocated with ACL 2016, August 11-12, Berlin, Germany*, pages 319–325.

Diederik Kingma and Jimmy Ba. 2014. Adam: A method for stochastic optimization. *arXiv preprint arXiv:1412.6980*.

Sadao Kurohashi. 1994. Improvements of japanese morphological analyzer juman. In *Proceedings of the Workshop on Sharable Natural Language Resources, 1994*, pages 22–28.

Xiaoqing Li, Jiajun Zhang, and Chengqing Zong. 2016. Towards zero unknown word in neural machine translation. In *IJCAI*, pages 2852–2858.

Minh-Thang Luong, Ilya Sutskever, Quoc V Le, Oriol Vinyals, and Wojciech Zaremba. 2015. Addressing the rare word problem in neural machine translation. In *Proceedings of ACL 2015*.

Toshiaki Nakazawa, Shohei Higashiyama, Chenchen Ding, Hideya Mino, Isao Goto, Graham Neubig, Hideto Kazawa, Yusuke Oda, Jun Harashima, and Sadao Kurohashi. 2017. Overview of the 4th Workshop on Asian Translation. In *Proceedings of the 4th Workshop on Asian Translation (WAT2017)*, Taipei, Taiwan.

Toshiaki Nakazawa, Hideya Mino, Chenchen Ding, Isao Goto, Graham Neubig, Sadao Kurohashi, and Eiichiro Sumita. 2016. Overview of the 3rd workshop on asian translation. In *Proceedings of the 3rd Workshop on Asian Translation (WAT2016)*, Osaka, Japan.

Rico Sennrich, Barry Haddow, and Alexandra Birch. 2015. Neural machine translation of rare words with subword units. *arXiv preprint arXiv:1508.07909*.

Mo Shen, Li Wingmui, HyunJeong Choe, Chenhui Chu, Daisuke Kawahara, and Sadao Kurohashi. 2016. Consistent word segmentation, part-of-speech tagging and dependency labelling annotation for chinese language. In *Proceedings of the 26th International Conference on Computational Linguistics*, Osaka, Japan. Association for Computational Linguistics.

Nitish Srivastava, Geoffrey E Hinton, Alex Krizhevsky, Ilya Sutskever, and Ruslan Salakhutdinov. 2014. Dropout: a simple way to prevent neural networks from overfitting. *Journal of Machine Learning Research*, 15(1):1929–1958.

Seiya Tokui, Kenta Oono, Shohei Hido, and Justin Clayton. 2015. Chainer: a next-generation open source framework for deep learning. In *Proceedings of Workshop on Machine Learning Systems (LearningSys) in The Twenty-ninth Annual Conference on Neural Information Processing Systems (NIPS)*.

Ashish Vaswani, Noam Shazeer, Niki Parmar, Jakob Uszkoreit, Llion Jones, Aidan N. Gomez, Lukasz Kaiser, and Illia Polosukhin. 2017a. Attention is all you need.

Ashish Vaswani, Noam Shazeer, Niki Parmar, Jakob Uszkoreit, Llion Jones, Aidan N. Gomez, Lukasz Kaiser, and Illia Polosukhin. 2017b. Attention is all you need. *CoRR*, abs/1706.03762.

Yonghui Wu, Mike Schuster, Zhifeng Chen, Quoc V. Le, Mohammad Norouzi, Wolfgang Macherey, Maxim Krikun, Yuan Cao, Qin Gao, Klaus Macherey, Jeff Klingner, Apurva Shah, Melvin Johnson, Xiaobing Liu, ukasz Kaiser, Stephan Gouws, Yoshikiyo Kato, Taku Kudo, Hideto Kazawa, Keith Stevens, George Kurian, Nishant Patil, Wei Wang, Cliff Young, Jason Smith, Jason Riesa, Alex Rudnick, Oriol Vinyals, Greg Corrado, Macduff Hughes, and Jeffrey Dean. 2016. Google's neural machine translation system: Bridging the gap between human and machine translation. *CoRR*, abs/1609.08144.

Wojciech Zaremba, Ilya Sutskever, and Oriol Vinyals. 2014. Recurrent neural network regularization. *arXiv preprint arXiv:1409.2329*.

CUNI NMT System for WAT 2017 Translation Tasks

Tom Kocmi   **Dušan Variš**   **Ondřej Bojar**
Charles University,
Faculty of Mathematics and Physics
Institute of Formal and Applied Linguistics
{kocmi,varis,bojar}@ufal.mff.cuni.cz

Abstract

The paper presents this year's CUNI submissions to the WAT 2017 Translation Task focusing on the Japanese-English translation, namely Scientific papers subtask, Patents subtask and Newswire subtask. We compare two neural network architectures, the standard sequence-to-sequence with attention (Seq2Seq) (Bahdanau et al., 2014) and an architecture using convolutional sentence encoder (FB-Conv2Seq) described by Gehring et al. (2017), both implemented in the NMT framework Neural Monkey[1] that we currently participate in developing. We also compare various types of preprocessing of the source Japanese sentences and their impact on the overall results. Furthermore, we include the results of our experiments with out-of-domain data obtained by combining the corpora provided for each subtask.

1 Introduction

With neural machine translation (NMT) currently becoming the leading paradigm in the field of machine translation, many novel NMT architectures with state-of-the-art results are being proposed. In the past, there were reports on large scale evaluation (Britz et al., 2017), however, the experiments were performed on a limited number of language pairs from related language families (English→German, English→French) or focused on a subset of possible NMT architectures, leaving room for further exploration.

One of the downsides of NMT is the limited allowable size of both input and output vocabularies. Various solutions for dealing with potential out-of-vocabulary (OOV) tokens were proposed either by using a back-off dictionary look-up (Luong et al., 2015), character-level translation of unknown words (Luong and Manning, 2016) or recently quite popular translation via subword units generated by byte pair encoding (Sennrich et al., 2016c). However, in the case of Japanese which has no clear definition of a word unit, there has been less research on how a particular preprocessing can influence the overall NMT performance.

In this system description paper we compare two sequence-to-sequence architectures, one using a recurrent encoder and one using a convolutional encoder. We also report results of our experiments with preprocessing of Japanese. Furthermore, we report how including additional out-of-domain training data influence the performance of NMT.

2 Dataset Preparation

In this section we describe the methods we used for preprocessing both Japanese and English.

Due to Japanese being an unsegmented language with no clear definition of word boundaries, proper text segmentation is essential. We used MeCab[2] (Kudo et al., 2004) with the UniDic[3] dictionary to perform the tokenization.

For English, we used morphological analyser MorphoDiTa[4] (Straková et al., 2014) to tokenize English training sentences. Based on the generated lemmas, we also performed truecasing of the target side of the training data.

To reduce the vocabulary size, we use byte pair encoding (BPE; Sennrich et al., 2016c) which breaks all words into subword units. The vocabulary is initialized with all alphabet characters

---

[1]http://ufal.mff.cuni.cz/neuralmonkey

[2]http://taku910.github.io/mecab/
[3]https://osdn.net/projects/unidic/
[4]https://github.com/ufal/morphodita/

Proceedings of the 4th Workshop on Asian Translation, pages 154–159,
Taipei, Taiwan, November 27, 2017. ©2017 AFNLP

present in the training data and larger units are added on the basis of corpus statistics. Frequent words make it to the vocabulary, less frequent words are (deterministically) broken into smaller units from the vocabulary. We generated separate BPE merges for each dataset, both source and target side.

Because the BPE algorithm, when generating the vocabulary, performs its own (subword) segmentation, we decided to compare a system trained on the tokenized Japanese (which was then further segmented by BPE) with a system that was segmented only via BPE. Additionally, we also performed a comparison with a system with Japanese text transcribed in Latin alphabet. The romanization was done by generating Hiragana transcription of each token using MeCab and then transcribing these tokens to Romaji using jaconv.[5] The resulting text was then also further segmented by BPE. The results are discussed in Section 4.1

3   Architecture Description

We use Neural Monkey[6] (Helcl and Libovický, 2017), an open-source NMT and general sequence-to-sequence learning toolkit built using the TensorFlow (Abadi et al., 2015) machine learning library.

Neural Monkey is flexible in model configuration supporting the combination of different encoder and decoder architectures as well as solving various tasks and metrics.

We perform most of the experiments on the 8GB GPU NVIDIA GeForce GTX 1080. For the preprocessing of data and final inference, we use our cluster of CPUs.

The main hyperparameters of the neural network are set as follows. We use the batch size of 60. As the optimization algorithm we use Adam (Kingma and Ba, 2014) with initial learning rate of 0.0001. We used only the non-ensembled left-to-right run (i.e. no right-to-left rescoring as done by Sennrich et al. 2016a) with beam size of 20, taking just the single-best output.

We limit the vocabulary size to 30,000 subword units. The vocabulary is constructed separately for the source and target side of the corpus.

We compare two different architectures. We describe both of them in more details as well as the hyperparameters used during the training in the following sections.

3.1   Sequence to Sequence

Our main architecture is the standard encoder-decoder architecture with attention as proposed by Bahdanau et al. (2014).

The encoder is a bidirectional recurrent neural network (BiRNN) using Gated Recurrent Units (GRU; Cho et al., 2014). In each step, it takes an embedded token from the input sequence and its previous output and outputs a representation of the token. The encoder works in both directions; the resulting vector representations at corresponding positions are concatenated. Additionally, the final outputs of both the forward and backward run are concatenated and used as the initial state of the decoder.[7]

The decoder is a standard RNN with the conditional GRU (Calixto et al., 2017) recurrent unit. At each decoding step, it takes its previous hidden state and the embedding of the token produced in the previous step as the input and produces the output vector. This vector is used to compute the attention distribution vector over the encoder outputs. The RNN output and the attention distribution vector are then used as the input of a linear layer to produce the distribution over the target vocabulary. During training, the previously generated token is replaced by the token present in the reference translation. The architecture overview is in Figure 1.

We have used the following setup of network hyperparameters. The encoder uses embeddings of size 500 and the hidden state of bidirectional GRU network of size 600 in both directions. Dropout (Srivastava et al., 2014) is turned off and the maximum length of the source sentence is set to 50 tokens. The size of the decoder hidden state is 600 and the output embedding is 500. In this case, dropout is also turned off. The maximum output length is 50 tokens. In this paper, we will refer to this architecture as *Seq2Seq*.

3.2   Convolutional Encoder

The second architecture is a hybrid system using convolutional encoder and recurrent decoder.

We use the convolutional encoder defined by Gehring et al. (2017). First, the input sequence

---

[5]https://github.com/ikegami-yukino/jaconv
[6]http://ufal.mff.cuni.cz/neuralmonkey

[7]The concatenated final states are transformed to match the size of the decoder hidden state.

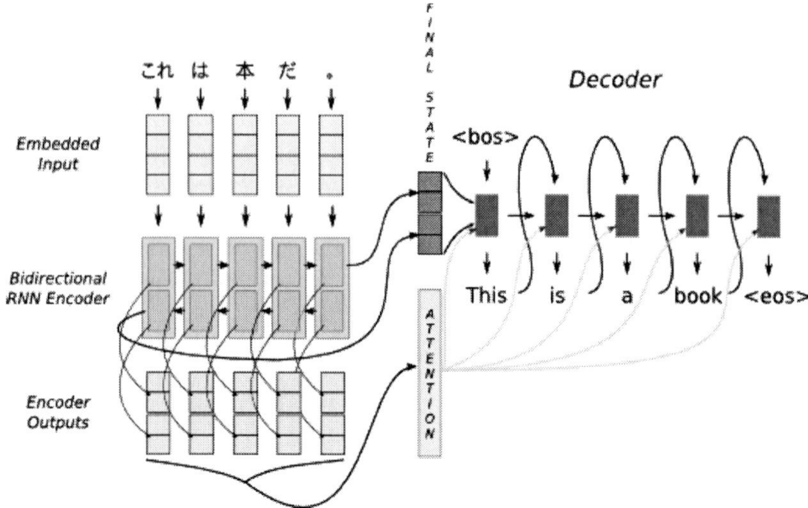

Figure 1: Simplified illustration of the standard RNN encoder-decoder architecture. Labels describing parts of the network are in italics. *<bos>* and *<eos>* are special tokens marking the beginning and end of the sentence.

of tokens $\mathbf{x} = (x_1, ..., x_n)$ is assigned a sequence of embeddings $\mathbf{w} = (w_1, ..., w_n)$ where $w_i \in \mathbb{R}^f$ is produced by embedding matrix $\mathsf{D} \in \mathbb{R}^{|V| \times f}$. When compared to the RNN encoder, the convolutional encoder does not explicitly model positions of the tokens in the input sequence. Therefore, we include this information using positional embeddings. We model the information about the position in the input sequence via $\mathbf{p} = (p_1, ..., p_n)^8$ where $p_i \in \mathbb{R}^f$. The resulting input sequence embedding is computed as $\mathbf{e} = (w_1 + p_1, ..., w_n + p_n)$.

The encoder is a convolutional network stacking several convolution blocks over each other. Each block contains a one dimensional convolution followed by a nonlinearity. The convolution with kernel size k and stride 1 with SAME padding is applied on the input sequence using d input channels and $2 \times d$ output channels. This output is then fed to the Gated Linear Unit (GLU; Dauphin et al., 2016) which substitutes a nonlinearity between the convolution blocks. Additionally, residual connections are added to the produced output. At the final layer, we get the encoded sequence $\mathbf{y} = (y_1, ..., y_n)$ where $y_i \in \mathbb{R}^d$.

We use same decoder as in the previous section. The initial decoder state $s \in \mathbb{R}^d$ is created by picking element-wise maximum across the length

of the encoder output sequence $\mathbf{y}$. We tried other methods for creating the initial decoder state and this one produced the best results. Figure 2 shows the overview of the encoder architecture.

In the experiments we use encoder with the embedding size of 500 and maximum length of 50 tokens per sentence. The encoder uses 600 input features in each of its 6 convolutional layers with the kernel size of 5. Dropout is turned off. For the rest of this paper we will refer to this architecture as *FBConv2Seq*.

4 Experiments

In this section we describe all experiments we conducted for the WAT 2017 Translation Task. We report results over the development set.

4.1 Japanese Tokenization

We experimented with various tokenization methods of the Japanese source side. In Table 1 we compare untokenized, tokenized and romanized Japanese side. This experiment was evaluated over the top 1 million training examples in the ASPEC dataset.

4.2 Architecture Comparison

In Table 2 we compare the architectures we described in Section 3. We ran experiments on 4 different datasets. The JPO, JIJI, ASPEC with 1 million best sentences were used with tokenized

---

[8]Another option is to use the sine and cosine functions of different frequencies (Vaswani et al., 2017) instead of trainable positional embeddings.

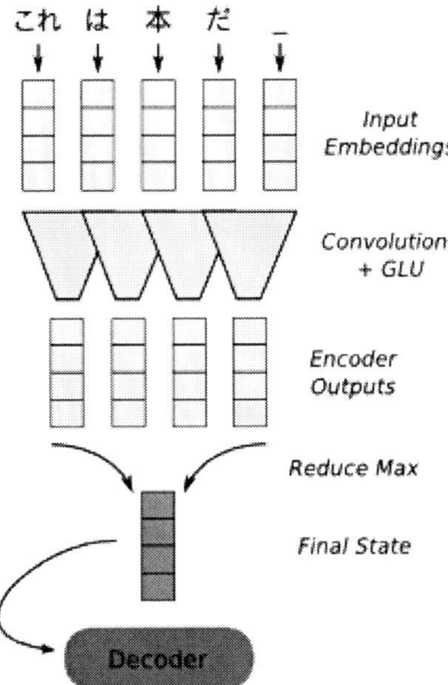

Figure 2: Illustration of the encoder used in the FBConv2Seq architecture. The attention over the *Encoder Outputs* is computed in a similar fashion as in Seq2Seq architecture and is omitted for simplicity.

Tokenization	BLEU
Untokenized	24.69
Tokenized	26.56
Romanized	25.46

Table 1: Comparison of various tokenization methods measured on the ASPEC dataset.

Japanese. The dataset ASPEC 3M was not tokenized by MeCab.

After examination of the Table 2, we can see that in most cases the Seq2Seq model (Bahdanau et al., 2014) outperforms the FBConv2Seq architecture. On the other hand, the FBConv2Seq model performed better on the untokenized corpus. This might suggest that the model has an advantage in processing inputs which are not properly segmented thanks to the convolutional nature of the encoder. This could be valuable for languages that cannot be segmented.

4.3 ASPEC Size of Data

The ASPEC dataset consists of 3 millions of English to Japanese sentence pairs ordered with a decreasing accuracy of the translation. It is a well known fact about neural networks that the more

Corpora	Seq2Seq	FBConv2Seq
JPO	**35.40 BLEU**	33.87 BLEU
JIJI	**16.40 BLEU**	13.72 BLEU
ASPEC 1M	**26.56 BLEU**	22.29 BLEU
ASPEC 3M untok.	18.14 BLEU	**19.16 BLEU**

Table 2: Comparison of two examined architectures.

Corpora	In-domain	Combined corpora
JPO (1M)	**34.95 BLEU**	33.62 BLEU
JIJI (0.2M)	**16.40 BLEU**	14.19 BLEU
ASPEC (2M)	23.19 BLEU	**23.46 BLEU**

Table 3: Comparison of in-domain data only and combined corpora.

data is available, the better performance they can get. In this experiment we try to compare the influence of the size of dataset and the quality of the training pairs. We decided to experiment with subcorpora containing 1, 1.5, 2, 2.5 and 3 million best sentence pairs. We refer to them as ASPEC 1M, ASPEC 1.5M, ASPEC 2M, ASPEC 2.5M, ASPEC 3M respectively.

For simplicity, the experiment was performed with untokenized Japanese side and we used the Seq2Seq architecture. All corpora are shuffled in order to overcome the ordering by the quality of translation.

The results presented in Figure 3 show a clear picture that the overall quality of the training data is more important than the total amount of the data.

4.4 Corpus Combination

In the previous section, we experimented with the quality of the training corpora. In this experiment we show whether more data can help in various domains or if it is also a burden as shown in the previous section comparing quality of the data.

We combined tokenized corpora for JPO (1 million sentences), JIJI (200 thousand sentences) and 2 million of the best sentences from ASPEC. The resulting corpus was shuffled.

The results in Table 3 suggest that the domain is important for both the JPO and JIJI datasets. Interestingly, it improved the score of the ASPEC 2M.

There is also another explanation which is more plausible with respect to the experiments in the previous section. The training data in JPO and JIJI have better quality than the data in ASPEC 2M, which leads to the worse performance on those datasets and on the other hand cleaner data helps

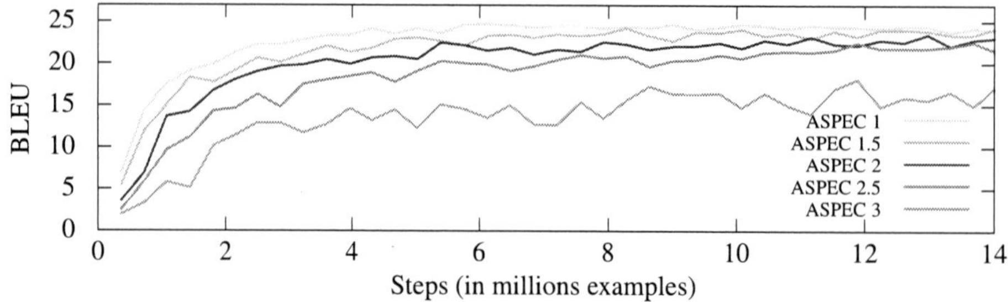

Figure 3: Learning curves over different sizes of ASPEC data.

Corpora	Results
JPO	35.35 BLEU
JIJI	16.40 BLEU
ASPEC	25.56 BLEU

Table 4: Performance of the final models on the development data.

ASPEC to increase the performance.

More research on this topic is needed to answer which of the explanations is more plausible. In future work, we want to experiment with combined corpora of JPO, JIJI and only 1 million of the cleanest sentences from ASPEC.

4.5 Official Results

Based on the previous experiments we decided to use the tokenized and shuffled in-domain training data for each of the tasks. For the Translation Task submission, we chose the Seq2Seq architecture, because it had a better overall performance. For the ASPEC dataset, we decided to train only on the 1 million cleanest training data. The results of the evaluation done on the corresponding development datasets are in Table 4.

The results of Translation Task are available on the WAT 2017 website.[9] Our system performed mostly on average. It was beaten by more sophisticated architectures using more recent state-of-the art techniques.

5 Summary

In this system description paper, we presented initial results of our research in Japanese-English NMT. We compared two different architectures implemented on NMT framework, Neural Monkey, however, as the official results of the WAT

2017 Training Task suggest, future improvements needs to be done to catch-up with the current state of the art.

We performed experiments with different input language tokenization combined with the byte-pair-encoding subword segmentation method. In the future, we plan to explore other tokenization options (e.g. splitting to bunsetsu) together with using a shared vocabulary for both the source and target languages. We are curious, whether the latter will bring an improvement when combined with romanization of Japanese.

Lastly, we made several experiments with dataset combination suggesting that including additional out-of-domain data is generally harmful for the NMT system. As the next step we plan to investigate options for creating additional synthetic data and their impact on the overall performance as suggested by Sennrich et al. (2016b).

Acknowledgments

This work has been in part supported by the European Union's Horizon 2020 research and innovation programme under grant agreements No 644402 (HimL) and 645452 (QT21), by the LINDAT/CLARIN project of the Ministry of Education, Youth and Sports of the Czech Republic (projects LM2015071 and OP VVV VI CZ.02.1.01/0.0/0.0/16_013/0001781), by the Charles University Research Programme "Progres" Q18+Q48, by the Charles University SVV project number 260 453 and by the grant GAUK 8502/2016.

References

Martín Abadi, Ashish Agarwal, Paul Barham, Eugene Brevdo, Zhifeng Chen, Craig Citro, Greg S. Cor-

---

rado, Andy Davis, Jeffrey Dean, Matthieu Devin, Sanjay Ghemawat, Ian Goodfellow, Andrew Harp, Geoffrey Irving, Michael Isard, Yangqing Jia, Rafal Jozefowicz, Lukasz Kaiser, Manjunath Kudlur, Josh Levenberg, Dan Mané, Rajat Monga, Sherry Moore, Derek Murray, Chris Olah, Mike Schuster, Jonathon Shlens, Benoit Steiner, Ilya Sutskever, Kunal Talwar, Paul Tucker, Vincent Vanhoucke, Vijay Vasudevan, Fernanda Viégas, Oriol Vinyals, Pete Warden, Martin Wattenberg, Martin Wicke, Yuan Yu, and Xiaoqiang Zheng. 2015. TensorFlow: Large-scale machine learning on heterogeneous systems. Software available from tensorflow.org.

Dzmitry Bahdanau, Kyunghyun Cho, and Yoshua Bengio. 2014. Neural machine translation by jointly learning to align and translate. In *ICLR 2015*.

Denny Britz, Anna Goldie, Minh-Thang Luong, and Quoc V. Le. 2017. Massive exploration of neural machine translation architectures. *CoRR*, abs/1703.03906.

Iacer Calixto, Qun Liu, and Nick Campbell. 2017. Doubly-attentive decoder for multi-modal neural machine translation. In *Proceedings of the 55th Annual Meeting of the Association for Computational Linguistics, ACL 2017, Vancouver, Canada, July 30 - August 4, Volume 1: Long Papers*, pages 1913–1924.

Kyunghyun Cho, Bart van Merrienboer, Dzmitry Bahdanau, and Yoshua Bengio. 2014. On the properties of neural machine translation: Encoder-decoder approaches. In *Proceedings of SSST@EMNLP 2014, Eighth Workshop on Syntax, Semantics and Structure in Statistical Translation, Doha, Qatar, 25 October 2014*, pages 103–111.

Yann N Dauphin, Angela Fan, Michael Auli, and David Grangier. 2016. Language modeling with gated convolutional networks. *arXiv preprint arXiv:1612.08083*.

Jonas Gehring, Michael Auli, David Grangier, Denis Yarats, and Yann Dauphin. 2017. Convolutional sequence to sequence learning.

Jindřich Helcl and Jindřich Libovický. 2017. Neural Monkey: An Open-source Tool for Sequence Learning. *The Prague Bulletin of Mathematical Linguistics*, 107:5–17.

Diederik P. Kingma and Jimmy Ba. 2014. Adam: A method for stochastic optimization. *CoRR*, abs/1412.6980.

Taku Kudo, Kaoru Yamamoto, and Yuji Matsumoto. 2004. Applying conditional random fields to japanese morphological analysis. In *Proceedings of EMNLP 2004*, pages 230–237, Barcelona, Spain. Association for Computational Linguistics.

Minh-Thang Luong and Christopher D. Manning. 2016. Achieving open vocabulary neural machine translation with hybrid word-character models. In *Proceedings of the 54th Annual Meeting of the Association for Computational Linguistics, ACL 2016, August 7-12, 2016, Berlin, Germany, Volume 1: Long Papers*.

Thang Luong, Hieu Pham, and Christopher D. Manning. 2015. Effective approaches to attention-based neural machine translation. In *Proceedings of the 2015 Conference on Empirical Methods in Natural Language Processing, EMNLP 2015, Lisbon, Portugal, September 17-21, 2015*, pages 1412–1421.

Rico Sennrich, Barry Haddow, and Alexandra Birch. 2016a. Edinburgh Neural Machine Translation Systems for WMT 16. In *Proceedings of the First Conference on Machine Translation*, pages 646–654, Berlin, Germany. Association for Computational Linguistics.

Rico Sennrich, Barry Haddow, and Alexandra Birch. 2016b. Improving neural machine translation models with monolingual data. In *Proceedings of the 54th Annual Meeting of the Association for Computational Linguistics, ACL 2016, August 7-12, 2016, Berlin, Germany, Volume 1: Long Papers*.

Rico Sennrich, Barry Haddow, and Alexandra Birch. 2016c. Neural machine translation of rare words with subword units. In *Proceedings of the 54th Annual Meeting of the Association for Computational Linguistics (Volume 1: Long Papers)*, pages 1715–1725, Berlin, Germany. Association for Computational Linguistics.

Nitish Srivastava, Geoffrey Hinton, Alex Krizhevsky, Ilya Sutskever, and Ruslan Salakhutdinov. 2014. Dropout: A simple way to prevent neural networks from overfitting. *Journal of Machine Learning Research*, 15:1929–1958.

Jana Straková, Milan Straka, and Jan Hajič. 2014. Open-Source Tools for Morphology, Lemmatization, POS Tagging and Named Entity Recognition. In *Proceedings of 52nd Annual Meeting of the Association for Computational Linguistics: System Demonstrations*, pages 13–18, Baltimore, Maryland. Association for Computational Linguistics.

Ashish Vaswani, Noam Shazeer, Niki Parmar, Jakob Uszkoreit, Llion Jones, Aidan N. Gomez, Lukasz Kaiser, and Illia Polosukhin. 2017. Attention is all you need.

Tokyo Metropolitan University Neural Machine Translation System for WAT 2017

Yukio Matsumura and **Mamoru Komachi**

Tokyo Metropolitan University
Tokyo, Japan
matsumura-yukio@ed.tmu.ac.jp
komachi@tmu.ac.jp

Abstract

In this paper, we describe our neural machine translation (NMT) system, which is based on the attention-based NMT (Luong et al., 2015) and uses long short-term memories (LSTM) as RNN. We implemented beam search and ensemble decoding in the NMT system. The system was tested on the 4th Workshop on Asian Translation (WAT 2017) (Nakazawa et al., 2017) shared tasks. In our experiments, we participated in the scientific paper subtasks and attempted Japanese-English, English-Japanese, and Japanese-Chinese translation tasks. The experimental results showed that implementation of beam search and ensemble decoding can effectively improve the translation quality.

1 Introduction

Recently, neural machine translation (NMT) has gained popularity in the field of machine translation. The conventional encoder-decoder NMT (Sutskever et al., 2014; Cho et al., 2014) uses two recurrent neural networks (RNN); one is an encoder, which encodes a source sequence into a fixed-length vector; the other is a decoder, which decodes this vector into a target sequence. Attention-based NMT (Bahdanau et al., 2015; Luong et al., 2015) can predict output words by using the weights of each hidden state of the encoder as the context vector, thereby improving the adequacy of the translation.

Despite the success of attention-based models, several open questions remain in NMT. In general, a unique output word is predicted at each time step. Therefore, if a wrong word is predicted, subsequent words will not be correctly output. To enable better predictions, best practices such as beam search and ensemble decoding are recommended to improve the robustness of the predictions. Beam search keeps better hypotheses during decoding, while ensemble decoding reduces the variance of output during decoding.

In this paper, we describe the NMT system that was tested on the shared tasks at 4th Workshop on Asian Translation (WAT 2017) (Nakazawa et al., 2017). We implemented beam search and ensemble decoding in our NMT system. We applied our NMT system to Japanese-English, English-Japanese, and Japanese-Chinese scientific paper translation subtasks. The experimental results show that beam search and ensemble decoding improve the translation accuracy by 3.55 points in Japanese-English translation and 3.28 points in English-Japanese translation in terms of BLEU (Papineni et al., 2002) scores.

2 Neural Machine Translation

Herein, we describe the architecture of our NMT system as shown in Figure 1. The designed system is based on the attention-based NMT (Luong et al., 2015) and uses long short-term memories (LSTM) as RNN. Our NMT system comprises mainly two components:

- Encoder : one-layer bi-directional LSTM

- Decoder : one-layer uni-directional LSTM

2.1 Encoder

The source sentence is converted into a sequence of one-hot word vectors ($X = [x_1, \cdots, x_{|X|}]$) where $|X|$ is the length of source sentence.

At each time step i, the source word embedding vector e_i^s is computed by the following equation.

$$e_i^s = \tanh(W_x x_i) \tag{1}$$

Proceedings of the 4th Workshop on Asian Translation, pages 160–166,
Taipei, Taiwan, November 27, 2017. ©2017 AFNLP

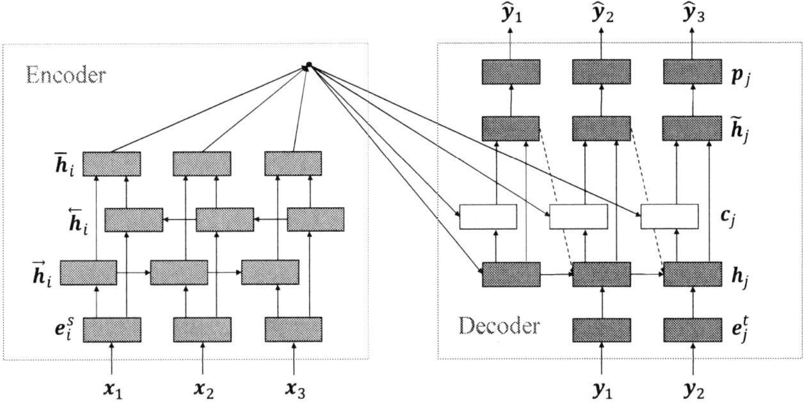

Figure 1: The architecture of our NMT system.

where $\boldsymbol{W}_x \in \mathbb{R}^{q \times v_s}$ is a weight matrix. q is the dimension of the word embeddings and v_s is the size of source vocabulary.

The hidden state $\bar{\boldsymbol{h}}_i$ of the encoder is computed as given by the following equation.

$$\bar{\boldsymbol{h}}_i = \overrightarrow{\boldsymbol{h}}_i + \overleftarrow{\boldsymbol{h}}_i. \tag{2}$$

Here, the forward state $\overrightarrow{\boldsymbol{h}}_i$ and the backward state $\overleftarrow{\boldsymbol{h}}_i$ are computed by

$$\overrightarrow{\boldsymbol{h}}_i = \text{LSTM}(e_i^s, \overrightarrow{\boldsymbol{h}_{i-1}}) \tag{3}$$

and

$$\overleftarrow{\boldsymbol{h}}_i = \text{LSTM}(e_i^s, \overleftarrow{\boldsymbol{h}_{i+1}}). \tag{4}$$

Note that the computation of hidden state $\bar{\boldsymbol{h}}_i$ of the encoder can be regarded as an addition instead of a concatenation.

2.2 Decoder

As with the source sentence, the target sentence is converted into a sequence of one-hot word vectors ($\boldsymbol{Y} = [\boldsymbol{y}_1, \cdots, \boldsymbol{y}_{|Y|}]$) where $|\boldsymbol{Y}|$ is the length of target sentence.

At each time step j, the hidden state $\boldsymbol{h}_j$ of the decoder is represented as

$$\boldsymbol{h}_j = \text{LSTM}([e_{j-1}^t : \tilde{\boldsymbol{h}}_{j-1}], \boldsymbol{h}_{j-1}) \tag{5}$$

where e_{j-1}^t is the target word embedding vector, $\tilde{\boldsymbol{h}}_{j-1}$ is the attentional hidden state, and $\boldsymbol{h}_{j-1}$ is the hidden state at the previous time step.

The target word embedding vector e_j^t is computed by

$$e_j^t = \tanh(\boldsymbol{W}_y \boldsymbol{y}_j) \tag{6}$$

where $\boldsymbol{W}_y \in \mathbb{R}^{q \times v_t}$ is a weight matrix. v_t is the target vocabulary size. The attentional hidden state $\tilde{\boldsymbol{h}}_j$ is represented as

$$\tilde{\boldsymbol{h}}_j = \tanh(\boldsymbol{W}_a[\boldsymbol{h}_j : \boldsymbol{c}_j] + \boldsymbol{b}_a) \tag{7}$$

where $\boldsymbol{W}_a \in \mathbb{R}^{r \times 2r}$ is a weight matrix and $\boldsymbol{b}_a \in \mathbb{R}^r$ is a bias vector. r is the number of hidden units.

The context vector $\boldsymbol{c}_j$ is a weighted sum of each hidden state $\bar{\boldsymbol{h}}_i$ of the encoder. It is represented as

$$\boldsymbol{c}_j = \sum_{i=1}^{|X|} \alpha_{ij} \bar{\boldsymbol{h}}_i. \tag{8}$$

Its weight α_{ij} is a normalized probability distribution, which is computed using a dot product of hidden states, as follows:

$$\alpha_{ij} = \frac{\exp(\bar{\boldsymbol{h}}_i^{\mathrm{T}} \boldsymbol{h}_j)}{\sum_{k=1}^{|X|} \exp(\bar{\boldsymbol{h}}_k^{\mathrm{T}} \boldsymbol{h}_j)}. \tag{9}$$

The conditional probability of the output word $\hat{\boldsymbol{y}}_j$ is computed by

$$p(\hat{\boldsymbol{y}}_j | \boldsymbol{Y}_{<j}, \boldsymbol{X}) = \text{softmax}(\boldsymbol{W}_p \bar{\boldsymbol{h}}_j + \boldsymbol{b}_p) \tag{10}$$

where $\boldsymbol{W}_p \in \mathbb{R}^{v_t \times r}$ is a weight matrix and $\boldsymbol{b}_p \in \mathbb{R}^{v_t}$ is a bias vector.

Incidentally, the rare words that did not fit in the vocabulary are replaced with unknown tokens "<unk>". When the unknown word is predicted, our NMT system does not process it and outputs this unknown token as it is.

	Japenese-English	Japanese-Chinese
train	1,456,278	672,315
dev	1,790	2,741
test	1,812	2,300

Table 1: Numbers of parallel sentences.

2.3 Training

The objective function is defined by

$$\mathcal{L}(\boldsymbol{\theta}) = \frac{1}{D} \sum_{d=1}^{D} \sum_{j=1}^{|\boldsymbol{Y}|} \log p(y_j^{(d)} | \boldsymbol{Y}_{<j}^{(d)}, \boldsymbol{X}^{(d)}, \boldsymbol{\theta}) \tag{11}$$

where D is the number of data and $\boldsymbol{\theta}$ are the model parameters. On training, this objective function is maximized. The model parameters of word embedding are initialized using Word2Vec (Mikolov et al., 2013). The other model parameters are randomly initialized.

2.4 Testing

In general, a unique output word is predicted at each time step. Then the next output word is predicted on the premise that this unique output word is correct. Therefore, if a wrong word is once predicted, then it is difficult to correctly output subsequent words. To make better predictions, we implemented beam search and ensemble decoder.

2.4.1 Beam Search

In general, the word that has the highest probability is output. In beam search, we keep hypotheses of beam size n at each time step. At the subsequent time step, for each hypothesis, we compute n hypotheses; then, we keep n hypotheses in total n^2 hypotheses. Adopting this approach reduces the risk of generating wrong sentences.

2.4.2 Ensemble Decoding

In ensemble decoding, the conditional probability of the output word $\hat{y}_j$ is the average of each model's score. It is computed by

$$p(\hat{y}_j | \boldsymbol{Y}_{<j}, \boldsymbol{X}) = \frac{1}{M} \sum_{m=1}^{M} p^{(m)}(\hat{y}_j | \boldsymbol{Y}_{<j}, \boldsymbol{X}) \tag{12}$$

where M is the number of models. Adopting this approach reduces the risk of predicting a wrong word at each time step.

3 Experiments

We experimented our NMT system on Japanese-English, English-Japanese, and Japanese-Chinese scientific paper translation subtasks.

3.1 Datasets

We used the Japanese-English and Japanese-Chinese parallel corpora in Asian Scientific Paper Excerpt Corpus (ASPEC) (Nakazawa et al., 2014). As regards the Japanese-English parallel corpus, Japanese sentences were segmented by the morphological analyzer MeCab[1] (version 0.996, IPADIC) and English sentences were tokenized by tokenizer.perl of Moses[2]. On the other hand, as regards the Japanese-Chinese parallel corpus, Japanese and Chinese sentences were tokenized by SentencePiece[3]. The vocabulary size of the tokenizer was set to 50,000.

As regards the training data in Japanese-English parallel corpus, we used only the first 1.5 million sentences sorted by sentence-alignment similarity; sentences with more than 60 words were excluded. On the other hand, as regards the training data in Japanese-Chinese parallel corpus, we used all the sentences. Table 1 shows the numbers of the sentences in each parallel corpus.

3.2 Japanese-English and English-Japanese translation tasks

Settings In these tasks, we conducted the experiment using the following configuration:

- Number of hidden units: 1,024

- Word embedding dimensionality: 512

- Source vocabulary size: 100,000

- Target vocabulary size: 30,000

- Minibatch size: 128

- Optimizer: Adagrad

- Initial learning rate: 0.01

- Dropout rate: $\{0.1, 0.2, 0.3, 0.4, 0.5\}$

- Beam size: $\{1, 2, 5, 10, 20\}$

---

[1] https://github.com/taku910/mecab
[2] http://www.statmt.org/moses/
[3] https://github.com/google/sentencepiece

Japanese-English				
Model	BLEU	RIBES	AMFM	HUMAN
Previous system (Yamagishi et al., 2016)	18.45	0.711542	0.546880	-
beam 1	21.00	0.725284	0.585710	+56.750
beam 2	22.21	0.733571	0.591740	-
beam 5	22.85	0.737631	0.595180	-
beam 10	22.99	0.739629	0.595030	-
beam 20	23.03	0.741175	0.595260	+61.000
5 ensemble + beam 1	22.78	0.738325	0.587630	-
5 ensemble + beam 2	24.02	0.743581	0.596840	-
5 ensemble + beam 5	24.46	**0.744955**	**0.597760**	-
5 ensemble + beam 10	**24.55**	0.744928	0.596360	-

Table 2: Japanese-English translation results.

English-Japanese				
Model	BLEU	RIBES	AMFM	HUMAN
beam 1	33.72	0.811057	0.740620	+50.750
beam 2	34.54	0.817303	0.744730	-
beam 5	35.10	0.820389	0.744370	-
beam 10	35.30	0.821341	0.744660	-
beam 20	35.32	0.821563	0.744890	+56.500
5 ensemble + beam 1	35.63	0.825683	**0.751660**	-
5 ensemble + beam 2	36.35	0.829732	0.750950	-
5 ensemble + beam 5	36.90	0.831559	0.750360	-
5 ensemble + beam 10	**37.00**	**0.832569**	0.749410	-

Table 3: English-Japanese translation results.

We trained five models with different dropout rates for each task. Then, we selected the best model based on the development set for a single model. The best dropout rate of 0.2 was achieved in a preliminary experiment. We applied various beam sizes during testing. In addition, we ensembled five trained models.

Results Tables 2 and 3 show the translation accuracy in BLEU (Papineni et al., 2002), RIBES (Isozaki et al., 2010), AMFM (Banchs and Li, 2011) and HUMAN evaluation scores. In the "Model" column, "beam n" indicates the model with the beam size of n, "n ensemble" indicates the model ensembled by n trained models on testing. "Previous system" in Table 2 indicates our previous NMT system for WAT 2016 (Yamagishi et al., 2016). This system is based on the attention-based NMT (Bahdanau et al., 2015) and did not implement dropout, beam search, and ensemble decoding.

The results show that beam search and ensemble decoding improve the translation accuracy by 3.55 points in Japanese-English translation and 3.28 points in English-Japanese translation in BLEU scores. As regards Japanese-English translation, our NMT system improved the translation accuracy by 6.10 points compared with our previous NMT system. From a BLEU score standpoint, with increasing beam size, the translation accuracy is enhanced. However, it does not always improve translation accuracy in other metrics.

Table 4 shows examples of outputs of Japanese-English translations. In Example 1, the output is significantly poor when the beam size is 1. However, by increasing the beam size, the output is improves significantly. In Example 2, increasing the beam size does not improve the output; however, by ensemble decoding, the output is improved. The experimental results indicate that beam search and ensemble decoding can effectively improve the translation quality.

Example 1	
Source	単純 桁 橋 より 接合 金具 を 始め 多種 部材 を 組合せる ため , 工法 が 複雑 で ある 。
beam1	since a joint metal
beam20	the method is complicated in order to combine a joint metal metal fitting to a simple girder bridge and a lot of member .
5ensemble + beam10	the method is complicated in order to combine various kinds of members from simple girder bridges to combine various kinds of members .
Reference	the construction was more complicated than simple girder bridge because of combinating various members including connecters .
Example 2	
Source	小型 甲殻 類 では , アミ 類 の アカイソアミ , ワレカラ 類 の ニッポンワレカラ と ツガルワレカラ は 茨城 県 で 初めて 確認 された 。
beam1	<unk> , <unk> , <unk> , <unk> , <unk> , <unk> , <unk> , <unk> , <unk> , <unk> , <unk> , <unk> , <unk> , <unk> , <unk> , <unk> , <unk> , <unk> , <unk> , <unk> , <unk> , <unk> , <unk> , <unk> , <unk> , <unk> , <unk> and <unk> , <unk> and <unk> ,
beam20	<unk> , <unk> and <unk> of <unk> , <unk> , <unk> , <unk> , <unk> , <unk> , <unk> , <unk> , <unk> , <unk> , <unk> , <unk> , <unk> , <unk> , <unk> , <unk> , <unk> , <unk> , <unk> , <unk> and <unk> , respectively , in Ibaraki Prefecture , for the first time .
5ensemble + beam10	in small crustaceans , <unk> and <unk> of <unk> and <unk> were confirmed for the first time in Ibaraki Prefecture .
Reference	among the small-type Crustacea , Paracanthomysis hispida of Mysidae , and Caprella japonica and C. tsugarensis of Caprellidae were confirmed for the first time in Ibaraki Prefecture .

Table 4: Examples of outputs of Japanese-English translation.

3.3 Japanese-Chinese translation task

Settings In this task, we conducted the experiment using the following configuration:

- Number of hidden units: 1,024

- Word embedding dimensionality: 1,024

- Source vocabulary size: 30,000

- Target vocabulary size: 30,000

- Minibatch size: 64

- Optimizer: Adagrad

- Initial learning rate: 0.01

- Dropout rate: 0.1

- Beam size: 1

Japanese-Chinese			
BLEU	RIBES	AMFM	HUMAN
22.92	0.798681	0.700030	+4.250

Table 5: Japanese-Chinese translation result.

Results Table 5 shows the translation accuracy in terms of BLEU, RIBES, AMFM, and HUMAN evaluation scores. The experimental result indicates that the translation quality is significantly poor compared with the other NMT systems in this task at WAT 2017. As regards this task, because this research is in its infancy, so we could not apply the proper settings. Therefore, we will attempt to pre- or post-process a corpus properly, tune the hyper parameters, and improve the translation quality.

4 Conclusion

In this paper, we described our NMT system, which is based on the attention-based NMT and uses long short-term memories as RNN. We evaluated our NMT system on Japanese-English, English-Japanese, and Japanese-Chinese scientific paper translation subtasks at WAT 2017. The experimental results show that the implementation of beam search and ensemble decoding can effectively improve the translation quality.

In our future work, we will attempt to use the byte pair encoding (BPE) (Sennrich et al., 2016) and compare it with SentencePiece that was explored in this work. In addition, we plan to implement the adversarial NMT (Wu et al., 2017; Yang et al., 2017), which is based on generative adversarial networks (GAN). GAN consist of two networks; one is a discriminator, which distinguishes whether the input data is real or not; the other is a generator, which generates the data that the discriminator cannot distinguish. This approach attempts to generate high quality translations that are comparable to human translations.

Acknowledgement

We express our sincere gratitude to Hayahide Yamagishi, Satoru Katsumata, Michiki Kurosawa, Hiroki Shimanaka, and Longtu Zhang for their support in the tuning of hyper parameters.

References

Dzmitry Bahdanau, Kyunghyun Cho, and Yoshua Bengio. 2015. Neural Machine Translation by Jointly Learning to Align and Translate. In *Proceedings of the 3rd International Conference on Learning Representations (ICLR2015)*.

Rafael E Banchs and Haizhou Li. 2011. AM-FM: A Semantic Framework for Translation Quality Assessment. In *Proceedings of the 49th Annual Meeting of the Association for Computational Linguistics: Human Language Technologies*, pages 153–158, Portland, Oregon, USA. Association for Computational Linguistics.

Kyunghyun Cho, Bart van Merrienboer, Caglar Gulcehre, Dzmitry Bahdanau, Fethi Bougares, Holger Schwenk, and Yoshua Bengio. 2014. Learning Phrase Representations using RNN Encoder–Decoder for Statistical Machine Translation. In *Proceedings of the 2014 Conference on Empirical Methods in Natural Language Processing (EMNLP)*, pages 1724–1734, Doha, Qatar. Association for Computational Linguistics.

Hideki Isozaki, Tsutomu Hirao, Kevin Duh, Katsuhito Sudoh, and Hajime Tsukada. 2010. Automatic Evaluation of Translation Quality for Distant Language Pairs. In *Proceedings of the 2010 Conference on Empirical Methods in Natural Language Processing*, pages 944–952, Cambridge, Massachusetts. Association for Computational Linguistics.

Thang Luong, Hieu Pham, and Christopher D Manning. 2015. Effective Approaches to Attention-based Neural Machine Translation. In *Proceedings of the 2015 Conference on Empirical Methods in Natural Language Processing*, pages 1412–1421, Lisbon, Portugal. Association for Computational Linguistics.

Tomas Mikolov, Ilya Sutskever, Kai Chen, Greg S Corrado, and Jeff Dean. 2013. Distributed Representations of Words and Phrases and their Compositionality. In C J C Burges, L Bottou, M Welling, Z Ghahramani, and K Q Weinberger, editors, *Advances in Neural Information Processing Systems 26 (NIPS2013)*, pages 3111–3119. Curran Associates, Inc.

Toshiaki Nakazawa, Shohei Higashiyama, Chenchen Ding, Hideya Mino, Isao Goto, Graham Neubig, Hideto Kazawa, Yusuke Oda, Jun Harashima, and Sadao Kurohashi. 2017. Overview of the 4th Workshop on Asian Translation. In *Proceedings of the 4th Workshop on Asian Translation (WAT2017)*, Taipei, Taiwan.

Toshiaki Nakazawa, Manabu Yaguchi, Kiyotaka Uchimoto, Masao Utiyama, Eiichiro Sumita, Sadao Kurohashi, and Hitoshi Isahara. 2014. ASPEC : Asian Scientific Paper Excerpt Corpus. In *Proceedings of the Tenth International Conference on Language Resources and Evaluation (LREC)*, pages 2204–2208.

Kishore Papineni, Salim Roukos, Todd Ward, and Wei-Jing Zhu. 2002. Bleu: a Method for Automatic Evaluation of Machine Translation. In *Proceedings of 40th Annual Meeting of the Association for Computational Linguistics*, pages 311–318, Philadelphia, Pennsylvania, USA. Association for Computational Linguistics.

Rico Sennrich, Barry Haddow, and Alexandra Birch. 2016. Neural Machine Translation of Rare Words with Subword Units. In *Proceedings of the 54th Annual Meeting of the Association for Computational Linguistics (Volume 1: Long Papers)*, pages 1715–1725, Berlin, Germany. Association for Computational Linguistics.

Ilya Sutskever, Oriol Vinyals, and Quoc V Le. 2014. Sequence to Sequence Learning with Neural Networks. In Z Ghahramani, M Welling, C Cortes, N D Lawrence, and K Q Weinberger, editors, *Advances in Neural Information Processing Systems 27 (NIPS2014)*, pages 3104–3112. Curran Associates, Inc.

Lijun Wu, Yingce Xia, Li Zhao, Fei Tian, Tao Qin, Jianhuang Lai, and Tie-yan Liu. 2017. Adversarial Neural Machine Translation. *arXiv*, abs/1704.06933.

Hayahide Yamagishi, Shin Kanouchi, Takayuki Sato, and Mamoru Komachi. 2016. Controlling the Voice of a Sentence in Japanese-to-English Neural Machine Translation. In *Proceedings of the 3rd Workshop on Asian Translation (WAT2016)*, pages 203–210, Osaka, Japan. The COLING 2016 Organizing Committee.

Zhen Yang, Wei Chen, Feng Wang, and Bo Xu. 2017. Improving Neural Machine Translation with Conditional Sequence Generative Adversarial Nets. *arXiv*, abs/1703.0.

Comparing Recurrent and Convolutional Architectures for English-Hindi Neural Machine Translation

Sandhya Singh, Ritesh Panjwani, Anoop Kunchukuttan, Pushpak Bhattacharyya
Center for Indian Language Technology
Department of Computer Science & Engineering
Indian Institute of Technology Bombay
{sandhya, ritesh, anoopk, pb}@cse.iitb.ac.in

Abstract

In this paper, we empirically compare the two encoder-decoder neural machine translation architectures: convolutional sequence to sequence model (ConvS2S) and recurrent sequence to sequence model (RNNS2S) for English-Hindi language pair as part of IIT Bombay's submission to WAT2017 shared task. We report the results for both English-Hindi and Hindi-English direction of language pair.

1 Introduction

Neural Machine Translation (NMT) systems are currently being widely investigated in the research community due to the benefits of distributed representation and continuous space modeling in generating more fluent outputs. In this paper, we report the results of our experiments with NMT for English-Hindi language pair for the shared task in the 4th Workshop on Asian Translation (Nakazawa et al., 2017). Hindi is the most widely spoken language in the Indian subcontinent, while English is a major link language in India as well across the world. Hence, English-Hindi is an important language pair for machine translation.

In this work, we focus on comparing two variants of the encoder decoder architectures. Section 2 describes our systems. Section 3 describes the experimental setup. Section 4 describes the results and observations of our experiments. Section 5 concludes the report.

2 System Description

We trained Neural Machine Transaltion systems using the encoder-decoder architecture with attention (Bahdanau et al., 2014) for English-Hindi as well Hindi-English translation. We compared convolutional neural network (ConvS2S) (Gehring et al., 2017) and recurrent neural network (RNNS2S) (Bahdanau et al., 2014) based sequence to sequence learning architectures. While RNN based architectures have proved to be successful and produce state-of-the-art results for machine translation, they take a long time to train. The temporal dependencies between the elements in the sequence due to the RNN state vector requires sequential processing. On the other hand, different parts of the sequence can be processed in parallel using a ConvS2S. Hence, it is appealing to explore ConvS2S as the basis of an architecture to speed up training and decoding. Recent work (Gehring et al., 2017) has shown that a purely CNN based encoder-decoder network is competitive with a RNN based network.

2.1 Recurrent sequence to sequence model (RNNS2S)

Recurrent sequence to sequence model (Bahdanau et al., 2014) is currently the most popular method for neural machine translation. It is been shown to be useful for other sequence to sequence tasks like image captioning (Vinyals et al., 2015), language modeling, question answering (Wang and Nyberg, 2015) *etc*. The typical architecture encodes the sequence of source word embeddings to generate annotations for the source words. The encoder is typically a bi-directional RNN layer of LSTM or GRU units. The final state of the encoder is used to initialize the decoder. The decoder is also an RNN which generates one output token at a time. Each output token is predicted based on the decoder state, previous output word and the context vector. The context vector encodes source information required for predicting the words, and is generated using an attention mechanism on the source word annotations. Please refer to Bahdanau et al. (2014) for an detailed description of the method.

Proceedings of the 4th Workshop on Asian Translation, pages 167–170,
Taipei, Taiwan, November 27, 2017. ©2017 AFNLP

2.2 Convolutional sequence to sequence model (ConvS2S)

In convolutional sequence to sequence model (Gehring et al., 2017), the input sequence is encoded into distributional vector space using a CNN and decoded back to output sequence again using CNN instead of RNN (Sutskever et al., 2014). Each input element embedding is combined with its positional embedding (signifies the position of the input element). Positional embeddings help the network to realize what part of input it is dealing with, currently.

Encoder-Decoder. Both the encoder and decoder are CNN blocks along with a multi-step attention mechanism with multiple 'hops' (Sukhbaatar et al., 2015). Each block consists of one dimensional convolutions followed by a Gated Linear Unit (GLU) non-linearity (Dauphin et al., 2016). GLU is a gating function over the outputs of the convolutions. The multi-step attention mechanism suggests that the attention mechanism is applied to every layer in the decoder. The attention of the first layer gives contextual information which is then given as an input to the next layer that considers this information while calculating the attention weights of the current layer.

Set	# Sentences	# Tokens	
		En	Hi
Train	1,492,827	20,666,365	22,164,816
Test	2,507	49,394	57,037
Development	520	10,656	10,174

Table 1: Statistics of data sets

Method	BLEU	RIBES	AMFM	HUMAN
RNNS2S	11.55	0.6829	0.5570	21
ConvS2S	**13.76**	**0.6975**	-	-

Table 2: Hindi to English Translation

Method	BLEU	RIBES	AMFM	HUMAN
RNNS2S	**12.23**	0.6886	0.6248	28.75
ConvS2S	11.73	**0.6903**	-	-

Table 3: English to Hindi Translation

3 Experimental Setup

3.1 Data

The data for WAT2017 shared task for English-Hindi language is a mix domain data collected

Encoder	Decoder	BLEU	
		En-Hi	Hi-En
4	3	7.84	8.67
9	5	11.43	13.05
13	7	**11.73**	**13.76**

Table 4: Different number of encoder and decoder layers in ConvS2S in terms of BLEU.

from different sources at CFILT[1] lab. The data provided was in tokenized format using moses tokenizer for English side and Indic NLP library[2] for Hindi side of the parallel data. The training data was further cleaned for a sentence length of 100 words. Table-1 shows data statistics used for the experiments.

3.2 Training

The RNNS2S model was trained using Nematus[3] framework. To handle rare words, subword[4] technique was used through byte pair encoding(BPE) Shibata et al. (1999) with 16000 BPE operations. Since there is no similarity between English and Hindi language vocabulary, both the languages were trained separately for BPE. The encoder and decoder hidden layer size was kept at 512 and word embedding size as 256. The model was trained with a batch size of 40 sentences and maximum sentence length of 100 using AdaDelta (Zeiler, 2012) optimizer with a learning rate of 0.0001 and no dropout setting. The output parameters were saved after every 10000 iterations. The decoding was done using a beam size of 12 and ensemble of last 3 models and the best model taken together.

The ConvS2S model was trained using Fairseq[5], an open source library developed by Facebook for neural machine translation using CNN or RNN networks. For handling the rare words, the source side and target side corpora were segmented using byte pair encoding (BPE) (Shibata et al., 1999). The baseline model with 4 encoder layers and 3 decoder layers was trained using *nag* optimizer (Gehring et al., 2017) with a learning rate of 0.25 with 0.2 as its dropout value and gradient clipping was also applied.

---

[1] http://www.cfilt.iitb.ac.in/
[2] http://anoopkunchukuttan.github.io/indic_nlp_library/
[3] https://github.com/EdinburghNLP/nematus
[4] https://github.com/rsennrich/subword-nmt
[5] https://github.com/facebookresearch/fairseq

Team	BLEU	RIBES	AM-FM	Pairwise	Adequacy
2016 Best	18.72	71.68	67.07	57.25	3.36
XMUNLP	21.39	74.97	68.88	64.5	3.86
IITB-MTG (RNNS2S)	12.23	68.86	62.48	28.75	2.68
IITB-MTG (ConvS2S)	11.73	69.03	-	-	-

Table 5: English to Hindi Translation Systems at WAT2017

Team	BLEU	RIBES	AM-FM	Pairwise	Adequacy
XMUNLP	22.44	75.09	62.95	68.25	3.51
IITB-MTG (RNNS2S)	11.55	68.29	55.7	21	2.29
IITB-MTG (ConvS2S)	13.76	69.75	-	-	-

Table 6: Hindi to English Translation Systems at WAT2017

The inferencing was done using beam search with a beam size of 10 for both Hindi-English and English-Hindi translation task. The model was also trained with more number of layers in the encoder and the decoder. The resulting BLEU scores for different number of encoder and decoder layers are shown in Table 4. The best results were obtained when the number of encoder layers were set to 13 and decoder layers to 7, with learning rate of 0.1 and no dropout regularization. The resulting BLEU scores with this setting for Hindi-English and English-Hindi are shown in Table 2 and Table 3 respectively.

4 Results and Observation

The Table 2 and the Table 3 shows the different evaluation metrics such as Bilingual Evaluation Understudy (BLEU) (Papineni et al., 2002), Rank-based Intuitive Bilingual Evaluation Score (RIBES) (Group et al., 2013), Adequacy-Fluency Metrics (AMFM) (Banchs et al., 2015) (N/A for ConvS2S model) and human evaluation score (HUMAN) (N/A for ConvS2S model) for Hindi-English and English-Hindi translation pairs.

In Hindi to English translation, the ConvS2S model outperforms the RNNS2S model in terms of BLEU score and the RIBES score. On the other hand, in English to Hindi translation, the RNNS2S model performs better than the ConvS2S model in terms of BLEU score and the RIBES score is at par with the ConvS2S model.

The JPO Adequacy and pairwise evaluation of our RNNS2S output was compared against WAT2016 best system. Table 5 and table 6 show the evaluation results of all other systems in comparison to our submission. The results clearly in-

dicate the scope of fine tuning our system parameters. Due to time constraint, the ConvS2S output could not be submitted for manual evaluation. But the increasing trend of BLEU Scores have motivated us to continue our experimentation for a deeper analysis.

Further experimentation is required to see if the ConvS2S can perform better on English-Hindi as well. One way to test this is by increasing the number of encoder and/or decoder layers even further. This is because, in the Table 4 we can clearly observe that the BLEU scores increases when number of encoder and decoder layers are increased. More experiments are required with RNNS2S architecture as well.

5 Conclusion

In our system submission, we compared two sequence to sequence architectures: RNN based and CNN based for the English-Hindi language pairs. The BLEU scores of CNN architecture improves by further tunning the parameters.

In future, we would like to investigate the threshold of hyperparameters for RNNS2S and ConvS2S architectures for this language pair keeping processing time in consideration.

References

Dzmitry Bahdanau, Kyunghyun Cho, and Yoshua Bengio. 2014. Neural machine translation by jointly learning to align and translate. *arXiv preprint arXiv:1409.0473*.

Rafael E Banchs, Luis F D'Haro, and Haizhou Li. 2015. Adequacy-fluency metrics: Evaluating mt in the continuous space model framework. *IEEE*

Transactions on Audio, Speech, and Language Processing, 23(3):472–482.

Yann N Dauphin, Angela Fan, Michael Auli, and David Grangier. 2016. Language modeling with gated convolutional networks. *arXiv preprint arXiv:1612.08083*.

Jonas Gehring, Michael Auli, David Grangier, Denis Yarats, and Yann N Dauphin. 2017. Convolutional sequence to sequence learning. *arXiv preprint arXiv:1705.03122*.

Linguistic Intelligence Research Group et al. 2013. Ntt communication science laboratories. ribes: Rank-based intuitive bilingual evaluation score.

Toshiaki Nakazawa, Shohei Higashiyama, Chenchen Ding, Hideya Mino, Isao Goto, Graham Neubig, Hideto Kazawa, Yusuke Oda, Jun Harashima, and Sadao Kurohashi. 2017. Overview of the 4th workshop on asian translation. In *Proceedings of the 4th Workshop on Asian Translation (WAT2017)*, Taipei, Taiwan.

Kishore Papineni, Salim Roukos, Todd Ward, and Wei-Jing Zhu. 2002. Bleu: a method for automatic evaluation of machine translation. In *Proceedings of the 40th annual meeting on association for computational linguistics*, pages 311–318. Association for Computational Linguistics.

Yusuxke Shibata, Takuya Kida, Shuichi Fukamachi, Masayuki Takeda, Ayumi Shinohara, Takeshi Shinohara, and Setsuo Arikawa. 1999. Byte pair encoding: A text compression scheme that accelerates pattern matching. Technical report, Technical Report DOI-TR-161, Department of Informatics, Kyushu University.

Sainbayar Sukhbaatar, Jason Weston, Rob Fergus, et al. 2015. End-to-end memory networks. In *Advances in neural information processing systems*, pages 2440–2448.

Ilya Sutskever, Oriol Vinyals, and Quoc V Le. 2014. Sequence to sequence learning with neural networks. In *Advances in neural information processing systems*, pages 3104–3112.

Oriol Vinyals, Alexander Toshev, Samy Bengio, and Dumitru Erhan. 2015. Show and tell: A neural image caption generator. In *Proceedings of the IEEE conference on computer vision and pattern recognition*, pages 3156–3164.

Di Wang and Eric Nyberg. 2015. A long short-term memory model for answer sentence selection in question answering. In *Proceedings of the 53rd Annual Meeting of the Association for Computational Linguistics and the 7th International Joint Conference on Natural Language Processing (Volume 2: Short Papers)*, volume 2, pages 707–712.

Matthew D Zeiler. 2012. Adadelta: an adaptive learning rate method. *arXiv preprint arXiv:1212.5701*.

Author Index